IF MINDS MATTER

A Foreword to the Future

Volume Two: Designs for Change

EDITED BY

Arthur L. Costa

James Bellanca

Robin Fogarty

IRI/Skylight Publishing, Inc.
Palatine, Illinois

The publisher gratefully acknowledges the following for permission to reprint material in this book:

In "The Art of Strategic Connections" Figure 2 appears in *Tomorrow's Classroom Today* by F. Brownlie, S. Close, and L. Wingren, 1990, and is reprinted with permission from Pembroke Publishers Ltd.

Portions of "Interactive Strategies for Enhancing Thinking and Writing" appear in *Practical Ideas for Teaching Writing as a Process* by C. B. Olson (Ed.), 1992 and are reprinted with permission from the California State Department of Education.

Portions of "How Do We Know We're Getting Better?" appear in *Reading and Responding Grade 6* by S. Jeroski, F. Brownlie, and L. Kaser, 1991 and are reprinted by permission of Nelson Canada, a division of Thomson Canada Limited.

In "The Art of Strategic Connections" Figure 3b appears in *Reading and Responding Grade 4* by S. Jeroski, F. Brownlie, and L. Kaser, 1990 and is reprinted by permission of Nelson Canada, a division of Thomson Canada Limited.

In "Cooperative Learning: A Natural Way to Learn," Figure 6 is reprinted with permission of Peggy Marketello, Susan M. Nerton, and Joannne Roster.

If Minds Matter: A Foreword to the Future
Volume Two: Designs for Change
Second Printing

Published by IRI/Skylight Publishing, Inc.
200 E. Wood Street, Suite 274, Palatine, Illinois 60067
800-348-4474 (in northern Illinois 708-991-6300)
FAX 708-991-6420

Editing: Julia E. Noblitt, Naomi Cohn, Lorraine Murray, Sharon Nowakowski, Marijke Rijsberman
Type Composition: Donna Ramirez
Book Design: Bruce Leckie
Cover Design: David Stockman
Typesetting: Bruce Leckie, Jamie Bellanca, Donna Ramirez

Printed in the United States of America
ISBN 0-932935-40-0
1399-08-94

ACKNOWLEDGMENTS

The orchestration required to publish a two-volume collection—involving four dozen authors who are scattered throughout the continental United States, Hawaii, and into the provinces of Canada—has been a monumental task. Naturally, a project of this scope involves the cooperation and commitment of the players at every level of the production process. However, one person is ultimately in charge; there is only one conductor. In this production of *If Minds Matter: A Foreword to the Future*, that one person has been Julia Noblitt, Senior Editor. Thanks to her expertise, the various elements were gingerly synchronized: assignments were set, monitored, revised, juggled, and adjusted and the production schedule was meticulously met. For this, we are forever indebted to Julie.

Responding to Julie's leadership, we would like to acknowledge the other key players instrumental in crafting these volumes. First, we'd like to thank the authors for their valiant efforts in following our guidelines, meeting our standards, and providing exceptional and enlightening text—all within stringent timelines. As in any concerted effort, the diversity and multitude of the various authored parts have created a synergy evidenced in the finished product.

In addition to the authoring efforts, we would like to acknowledge our production and editing staff for commendable teamwork: Naomi Cohn, Lorraine Murray, Sharon Nowakowski, and Marijke Rijsberman comprised our editorial team. Working at breakneck speed, and yet with the deliberation and care necessary for final copy, they skillfully edited the work of our authors. Also, a note of appreciation is in order for Sandi Schroeder for meeting our indexing needs.

To Bruce Leckie, lead designer on this project, we extend our thanks for the layout design and for the hours of fine tuning required to make it all fit. Working closely with him, we would like to acknowledge Jamie Bellanca for his patience in formatting and revising chapters that were each unique in style and form. Also, in the production and design department, we'd like to thank Donna Ramirez for her seemingly effortless ability to input a never-ending stream of text. And, a special thank you to Dave Stockman for his inspired cover design. We extend our appreciation to both Dave and Kim Overton for handling all the other production in progress. Without their efforts, making our publication deadlines would have been impossible.

Two final notes of appreciation must not be overlooked. At the earliest conception of the project, we approached Ralph Tyler and asked if he would write an introduction to our work because of his esteemed and historic role in instruction and curriculum development. He graciously accepted our invitation and to him we are forever grateful. Similarly, at the close of the project, we approached Elliot Eisner and asked if he would write a foreword to our work because of his well-known role as a connoisseur in curriculum and program evalua-

tion. He, too, graciously accepted our invitation and to him we are also forever grateful.

In any extraordinary human endeavor, the results speak for themselves. Many hands and hearts have shaped these volumes … as if minds mattered. To all involved in this labor of love, we thank you.

Art Costa,
James Bellanca &
Robin Fogarty

FOREWORD

A t at time when American educators are being riddled by proposals to emphasize content as if it could be separated from the mental processes that give it meaning, *If Minds Matter: A Foreword to the Future* is welcome. From my perspective, the development, even the invention of mind is one of education's major aims. The term *invention* with respect to mind is not a common locution. The ordinary person views mind as something that humans are born with, just as they are born with hands and feet. The idea that mind is a form of cultural achievement, an invented process influenced by the opportunities a child has had to learn is not a common view. Yet, in a very real sense, mind is not something like brain: brain is biological but mind is significantly cultural. The curricula that we provide in schools, the ways in which we teach, the opportunities given to children in the course of their development are opportunities that shape the kinds of minds children will come to own. When we define the curriculum we are defining those opportunities. Decisions that educators and laypeople make about the content of school programs—what is included and what is left out—are decisions about the kinds of content about which children will have an opportunity to think and the kind of cognitive processes they will have an opportunity to develop. Hence the educator's task in the broadest sense is to generate those conditions that bring mind into being, in part by recognizing the ways in which people can learn to think.

I said earlier that attention to the development of mind has not been salient in the current debate about the aims of education or the content of curriculum. The generally conservative picture of the mission of schools that now prevails is one that emphasizes the acquisition of information. Becoming "culturally literate" is, unfortunately, often related to the acquisition of dictionary knowledge concerning supposedly key events. While there is no question that the processes of thinking require a content, the content can be thought about in ways that are shallow or deep, imaginative or routine, analytic or pedestrian, integrated or fragmented. As Whitehead once said, the merely well-informed man is the greatest bore on earth.

Given the prevailing climate, we all need to remind ourselves that whatever children are able to become will be significantly influenced by the quality of the programs they encounter in school and the character of the teaching that mediates it. Like the systole and diastole of a beating heart, curriculum and teaching are at the core of education. *If Minds Matter* reminds us of the importance of these processes and the creative role that teachers and educational policy makers can perform in shaping the opportunities children will have to invent their own minds.

The creation of those opportunities will in the final analysis require far more than attention to the curriculum per se, or to the quality of teaching. Neither curriculum nor teaching functions independently of the "biological" environment in which they are housed. The school is, in a sense, a kind of biological environment for curriculum and for teachers. The school provides its own constraints and its own incentives. What teachers are able to emphasize and what the curriculum can become is only in part influenced by our educational aspirations. It is also influenced by the habits that we as teachers harbor, the traditions within which schools function, and the expectations of the community and the students we teach. Put another way, our most noble aspirations to reform education so that mind can be invented in its fullest sense will be tempered by considerations beyond the classroom, indeed beyond the school itself. For example, the communities within which schools reside need to understand that the long-term goal of education is no small victory in an economic arms race with foreign nations, but the invention of the kind of mentality that our culture needs to remain viable, civil, and humane.

This mentality, in its best sense, is not some homogenized uniformity measurable through standardized achievement tests. At its very best, the practice of education cultivates what is distinctive, what is unique about individuals. It is through such uniqueness— what in other contexts I have called productive idiosyncrasy—that the culture itself thrives. A well-developed mind will possess unique features from which the culture is nourished. In a sense, we feed each other precisely from those unique personal aptitudes that we ourselves do not possess. Thus, the aims of education are closely related not only to the invention of mind, but to the invention of individual minds, minds that have a personal signature, minds that see and act upon the world in uniquely individual ways.

The aim of education is not the reduction of heterogeneity in the service of standard attainment, but just the opposite. The goal of schooling is to increase variability among the young while at the same time the magnitude of the mean.

Such an ambition will of course play havoc with simple efforts at assessment. It will create a labor-intensive demand in matters of evaluation, and it will de-standardize what we think schools ought to be about. It is not clear to me whether our own culture, steeped as it is in a meritocratic tradition, will be willing to accept such a personalistic view of the deepest ends of education. We have grown accustomed, I am afraid, to simple answers and to quantitative indices of achievement. We tend to import into education the language of the marketplace and the images of battle.

We need different metaphors, indeed different paradigms. We need images of education that harken to the kinder, gentler America we have heard about. I believe schools have a major contribution to make in realizing such a social ambition. Attention to the potential of mind as a primary educational aim is one of the important steps we can take to move in that direction. Yet as important as it is, it is a limited step. What we do or try to do in classrooms is only a part of the task. As educators, we need to direct our efforts toward the public at large so that they can help us alter the blinkered vision that now seems to drive our schools.

If Minds Matter is an important legitimation of the conviction that mind does indeed matter. Whether it can matter enough to shape school policies will depend not only on what we do in school, but what we can help our constituency come to understand about the deeper purposes of education. *If Minds Matter* has the potential to help us do that. If that potential is realized, it will certainly be an important contribution, not only to the educational literature but even more important, to the practice of education.

Elliot W. Eisner
Stanford University
February, 1992

ANNOTATED CONTENTS

—

VOLUME II

Designs for Change

SECTION ONE

CREATING THE THOUGHTFUL CLASSROOM

Cognitive instruction research includes several major areas: explicit skill instruction, cognitive organizers, metacognition, and transfer of learning. Criteria for explicit instruction in thinking skills are examined and specific programs are categorized. Next, the emergence of cognitive organizers as significant cognitive tools is briefly noted. A substantial section on metacognition as a superordinate kind of thinking is also included. A metacognitive framework for planning, monitoring, and evaluating learning is explained. Finally, current work in the area of transfer of learning is discussed as cognitive instruction moves in a new direction.

Thinking is the bridge that links students' experiences with the curriculum. This bridge is activated by the use of teaching/learning strategies in the classroom. This chapter weaves the attributes of a thoughtful classroom with the attributes of a strategy, then moves on to discuss implementation issues: How do teachers begin to use strategies in their teaching? How do teachers monitor the strategies they teach? How can students be involved in monitoring the effectiveness of the strategies they are learning?

Creating the Thoughtful Classroom describes the change process and the staff development component used by a suburban K-12 school district to facilitate the use of instructional strategies that promote thinking. The article demonstrates that an entire district can move forward in an area of focus when careful attention is given to the change process.

This chapter focuses on enhancing the development of higher-order thinking skills through the use of cooperative learning strategies. Content includes a definition of "higher-order thinking" skills; what thinking paths are and how they are developed;

ligences. The particular context of schools favors certain abilities over others. The standard curriculum stresses language and logic; other capacities receive only cursory acknowledgment despite their importance in other contexts, especially later in life. MI Theory suggests educational practices that diverge considerably from the current push toward standardization of curriculum, pedagogy, and assessment. In particular, MI Theory calls for broadening the school curriculum, emphasizing the divergent paths that students can take toward understanding, and diversifying assessment.

This chapter is concerned with practical implications of the theory of multiple intelligences for restructuring schools in three areas. The first is the curriculum (teaching FOR multiple intelligences). We need to be sure that the basic skills/capacities of the different ways of knowing are being taught in our schools. Second is instructional practices and methodologies (teaching WITH multiple intelligences). We need to be presenting academic material in a wide variety of ways to address and stimulate all intelligence areas. The third concern is reinventing the learning process itself (teaching ABOUT multiple intelligences). Here we are concerned not only with helping students learn about their multiple ways of knowing, but with such things as assessment of various intelligence strengths and weaknesses, as well as assessing academic progress using multiple intelligences.

Unique opportunities exist in the middle school classroom for teaching thinking. Fundamental aspects of the middle school concept include a curriculum model that integrates content, skills, and personal development as well as team approaches to instruction. Within this milieu, strategies appropriate for teaching thinking include: clarifying purposes; providing motivation, readiness, and goal-setting; utilizing recall strategies; providing transitions; moving from concrete to abstract; using wait-time; facilitating student-to-student interaction; assigning team tasks; creating simulation and game techniques; and focusing on affective issues.

What will classrooms look like in 2001? The author shows how the best instructional practices used by outstanding practitioners in today's classrooms could become the norm in the next century. He identifies the major blocks to this evolution and suggests a practical vision for the classroom in the year 2001.

SECTION TWO

CREATING COOPERATIVE LEARNERS

The use of cooperative learning in schools is unique in its theoretical and research support. The comparison of cooperative, competitive, and individualistic efforts is the oldest research tradition in American social psychology. The impact of cooperative learning on a wide variety of educational outcomes has been studied. One set of outcomes involves effort to achieve. A second set of outcomes involves interpersonal attraction, desegregation, mainstreaming, and social support. A third set of outcomes involves psychological adjustment and health, social competencies, and self-esteem. The validity, breadth, and power of social interdependence theory make it a key aspect of schooling. The use of cooperative learning is part of changing schools from a competitive/individualistic to a high-performance cooperative-team organizational structure.

SECTION THREE

ASSESSING SIGNIFICANT OUTCOMES

practices in classroom assessment where students are encouraged to: make critical choices about reading, responding, and representing; make connections to previous knowledge and experience; personalize their responses to deepen their understanding; and engage in thoughtful interactions. Samples are drawn from a variety of contexts in elementary school classrooms.

This chapter describes a systematic process for planning and conducting more thoughtful and sound classroom assessments. The authors briefly describe assessment methods appropriate for use by classroom teachers, organized in a Framework of Assessment Approaches. They examine principles of sound classroom assessment and present an Assessment Planning Chart. They also illustrate the planning process, framework, planning chart, and seven of the assessment methods in use.

Accepting the premise that transfer of learning is the most significant learner outcome, this chapter outlines a model for tracking and assessing that transfer. Transfer of learning is depicted along a continuum that includes six situational dispositions toward transfer: overlooking, duplicating, replicating, integrating, mapping, and innovating. Each disposition is illustrated metaphorically and specific student behaviors are listed for teachers to look for and listen for as they systematically track student transfer. Key metacognitive questions are suggested to move students along the transfer continuum. In closing, it is suggested that the model may be used as a metacognitive tool for student self-assessment.

INTRODUCTION

—

Ralph Tyler

Profound changes have taken place in educational thought since the beginning of the 20th century. In earlier times, social change was relatively slow and the school was generally viewed as the institution to teach children the information and skills of the adults so that the children would be able to take their places and carry on successfully the activities of their parents' generation. However, the increasing tempo of change in American society has resulted in a situation in which each new generation faces problems not faced by their parents. Schools that only prepared children to carry on the activities of their parents and to meet the problems that their parents had encountered became inadequate.

Fortunately, at the beginning of the 20th century a few educators recognized the need for new conceptions of the tasks and procedures of schools that took into account such social change. In their speaking and writing, they led the development of a reformulation of the role and practices of a school that would be appropriate for a constantly changing society. Four major emphases were stressed in this formulation. (1) The role of the school is no longer that of preparing the child to fit into a static society, but is to educate students to take part in improving society. (2) The curriculum of the school should no longer focus on the memorization of facts and the development of fixed habits, but should emphasize identifying and solving social problems and developing constructive, flexible habits. (3) The activities of the school should no longer be largely limited to reading, listening, and repetitive practice, but should include experiences in which children work cooperatively with others in socially important learning activities carried on beyond the classroom. (4) The evaluation of student learning should no longer be largely restricted to paper-and-pencil tests, but should be based mainly on the child's work in conducting and completing projects requiring the use of the learning that schools are expected to teach.

This reformulation has been developed by educators who are continually seeking to make educational thought and practice appropriate for the needs of society. Perhaps twenty percent of American educators have these views to guide their work. Fifty years hence, it is likely that as many as eighty percent of American public schools will be undertaking such changes.

This book not only defines and describes these profound changes in educational thought but also presents examples of how these changes are embodied in excellent schools and other learning communities. It is an important and exciting presentation.

CREATING THE
THOUGHTFUL CLASSROOM

"How was your day, Kate?" asked her mother.

"Great!" Kate beamed. "I got two hundreds."

"Oh, that's wonderful. For what?"

"I spelled out the words I memorized and I circled all the right state flowers."

"That's great," said Kate's mother.

[Later that day.] "I'm pleased to report that Kate does excellent work," said the fourth-grade teacher. "She is a wonderful child. She has a record string of sixty-seven spelling words without a miss, and her seatwork is always 90-100% correct. Look here. She did so well matching the flowers and states."

Mrs. Smith nodded. "That is very nice. She works hard every night to do the worksheets and memorize her vocabulary."

"Do you have any questions, Mrs. Smith?"

"Why yes. I was wondering about Kate's problem-solving skills. She doesn't seem do have much patience when I ask her to apply some of the math facts to actual problems."

"Oh, I wouldn't worry about that. She'll get the chance to do problem solving when she's older. Right now we are not as concerned about application as we are in building a base of knowledge and facts. There is just so much to cover."

In contrast to this teacher's defense of memorization of facts, the Minister of Intellectual Development for Venezuela, Luis Alberto Machado, stated in 1984 that the level of the development of a country is determined mostly by the level of development of its people's intelligence.

The schools of the 21st century have a commitment to the development of the mind as the central role. Gazing into an uncertain future, these mandates help us realize that fundamental to each student's productivity, happiness, and survival in the next century will be a range of complex intellectual skills: the ability to seek, pose, and solve problems; to retrieve, organize, and derive meaning from a vast quantity of rapidly changing hi-tech information; to collaboratively envision, dream, and create new products and new solutions; and to be seriously concerned about the perspectives, conditions, and well-being of their fellow human beings.

This section opens with a research piece delineating the theoretical basis for instructional methodologies that highlight cognitive skills and strategies. As scenarios of thoughtful classrooms emerge, the picture includes: techniques for explicit skill instruction; strategies that employ graphic organizers to represent student thinking; and interactive methods that invite all students into the learning. One chapter discusses the role of technology as a thinking tool, while other chapters expand on the broader view of intelligence which suggests multiple ways of knowing. This section outlines cognitive strategies to foster thoughtful classrooms. It closes with two scenarios depicting future school models: a middle school as an emergent model for the next decade, and a portrait of an evolving classroom for the year 2001.

COGNITION IN PRACTICE

—

James Bellanca and Robin Fogarty

Cognitive instruction research embodies four distinct areas of study: explicit skill instruction, cognitive organizers, meta-cognition and transfer of learning. Each of these areas has its own body of literature as well as works that encompass all four areas.

EXPLICIT THINKING SKILLS

A steady current of experts favor explicit skill instruction for the thinking curriculum. In some areas, consensus among the many thinking skills advocates embodies these beliefs (Costa, 1985a):

- Thinking is most often taught indirectly, but a direct approach is needed.

- Learning how to think is not an automatic by-product of studying certain subjects.

- Students will not learn to think better simply by being asked to think about a subject or topic.

- Youngsters do not learn how to engage in critical thinking by themselves.

- There is little reason to believe that competency in critical thinking can be an incidental outcome of instruction directed, or apparently directed, at other ends.

- Instructions for the skills must be direct and systematic prior to, during, and following students' introduction to and use of them in the classroom.

However, there seem to be two obstacles impeding the momentum of a stronger flow toward consensus on how to teach thinking explicitly. The first obstacle is a philosophical issue that must be addressed before the second obstacle can even be approached. This primary issue is the debate over whether explicit thinking skills should be taught separate from or infused into the existing subject area curriculum. There are, of course, pros and cons for each instance. (See Figure 1.)

Although both approaches are successfully implemented in various settings, we favor the infused model. Our focus is always and foremost on the *transfer of learning* for all children, and the infused model eases the way for fruitful transfer, creative application, and relevant student use throughout the curriculum. The separate model seems to reinforce for students the "little boxes" theory of curriculum: in little boxes, math is not art, art is not science, and think-

THINKING SKILLS PROGRAMS

	PROS	CONS
Thinking Infused Into Content	• Easy transfer • Carries content	• Teachers may be unskilled in the teaching skills
Thinking Taught Separately	• Spot and slot for thinking • Targeted to test and grade • Easy staff development	• No Time • No transfer

Figure 1   Thinking Skills: Infused or Separate

ing is not any of these—the curricula are fragmented.

However, once the decision has been made in terms of how to deliberately include thinking in the curricula, the next obstacle stubbornly emerges: How does one know which program is best? An overview of the spectrum of thinking models provides some food for thought. Just as in cooperative learning, the various programs tend to cluster into four distinct categories: the conceptual models, the strategic approaches, the curriculum packages, and the model-building designs. Figure 2 presents the thinking skill programs as they cluster in patterns.

The major categories that delineate the four types of thinking skills programs have definite characteristics that distinguish one from the other.

CLUSTERS OF THINKING SKILLS PROGRAMS

CONCEPTUAL MODELS

Patterns for Thinking—Patterns for Transfer - *Fogarty and Bellanca*

Tactics in Thinking- *Marzano and Arredondo*

Dimensions in Thinking - *Marzano*

Thoughtful Education Training Series - *Hansen, Silver, and Strong*

Teaching for Intelligent Behavior - *Costa*

Models of Teaching - *Joyce & Weil*

STRATEGIC/SKILLS APPROACH

CoRT - *de Bono*

Catch Them Thinking - *Bellanca and Fogarty*

Start Them Thinking - *Fogarty and Opeka*

Teach Them Thinking - *Fogarty and Bellanca*

Synectics - *Gordon*

Strategic Reasoning - *Upton*

Practical Strategies for Teaching Thinking - *Beyer*

Project Impact - *Winocur*

CURRICULUM PACKAGES

Philosophy in the Classroom - *Lipman et al.*

Instrumental Enrichment - *Feurerstein*

HOTS - *Pogrow*

SOI - *Meeker*

Great Books - *Will*

Future Problem Solving - *Torrence*

Odyssey - *Project Zero (Harvard)*

Critical Thinking - *Black and Black*

MODEL BUILDING WITH PROTOTYPES

Knowledge as Design - *Perkins*

Keep Them Thinking I, II, III - *Opeka, Fogarty, Bellanca*

Breakthrough - *Jones*

Guided Design - *Nardi, Wales*

Connections - *Perkins et al.*

Creative Problem Solving - *Parnes*

Cooperative Think Tank - *Bellanca & Fogarty*

Figure 2   Major Categories of Thinking Skills Programs

Each program has a flavor of its own, yet each category is also easily recognized by its distinguishing critical attributes.

Conceptual Models

In the conceptual models, broad guidelines set the framework within which more specific ideas are set forth. For example, in *Patterns for Thinking—Patterns for Transfer*, the four broad guidelines framing the program are teaching *for, of, with*, and *about* thinking: setting the climate *for* thinking, teaching the explicit skills *of* thinking, structuring interactions to teach *with* thinking, and teaching metacognitively *about* thinking. Within that framework, specific thinking skills and strategies are used to demonstrate the conceptual model.

Likewise, in *Models of Teaching*, Joyce and Weil conceptualize instructional models into families: information processing, personal, social, and behavioral. Within that framework, specific models are explored. For example, within the personal family the synectics approach is elaborated. It begins with a scenario that presents the model, followed by an introduction to the basic structures, theory, demonstration, practice, and feedback. It ends with coaching and extended application that help teachers learn the instructional techniques.

While conceptual models allow great freedom on the part of the teacher for innovative and highly relevant content-specific use, less skilled or less confident staff may find the freedom within the conceptual structure too ambiguous.

Strategic/Skills Approach

The strategic/skills approach, on the other hand, provides tried and true, teacher-tested techniques that are ready for immediate use. In the strategic/skills approach, a menu of specific and fully delineated methods are presented to the teacher for explicit instructional use.

Usually, these strategies/skills are introduced in what is often called a "content-free" lesson. In reality, this content-free lesson does indeed have a content focus. However, the content is usually familiar, almost generic in nature. It is used merely as a vehicle to carry the strategy or skill under study.

For example, in teaching the explicit thinking skill of classification, the familiar content focus might be on solids, liquids, and gases. Using these generic categories, the classification skill, not the science, becomes the focus of the lesson.

Similarly, in teaching the strategy PMI (plus, minus, interesting), de Bono uses the generic or familiar content of buses. The initial lesson requires students to generate pluses, minuses, and interesting aspects of buses that have no seats. Again, by using content that is simple and well-known, the emphasis can be placed on the PMI strategy itself.

While the strategic/skills approach usually has immediate appeal to practitioners because it easily applies directly to the classroom, caution must be taken that the strategies and skills lessons are not merely used as a cutesy Friday afternoon activity. If the strategy or skill is used only once as modeled in the teacher training, it is an *activity*. If, however, teachers introduce the strategy or skill as modeled, practice it in another situation, and transfer it into still another situation, then and only then can we call it a *strategy*. An activity is a one-time shot. A strategy is placed in our repertoire of instructional techniques, our tool kit to be used over and over, whenever appropriate.

Curriculum Packages

Curriculum packages provide a ready-made set of materials for classroom use. These materials are, more often than not, specifically designed for explicit instruction as separate and disparate pieces in the classroom. While the curriculum package provides a neat and tidy unit for deliberate placement in the instructional day, "a spot and a slot" for explicitly addressing thinking skills and strategies, often the subsequent transfer needed for continued and relevant use does not occur.

Examples of the curriculum packages might include Feuerstein's *Instrumental Enrichment*, in which specific and strategic thinking techniques are taught through pencil-and-paper tasks. By metacognitively processing and talking about how students approached a particular task, future application and transfer are mediated for the students.

Another curriculum package is Lipman's *Philosophy for Children* program, in which skillfully written, highly motivating, and extremely relevant scenarios are used to engage students in Socratic dialogue. Using the fictional situations as springboards, further discussion is encouraged as students attempt to draw philosophical principles into other academic situations or into life's circumstances.

While curriculum packages have strong appeal because of their completeness as a package, their use can be limiting if transfer is not addressed with vigor.

Model Building with Prototypes

The final cluster of thinking skills programs, model building with prototypes, provides a generic piece or model as a prototype. That is, the generalizable model is presented through a content-specific lesson, with the implicit understanding that it is a model and should be used as such. Transfer to other content is built in explicitly. Examples of model building with prototypes are the *Breakthrough* program by Jones and *Knowledge as Design* by Perkins.

In the *Breakthrough* program, for example, a lesson on garbage is presented in a fully designed, ready-to-use lesson format. However, in model building a specific prototype is set up. The lesson features specific strategies for modeling collaborative learning, reciprocal teaching, and cognitive mapping. The expectation is that although garbage is the lesson's content focus, the real lesson extends beyond that with definite attention to instructional methodology.

Perkins' *Knowledge as Design* uses the same model-building approach. Perkins poses four questions that can be applied across content, subject matter, and life situations:

- What is its purpose (or purposes)?
- What is its structure?
- What are the model cases of it?
- What are arguments that explain and evaluate it?

Through these four questions, a model for thinking emerges. Perkins claims these questions can be applied to ecology, Boyle's law, the Bill of Rights, and to understanding a common screwdriver.

THINKING SKILLS PROGRAMS

Briefly, without belaboring the decision-making processes that must be employed to reach consensus, there are some major considerations to weigh in the selection of a program. (See Figure 3.)

Considerations For Selecting a Program

- What is the purpose of the program?
- Should an explicit thinking skills program be introduced separate from or infused into the subject matter content?
- What are the experiences and competencies of the teachers?
- What are the available resources in terms of time and funds for training and materials?
- What is the commitment level for long-term change toward cognitive instruction?
- What kinds of results are expected?

How to Teach the Skills

After consideration of these key issues, program selection becomes easier. By targeting needs and expectations, several programs will seem more appropriate than others. Once the final choice is made, the subsequent decisions on how to teach the skills fall into place. A model of what is required to teach explicit thinking skills, according to Beyer (1987), is provided in Figure 4.

The research on the need for explicit attention to thinking in the curriculum is clear:

Knowing that…

…schools do make a difference (Edmonds, 1997),

…intelligence is modifiable (Feuerstein, 1980),

…learners can monitor and control their own performance (Brown, 1978),

…learners are active, strategic, planful, and constructive (Anderson, Hiebert, Scott, & Wilkinson, 1984),

THINKING SKILLS PROGRAMS		
Type	**Pros**	**Cons**
Conceptual Models	• Deep understanding results in creative application • Can easily adapt, mix, and match the best from many models	• Full commitment to long-term change from building or district • Needs explicit attention to transfer
Strategic/Skills Approach	• Easy for teachers to learn • Immediate application • Transfer power inherent (if noted explicitly)	• Can appear "cutesy" • Superficial activities rather than generic, transferable strategies for the instructional repertoire
Curriculum Packages	• Stand alone • Spot and slot in curriculum • Teacher's preparation minimal	• Narrow in focus • Needs (and often overlooks) attention to transfer • Separated from content; more to teach
Model Building with Prototypes	• Procedural learning or heuristics taught and modeled for easy application and transfer • Straightforward approach with transfer built in	• Can be narrow in focus • Transfer embedded but can be slighted

Figure 3   Pros and Cons of Thinking Skills Programs

then cognitive instruction must include explicitness in both the thinking skill and the transfer of the thinking skill.

COGNITIVE ORGANIZERS

The concept of cognitive organizers is rooted in Ausubel's (1978) theory of "meaningful reception learning." Simply put, Ausubel believes that information is naturally stored hierarchically in the brain. For instance, highly generalized concepts seem to cluster together, followed by less inclusive concepts, and finally specific facts and details.

Ausubel advocates the idea of the advance organizer in which information is graphically displayed prior to the reading of the text. In Ausubel's terms,

HOW TO TEACH EXPLICIT SKILLS

1. Examples (or Products).
2. Introduction to components of the thinking skill in a systematic manner.
3. Demonstration of the basic attributes of the skill.
4. Discussion of the operation and how to do the operation.
5. Opportunity for related practice and feedback.
6. A broadening of the skill beyond the original components.
7. Generalization of the skill with application in a variety of situations.

EXPLICIT SKILL INFORMATION

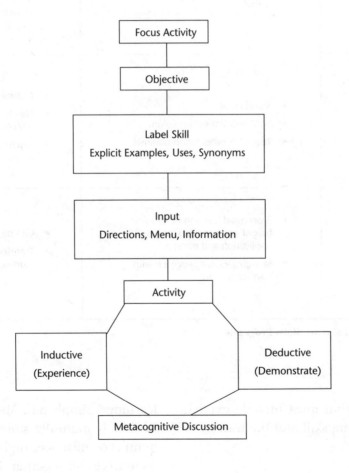

(Based on Beyer's model)

Figure 4   Explicit Skill Instruction Model

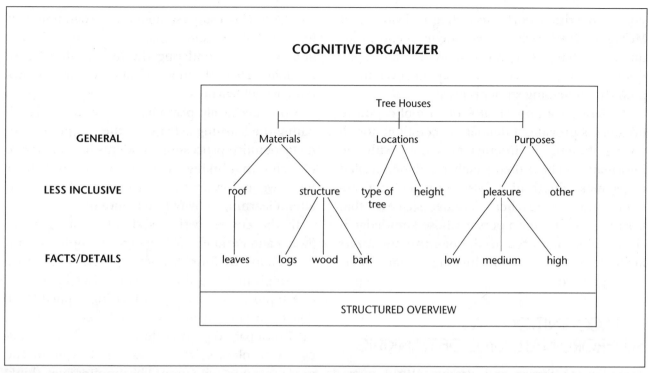

Figure 5   Structured Overview

this advance visual depicts information in hierarchical order and is called a *structured overview* (see Figure 5).

The structured overview always shows vocabulary in relation to more inclusive vocabulary. However don't think of the cognitive structure as passive. It is really quite dynamic. As new information and experiences are assimilated by the learner, it is reorganized cognitively and the graphic display reflects the shifts.

Mapping

Cognitive maps, or organizers, as studied by Armbruster and Anderson (1980), Dansereau et al. (1979), Davidson (1982), and Vaughn (1982), demonstrate success in improving the retention of information. Lyman and McTighe (1988) demonstrate the use of cognitive maps in a discussion of theory-embedded tools for cognitive instruction. They suggest that the ability to organize information and ideas is fundamental to thinking. Graphic displays or cognitive maps aid in the development of organizational skills for students of all ages and abilities across all content.

Cognitive organizers provide a holistic picture of the concept, complete with relationships and interrelationships. Lyman and McTighe suggest that cognitive maps help students:

- represent abstract or implicit information in more concrete forms,
- depict the relationships between facts and concepts,
- generate elaborate ideas, and
- relate new information to prior knowledge.

Maps and Minds—Together

From kindergarten to college, cognitive organizers are employed to help students organize, retain, and assimilate concepts and ideas. Perhaps the most widely used cognitive organizer is the web, which targets a concept and provides structures for analyzing attributes. Other types of maps include sequence chains, vector charts, story maps, analogy links, flow charts, matrices, Venn diagrams, and ranking ladders. These cognitive organizers provide frameworks for class or small-group discussions and written work. According to Lyman and McTighe (1988), when used in conjunction with think-pair-share cooperative strategies and meta-cognitive cues, these cognitive maps are even more powerful in helping students learn.

Perhaps most importantly, the use of cognitive organizers provides a deliberate technique for allowing students to interact personally with the information. These theory-embedded tools, called maps, make the thinking visible for both the students and the teacher. Ausubel suggests that learning is easier for a person whose knowledge is clear, stable, and organized. Cognitive organizers facilitate just that sort of thinking—clear, stable, and organized.

METACOGNITION—A SUPERORDINATE KIND OF THINKING

According to Swartz and Perkins (1989), meta-cognition refers to knowledge about, awareness of, and control over one's own mind and thinking. Costa (1985a) calls this "thinking about thinking." Marzano and Arredondo (1986) also speak of awareness and control over one's own thinking, while Brown (1978) describes the metacognitive process in relationship to the reading process.

They allude to the good reader who reads and reads and reads and suddenly hears a little voice inside his or her head saying, "I don't know what I just read." The words on the page had been read; they had been spoken in the mind, but in a "word-calling" sense, no meaning had been conveyed. Suddenly, the reader becomes aware of this deficit. Good readers realize they have lost contact with the context of the text, and their minds signal them to adapt a recovery strategy: reread the beginning of the paragraph, recall a thought, scan the text for key words...

On the other hand, poor readers read and read and read and never know they don't know. They don't notice that they are getting no meaning from the text because they never have gotten meaning from text. They word-call in their minds, but they are nonreaders in the real sense of reading.

Learning to understand and articulate our own mental processes is a necessary link to fruitful trans-fer—or as Costa suggests about metacognition, having the ability to know what we know and what we don't know and wondering why we are doing what we are doing. That's the metacognition we want to promote for all learners.

More specifically, planning, monitoring, and evaluating the learning activity are the components of metacognitive processing. Students become aware of their own thinking and what goes on inside their heads when they are thinking prior to, during, and after a learning activity (see Figure 6).

In the current writings about metacognition, Swartz and Perkins (1989) gauge the sophistication of thinking by four distinctive levels that are increasingly metacognitive in nature (see Figure 7).

A sophisticated example of paying explicit attention to metacognition is seen in Whimbey's model (1975) of paired partner think-alouds. In this strategy, a problem solver thinks aloud as he or she works through a situation. The monitor cues thinking aloud with specific questions or prompts. Thus, instead of tacitly solving the problem, unaware of the strategies used, awareness is brought to a conscious level. In addition, over time, strategic use is mapped out by both the problem solver and the monitor as problem-solving patterns emerge. Reflective use is inherent in the think-aloud technique. In fact, all four metacognitive levels are clearly evidenced in the strategy.

By using metacognitive prompts we can help students monitor and direct their own thinking as they move toward reflective thinking. Beyond teaching about thinking, metacognitive questions also promote the kind of metaphorical thoughts, generalizations, and mindful abstractions that Perkins and Salomon (1988) suggest are powerful bridges for complex transfer.

In addition, Beyer elaborates on a cueing technique to prompt metacognition. Questions Beyer (1987) suggests to foster metacognitive behavior are:

- What am I doing?
- Why am I doing it?
- What other way can I do it?
- How does it work? Can I do it again or another way?

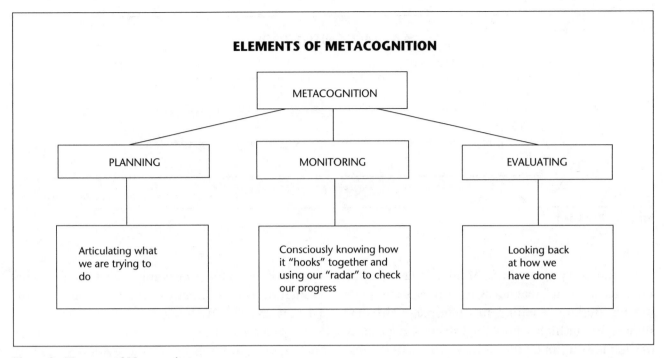

Figure 6   Elements of Metacogniton

• How would I help someone else do it?

These questions and similar questions lead students to examine their own thinking and behavior in ways that press the generalization process. Additional lead-ins that may be discussed within the group or reflected upon individually in a log entry are:

• How is _____ like _____?

• I wish I'd known this when _____.

• Next time, I am going to…

Mrs. Potter's Questions (Fogarty & Bellanca, 1989) are standard metacognitive questions that promote reflective thinking and foster future applications. They are suggested for repeated use to process student thinking during cooperative learning tasks in the classroom.

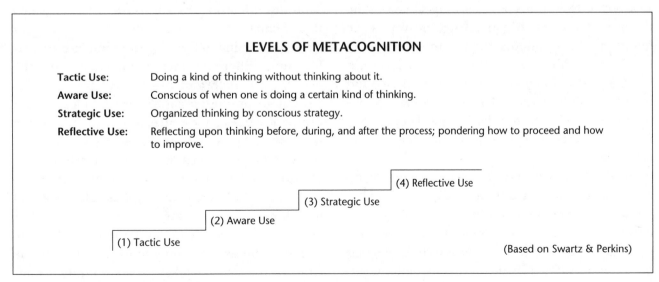

Figure 7   Levels of Metacognition

A METACOGNITIVE TOOL

Affective: How did it feel?

P(+)	
M(-)	
I(?)	

(PMI- based on de Bono's work)

Figure 8 PMI Chart

As the story goes, Mrs. Mimi Potter was Jim Bellanca's "critic" teacher when Jim was completing his student teaching in Champaign-Urbana, Illinois. In this high school English class, regardless of what lesson Jim taught or how successful the lesson seemed, Mrs. Potter would always sit Jim down and ask him to reflect on these questions:

What were you trying to do?

What do you think went well?

What would you do differently next time?

Do you need any help?

In the self-analysis and in answering these four questions, Jim was asked to reflect on his own teaching behavior for future transfer and successful use. Inadvertently, in Jim's own teaching situations, he discovered that he began asking the very same questions of his students. In turn, they became reflective about their own thinking and behavior in his classes. Mrs. Potter's Questions can be posted and used repeatedly as reminders of the metacognitive nature needed for the transfer process. They can easily become part of the processing that follows a cooperative task.

In addition, Beyer (1987) suggests modeling direct instruction of a thinking skill and thinking guides to promote planning, monitoring, and evaluating. A viable tool that students can readily use to assess their own behavior is a strategy based on de Bono's PMI (1970). In this procedure, students look at the affective, cognitive, and meta-

cognitive levels for processing their thinking. This evaluation is tied directly to the learning situation (see Figures 8 & 9).

Regardless of the means or measures used for the metacognitive process, the evidence is clear that explicit attention to the metacognitive—the stuff beyond the cognitive answers—promotes transfer and application of knowledge, skills, concepts, and positive attitudes in novel situations.

BO PEEP, LOST SHEEP, AND THE GOOD SHEPHERD—TALES OF TRANSFER

Isn't all learning for transfer? The question is so generic to the teaching/learning process, one wonders why talk of transfer has become this seemingly unending tale of controversy and confusion. To transfer learning means to use what is learned in one situation in another situation that is either quite like the initial learning situation or even perhaps quite different from the situation in which the learning originally took place.

That seems quite straightforward. In learning to drive one car, we, in essence, transfer that learning to driving all cars. In learning to survey a book, we learn the art of survey as an overview methodology. Of course, we learn things so we can use that learning in other places. Learning has relevance and usefulness.

However, as the tale of transfer unfolds, the complexity of the issue becomes more evident, and the concern for transfer takes on added dimensions. On the one hand, experts over the past twenty-five

LEVELS OF PROCESSING

Cognitive: Assessing answers or strategies.

What answer did you get?

What else?

Tell me more.

Give an example.

Please illustrate.

Metacognitive: Why bother? How can I use this?

Can I:

Duplicate?

Replicate?

Integrate?

Map?

Innovate?

Figure 9   Comparing Cognitive and Metacognitive Questions

years seem to agree that there is a natural dichotomy to this concept called transfer. There appears to be transfer that is simple and another type of transfer that is more complex. The research suggests many terms to describe this dichotomy. For the simple transfer there is: simple (Fogarty, 1989), near (Wittrock, 1967), horizontal (Joyce & Showers, 1983), automatic (Perkins, 1986), lowroad (Perkins & Salomon, 1988), similar (Hunter, 1973; Beyer, 1987), spontaneous (Sternberg, 1984), and practiced (Feuerstein, 1980). For the complex trans-

fer there is: complex (Fogarty, 1989), far (Wittrock, 1967), vertical (Joyce & Showers, 1983), mindful (Perkins, 1986), highroad (Perkins & Salomon, 1988), cued (Beyer, 1987) guided and scaffolded (Sternberg, 1984), and mediated (Feuerstein, 1980) (see Figure 10).

This distinction between simple and complex transfer seems to be fairly easy to sense and deal with. Yet there is another dichotomy in thinking about transfer that takes precedence over all else. In fact, to explore the division in thinking, the con-

DICHOTOMY IN TRANSFER

Low Level	High Level
simple	complex
near	far
horizontal	vertical
automatic	mindful
lowroad	highroad
similar	cued
spontaneous	guided and scaffolded
practiced	mediated

Figure 10   Types of Transfer

troversy over whether transfer is best served with generalized teaching rather than with teaching that has a content-specific focus, we must look historically into the issue.

Bo Peep Theory

"Leave them alone and they'll come home wagging their tails behind them." According to Perkins (1986), this represents the standard instructional practice today. It is the basic position that holds the educational community in its grip at the present time—teach the content, give students practice that is both immediate and spaced over time, and the transfer of learning is sure to follow.

For example, by teaching students the periodic table of elements and giving them practice in recognizing and analyzing the atomic structure of the elements, it is presumed that this factual information somehow transfers into relevant application. With sufficient and varied practice, this may actually occur. Then again, it may not. It may also be presumed that students who learn the periodic table of elements also somehow transfer concepts about patterns, symbolic notation, and about charting information by simply working with the actual table in fact-oriented tasks. While there is some possibility of the first presumption occurring as a result of varied practice, there is slim possibility of the second type of transfer occurring. Bo Peep has lost her sheep here.

Lost Sheep Theory

In fact, according to Fogarty, Perkins, and Barell (1991), over time, transfer has become the lost sheep of the education community. Let's unravel the tale from the beginning to see how this lost sheep theory has evolved to the point that it somehow overrides all other evidence.

Historically, the educational dogma dictating curricula adhered to the idea that Latin, geometry, and the like train the mind. However, in the early 1900s Thorndike and others presented convincing evidence that suggested that training the faculties indeed did not transfer in generalized ways. These researchers favored schooling in which the initial learning situation simulated as closely as possible the anticipated transfer situation. In fact, they advocated learning that encompassed identical elements for the two situations. Training would be specific and transfer would occur.

Diametrically opposed to that view was the position advocated by Polya in the early 1900s that a general, generic, heuristic approach to problem solving in math was the key to the transfer of learning in diverse settings. The arguments for transfer from specific, similar contexts versus transfer from generalizable heuristics began. Unfortunately, buried within the embers of the fading controversy is one illuminating fact. Neither side—context-bound, specific training nor generalizable principles and rules—shows overwhelming and convincing evidence of transfer.

Perkins' summation: "Transfer ain't that great, right now. We're not getting the transfer we want." In fact, the transfer is so lacking and so rare that transfer has become what Perkins now calls the "lost sheep" of education. The attitude is: if it doesn't work, if we can't seem to get the transfer we want, then let's just do better in highly focused subject-oriented lessons. Thus, transfer has been ignored. If transfer can't be there, it's not a big issue. Let's just teach well what we can teach.

Good Shepherd Theory

Fortunately, the transfer embers, close to becoming forgotten ashes, have recently been stirred by the winds of curricular change. A number of voices from the thinking skills movement are focusing on the transfer issue again, igniting sparks of urgent concern and emerging agreements. While the controversy surrounding transfer as context-bound or transfer as generalizable remains a somewhat unresolved issue, agreements about transfer of learning do show evidence of promise for the educational community.

Teaching Latin does not seem to transfer inherently in terms of a more disciplined mind, yet it is now agreed that Latin may not have transferred because Latin had not been taught to cultivate transfer. And while teaching general heuristics such as steps to math problem solving do not seem to transfer into problem-solving steps in the writing process even though transfer had been expected, intricate and powerful implications have emerged from work in both areas.

TRANSFER TACTICS		
	ANTICIPATORY	RETRIEVAL
HIGHROAD	• abstracting rules • anticipating applications	• reflect by generalizing the problem • focus retrieval in one particular context • make metaphors
LOWROAD	• immediate practice • varied practice • matching lesson target and outcome	• varied practice performed over time (Based on David Perkins' work)

Figure 11   Transfer Tactics

In essence, what current transfer research suggests is that when teachers pay attention to transfer in contextual learning situations, transfer does occur. And when general, bare strategies are accompanied with self-monitoring techniques, transfer does in fact occur. In both context-bound teaching and a general heuristics approach, transfer must be shepherded.

Thus, there is Perkins' Good Shepherd theory: when transfer is provoked, practiced, and reflected on, transfer is fairly easy to get. Transfer can be mediated. With the Good Shepherd theory comes new hope for transfer. And with that new hope, of course, comes a new responsibility toward teaching for transfer—for after all, isn't all learning for transfer?

Hugging and Bridging for Transfer

To get transfer, to change Perkins' summation "transfer ain't that great, right now," to "transfer is greater than ever, right now," a close look at transfer reveals two critical elements that foster the transfer phenomenon. Perkins and Salomon (1988) refer to lowroad, automatic transfer and highroad, abstracted transfer. They further describe two mediation strategies for lowroad/highroad transfer which they label *hugging* and *bridging.*

Hugging means teaching so as to better meet the resemblance conditions for lowroad or automatic transfer. Bridging means teaching to better meet the conditions for highroad transfer by mediating the needed processes of abstraction and making connections (Perkins & Salomon, 1988).

While Beyer refers to mediation as cueing what to do, when to do it, and how to do it, his cues take the content lesson's thinking skills into new contexts. Perkins et al. (1989) further suggest that anticipatory tactics and retrieval tactics promote transfer (see Figure 11).

The Transfer Curriculum

In looking at the transfer of learning by adult learners in staff development programs, Joyce and Showers (1983) suggest that, while horizontal transfer shifts directly into the classroom teaching situation, vertical transfer requires adaptation to fit the conditions. Highroad transfer requires understanding the purpose and rationale of the skill and know-how to adapt it with executive control. Still, looking at adult learners, Fogarty (1989) suggests a continuum of transfer behavior within the dichotomy of simple and complex transfer. The learner levels, originally indicative of adult creative transfer, are also similarly applied to student transfer as depicted in Figures 12 and 13.

Awareness of the learner's transfer level and monitoring of that transfer through appropriate cueing questions seem to promote creative transfer, which is increasingly complex. For example, for the learner who is simply "duplicating" the learned skill or strategy, which is a somewhat low level of transfer, the teacher might cue with a question such as, "Can you think of an adjustment you can make so that this idea is useful in another context?" This cue may be enough to spark movement toward *replicated* transfer in which learners personally tailor the idea to suit their needs.

This reflective questioning based on transfer levels is analogous to a student who always draws figures in an identical way, almost as if they were produced in a cookie-cutter fashion. Simply by suggesting that the learner might change the eyes or hair on the figure, or even the size of it, the teacher propels the student toward creative divergence and more complex transfer. The metacognitive reflection questions can be self-monitored or peer-monitored with both adult and student learners. Note the shifts that are required as one wrestles with the transfer cueing questions in Figure 14.

Shepherding Transfer

Some of the current thinking on transfer is addressed by Perkins et al. (1989). They look at the topic of teaching for transfer as the key to more thoughtful instruction. By focusing curricula on the "somethings" to be transferred (the knowledge, skills, concepts, principles, attitudes, and dispositions) and the "somewheres" that teachers want them transferred to (within content, across disciplines, and into life), instruction is expertly tailored by mediating the "somehows" of the hugging and bridging strategies.

By working with the model of "somethings" to transfer "somewhere," the instructional strategies of the "somehows" take on greater emphasis in the teaching/learning situation. In essence, the curricula is shaped with the pieces, which have what Fogarty calls transfer power, and teaching for transfer becomes an explicit part of the lesson (see Figure 15).

Knowing that the Bo Peep theory leads only to the loss of one of the key aspects of the learning situation, the transfer of learning; knowing that by ignoring transfer as the lost sheep of the instructional cycle, we again miss the essence of learning, which of course is the transfer, use, and application of learning in new settings; and knowing that if we pay attention to transfer and guide it like a good shepherd herds sheep, then we will take learning to new heights for learners of all ages and in all situations—knowing all this, we can pay attention to transfer, for isn't all learning for transfer?

CONCLUSION

The four realms of cognitive research tie together to provide practitioners with the tools to teach for thoughtfulness. Based on the context of teaching for transfer, these tools provide rich opportunity for teachers to shift from a conceptually poor recall agenda to a fertile format for mindfulness.

TEACHER LEVELS OF TRANSFER

Ollie

the Head-in-the-sand Ostrich

OVERLOOKS

Does nothing; unaware of relevance and misses appropriate applications; overlooks intentionally. (persists)

"Great session but this wouldn't work with my kids or content" ... "I chose not to... because..."

Dan

the Drilling Woodpecker

DUPLICATES

Drills and practices exactly as presented; Drill! Drill! Then stops; uses as an activity rather than as a strategy, duplicates. (observes)

"Could I have a copy of that transparency?"

Laura

the Look-alike Penguin

REPLICATES

Tailors to kids and content, but applies in similar content; all look-alike, does not transfer into new situation; replicates. (differentiates)

"I use the web for every character analysis."

Jonathan

Livingston Seagull

INTEGRATES

Raised consciousness; acute awareness; deliberate refinement; integrates subtly with existing repertoire. (combines)

"I haven't used any of your ideas, but I'm wording my questions carefully. I've always done this, but now I'm doing more of it."

Cathy

the Carrier Pigeon

MAPS

Consciously transfers ideas to various situations, contents; carries strategy as part of available repertoire; maps. (associates)

"I'm using the webbing strategy for everything."

Samantha

the Soaring Eagle

INNOVATES

Innovates; flies with an idea; takes it into action beyond the initial conception; creates, enhances, invents; takes risks. (diverges)

"You have changed my teaching forever. I can never go back to what I used to do. I know too much. I'm too excited."

Figure 12 Teacher Transfer

STUDENT LEVELS OF TRANSFER

Ollie

the Head-in-the-sand Ostrich

OVERLOOKS

Misses appropriate opportunity; overlooks; persists in former way.

"I get it right on the dittos, but I forget to use punctuation when I write an essay." (Doesn't connect appropriateness.)

Dan

the Drilling Woodpecker

DUPLICATES

Performs the drill exactly as practiced; duplicates.

"Yours is not to question why—just invert and multiply." (When dividing fractions, has no understanding of what she or he is doing.)

Laura

the Look-alike Penguin

REPLICATES

Tailors but applies only in similar situation; all look-alike; replicates.

"Paragraphing means I must have three 'indents' per page." (Tailors into own story or essay, but paragraphs inappropriately.)

Jonathan

Livingston Seagull

INTEGRATES

Is aware; integrates; combines with other ideas and situations.

"I always try to guess (predict) what's going to happen next on T.V. shows." (Connects to prior knowledge and experience.)

Cathy

the Carrier Pigeon

MAPS

Carries strategy to other content and situations. Associates and maps.

Parent-related story—"Tina suggested we brainstorm about our vacation ideas and rank them to help us decide." (Carries new skills into life situations.)

Samantha

the Soaring Eagle

INNOVATES

Innovates; takes ideas beyond initial conception; risks; diverges.

"After studying flow charts for computer class student constructs a Rube Goldberg type invention." (Innovates; invents; diverges; goes beyond and creates novel.)

Figure 13   Student Transfer

TRANSFER CUEING QUESTIONS

OVERLOOKING
Think of an instance when the skill or strategy would be inappropriate.
"I would not use _____ when_____."

DUPLICATING
Think of an "opportunity passed" when you could have used the skill or strategy.
"I wish I'd known about _____ when _____."

REPLICATING
Think of an adjustment that will make your application of _____ more relevant.
"Next time I'm going to _____."

INTEGRATING
Think of an analogy for the skill or strategy.
"_____ is like _____ because both _____."

MAPPING
Think of an opportunity to use the new idea.
"A strategy to carry across is _____."

INNOVATING
Think of an application for a "real-life" setting.
"What if _____."

Figure 14   Transfer Cueing Questions

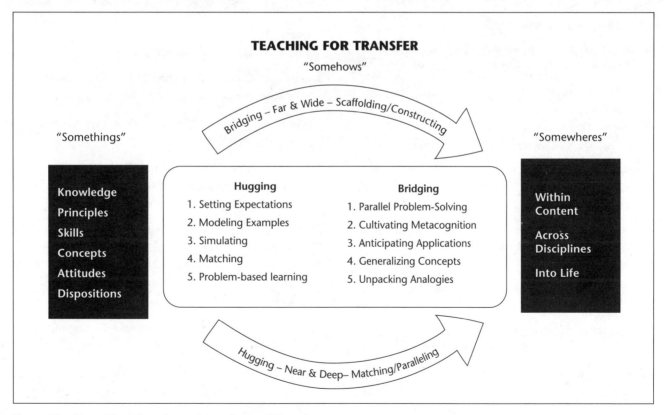

Figure 15   Somethings, Somehows, Somewheres of Transfer

REFERENCES

Adams, M. et al. (1986). *Odyssey: A curriculum for thinking.* Watertown, MA: Mastery Education Corporation.

Anderson, R., Hiebert, E., Scott, J., & Wilkinson, I. (1984). *Becoming a nation of readers: The report of the Commission on Reading.* Washington, DC: The National Institute of Education.

Armbruster, B., & Anderson, T. (1980). *The effect of mapping on the free recall of expository test.* (Technical Report 160). Urbana Champaign: Center for the Study of Reading, University of Illinois.

Ausubel, D. (1978). *Educational psychology: A cognitive view.* (2nd ed.). New York: Holt, Rinehart, & Winston.

Bellanca, J. (1990). *Keep them thinking: Level III.* Palatine, IL: Skylight Publishing.

Bellanca, J., and Fogarty, R. (1990). *Blueprints for thinking in the cooperative classroom.* Palatine, IL: Skylight.

Bellanca, J., & Fogarty, R. (1986). *Catch them thinking: A handbook of classroom strategies.* Palatine, IL: Skylight Publishing.

Beyer, B. K. (1987). *Practical strategies for the teaching of thinking.* Boston: Allyn & Bacon.

Black, H., & Black, S. (1987). *Building thinking skills: Books 1-3.* Pacific Grove, CA: Midwest Publications.

Brown, A. L. (1978). Knowing when, where, and how to remember: A problem of metacognition. In R. Glaser (Ed.), *Advances in instruction psychology* (1). Hillsdale, NJ: Lawrence Erlbaum Associates.

Brown, A., & Campione, J. (1990). Communities of learning and thinking, or a context by any other name. *Human Development, 21,* 108-125.

Costa, A. (Ed.). (1985a). *Developing minds.* Alexandria, VA: Association for Supervision and Curriculum Development.

Costa, A. (1985b). *Teaching for intelligent behavior: A course syllabus.* Orangevale, CA: Search Models Unlimited.

Crabbe, A. B. (1989). The future problem solving program. *Educational Leadership, 47*(1), 27-29.

Dansereau, E., et al. (1979). Development and evaluation of a learning strategy training program. *Journal of Educational Psychology, 71*(1), 64-73.

Davidson, J. (1982, October). The group mapping activity for instruction in reading and thinking. *Journal of Reading,* pp. 53-56.

de Bono, E. (1973). *Lateral thinking: Creativity step by step.* New York: Harper & Row.

de Bono, E. (1970). *Lateral thinking.* New York: Harper and Row.

Edmonds, R. (1979). Effective schools for the urban poor. *Educational Leadership, 37*(1), 15-18.

Feuerstein, R. (1980). *Instrumental enrichment.* Baltimore: University Park Press.

Fogarty, R. (1990). *Keep them thinking: Level II.* Palatine, IL: Skylight Publishing.

Fogarty, R. (1989). *From training to transfer: The role of creativity in the adult learner.* Doctoral dissertation, Loyola University of Chicago.

Fogarty, R., & Bellanca, J. (1989). *Patterns for thinking: Patterns for transfer.* Palatine, IL: Skylight Publishing.

Fogarty, R., & Bellanca, J. (1986). *Teach them thinking.* Palatine, IL: Skylight Publishing.

Fogarty, R., & Opeka, K. (1988). *Start them thinking.* Palatine, IL: Skylight Publishing.

Fogarty, R., Perkins, D., & Barell, J. (1991). *How to teach for transfer.* Palatine, IL: Skylight Publishing.

Gordon, W. J. (1961). *Synectics: The development of creative capacity.* New York: Harper & Row.

Hansen, J., Silver, H., & Strong, R. (1986). *Thoughtful education training series.* Moorestown, NJ: Hansen, Silver, Strong & Associates, Inc.

Harvard University. (1983, October). *Project intelligence: The development of procedures to enhance thinking skills.* Final report. Submitted to the Minister for the Development of Human Intelligence, Republic of Venezuela.

Hunter, M. (1973). *Teach for transfer.* El Segundo, CA: Tip Publications.

Jones, B., Tinzmann, M., & Thelan, J. (1990). *Breakthroughs: Strategy for thinking* (series). Columbus, OH: Zaner-Bloser.

Joyce, B., & Showers, B. (1983). *Power in staff development through research and training.* Alexandria, VA: Association for Supervision and Curriculum Development.

Joyce, B., Showers, B., & Rolheiser-Bennett, C. (1987, October). Staff development and student learning: A synthesis of research and models of teaching. *Educational Leadership, 45,* 17.

Joyce, B., & Weil, M. (1985). *Models of learning.* Englewood Cliffs, NJ: Prentice-Hall.

Lipman, M., Sharp, A., & Oscanyan, R. (1980). *Philosophy in the classroom* (2nd ed.). Philadelphia: Temple University Press.

Lyman, F., & McTighe, J. (1988, April). Cueing thinking in the classroom: The promise of theory-embedded tools. *Educational Leadership, 45* (7).

Marzano, R., & Arredondo, D.(1986). Restructuring schools through the teaching of thinking skills. *Educational Leadership, 43*(8), 23.

Marzano, R., Brandt, R., Hughes, C., Jones, B., Presseisen, B., Rankin, S., & Suhor, C. (1987). *Dimensions of thinking: A framework for curriculum and instruction.* Alexandria, VA: Association for Supervision and Curriculum Development.

Meeker, M. N. (1969). *The structure of intellect: Its interpretation and uses.* Columbus, OH: Charles E. Merrill.

Opeka, K. (1990). *Keep them thinking: Level I.* Palatine, IL: Skylight Publishing.

Parnes, S. (1975). *Aha! Insights into creative behavior.* Buffalo, NY: D.O.K.

Parnes, S. (1972). *Creativity: Unlocking human potential.* Buffalo, NY: D.O.K.

Perkins, D. N. (1986). *Knowledge as design.* Hillsdale, NJ: Lawrence Erlbaum Associates.

Perkins, D. N., & Salomon, G. (1988). Teaching for transfer. *Educational Leadership, 46*(1), 22-32.

Perkins, D. N., Mirman, J., Tishman, S., & Goodrich, H. (1991). *Connections: A program for integrating the teaching of thinking with instruction in the subject matters.* Unpublished material prepared by Project Zero, Harvard Graduate School of Education, Cambridge, MA, in conjunction with the Regional Lab of the Northeast and Islands, Andover, MA.

Pogrow, S. (1990). *HOTS: A validated thinking skills approach to using computers with at-risk students.* New York: Scholastic, Inc.

Sternberg, R. (1984). How can we teach intelligence? *Educational Leadership, 42*(1), 38-48.

Swartz, R. J., & Perkins, D. N. (1989). *Teaching thinking: Issues and approaches.* Pacific Grove, CA: Midwest Publications.

Torrance, E. P. (1978). Giftedness in solving future problems. *Journal of Creative Behavior, 12,* 75-86.

Upton, R. (1985). *Strategic reasoning.* Bloomington, IN: Innovative Sciences, Inc.

Vaughn, L. (1982, February). Use the construct procedure to foster active reading and learning. *Journal of Reading.*

Wales, C., Nardi, A., & Stager, R. (1987). *Thinking skills: Making a choice.* Morgantown: West Virginia University Center for Guided Design.

Whimbey, A. (1975). *Intelligence can be taught.* New York: E. P. Dutton.

Will, H. (1991). The junior great books program of interpretive reading and discussion. In A. Costa (Ed.), *Developing minds: Programs for teaching thinking* (rev. ed., Vol. 2, pp. 57-58). Alexandria, VA: Association for Supervision and Curriculum Development.

Winocur, S. (1983). *Project impact.* Costa Mesa, CA: Orange County School District.

Wittrock, M. (1967). Replacement and nonreplacement strategies in children's problem solving. *Journal of Educational Psychology, 58*(2), 69-74.

THE ART OF STRATEGIC CONNECTIONS

—

Faye Brownlie

As teachers build their classroom inquiry around their students, they weave curriculum content carefully together with processes that invite students to construct meaning.
—Brownlie, Close, & Wingren,1990

Thinking—its diversity in representation and its inherent complexity and apparent simplicity—permeates what we do in school. Thinking bridges the experiences of the students to the written curriculum. Strategies are essential links in thinking of and with our curriculum and in making learning more accessible to more students. In this chapter, I will build a shared view of how strategies can be connectors strengthening the personal scaffolding of a thoughtful curriculum. Strategies can be applied in all subject areas and work for all students, from novice to apprentice to master teacher. Strategies, as described here, are initially teacher-directed, but they enjoy the full realization of their utility when adopted by the students and used independently as learning strategies.

Each subtopic in this chapter will be developed around a different prereading framework. These frameworks link prior knowledge, focus reader/ writer interaction, and exemplify thinking in practice.

ATTRIBUTES OF A THOUGHTFUL CLASSROOM

Teachers today are inviting students to become members of a club—a thinking club in which members are active, constructive makers of meaning. Together in classrooms, working as master builder and apprentice, teachers and students build understanding. There are always many possible right answers. What is crucial in establishing the right-ness of an answer is the speaker's ability to explain his connections or his thinking to make explicit to the audience the way in which he has chosen to use bits of information to create an understanding. Differences in thinking are prized in such thinking clubs. Indeed, it is often these differences that enrich learning if minds are open to hear the surprises of another's thinking. This openness demands a respectful tone in a classroom, and a willingness on the part of all students and teachers to both participate in the construction and to hear and value one another's ideas.

Thinking classrooms are those in which inquiry is valued. Students frequently pose their own questions and learn to carry around in their back pockets those questions whose answers must develop over extended periods of time: "How can I be a faster racer?" "How can we prevent world hunger?" The uncertainty of the unknown is not viewed as an impediment to learning but rather as a challenge for future learning. It is essential to recognize that when we stop asking questions, we stop thinking.

In thoughtful classrooms, students learn how to question and how to search. Strategies and processes for the "how tos" of learning help them become increasingly more independent as questioners and as searchers.

Thoughtful learning also involves reflecting on what has been learned and how it has been learned. Students become aware of their ever-changing knowledge structures, which extend or regroup to fit new information. Students also become aware of how these patterns change with varying contexts and content. This personal reflection on content and process enables students to gain control over their thinking and to monitor and adjust their thinking as the need arises.

Teachers in thoughtful classrooms believe that all students can think, that learning is thinking, that we can all learn to think better, that interaction is fundamental to developing thought, and that teaching and learning in thoughtful classrooms is fun! They arrange for whole-group, small-collaborative-group, and individual experiences during learning sequences. They provide whatever support is necessary for learning to occur, encourage risk taking, and weave a community of learners. Indeed, it is this community of learners that drives the learning experience. Learning now fits the students, who are no longer force-fitted into a predetermined system.

In thoughtful classrooms, the dominant sound is not that of the teacher's voice. Teachers aim to increase the talk time for their students. Students are encouraged to talk with one another as well as with the teacher. The language of recitation is replaced with the language of inquiry and real conversation.

Finally, thoughtful classrooms choose content that is worth knowing. Challenge is implicit in the activities designed to promote interaction with this content. Although the content may be common to all, learners are provided with choice in representation of understanding, in strategies, in timing, in independent versus partner work, or in content within a theme. Students of all ages understand what they are doing and why they are doing it. Teachers also help learners connect the content to their prior knowledge and use it for future inquiry and for wise action.

ATTRIBUTES OF A STRATEGY

When teachers are changing their instructional practices in classrooms and beginning to use more teaching/learning strategies with their students, the change follows a pattern. Change first takes place when teachers get new things to do. In this case, the 'new things' are a set of strategies. As teachers work at extending their strategic repertoires, differences in their students' learning become more obvious. These differences alert them to the possibilities of making more informed choices about the strategies they use; fitting strategies to the goals of their instruction and to student needs; and matching 'how' and 'what' questions more frequently. This is a philosophical shift for many teachers, a shift from teacher as technician to teacher as decision maker. It is also the shift that marks the difference between providing teacher-proof material and material for teaching.

To help teachers make the shift, a strategy such as "Think of a Time" in teacher study groups is very useful. "Think of a Time" is an exercise focusing on the attributes of strategies and on the sophistication of the choice involved each time a teacher selects a strategy to facilitate thinking and learning. By constructing an attribute list together, teachers learn a strategy to use with their students through participation, reflection, and the construction of a personal set of questions or criteria to guide future practice. Questions such as, "How is what I am currently doing in my classroom meeting our learning goals?" can be a frame for change. (See Figure 1.)

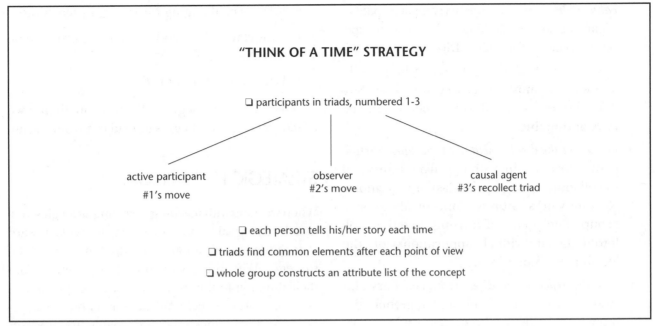

Figure 1 "Think of Time" Strategy

THE SCENARIO:
Imagine a Teacher Workshop

Form groups of three and number yourselves from 1 to 3. We are going to consider the concept of teaching/learning strategies from three points of view: as active participants, as observers, as causal agents. Each member of the triad tells the story of a past teaching experience. After each point of view has been given in your triad, you will consider common elements of the stories you have told. Finally, we will construct an attribute list of strategies that we can personally apply in our classes.

Think of a time when you *personally used* a teaching/learning strategy. In your triad, each tell your story. In your learning logs, identify two or three common elements or attributes of the strategy used in each of your stories.

Number ones rise, say goodbye, and find a new group. This time, think of a time when you *observed someone using* a teaching/learning strategy. In your new triad, each tell your story.

Then, in your learning logs, compare and add to your strategy attribute list. Notice how your thinking is sculpted as you change your point of view and as you move from group to group. Number twos stand, say goodbye, and find a new group. Now

think of a time when you *helped someone use* a teaching/learning strategy. Tell your stories.

How much are you learning about the people you are talking with? Think of how such learning would impact on the social networks of your classroom. Please reflect one more time on the common elements of a strategy. Number threes, call your initial group home.

Now that you are back in your original groups, compare notes on your attribute list and be prepared to help us construct a shared list. Consider which of the elements you have listed are critically important to making a strategy work. Talk about this for a moment in your triads, then we will work as a whole group.

The following list has been compiled after using "Think of a Time" with six different groups of primary and secondary school teachers.

A strategy:

- *is constructive.* A strategy is a vehicle to build understanding. Students use personal understanding, extend this to connect with their small group, and finally extend their understanding to connect with the whole class. Information becomes personally owned and reuseable in different situations.

- *values individuals.* All students can participate in a learning strategy, linking their personal experience to new information. Diversity is honored.

- *is supportive of risk taking.* A strategy helps build a climate of mutual respect and trust. Students are encouraged to be open to others' ways of thinking.

- *focuses on the development of social skills.* Participants move within a strategy from individual to collaborative groups to class organizations. No one works entirely alone or always in a group. The power of learning together, followed by individual applications of the learning is emphasized.

- *includes reflection and feedback.* Teachers and students examine, alone and together, the impact of the use of the strategy on learning.

- *is adaptable and transferable.* The pattern in any specific strategy is not fixed. Strategies adapt and change with purpose and with the growing expertise of the participants. Any strategy should be useable in many different contexts and contents.

- *strengthens with practice.* A strategy improves as a learning tool as learners become more competent with its use.

- *encourages independence.* A strategy is ultimately useful if learners can integrate the thinking behind the strategy into their own repertoires, and make use of it in other learning situations.

This strategy, "Think of a Time," is readily transferable. Together with a group of teachers, a teacher leader or an administrator could construct the group's attribute list. Then teachers can use this list to focus their reflections on the strategic learning opportunities available in their classrooms. The following questions are examples of those used in encouraging teacher reflection:

- What am I currently feeling very successful about in strategic learning?

- What is my evidence for this success?

- What does this strategy look like and sound like in my classroom?

- What is challenging for me in my teaching?

- How can I tell when I am making progress on this challenge?

- What kind of support do I need?

When teachers begin reflecting on their own practice, education begins to lead out from within.

STRATEGIC PLANNING

When working with teaching/learning strategies, ultimately the goal is to move the students toward independent application of the thinking behind the strategy. With this goal in mind, teachers explain their thinking to the students, modeling the choices available and the decisions made in choosing a particular strategy. Such modeling enables the students to use these considerations later to help make their own informed decisions about learning when the teacher is not there to guide them. The teacher thus explains the why of the strategy (what is the purpose? what do we hope to achieve?) and the how (the steps, a preview of what is going to happen, an advance framework to enable students to construct a "big picture"). (See Figure 2.)

The reasoning behind a strategy requires explicit instruction. Thus, the teacher teaches the strategy in context with the whole class, then reflects with the students on what they did and why. This can be risky for teachers, especially as this "sharing of all the cards" with the students may be new to them. We often do not feel comfortable when students give feedback on our teaching, even if it is constructive. Sometimes we have not reflected ourselves on reasons for the lesson design, or may be so used to choosing strategies that match our learning style that we unintentionally overlook those students who process information more easily in another style.

It is not our intent to focus only on students' preferred ways of thinking. The challenge is to build up an acknowledged student repertoire. Thus, it is critically important that we listen carefully to the students at this phase, helping them understand our choices and helping them recognize which parts of the learning sequence were most functional and applicable for

---

STRATEGIC PLANNING

SETTING THE STAGE

1. Identify the strategy to be taught.
2. Discuss the reasons why it is being taught.
3. Tell the steps of the strategy.

MODELING AND DIRECT INSTRUCTION

4. Teach the strategy in an appropriate context.
5. Provide opportunities for whole-group work, collaborative-group work, and individual work.
6. Reflect with your students on what you did and why.

GUIDED PRACTICE

7. Review the steps of the strategy with the students.
8. Establish criteria for effective use of the strategy.
9. Use the strategy in a variety of contexts and with a variety of texts.
10. Reflect with your students on their growing competency with the strategy.

ENCOURAGING INDEPENDENT APPLICATION

11. Provide opportunities for students to use the strategy independently in materials of their own choosing.
12. Encourage adaptation of the strategy to fit text, context, and personal style.
13. Monitor the student's expertise and independent application of the strategy.
14. Monitor the gradual diminishment of teacher support needed.

From *Tomorrow's Classroom Today* by F. Brownlie, S. Close, & L. Wingren: Pembroke, 1990. Reprinted with permission.

Figure 2 Strategic Planning

---

them. Such feedback empowers individual learners, and extends and refines a strategy beyond a recipe stage. When students consider the purpose of an activity within a classroom, they become more involved with meaningful issues and thus more motivated to participate and learn. This is a strong move away from things being done to students in classrooms, to events being planned with students in classrooms.

The effective use of strategies in classrooms takes time to develop. Working through a checklist of strategies, trying each one or two times, does not extend thinking across the curriculum or impact significantly on student learning. Effective change in thinking requires using a few strategies in a variety of contexts and with a variety of texts or contents over time. Students work with teachers to establish criteria for effective use of the strategy and monitor their use of this strategy and their subsequent learning. Some of my most effective staff development programs have focused on using six new strategies in one year, refining them to the stage where a teacher automatically can take a learning goal, consider the students involved, con-

sider the resources available, and apply the most appropriate strategy or strategy sequence.

The decision making involved in using strategies is fully realized when it is transfered to the students. Our goal is to support them in becoming independent learners. They need opportunities to apply the strategies themselves in materials and situations of their own choosing. They need not adopt our strategies, but they do need to adapt and refine them to suit their learning purposes and styles. Over time, with students of all ages, the amount of teacher support required in a strategic sequence will diminish. Students, too, will be able to choose a strategy that best fits their learning purposes from their own repertoires. Thus, both the content of the curriculum and the thinking processes of the curriculum are being personalized and learned. It is this "how to" of the processes that enables students to become lifelong learners.

Monitoring the Strategies We Teach
Perhaps the most unfamiliar element in the process of implementing strategic connections in

classrooms is the need to develop some practices for monitoring the effective use of the strategies. Reflection on and about practice is new to many of us.

The development of criteria for success is key in monitoring our development. Sometimes we use criteria from the outside. In this case, teachers could use the attributes of a strategy that we developed in teacher study groups. These attributes can be applied as personal frameworks for monitoring and enhancing our growth. Questions we use to guide our application of this framework include:

- Who is the audience?
- What is the purpose?
- What is the form?
- How do I tell if we are getting better at it?
- What are my criteria for success?
- Which elements of this strategy are clearly evident in my classroom—choice, active learning, practice, modeling of thinking?
- What do I need to do more of, more often?
- Which of these strategies most supports the thinking of my students?
- Have I provided ample opportunity for whole-group practice of the strategy and for individual choice in using the strategy?

Even more powerful is developing with your students, or with a colleague or a group of colleagues, your own list of attributes. This list then becomes a more relevant framework for monitoring and enhancing strategic growth. The more students know about the overarching classroom goals, the more easily and expertly they participate with you in evaluating the use of strategies to facilitate their learning.

Some teachers have been using Howard Gardner's theory of multiple intelligences as their framework for monitoring teaching/learning strategies in the classroom. A form, such as the one in Figure 3a, is completed at a natural break, such as the end of a day or the end of several classes. Some teachers choose to complete this independently: some choose to complete it with their students. Of course, the importance of completing a form such as this is that it enables us to reflect on our past decisions as teachers and to fuel wise action. If we

find we are spending an inordinate amount of instructional time around a cluster of intelligences, then the form should prompt us to consider a different strategic sequence that addresses several intelligences.

Some teachers have also used a form such as the one in Figure 3b to track the focus strategies they teach and the opportunities they provide students for independent application of the strategy.

Students Monitoring the Strategies They Use

The ultimate goal in teaching is to enable students to become independent, lifelong learners. Teachers must involve students in reflection on their thinking and on the use of strategies to help them think. The following student samples were collected from three different grade groups, each using the same strategy: "Listen—Sketch—Draft" (Brownlie, Close, & Wingren, 1990).

In a grade two/three class, the students were very used to reflecting on their thinking and to being actively involved in examining their learning. When a relief teacher came to their class, she asked them what they noticed about their thinking. Brent explained his drawing: "My ideas came from listening to the story, mixing that up in my brain, and remembering what I needed by drawing pictures." What he noticed about the story was "My think is nobodys perfect," an apt summary, considering the story he had heard was about an old lady who had lost her memory. When asked how the strategy had helped, he said, "it encrises [increases] your thinking." (See Figure 4.) Tricia understands that a thoughtful response to reading is moving beyond the story to personalize the meaning. (See Figure 5.)

Although this strategy was new to the students, they have ably applied their personal knowledge about how thinking works in reflecting on their use of the new strategy. Their representations show a developing understanding of how to connect stories to their lives.

These responses are from a grade three/four class:

I want to write to people. Not talking would make me think better. I was thinking about what I would do if I was a writer.

MONITORING MULTIPLE INTELLIGENCE STRATEGIES

Date: _____   Name/Class: _____

Record each time you practice or I teach using a different intelligence. Let's try to give examples.

Linguistic: _____

Visual: _____

Logical/Mathematical: _____

Body/Kinesthetic: _____

Musical/Rhythmical: _____

Interpersonal: _____

Intrapersonal: _____

*Did you have a preference for any intelligence or any combination?

_____

_____

*Were you surprised by any aspect of this record?

_____

_____

*What is your plan to expand your thinking?

_____

Figure 3a Monitoring Strategies Via Gardner's Intelligences

TRACKING FOCUS STRATEGIES

Name: _____   Date: _____

Date/ Month	Strategy	Shared Selection	Independent Application
September			
October			
November			
December			
January			
February			
March			
April			
May			
June			

From *Reading and Responding: Evaluation Resources for Your Classroom (Grade 4)* by S. Jeroski, F. Brownlie, and L. Kaser: Nelson Canada, 1990. Reprinted with permission.

Figure 3b Teacher's Record

What I noticed about my thinking.

My think is nobodys perfict

and it encriBes your thinking. ✓

Brent

Figure 4 Brent's Drawing

I was thinking about the story and if it was true.

I think it's good but it's nicer to draw good colour pictures.

Neks time it mite be eseyr. The picjer was esey. [Next time it might be easier. The picture was easy.]

The students have linked their thinking to real world purposes—writing and truth. They acknowledge the challenge and give advice for color pictures and more practice to make it easier. Their ability to articulate these thoughts enhances their monitoring of their necessary conditions for learning.

Finally, these reflections with the same strategy, are from a grade nine class:

When other people are talking I notice that I can put all of my effort to remembering or imagining, but when I read fifty percent goes to reading and fifty percent to imagining which means I don't remember as well; if its a good story, but if its dull my mind wanders.

Jamie is definitely a social learner!

I notice about my thinking that when someone is reading to me, I make up pictures about it in my head which often pertain to my life.

Stephen acknowledges both the images he uses in listening and the personal connections he makes as he extends beyond the text.

My thinking gets side-tracked to what the tape or the people are saying. My thoughts get mixed up and unclear before getting into the story.

For Sabrina, making meaning requires some time and distance.

It is evident from the student samples that they are internalizing what is valued in the classroom. As they reflect on their thinking and their use of strategies, teachers use the information to monitor their students' developing independence and to provide appropriate instructional support.

To close, see Figure 6, Alanna's poem reflecting on her thinking and learning at the end of her first full year of school. Alanna is definitely uncovering the mysteries of lifelong learning!

	What I noticed about my thinking.
Michelle	that I was biloing My thinking up
Jennifer	My dran was geting good rchers in my head
Tricia	I wos Thinking aubat the story and I icpandr

Figure 5 Michelle, Jennifer, Tricia

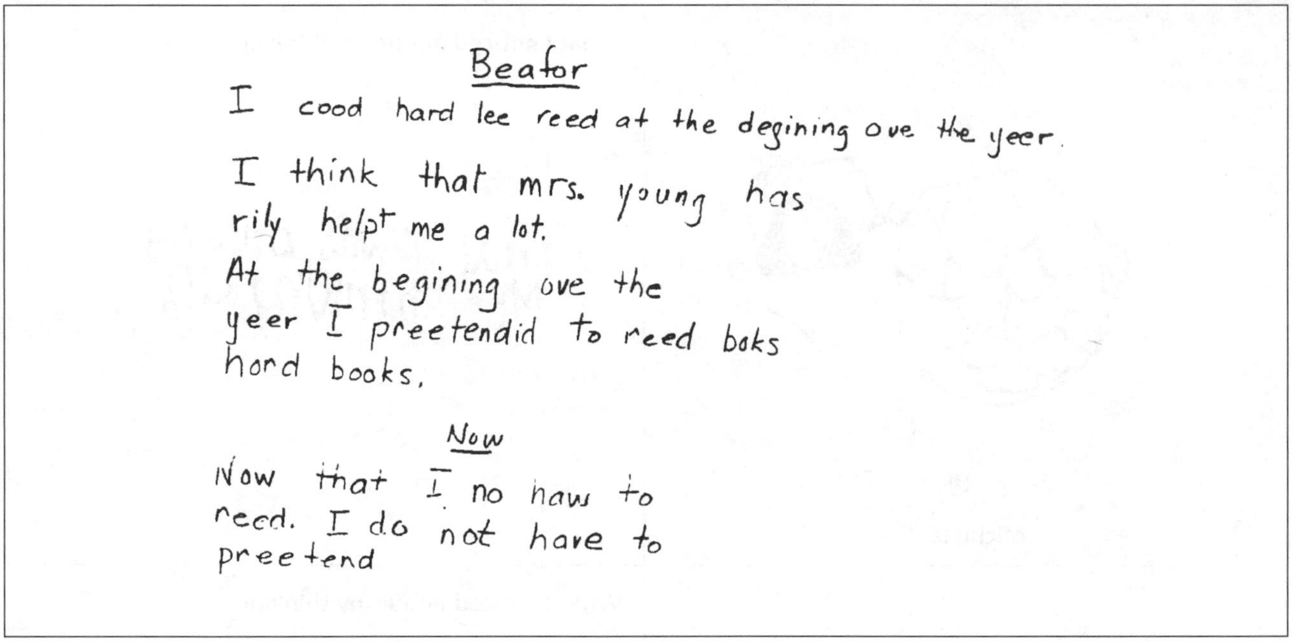

<u>Beafor</u>

I cood hard lee reed at the degining ove the yeer.

I think that mrs. young has rily helpt me a lot.

At the begining ove the yeer I preetendid to reed boks hord books.

Now

Now that I no haw to reed. I do not have to preetend

Figure 6   Alanna's Poem

REFERENCES

Brown, R. (1991). *Schools of thought.* San Francisco: Jossey-Bass.

Brownlie, F., Close, S., & Wingren, L. (1990). *Tomorrow's classroom today: Strategies for creating active readers, writers, and thinkers.* Portsmouth, NH: Heinemann and Makham, Ontario: Pembroke.

Brownlie, F., Close, S., & Wingren, L. (1988). *Reaching for higher thought: Reading, writing, thinking strategies.* Edmonton, AL: Arnold Publishing.

D'Arcy, P. (1989). *Making sense, shaping meaning: Writing in the context of a capacity-based approach to learning.* Portsmouth, NH: Boynton/Cook Publishers.

Eisner, E. (1991). *The enlightened eye.* New York: Macmillan.

Gardner, H. (1983). *Frames of mind: The theory of multiple intelligence.* New York: Basic Books.

Jeroski, S., Brownlie, F., & Kaser, L. (1990). *Reading and responding: Evaluation resources for your classroom.* (Three volumes: Grades 4, 5, & 6). Toronto, ON: Nelson, Canada. (Available in the U.S. from The Wright Group. Bothel, WA).

Jeroski, S., Brownlie, F., & Kaser, L. (1991). *Reading and responding: Evaluation resources for your classroom.* (Two volumes: Late primary and Primary). Toronto, ON: Nelson Canada. (Available in the U.S. from The Wright Group. Bothel, WA).

Ministry of Education. (1991). *Thinking in the classroom: Resources for teachers.* Victoria, BC: Ministry of Education.

Smith, F. (1991). *To think.* Columbia, New York: Teachers College Press.

CREATING THE THOUGHTFUL CLASSROOM

—

Jean Speer Cameron

Today's classroom in which children are not challenged to be thinkers looks very much like the classroom in which those who are attempting to restructure education spent their school years. The room is organized with five rows of desks, six desks in each row. The teacher's desk is usually located in the front of the room. In another area of the room, a cluster of small chairs is grouped around an adult chair. A rug is on the floor in another area. A glance into the room would show the majority of the children sitting at their desks doing seat work while another small group of children gathers around the teacher for a twenty-minute reading lesson. Except for the sound of a child reading to the teacher, the room is quiet. Occasionally, a child leaves the row of seats to sharpen a pencil or to put the appropriate card in the washroom slot. The activities in the room are controlled by the teacher, and the children comply with expectations. Learning is occurring, but with little involvement by the children and much control by the teacher.

The classroom in which children are challenged to be thinkers and learners has a different appearance. The furniture is in a flexible arrangement so

it can be rearranged to support a variety of class activities. Sometimes the desks are in rows, but more often they are grouped by pairs or are in groups of four or five. The teacher's desk is tucked away in a corner. Most of the instruction is directed to the entire class, reducing the need for seat work while the teacher works with a small group of children. On the chalkboard is a web representing the brainstorming the children participated in to develop ideas for writing a story. The physical space of the classroom is enriched by a multitude of student-generated projects attached to the walls, ceiling, windows, and any other available spaces. There is a hum of activity as children read to each other and share stories they have written. A casual observer might have difficulty locating the teacher, who has joined the children working in the science corner.

Teachers whose classrooms look like the first one are often well-trained in management skills. They are respected by their peers, parents, and administrators for directing children through the objectives of the curriculum. The children are not unhappy in these classrooms when the teacher is a caring, nurturing individual. However, a lesson that these children learn early is that those who are most successful in school are those who comply with the rules, work quietly, complete what is asked of them, and learn the facts that are taught to them. School is not a place to question, analyze, create, synthesize, or evaluate. This traditional classroom, with its emphasis on compliance, no longer prepares children to be productive citizens in the global, technological society of the twenty-first century. Today's children live in a world in which the information explosion requires that citizens learn how to manage information, not memorize facts. To manage information, children need to learn not only content, but also processing skills and how to work in a cooperative, teaming approach.

To create the necessary changes in which instruction is delivered requires a systematic process. Michael Fullan suggested a model for change in a 1989 presentation to the Illinois Association for Supervision and Curriculum Development Fall Conference. It provided direction for a public school district in Illinois that was attempting a major change. Fullan's model of change included three separate phases—initiation, implementation, and institutionalization. The initiation phase involves those events that lead up to and include a decision to proceed with a change. The first experiences of putting the idea into practice are the implementation phase. Institutionalization has to do with whether or not the change becomes an ongoing part of the system. Within each of the three phases Fullan described a set of success factors.

Fullan's model provided the guidelines needed for the change process that had just begun in Elmhurst Community District 205 in Elmhurst, Illinois. District 205 includes grades kindergarten through twelve, with a teaching staff of approximately 400 and a student enrollment of 6,000. Prior to the initiation of a thinking skills program in the district, instruction in many classrooms was similar to the traditional classroom described above. Through reading articles in educational journals and participating in professional growth activities, some teachers had become aware of the thinking skills movement. Other teachers had developed, through their own experiences, a style of teaching that valued students as thinkers.

INITIATE INNOVATION – PHASE I

In the initiation stage Fullan described the change success factors as:

- a linking of the change to a high-profile need,
- a clear model of procedures for implementation,
- a strong advocate who provides both pressure and support, and
- an active, short start-up period.

Link Change to High-Profile Need

The development of a high-profile need for change across the district was created when—through the efforts of the central office administration—the following instructional goal was adopted for the district:

> *To improve student achievement through a focus on the instructional, classroom management, and communication skills that foster cognitive instruction and higher-level thinking.*

A task of the change agent in the initiation stage is to create the high-profile need. Thinking skills were not perceived by most staff in District 205 as a high-profile need prior to the writing of the district instructional goal. That perception changed as the goal shifted to the building and individual levels. Once an instructional goal has been approved by the Board of Education, principals work with their staff to incorporate the district goal into the building's goals and activities. For example, each teacher's professional goals are developed in collaboration with the supervisor to support building and district goals. This process provides the mechanism for bringing a high-profile need of thinking skills into the goals of the schools and the staff members.

Set Model for Change

Progress toward fulfilling an instructional goal on thinking requires a consideration of the current curriculum, the needs of the teacher, and the structure of the district. Though teachers say they value the teaching of thinking skills, often their first real concern is that there is not enough time in the school year to teach the current curriculum. An approach to the teaching of thinking that supports the curriculum and values the concerns of the teacher is one more likely to be implemented. Fullan referred to Seymour Sarson's statement that educational change depends on what teachers do and think—it's as simple and as complex as that.

Though several models for thinking were reviewed for possible implementation, the one that seemed most appropriate for use in District 205 was one that focused on teaching strategies to enhance thinking within the curriculum, rather than adding to the already crowded curriculum. The teaching strategies in the adopted model were appropriate across grade levels and content areas, an important dimension in a K-12 district.

The training model focuses on four essential elements that promote thinking in the classroom—setting the climate for thinking, structuring interaction with thinking, teaching explicit skills of thinking, and using metacognitive processing about thinking. The training for teachers is organized to support transfer from the work session to the classroom. Since teachers provide the framework for a thinking classroom, they are asked to consider the following groups of questions (from Fogarty & Bellanca, 1989) as they adjust their instruction to promote thinking.

Setting the Climate for Thinking   Setting a safe climate for thinking by modeling risk taking and acceptance.

- Does the room arrangement invite interaction, openness, flexibility?
- What verbal and nonverbal messages are you communicating?
- Are you modeling the teacher as a learner?
- Do you LISTEN?
- Do you energize and motivate?
- Do you tolerate the noise, movement, and failure that sometimes accompany a thinking environment?
- Do you set an atmosphere of expectancy and focus?
- Do you project high expectations?
- Do you treat students as thinkers?

Structuring Interaction with Thinking   Getting students to process the information and interact with the material in experiential activities.

- Do you structure groups to accommodate various learning situations and learning styles?
- Do you model the teacher as a participant?
- Do you invite involvement through forced responses?
- Do you set clear rules and objectives for students to target?
- Do you assign roles and responsibilities to foster accountability and cooperative efforts?
- Do you listen, observe, and facilitate interaction to foster thinking in the classroom?

Teaching Explicit Skills of Thinking   Teaching the thinking skill explicitly to students and bridging skill application into relevant situations.

- Do you teach the micro-skills of thinking explicitly?
- Do you define terms and post the objective?
- Do you vary the learning input to meet different learning styles and different rates of learning?
- Do you provide opportunities for students to process the material?
- Do you build in guided practice with monitoring and feedback?
- Do you value thinking enough to set time priorities to teach the skills?

Using Metacognitive Processing About Thinking Getting students to think about their thinking and deliberately bring their thinking patterns to a conscious level.

- Do you process learning activities with students?
- Do you help them track their thinking patterns by inviting them to verbalize how they did what they did?
- Do you lead them into metacognitive processing by providing time to reflect in writing about their thinking strategies?
- Do you help students make the connections between new learning and past experiences?
- Do you guide them to extend new learning with relevant situations both in and out of the classroom?

- Do you bridge learning to help students make the transfer?
- Do you provide visual formats and ask metacognitive questions?

Advocate Change

In the initiation phase of change, the vision and support of a strong advocate is an essential component. The change advocate in the District 205 process—to facilitate instruction that supports students as thinkers—came through the director of instruction, a position in the superintendent's cabinet. The superintendent had reorganized the central office responsibilities and created the Office of Instruction and Human Resource Development to connect the instructional needs of staff with appropriate professional growth activities. Though the instructional goal had been developed primarily by the director of instruction, the support of the superintendent and the Board of Education validated its importance to the district staff. The director of instruction was able to work with the staff development committee and other district administrators in the implementation of the goal.

Initiate Action

Though a multi-year plan was developed to initiate the goal, the first year of the plan began with a focus group of teachers and administrators from each of the district's twelve schools. Each of the schools in District 205 was expected to form a team of volunteer teachers and the building principal to participate in a series of workshops related to instructional strategies that enhance a thinking classroom. The four full-day workshops were scheduled in a classroom at one of the district's elementary schools, with the first workshop held in October and the last in May. Teams were expected to participate in all four sessions along with the superintendent and the director of instruction. The funding for the activity was obtained through the state staff development grant and covered the costs of the consultant, materials, and substitutes for teachers.

Since the first training is a pivotal one for the outcome of the project, the details for the first session had to be carefully planned. Twelve teams in District 205 began a project based on an instructional goal and an overview of a training package

that had been presented to them prior to volunteering for the project. The initial training session needed to capture their enthusiasm and provide them with a vision of how their participation could be a change model for instruction. Important factors to consider were the consultant's skills in establishing a climate that supported the adult learner as a thinker, the training materials and activities, the readiness level of the volunteers, the participants' affective needs as learners, and the wide range of skills represented by the learners. District 205 volunteers included teachers with tenure in the district and newer teachers.

In the first training session, the expectation was established that all participants, teachers *and* administrators, would be actively involved in the activities and would commit to using the strategies within their workplace prior to the next session. The expectation that change would occur as a result of the training was also a critical component of the beginning session. Each participant was asked to use several activities from the training and to bring back artifacts to share at the next training session. Transfer from training to the workplace was established as an expectation of participation.

During the first year of the training, enthusiasm for the implementation of the strategies presented during the District 205 workshops increased as team members shared their success stories with each other and with other teams. In each session, participants practiced a few skills in each of the four essential elements of the thinking classroom. They then used them with their students. They were excited about positive student reaction to paired partners and cooperative groups. They brought back to the training sessions samples of brainstorming, huge sheets of newsprint covered with webs. The teacher's new role in stressing student interaction with each other and the materials of learning was not always comfortable. But, in the training sessions, participants discussed their successes and received support when new strategies had not worked as planned.

Several factors of the thinking skills model and similar trainings increased participants' enthusiasm for a change project. The strategies teachers transferred into the classroom fit into their repertoire. They often were not new strategies but a validation of an approach already in use. Though the thinking skills strategies slowed down the delivery of curriculum, their use did not expand it. Of great importance to teachers, they often received support from students when attempting the strategies. Teachers were encouraged to continue working with the strategies when administrators incorporated the strategies into the activities that they directed. Administrators used the strategies in team and building meetings and administrator work sessions.

The last workshop training session with the consultant was used by each team to develop an action plan for the continued implementation of the instructional strategies at each building. These plans were used to refine the district instructional goal for the second year of the program.

IMPLEMENT INNOVATION – PHASE II

Change is a process that occurs over a period of extended time. The first year of training in the District 205 thinking program was the first step in a plan that has continued for six years. Fullan described several essential factors in the implementation of an innovation:

- orchestration of the network for change,
- empowerment of others to share in the problem solving and decision making,
- pressure and support in a delicate balance,
- training and coaching in the innovation, and
- reinforcement with early and frequent recognition and rewards.

The success of a program, as evidenced by transfer of instructional strategies in classrooms across a district, reflects attention to Fullan's implementation of innovation factors.

Orchestrate The Network

Inherent in the orchestration of an activity is a plan that includes a director and players, each with specific roles and responsibilities for creating the desired change. The orchestration plan in District 205 began with the training of the volunteer teams at each building. These teams developed action plans for implementation, which differed somewhat from team to team. Some teams chose to meet periodically during the following year to discuss the strategies that they were using and to encourage each other. Others decided to select several of the strategies for a presentation to other staff members at their school. All teams defined the need to continue meeting in some format during the second year to move forward in using the strategies.

The focus from the district perspective was to create the network for change at several levels. At the building level, the teams were expected to continue using the instructional strategies during year two within their own classrooms. Additional volunteers were solicited from each building to participate in another four days of district training during year two.

Empower Others

Those who were involved in the first training were asked to assume the role of peer coach for the additional staff at their buildings participating in the second training. Prior to the second training, a review session was held for those previously trained at each building to discuss the strategies that would be presented in the workshops. This had two purposes. It served as a review of the strategies for the first group, and it provided them with a focus for sharing with the new teachers involved. Those beginning the training were asked to practice the instructional strategies presented and to invite teachers from the first training to visit their classrooms. This helped develop a dialogue related to the implementation of the skills.

Since the number of high school teachers in the first training for District 205 was smaller in proportion to the total number of teachers than at the elementary or junior highs, the high school principal requested that the training be provided for an expanded group of high school staff members. Each department chair was expected to participate in the training along with a volunteer member from each department. The high school principal and assistant principal made a commitment to participate in the workshops with the groups of teachers. Though the department chairs were required to attend, other staff members had the opportunity to volunteer. The high school workshops put stress on the substitute staff and the building facilities, but the consultant was able to work through these distractions.

Balance Pressure and Support

The delicate balance of pressure and support that Fullan described is essential in the implementation of change. In the second year of the training, support for the program was maintained at various levels. Across the entire district, principals and the teams who participated in the first training worked together to implement the strategies. Principals and trained staff members met before school to share ideas related to implementation of the strategies. They made presentations at faculty meetings for other staff members and shared materials from the training sessions. Support for District 205 teams also came from the continued district focus on their instructional goal, which incorporated teaching strategies related to climate setting, student interaction, explicit thinking skills, and metacognition. Scheduling the thinking skills consultant for more intense training workshops at the high school level validated the district's continued support. The training continued at the elementary and junior high schools though it was delivered by a district administrator.

Pressure was also placed on those who were involved in the first training to continue using the thinking strategies as peer coaches for those in the second training. Prior to the training sessions at the District 205 elementary and junior high schools, the district trainer met with the peer coaches to review the strategies that would be presented, to encourage sharing how they were using the strategies, and to brainstorm ways they could support those people beginning the training.

Throughout District 205 a variety of methods were used to maintain enthusiasm for the program. Building principals worked with their teams to find ways of sharing the thinking strategies through grade level, department, and building meetings. A teacher and principal who had been involved in the first year of training prepared a videotape for presentation to the Board of Education. It demonstrated the strategies in a fourth grade class. A two-hour overview of the program was presented by the consultant for all teachers in the district as part of an institute day. Following the session, those who had previously participated in the training or who were currently involved in the training were invited to a special "reunion" session with the consultant.

At the conclusion of the first intense year of training at the high school, the principal required each department to select at least five of the thinking skills strategies to focus on during the next school year. Those who participated in the training were expected to share the strategies with others within the department and to demonstrate implementation of the skills. The high school plan for the third year included continued training from the program consultant, and it required all new staff members and volunteers from the tenure staff to participate.

Train and Coach

As teachers began to develop a level of expertise in the use of the thinking strategies, there emerged at the elementary level two who had reorganized the material into a succinct format that seemed to facilitate the use of the skills in their third and fifth grade classrooms. These two enthusiastic teachers were willing to present workshops to other elementary teachers. For the next three years, those who had not already participated in workshops at the elementary level and teachers new to the district worked with the district trainers in workshops. The training was consolidated into two half-day sessions scheduled over a month to allow for practice with the strategies between sessions. As previously, those at a building who had participated in earlier trainings were expected to serve as peer coaches for those in the current sessions. A trained teacher has paired with a teacher just beginning training in the building. They periodically met to share their use of strategies and to plan classroom visits to observe each other implementing the strategies with students.

At the high school level, a science teacher emerged as one who was able to implement the program very successfully in his classroom and who also had the skills to present the strategies to his peers. After the initial years of training with the program consultant, the continuing training at the high school level was assumed by the science teacher, who used a format similar to the one developed for the elementary teachers.

Reinforce with Recognition and Rewards

Successful implementation of an innovation requires reinforcement with early and frequent recognition and rewards. Attention was given to this requirement at the building level and district level as the program was implemented. The teams at each building who participated in the first year of training were recognized as the experts and were expected to continue a leadership role as other teachers began using the skills. In each successive training session the new experts were added as building resources. Teachers were selected from the experts to continue the training workshops. Several networking sessions were scheduled across the district so those who had participated in the training could share the strategies they were using successfully and receive additional support to continue the thinking strategies focus. The consultant scheduled a reunion with teachers who had participated in the training. A financial incentive was developed by the district in order to reimburse the teachers who had emerged as trainers.

At the district level, recognition was given to participants through a presentation to the Board of Education. Teachers prepared a videotape demonstrating thinking strategies in the classroom. It was shown to the board and also used in subsequent training sessions. Slides were taken throughout the district, illustrating the application of thinking strategies in the classroom. This slide presentation was developed primarily for the board as an evaluation of the training to demonstrate there had been transfer from the workshops to instruction. It was also used in presentations for other educational agencies at the local and national levels.

Those who participated in the training originally have continued to receive recognition for their efforts. The teachers who emerged as trainers have participated in workshops at the national level and have enhanced their presentation skills. As they have continued to train their peers, they have also contracted with other organizations to teach thinking skills. The district continues to receive inquiries and visits from other educators about the process used to implement the thinking skills program and the transfer of the training into the classrooms.

Validation from the board and the administration that the teachers who participated in the thinking skills program have made a significant impact on changes in classroom instruction provides reinforcement that supports continuation of the program. The early and frequent recognition and rewards were an important component in support of change.

INSTITUTIONALIZE INNOVATION– PHASE III

Even though the components for initiation and implementation of an innovation are followed, the continuation of a change requires that the innovation become institutionalized. Fullan suggested that for this to happen the innovation must be

- embedded both politically and economically as part of a system,

- linked to instruction and have widespread use, and

- provided with continuing assistance.

Since classroom instruction that facilitates thinking strategies depends on how teachers teach, specific attention must be given to an ongoing process that will maintain those strategies as district and building priorities.

Embed Innovation

In order to maintain a focus on thinking skills, District 205 had to develop a plan for embedding the program politically and economically into the ethos of the system. The focus on thinking began with the development of a district instructional goal. After five years, most teachers in the district had participated in the training, and instructional strategies across the district reflected the thinking focus. District administrators and teachers were hesitant to eliminate a specific instructional goal related to thinking. But, they also realized that at some point other goals would need to be stressed. Consequently, after five years, rather than have a thinking-related instructional goal, the introduction to the instructional goals document was changed to read:

The District 205 instructional goals have been developed to support effective teaching strategies and district curricular needs. Continuing major emphases of instruction are the promotion of a thinking environment in each classroom and the integration of objectives and content across curricular areas.

This continuation of focus politically embeds the continuation of thinking strategies in the classroom since instructional goals direct building and individual goals.

As the umbrella for all other instructional goals, thinking skills also are embedded economically as part of the system. In the first years of the program the major portion of the Illinois State Staff Development Grant was allocated for the thinking skills training. Though other instructional goals need to be supported from the grant funds, the maintenance of the thinking skills training and emphasis has necessitated some use of state funds along with district and building professional growth funds.

Link Instruction

Fullan also stated that institutionalization of an innovation requires linkage to instruction and widespread use. If the innovation does not apply to what teachers do and is not used by a majority of the staff, there is little chance that it will become embedded in the system. The process for change that was implemented with the thinking skills training supported teachers in the transfer of the strategies into the day-by-day routine of teaching. After several years of training in the use of thinking skills strategies, almost all teachers in the district had participated in the workshops.

As other innovative instructional strategies came into the district, they were directly linked to the thinking skills strategies. Establishing a climate for thinking, providing opportunities for students to interact with each other and the tools of learning, developing metacognitive skills, and teaching ex-

plicit thinking skills all were important components of new programs adopted by the district. The revised mathematics program stresses problem solving and the use of manipulatives for teaching concepts. The newly adopted language arts program requires the use of a process approach to writing instruction. Children must use brainstorming and webbing skills in the prewriting component. Paired partners and cooperative groups are used during the conferencing sessions for editing. A literature-based reading program with an emphasis on whole language and integrated instruction also requires teachers to continue using the strategies presented in the thinking training. The traditional textbook-driven science program was revised to reflect a "hands-on/minds-on" philosophy.

Though each program shift has been a major change, teachers have adjusted with minimum frustration since the thinking skills workshops provided them with the basic instructional strategies needed to implement the new programs. Thinking strategies have become linked to instruction across all major content areas and are supporting effective instruction. These strategies provide a common link at the elementary, middle school, and high school levels, as teachers and teams attempt to deliver content through interdisciplinary units.

Continue To Assist

Institutionalization of an innovation requires that assistance be a continuous process. Innovations do not become traditions unless specific plans are developed to support valued change. As teachers retire and new teachers enter the system, a process must be in place to inculcate the beginning teachers into the district's traditions. Two formalized programs in District 205 assure that innovation is institutionalized. All teachers new to the district are assigned a mentor for their first teaching year. Veteran teachers apply to be mentors and participate in a training session prior to an assignment. These veteran teachers work with the new teachers throughout their first year to assist them with all facets of working in the district and delivering content to students. Mentors are expected to have participated in thinking skills workshops and to establish with new teachers the district's focus on facilitating a classroom in which students are thinkers.

During their first year, new teachers also participate in a new teacher induction program (NTIP). The NTIP workshops provide training in programs that are important to the district. As the new teachers participate in the workshops, their mentors assume the role of peer coach. The new teachers attend workshops on thinking skills, process writing, mathematics problem solving and manipulatives, teaming, and interdisciplinary units.

The experiences of the District 205 staff in creating the thoughtful classroom demonstrate that change requires a long-term commitment to a vision and a process. As Fullan has suggested, educators who want to be change facilitators must be willing to work with the process from initiation to implementation and through institutionaliza-

tion. Also, the institutionalization of change is an ongoing process that requires a continuing focus.

For Elmhurst District 205, the commitment to a change process has been the key factor in the reshaping of instruction. A walk down the halls of the schools in the district would give even the casual observer the sense that in these rooms children are involved learners. The furniture is arranged in a flexible manner so children can work in groups or pairs. Most instruction is presented to the whole group with some flexible groups to meet special needs. All available spaces in the rooms are used to display children's work and materials for learning. There is a hum of activity as children and teachers share the excitement of learning and thinking. The district's commitment to an ongoing change process has provided the children an enriched learning experience.

———

REFERENCES

Costa, A. (1984). *Developing minds: A resource book for teaching thinking.* Alexandria, VA: Association for Supervision and Curriculum Development.

Fogarty, R. (1991). *The mindful school: How to integrate the curricula.* Palatine, IL: Skylight Publishing, Inc.

Fogarty, R., & Bellanca, J. (1989). *Patterns for thinking: Patterns for transfer.* Palatine, IL: IRI Group.

Fullan, M. S. (1987, September). *Meaning of educational change.* Paper presented at the Illinois Association for Supervision and Curriculum Development Fall Conference, Matteson, IL.

Fullan, M. S. (1982). *The meaning of educational change.* Columbia, NY: Teachers College Press.

Fullan, M. S., & Stiegelbauer, S. (1991). *The new meaning of educational change.* Columbia, NY: Teachers College Press.

Joyce, B. (Ed.). (1990). *Changing school culture through staff development.* Alexandria, VA: Association for Supervision and Curriculum Development.

Joyce, B., & Showers, B. (1988). *Student achievement through staff development.* White Plains, NY: Longman, Inc.

Marzano, R. R., et al. (1988). *Dimensions of thinking: A framework for curriculum and instruction.* Alexandria, VA: Association for Supervision and Curriculum Development.

Resnick, L. B., & Klopfer, L. E. (Eds.). (1989). *Toward the thinking curriculum: Current cognitive research.* Alexandria, VA: Association for Supervision and Curriculum Development.

COGNITION AND COOPERATION: PARTNERS IN EXCELLENCE

—

Jacqueline Rhoades and Margaret McCabe

Studies have consistently suggested that many of our students are not developing the skills necessary for problem solving and decision making. Curriculum requirements mandated at the state and local levels appear to be increasing nationwide, and covering the required material often seems to be an impossible task. Students have seldom been treated as thinking people. Instead, they seem to have been viewed as "empty heads" to be filled with specific knowledge and facts for regurgitation on tests and in classroom discussions.

Students learn at a very young age that to be successful in school they must determine what the "right" answers are, then give those answers on assignments and tests. But teaching facts alone is no longer as relevant as it once was. The body of knowledge in some fields is doubling and tripling in two to three years. In other fields, knowledge is doubling in a matter of months. "Facts" as we know them and information relevant today may very likely be obsolete tomorrow. Taking the time to help students develop thinking skills helps them learn how to learn, which is the most powerful skill we can give our young people.

We are gaining significant knowledge about how the brain works, what thinking is, and how thinking occurs. In fact, there is a plethora of research, theories, and ideas. Still, there is no common definition of *thinking* among leading researchers and theorists.

Webster and American Heritage define the verb *think*:

> *To form or to have in the mind; to call to mind, i.e., remember; to reflect on or consider; to subject to the process of logical thought especially in order to reach a conclusion; to exercise the powers of judgment, conception, or inference as distinguished from simple sense perception; to create or devise.* (Gove, 1966, p. 2376; DeVinne, 1985, p. 1263)

This multifaceted definition, combined with research, leaves the field wide open for interpretation. Eventually, as we continue to learn more about how the brain and mind work, we will see more similarities than differences among our leading theorists. One similarity is theorists' views on the relationship between thinking and intelligence. Sternberg posits:

> *Thinking skills and intellectual skills that constitute intelligence overlap to a great extent. Most thinking*

skills are involved in intelligence. Although there is more to intelligence than just thinking skills. For example, intelligence is involved in making information processing automatic but thinking is not. To the contrary, information processing becomes automatic as the amount of thinking, or at least of conscious thinking, decreases. But the ties between thinking and intelligence are extremely close. (Baron & Sternberg, 1987, p. 196).

The concept of intelligence also lacks a common definition, being viewed as either a static or dynamic factor. It is generally agreed, however, that thinking is a component of intelligence and the more complex the thinking patterns the greater the possibility for higher intelligence. IQ assessments are seldom seen as the primary measure of a student's ability level or potential for learning. This perspective coincides with the broad definition developed by Wade and Tavris who view intelligence as "an inferred characteristic of an individual, usually defined as the ability to profit from experience, acquire knowledge, think abstractly, or adapt to changes in the environment" (1987).

This definition of intelligence has become more widely accepted. Earlier researchers concluded that IQ assessments measured overall learning and memory capacity. Their conclusion was based on high correlations between a student's IQ and that student's performance—that is, grades in school (Whimbey & Whimbey, 1975, p. 202). This conclusion led educators to believe that thinking skills could not be taught, which in turn limited the emphasis on teaching thinking.

Interestingly enough, it was Alfred Binet who first refuted this belief in 1901:

> *Some recent philosophers appear to have given their moral support to the deplorable verdict that the intelligence of an individual is a fixed quantity. ...We must protest and act against this brutal pessimism. A child's mind is like a field for which an expert farmer has advised a change in the method of cultivating, with the result that in place of desert land, we now have a harvest. It is in this particular sense, the one which is significant, that we say that the intelligence of children may be increased.* (cited in Whimbey & Whimbey, 1975, p. 113)

The concept of cognitive modifiability—that is, changing or enhancing an individual's level of intelligence—has been well established through the works of Reuven Feuerstein, Arthur Whimbey, Donald Meichenbaum, and others. In *Intelligence Can Be Taught*, Whimbey compared thinking skills to learning a sport (1975, p. 118). The overall skill is presented, and the subtasks are taught in a systematic manner. Take, for example, when tennis is taught. The rules of the game are presented, and the specific skills, such as how to hold the racket and footwork, are taught. Students practice the component skills, and, finally, after sufficient practice and corrective feedback, the game is mastered. So it is with thinking. An individual cannot practice an aspect of thinking without being exposed to that specific skill. A major task of educators, then, is to introduce general skills, teach the subcomponents necessary for understanding, and provide practice opportunities to obtain mastery. Within this theoretical framework, the process of teaching thinking begins.

For the purpose of this chapter, *thinking* is defined as a manifestation of intelligence and is viewed as a "series of mental strategies used by an individual to organize and manipulate previous learning experiences and perceptions in order to assimilate new knowledge, to formulate new ideas, and to make judgments" (Whimbey & Whimbey, 1975, p. 116). Thinking skills can be taught to increase students' intellectual abilities.

FRAME OF REFERENCE

Frame of reference provides a conceptual framework for the teaching of thinking skills. A frame of reference is the sum total of each individual's experience and knowledge. For example, in some parts of the United States a *soda* is a drink made with seltzer water and ice cream, and a *pop* is a carbonated drink sold in a can or bottle. But, in other locations the latter is called a *soda*. What each of these words means depends on a person's frame of reference.

Our ability to assimilate new information and to think about different concepts depends on our frame of reference. Using a computer as an analogy helps place this concept into perspective. A computer has the capacity to perform various tasks and solve different types of problems. But, until it is programmed to complete these tasks, the capacity for sorting information, making calculations, and solving problems is useless. The same is true of our students; they need to learn how to sort and combine information in order to retain and apply data and information in the given assignment (McCabe & Rhoades, 1989, p. 202).

A concrete example of this premise is the study of algebraic theory. If we have never been exposed to algebra, the equations are nothing more than a jumble of letters and numbers—it's a foreign language to us. Once we have studied algebra, however, the mystery is removed and the equation makes perfectly good sense.

For new information to be relevant, we must be able to either link it to past experience or have some basis for constructing new meanings. Each time we are exposed to a new way to think about something, we add another strategy or path to our thinking abilities. If there is nothing in our past experience or if we are unable to construct new meaning, we will not be able to make sense of the information.

For example, a sixth grade student was reading on a second grade level. She was a bright, likable youngster, who obviously had the capacity to be a good reader. Year after year she had been taught the phonetic sounds of letters. Mastery of phonetics was evidenced by her consistent ability to "sound out" letters. This student had also learned some words by sight, which provided a minimal amount of positive feedback to her. But, her reading problem remained a mystery until a new teacher talked with her about how she approached the task of decoding words phonetically. The teacher discovered that the student did not understand the concept of blending individual phonetic sounds into words. The student lacked the critical information to construct new meaning from the available information—how to integrate and blend phonetic sounds (Rhoades & McCabe, 1985, p. 6).

Teachers have the power to create a classroom environment that expands each student's frame of reference and teaches thinking skills. Thus, teachers have the power to increase a student's thinking paths, the network that functions as intelligence.

THINKING PATHS

The ability to think about new information is directly related to an individual's frame of reference. We need some sort of reference point to understand new information. Each time we are exposed to a new way to think about something, we add another strategy or path to our thinking abilities. The way we see and interpret the world around us is dependent on the network of thinking paths available. Some individuals may be viewed by others as slow or lacking common sense when, in fact, they have not had the opportunity to experience or learn alternative behaviors.

For example, a person who has written an extensive shopping list enters the market to purchase the items needed. The first item on the list is meat. The shopper takes a grocery cart and goes to the meat section on the north side of the store. The second item on the list is carrots. The shopper then goes to the produce section at the south side of the store. The next item on the list is milk, so the shopper proceeds to the dairy section on the east side of the store. The shopper then crisscrosses aisles to select other items. Some would say this behavior is stupid, when the fact may be that this person has never been taught the skill of organizing a list before shopping. The ability to organize is a thinking skill.

Thinking paths are formed from the first day we are born—some say even in the prenatal state—and continue to develop during one's lifetime. They cluster and connect into thinking banks, from which we can draw to assimilate new information and perceptions. The complexity of thinking paths depends on the type of input and feedback any given individual experiences. Assume it is winter and a child does not close the door after entering the house. Parents may respond to this behavior in a variety of ways.

PARENT #1: "Close the door." To the child, this is just another command to obey.

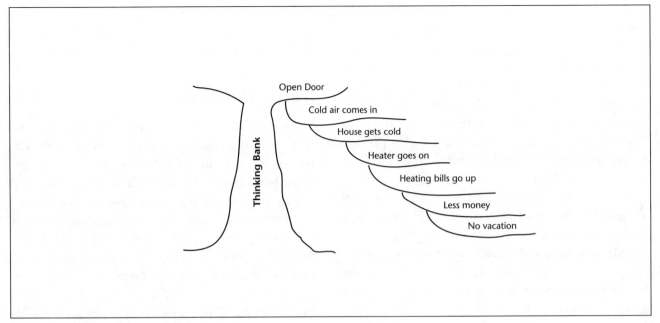

Figure 1 Thinking Paths

Parent #2: "Close the door; it's cold outside." The child begins to make a mental connection—if the door is open, cold air gets in the house.

Parent #3: "Close the door. It's cold outside, and the heater will come on." More information results in another mental connection.

Parent #4: "Close the door; it's cold outside. The heater will come on, and it will cost us money." The child can now make a series of mental connections and begin to learn about cause and effect.

Parent #5: "Close the door; it's cold outside. The heater will come on, and it will cost us money. If it happens too many times, we will not be able to go to Disneyland." The concepts of cause and effect now become relevant to the child's life.

In each of these instances the stimulus is identical. The parent's response is the critical factor in determining the child's resultant cognitive growth pattern. In other words, this child may be living in a command-only household, in which the reasons behind a given action are never explained. In the context of Benjamin Bloom's taxonomy, the first parent is communicating on level one—just the facts (Bloom, 1956).

These examples can be illustrated by envisioning the sum total of our thinking paths, or our "think-ing bank," as the trunk of a tree. From this, we can draw on experiences or past learning to assimilate new information. Each limb or branch represents a thinking path (see Figure 1).

Obviously, it is not appropriate for parents to always give detailed responses when communicating with their children. However, if the patterns, as outlined above, persist over a period of years, consider the difference in thinking power between the child of parent #1 and the child of parent #5. The latter child's long-term memory bank will be filled with options.

While early assimilation is an important factor in cognitive development, there is firm evidence that intelligence and thinking ability are not permanently fixed. When speaking of cognitively impaired individuals, Feuerstein said, "It is our conviction . . . that impairments do not reflect any real lack of capacity, but rather ineffective attitudes, faulty work habits, and inadequate modes of thinking—in other words, functions can be trained to operate more adequately" (1979).

Regardless of age, whether two or seventy-two years old, individuals may expand and enhance their intellectual functioning. Developing thinking paths can also be a lifelong process. Specific thinking strategies can be taught through the mediation process. Mediation can occur on a formal or informal basis. For example, a child may watch his father make a cake. He learns through a vicarious process the steps required to obtain the desired results. The mediation process becomes more formalized when the father notices his son watching and says such things as, "I am measuring two cups of flour," or "The directions say add two eggs." The auditory input from the father strengthens the mediation experience. If the child reads the directions, and measures and mixes the ingredients himself, the mediation experience is enhanced further. Three important variables when providing mediation are time, complexity, and conscious intent.

Time

Mediation requires interaction between two or more individuals. The mediator must invest time to share thought patterns. The amount of time required is related to the task at hand, the recipient's frame of reference, and the importance the individuals place on the subject at hand.

At home, time must be set aside for interaction between parents and children. A 1991 study reported that the average length of time parents and children interact on a daily basis is approximately fifteen minutes (California Task Force, 1991, p. 18). Three-quarters of this time is spent giving instructions and reprimands, leaving little, if any, time for building thinking skills.

While there have been serious attempts to alter instructional methodology in recent years, the vast majority of instruction involves independent tasks, affording little time and few opportunities to share thinking patterns. For students to learn new paths of thinking, a significant amount of time needs to be set aside in the instructional day to provide learning opportunities.

Complexity

While a knowledge base in any area is essential to understanding a concept, knowledge alone does not provide the ability to manipulate the information and to use it in everyday life. Acquiring facts, therefore, becomes the first step of many in becoming an intelligent human being.

Children raised in command-only households, whose parents seldom elaborate beyond "just the facts," are certainly at a disadvantage when entering school. Also, in many instances, the school environment continues this depressed pattern of stimulation. Research notes that ninety-three percent of the interaction between teacher and student during the school day falls within the knowledge category. A major challenge for our school system is to raise the level of complexity of the school environment beyond just the facts.

Conscious Intent

Mediation is enhanced when it is done with conscious intent. In other words, a skill is selected and a plan is developed to enhance the mediation process.

COOPERATIVE LEARNING AND THINKING

The cooperative learning process inherently facilitates the teaching of thinking skills. Cooperative learning requires students to work together to complete assignments, study academic content, and/or agree on responses for a worksheet or test. The teacher is no longer the sole mediator of learning. Each student in the group becomes a mediator when explaining personal thinking processes. When working in a group, students may not simply state their answers, they must share how they arrived at their answers. Through this explanation they help other students develop thinking paths because:

1. all students must think about their own thinking. Thinking about how one thinks is called *metacognition*, an important attribute in effective thinking. Teachers should be alert to aspects of metacognition and heighten students' awareness of the process by
   - modeling metacognition by sharing thought processes with students,
   - labeling spontaneous processes—for example, verbalizing thought processes while solving a problem, and
   - encouraging students to metacogitate about concrete objects.

2. students are sharing their *internal dialogue*—that is, what they said to themselves when con-

fronted with the specific question, problem, or situation.

3. sharing what they thought and how they actually arrived at their conclusions mediates the development of other students' thinking skills. It gives students alternatives to thinking about specific events, situations, problems, and content material. It provides new thinking paths, increasing the students' thinking banks from which they can draw when faced with the same or similar situation or problem.

The more thinking paths a person has, the more ways the person has to deal with new perceptions, experiences, and information. Our thinking paths are directed by our internal dialogue, the consistent self-talking that goes on in our minds. When confronted with any situation, we begin talking to ourselves about how best to approach it. Our minds search through past experiences to find a similar situation. We then discuss with ourselves how we dealt with that situation in the past and how successful or unsuccessful our actions were. The group-process experience develops thinking paths. If we have not had direct experience with a situation, our minds can search for examples and solutions provided by other group members.

Students should be taught the concepts of thinking paths, internal dialogue, and mediation. When explaining mediation and internal dialogue to students, it's important to point out that we each have different ways of thinking and approaching problems. The more ways we have of thinking, the greater our chances of finding successful solutions to problems and making good decisions in the future. While there are no right and wrong ways to think, different strategies work better in different situations. Thus, it is beneficial to have as many thinking strategies as possible.

Students need to know that effective thinkers talk to themselves continuously. This is called self-talk or internal dialogue. When we share how we arrived at our answers, we are sharing our internal dialogue. This, in turn, mediates the thought processes of other group members and gives everyone new ideas, new paths of thinking. In order to explain how we arrived at an answer, we must examine our own thinking processes. We must think about what we thought and how we thought it. Metacognition helps us become more effective thinkers (Whimbey, 1980). Because students enjoy the prospect of helping each other learn how to think differently, they approach their group discussions with enthusiasm.

Activities that enrich the mediation process include the following:

- Discuss the meaning of words. For example, have groups agree on a common definition of the word *surplus* when discussing government subsidy in relation to farming.

- Have the group "walk through" the thinking strategies they used in finding a solution to the problem.

- Ask the group to generate questions from a passage they have just read.

- Conduct self-evaluations. Ask group members to evaluate their academic or social performance in the group.

- Relate the past and present to the future. For example, relate how learning the Pythagorean theorem today will be useful to the student in the future.

WRAP-UPS

The wrap-up is another effective tool for teaching thinking paths. A wrap-up is a brief activity that immediately follows a cooperative lesson. It may be completed in small groups or with the whole class, and it may be written or oral. The wrap-up activity focuses on a social skills objective or an academic objective. It also provides students an opportunity to enhance their thinking and communication skills. The wrap-up provides closure by asking students to analyze their use of specific skills or what they learned from the academic content.

The wrap-up provides an opportunity for transference or bridging. Whatever the content of the wrap-up activity, internal dialogue is shared, and mediation and metacognition occur. The wrap-up can be structured to enhance any level of thinking desired, including recall, analysis, and synthesis of content information. The opportunities to develop thinking skills through wrap-up activities are infinite. Some examples of wrap-ups include the following:

- After completing this assignment, one question I have is ….
- I can use the information I learned today in the future by ….
- One way I contributed to my group was ….
- One new thing I learned was ….
- I disagree with ….because ….
- I felt the greatest strength of the character in this story was ….
- If I had lived in that era, I would feel ….
- One frustration I felt during this activity was ….
- One good feeling I had during this activity was ….
- The way I reached my conclusion was ….

HIGHER-LEVEL QUESTIONING

Infusing higher-level questioning into cooperative lessons is another powerful technique for building thinking skills. If we are to help students develop effective thinking skills, we need to move beyond asking questions that require mere recall of facts. One taxonomy that can be used is Bloom's (1956):

Knowledge: to define, recognize, recall, identify, label, and collect. Example: Name the last three U.S. Vice-Presidents.

Comprehension: to translate, interpret, explain, describe, summarize, and extrapolate. Example: Explain the importance of the Civil Rights Act.

Application: to apply, solve, experiment and predict. Example: Construct a chart showing the inflation percentages of the last ten years.

Analysis: to connect, relate, differentiate, classify, arrange, group, organize, distinguish, categorize, compare, and infer. Example: Listen to three television commercials and determine which parts are fact and which are inferences.

Synthesis: to produce, propose, design, plan, combine, formulate, compose, and hypothesize. Example: Using real issues in the community, write a speech for a candidate for mayor.

Evaluation: to appraise, judge, criticize, decide. Example: How does the author support the main premise?

Designing lessons that include questions that promote higher-level thinking should be a part of every teacher's overall plan. Following is just one example of how this can be accomplished easily, without purchasing extra materials. The content is a magazine ad showing a truck and the caption, "IT'S ALL TRUCK." Beneath this banner is a list of the truck's selling points, including its load capacity and horsepower. Give each group a copy of the advertisement and ask them to respond to the following:

KNOWLEDGE: Identify the make of the truck.

COMPREHENSION: Explain the significance of the caption, "IT'S ALL TRUCK."

APPLICATION: How could a farmer use this truck?

ANALYSIS: Some statements in the ad are facts and some are opinions. Write a list identifying which statements are facts and which are opinions.

SYNTHESIS: Write an ad to sell your bike.

EVALUATION: Based on your analysis of this ad, would you buy this truck? Why or why not?

These questions require the group members to apply the skills of a good thinker, to be aware of their own internal dialogue, and to share their internal dialogue. The questions, combined with the group process, promote effective thinking.

ASSESSING THINKING SKILLS THROUGH OBSERVATION

Effective thinking is not synonymous with knowledge. It cannot be called up from the recesses of memory on demand, such as Wednesday between 9:00 and 10:30 when a test is scheduled. Thinking occurs at all times—at odd times, out of the blue, in the middle of the night, in the midst of routine, and during trivial tasks.

Assessing thinking skills with a paper-and-pencil test places our students in untenable situations, but there is a technique teachers can use to measure thinking skills. It isn't perfect, but it seems fairer and more reliable than paper-and-pencil tests—observation. Through careful observation over an extended period of time, teachers can gain some idea of the effectiveness of a student's thinking processes. By using a list of effective thinking behaviors based on research by Luis Raths, Art Costa, Margaret McCabe, and Jacqueline Rhoades, we can begin to identify behaviors that are considered to be reflective of effective thinking.

First, a word of caution. While a list of behaviors associated with effective thinking can be a powerful guide, labeling any individual immediately sets up an expectation level, which in turn limits the individual's growth and progress. In reality, each person's thinking behaviors most likely fall somewhere on a continuum between what could be considered effective and ineffective thinking. Each person also exhibits strengths in some areas, weaknesses in others, and their strengths and weaknesses at different times. Rather than rating or grading students, use the following list as a guide to identify areas that seem to indicate a weakness in a student's thinking processes. Then design specific lessons to enhance those aspects. The important element is to provide experiences through which students can enhance and expand their thinking paths.

Obviously, making conclusions about others' thoughts, based solely on their behavior, would be nothing short of ridiculous. But, through observation, we can certainly tell if students are actualizing thinking behaviors in the classroom. Following are some qualities of students who exhibit effective thinking behaviors that may be used for observations (McCabe & Rhoades, 1989).

- Goal-oriented. Plans short- and long-range goals and develops plans to reach goals. This is true of class assignments as well as of other aspects of life. Considers possible consequences of behaviors.

- Self-initiator. Completes assignments with little or no prompting and encouraging.

- Open to ideas of others and to different ways of doing things. Considers new ideas and examines their strengths and weaknesses. Seeks new ideas from others and from readings.

- Listens to others with understanding and empathy. Is eager to listen to other points of view. Can clarify by asking questions and paraphrasing, and can detect indicators of feelings.

- Confident. Expresses own ideas freely and is not afraid to be wrong. Enthusiastically participates in class discussions.

Observation, as with all cooperative techniques, can become a powerful instructional tool, giving the teacher specific information from which to guide students into effective thinking habits.

CONCLUSION

Thinking skills are essential for a successful life. Different thinking strategies or thinking paths can easily be taught through cooperative learning, because cooperative learning strategies enhance the development of thinking skills.

REFERENCES

Baron, J. B., & Sternberg, R. J. (1987). *Teaching thinking skills: Theory and practice.* New York: N.H. Freeman.

Bloom, B. (1956). *Taxonomy of educational objectives.* New York: Longman.

Caine, R., & Caine, G. (1990, October). Understanding a brain-based approach to learning and teaching. *Educational Leadership, 48*(2), 66-70.

California Task Force to Promote Self-Esteem and Personal and Social Responsibility. (1991). *Toward a state of self-esteem.* Sacramento, CA: California State Department of Education.

Costa, A. (1991). Toward a model of human intellectual functioning. In A. Costa (Ed.), *Developing minds: A resource book for teaching thinking.* (pp. 137-140). (2nd ed.). Alexandria, VA: Association for Supervision and Curriculum Development.

Costa, A. (1984, November). Mediating the metacognitive. *Educational Leadership, 42*(3), 57-62.

DeVinne, P. B. (Ed.). (1985). *American heritage dictionary.* Boston: Houghton Mifflin.

Feuerstein, R. (1980). *Instrumental enrichment.* Baltimore, MD: University Park Press.

Feuerstein, R. (1979). *The dynamic assessment of retarded performers.* Baltimore, MD: University of Park Press.

Gove, P. B. (Ed.). (1966). *Webster's third new international dictionary.* Chicago: G & C Merriam.

McCabe, M., & Rhoades, J. (1989). *The nurturing classroom: Developing self-esteem, thinking skills, and responsibility through simple cooperation.* Willits, CA: ITA.

Meichenbaum, D. (1977). *Cognitive behavior modification.* New York: Plenum Press.

Presseisen, B., Sternberg, R., Kischer, K., Knight, C., & Feuerstein, R. (1990). *Learning and thinking styles: Classroom interaction.* Washington, DC: National Education Association and Research for Better Schools.

Rhoades, J., & McCabe, M. (1985). *Simple cooperation in the classroom.* Willits, CA: ITA.

Sternberg, R. (1984, September). How can we teach intelligence? *Educational Leadership, 42*(1), 38-47.

Wade, C., & Tavris, C. (1987). *Psychology.* New York: Harper & Row.

Wasserman, S. (1989, January). Reflections on measuring thinking while listening to Mozart's Jupiter symphony. *Phi Delta Kappan, 70,* 365-370.

Wasserman, S. (1987, February). Teaching for thinking: Luis E. Raths revisited. *Phi Delta Kappan, 68,* 460-465.

Whimbey, A. (1980, April). Students can learn to be better problem solvers. *Educational Leadership, 37*(7), 56-65.

Whimbey, A., & Whimbey, L. S. (1975). *Intelligence can be taught.* New York: Bantam Books.

The Nine Basics of Teaching Thinking

—

David Perkins and Robert Swartz

Everyone thinks. Thinking is a natural function of the human organism. It does not have to be taught any more than walking does. Yet throughout human history, people have sought to cultivate thinking. Socrates, Aristotle, Francis Bacon, and others set forth principles for good thinking. The noted American philosopher of education John Dewey emphasized the importance of thoughtful learning. Over the past two decades, educators, psychologists, and philosophers have worked hard to make the teaching of thinking more of a presence in public education. For something as natural as walking, thinking seems to be getting a lot of attention!

Why? And if thinking deserves attention, what kind of attention should it get? The answer to the first of these questions proves relatively easy. While everyone thinks after a fashion, people often do not think nearly as well as they might to serve their own best interests and those of others—to study well, to make important decisions in life, to solve problems, to respond inventively to circumstances, to exercise judgment free of bias and prejudice, and so on. So it is not thinking, per se, that attracts all the fuss, but improving thinking.

As to the second question, over the past several years, the two of us have been part of the contemporary effort to encourage more attention to the cultivation of thinking in schools. We believe that all students can learn to think better than they do—including the gifted ones and also those who are slow learners or at risk. We have participated both in research and in practical programs designed to help students think better. In these few pages, we try to boil down some basic principles about teaching thinking.

WHY, HOW, AND WHERE TO IMPROVE THINKING

Why Improve Thinking: Unfortunate Default Patterns

Since everyone thinks, why teach thinking? As already noted, thinking should be taught because most people do not think nearly as well as they might. Everyday experience gives us abundant evidence of this. Political speeches present endless examples of short-sighted reasoning. Many teachers also note that their students do not think very carefully about what they hear in classrooms or read in textbooks. In their oral and written work, students seldom show careful critical or creative thinking about the topic at hand. Moreover, testing by the National Assessment of Educational Progress and other programs underwrites teachers' impressions that students do not think nearly as well as we would like. Finally, we all occasionally see friends and colleagues make decisions that seem ill-considered or express views that seem narrow or biased (for a research-based perspective on short-falls in thinking, see Perkins & Salomon, 1988).

Of course, less-than-ideal thinking proves more readily visible in others than in ourselves. But here is a simple exercise that usually reveals some of our own shortcomings (Swartz & Parks, 1992a,b). Think of three or four decisions you have made in the last several weeks that turned out badly. Almost everyone has such experiences. Now review each decision. Ask yourself, "What went wrong?" And then ask yourself, "Is there something I could have done while making the decision so that it would have come out better?" Sometimes your answer may be "No." You did your best, but circumstances conspired against you. For other decisions, however, you are likely to find that you could have done a better job. Perhaps you could have explored more options and found a better one. Or you could have examined more fully and carefully the options you were considering.

It is useful to sum up the typical failings of human thinking into four *defaults*. A *default* is something that people fall into automatically, unless they make some effort to behave differently. Here are the principal defaults that plague our everyday thinking.

- *Hasty*: We reach conclusions and take actions without sufficient thought or attention to standards of judgment. Perhaps you did not give enough thinking time to some of the decisions that you have recently made.

- *Narrow*: Our thinking is blinkered. We fail to consider the other side of the case, the contrary evidence, alternative frames of reference and points of view, more imaginative possibilities, and so on. For instance, perhaps you did not search widely enough for options in one of your recent decisions and missed the best bet.

- *Fuzzy*: Our ideas are not clear, distinctions not sharp. Everything is all muddled. Perhaps you did not take a long, hard look at your priorities during a recent decision. And because you were fuzzy about what was most important, you made the wrong choice.

- *Sprawling*: Our thinking is disorganized, all over the place, fails to come to a point. Perhaps you faced a complicated decision recently and got lost in the maze of circumstances. Finally, in exasperation, you just did something; unfortunately, not the right thing.

Why do the defaults of hasty, narrow, fuzzy, and sprawling thinking plague Homo sapiens? After all, we're supposed to be smart! The answer lies in the complexities of human psychology. One factor is the usually high payoff of reflexive rather than reflective thinking. For much of everyday life, reflexive responses are good. They do the job quickly and save us time and effort. Unfortunately, when occasional problems and decisions require more reflection, the mind often defaults to a reflexive response anyway. By definition, hasty, a reflexive response, also tends to be narrow, relying on convention and past experience rather than on imaginative and unbiased exploration.

Another factor is the tender human ego. Often, we find ourselves invested in a particular viewpoint or group identity. It is difficult to think broadly and see matters from another perspective without threatening our self-image and self-confidence.

Still another factor recognizes the genuine complexity of the world. Many distinctions are subtle (between weight and mass in physics for instance), many priorities are obscure (which do you really want more, X or Y?), and many situations are labyrinthine (if I do A, he may do B, or C, or maybe D; and if he does B, I should …). Unless we work hard and systematically at maintaining distinctions and staying oriented, thinking tends to get fuzzy and sprawling.

All this is both bad news and good news. The bad news is that leanings toward less-than-ideal thinking are built into the human mind. It is natural not to think so well. The mind tends to slide toward hasty, narrow, fuzzy, and sprawling thinking in many circumstances.

The good news is that all this makes the goal of better thinking quite understandable. To a first approximation, better thinking is not anything technical or academic. It is giving thinking more time, making your thinking broad, and exercising care, precision, and systematic organization. Good thinking is everyday thinking done better. In summary:

Basic #1. *Why improve thinking? Because, by default, everyday human thinking tends to be hasty, narrow, fuzzy, and sprawling. We can help learners do better without recourse to any technical concept of good thinking.*

How To Improve Thinking: Thinking Organizers

The notion of the four thinking defaults brings into focus the challenge of teaching thinking. To help students counter the defaults, we need to help them give thinking more time, broaden their thinking, work for clarity and precision, and maintain some systematic organization.

How? The natural impulse is to give students experience with better patterns of thinking. To combat hastiness, let us engage students in discussion and writing that give thinking time. To broaden their thinking, let us engage them in activities that stretch their minds, such as arguing the side of a case opposite one's own or brainstorming. Such experiences benefit students and are to be applauded.

But they do not do the whole job. One of the most telling discoveries in recent efforts to teach thinking comes down to this: Mere experience is not enough. Even repeatedly experiencing a particular kind of thinking often does not help students get better at that kind of thinking. For example, engaging students in debates does not in itself necessarily make them better at debating or reasoning more generally.

Moreover, experiencing better thinking practices in a classroom context does not reliably lead students to putting that kind of thinking into action in other settings. For instance, students who have learned the importance of attending to both sides of a case through classroom debates do not necessarily show more attention to both sides of the case in other reasoning situations. Again, experience is not enough.

What goes wrong? The problem is that mere experience with better thinking practices often does not

make clear the point or importance of the revised practices. Nor does it give learners ways of reminding themselves later about those better practices. Like much else that happens in classrooms, the experience becomes "something you do on Fridays in English," or the like.

In our view, the answer to this dilemma is the use of *thinking organizers* to reorganize thinking. (One can also speak of thinking "frames"—see Perkins, 1986b,c). *Thinking organizers* are verbal or graphic symbols that remind us how to reorganize our thinking away from the four defaults and guide us along as we think. While some approaches to improving students' thinking do not emphasize thinking organizers, many do.

The idea of thinking organizers may sound esoteric, but it is not. Thinking organizers are quite commonplace, only we often do not recognize them for what they are. To appreciate both how ordinary thinking organizers are and how they do their work, let us look at a familiar example: the pro-con list. Many people occasionally jot down pros and cons to size up a yes-or-no decision. It's common to use a two-column chart, cons on the left and pros on the right, or vice versa.

Notice how this simple strategy works against the four defaults. First of all, the mere fact of drawing and filling a pro-con list guarantees that you are giving thinking time. Second, the pro-con list has built into it a strong call for even-handed thinking, which looks at both sides of the case. It sets aside a column for the pros and a column for the cons. Third, the pro-con list forces you to categorize factors either as pros or cons. Indeed, often factors emerge that are both pros and cons in different ways, so you need to add them to both lists. All this works against fuzzy thinking, bringing clarity to how different factors bear on the decision. Fourth, the pro-con list combats sprawling thinking by keeping you on track. It is hard to get lost in the problem with a clear delineation of pros and cons staring you in the face.

Let's generalize. A thinking organizer is a concrete, verbal, and/or graphic structure that guides thinking. Later, we will give some examples of thinking organizers especially useful for improving thinking through subject matter instruction. For now, we want to emphasize further how commonplace thinking organizers are, once you know how to recognize them. Here is a brief list of everyday thinking organizers.

- *Proverbs.* Proverbs and the like are a folk repository of thinking organizers. For instance, such sayings as "look before you leap" and "a stitch in time saves nine" work against the hasty thinking default. Such phrases as "use your imagination," "let's take a new approach," and "put yourself in his shoes" work against the narrow thinking default.

- *Analytical concepts and terms.* Many concepts and terms in English or other languages help us organize our thinking. For example, if you speak the "language of argument," you can ask another or yourself, "What's the claim here? And the arguments are what? Do you have any evidence for that generalization? Your first reason, how does that support your conclusion?"

- *Dispositional concepts and terms.* Many have pointed out that good thinking is more than technique. It's a matter of spirit or what are often more technically called "dispositions." Many concepts and terms in the English language express a commitment to kinds of thinking. We encourage people to be *fair, just, open-minded,* and *imaginative,* for example. Such terms do not have much analytical content in the way that *claim, evidence,* and *support* do. But they are loaded with affect. For example, the terms mentioned all appeal in one or another sense for broad rather than narrow thinking.

- *Familiar strategies.* Some thinking strategies are so familiar that they are a common part of our culture. Brainstorming is an obvious example, with its simple rules about not criticizing, piggybacking on one another's ideas, and so on. Another is the pro-con list. Yet another is the common counsel to find out someone's reasons behind an idea that seems odd, rather than rejecting it out of hand.

- *Common graphic organizers.* While the pro-con list is one common graphic organizer, there are others. For instance, people frequently make plans by listing steps. The list allows you to stand back, look at your plan, and revise it, helping you avoid fuzzy and sprawling thinking. In yet another example, people commonly use tables with two or more columns—for instance for budgets or supplies—organized by category or tasks and the people to whom they are assigned. Such tables help you clarify thinking that may initially be fuzzy and help you maintain some systematic organization, rather than getting lost in the many tradeoffs of complicated products.

With all these thinking organizers part of everyday culture, why don't we all think perfectly? Unfortunately, most knowledge people have is "passive" rather than "active." People know about it, but don't do anything with it. This applies to everyday thinking organizers as much as to other kinds of knowledge. For example, most people know such terms as *claim, reason, support, evidence,* and so on. Yet, in everyday reasoning or argument, people often make little use of such terms. This "language of argument" sees little use in ordinary classrooms as well.

This is unfortunate, but it does have a bright side. To a significant extent, the teaching of thinking does not involve teaching entirely new thinking organizers. It involves reminding people of what they already know, making it more explicit and emphatic, and exploring and emphasizing its importance. In summary:

Basic #2. *Better thinking depends on better organization. To improve thinking, we need to cultivate explicit use of the verbal and graphic organizers learners already know and introduce them to some they do not know.*

Where to Improve Thinking: Infusion into Content Area Instruction

Three broad approaches to teaching thinking have been practiced widely since the early 1980s: direct instruction in stand-alone thinking programs outside the regular curriculum (we can call this the teaching *of* thinking); the stimulation of higher-order thinking within regular content instruction (we can call this teaching *for* thinking); and infusion (Swartz, 1991a,b; Swartz & Perkins, 1990; regarding *for* and *of,* see Brandt, 1984; Costa, 1991a).

Stand-alone approaches include separate courses or minicourses (Baron & Sternberg, 1986; Nickerson, Perkins, & Smith, 1985). By and large, such programs focus on specific thinking organizers. Also, students typically think about issues that are not part of the subject matter. For example, in a well-known stand-alone program, students imagine that all cars are painted yellow. They think about the positive, negative, and interesting aspects of such a situation, applying a specific strategy called PMI (a thinking organizer), which they learn to use through this kind of practice. In another program, students compare and contrast objects in the school classroom by listing their similarities and differences. "Compare and contrast" is a verbal thinking organizer, typically reinforced by two-column charts or other graphic organizers. Students get better with practice and learn that insights can be discovered through such comparing and contrasting.

In teaching for thinking, the second approach, stimulating thinking in content area instruction has a distinctive character. It amounts to what the previous section called "giving students experiences" of better thinking practices within content areas. Teachers do not ask students to think about yellow cars or objects in the school classroom, but rather about topics in the subject matter of concern. Students might be challenged to write about why the plague spread so easily in medieval Europe, or how Macbeth compares to Hamlet, or to prepare themselves to discuss these questions in class. We see here a deliberate effort to move beyond questions that merely prompt recalling to more challenging higher-order or Socratic questions. This can stimulate some interesting and provocative thoughts. But instruction time gets spent solely on the content—what students are thinking about—with no direct attention to thinking organizers or reflection on the thinking itself. Thinking organizers may be used incidentally, for instance a compare-and-contrast chart, but without identifying them as general tools for organizing thinking. The treatment of thinking remains tacit and tends not to carry over to other settings.

Thus, the teaching *of* thinking and teaching *for* thinking both have their limitations. The first, with its stand-alone model, addresses thinking explicitly but does not contribute directly to deepening content area instruction. Moreover, in many school settings, time proves difficult to schedule. Teaching *for* thinking within content areas treats content more deeply and gives students experiences of better thinking, but without the direct cultivation of thinking. Recall from the last section that thinking needs direct attention to grow.

Infusion is a best-of-both-worlds approach. It involves the explicit attention to thinking, but in the context of content area instruction. It is the approach we recommend. The others may be used too, as valuable complements, but in our view infusion is an essential ingredient.

More specifically, infusion involves direct instruction in the use of effective thinking organizers during content instruction, supported by student reflection and attention to transfer of the thinking organizers to other situations. It also involves direct engagement with challenging and important questions about the content. The students apply the thinking organizers to the content, learning about both at once. Both improvement in thinking and enhanced content learning are the goal. Figure 1 expresses the relationships among the stand-alone, stimulation, and infusion approaches.

There are several approaches to infusion, although far fewer than to stand-alone instruction. Concerning our own work, we discuss infusion in *Teaching Thinking: Issues and Approaches*. Perkins has developed *Knowledge as Design* (1986a) and a recent overview of the importance of thoughtful learning, *Smart Schools* (1992). Perkins and colleagues have developed the *Connections* program (Mirman & Tishman, 1988; Perkins et al., in press; Tishman, 1991). Swartz has contributed infused science lessons to *Addison-Wesley Science* (1989), and Swartz and Parks have developed the program *Infusing Critical and Creative Thinking into Content Instruction* (1992a,b), which includes handbooks for elementary and secondary school teachers. Our comments here focus on the principles involved, principles that can be found in other materials or applied by committed and experienced teachers on their own.

What does the infusion approach actually look like in action? The way infusion plays itself out in the classroom can best be seen by looking at the

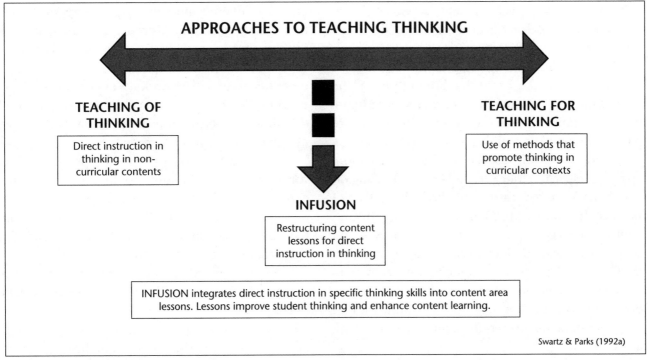

Figure 1   Approaches to Teaching Thinking

lesson on the extinction of the dinosaurs in Figure 2. Notice the engagement with a topic of prime importance in elementary and middle school science, but also the way direct instruction in the thinking being taught—causal explanation—weaves together with the content. Notice, in particular, the use of explicit verbal and graphic organizers, together with strategies for helping students reflect metacognitively on their thinking, as well as transfer of it to other contexts. Metacognition and transfer are important aspects of teaching thinking that we will discuss later.

Basic #3. *Infusion means direct and explicit attention to teaching thinking within content area instruction. Students' thinking benefits, and content learning proceeds with much more depth. Efforts to teach thinking should include infusion (stand-alone instruction and efforts to stimulate thinking during content instruction may be valuable complements).*

THE ART OF TEACHING THINKING

Attention to Skills, Processes, and Dispositions

Some approaches to the teaching of thinking emphasize very particular kinds of thinking, such as brainstorming, assessing the reliability of a witness' report, or identifying main themes of paragraphs. These relatively focused ways of organizing thinking might be called *thinking skills*.

Other approaches to the teaching of thinking emphasize larger, more encompassing thinking organizers, such as a three-step decision-making plan: (1) generate options; (2) assess each option in terms of consequences and payoffs; (3) synthesize the assessments to yield a decision. While the individual steps in this plan are relatively focused skills, we can call the overall plan a *thinking process*. In other words, thinking processes are larger organizations of thinking that are made up of thinking skills. Figure 3 illustrates this relationship for a particular thinking process, decision making, showing a number of the subskills that play themselves out as we work through an organized strategy for the process.

An ensemble of core skills can be organized into three basic categories: generating ideas, clarifying ideas, and assessing the reasonableness of ideas. (Swartz & Perkins, 1990). Skills in the first category are traditional creative thinking skills; in the second, traditional skills of analysis; and in the third,

THE EXTINCTION OF THE DINOSAURS

SCIENCE   GRADES

LESSON OBJECTIVES

CONTENT

Students will learn that there are different theories about the extinction of the dinosaurs and that the only scientific evidence we have today about what caused their extinction is from fossils and other prehistoric remains.

THINKING SKILL

Students will learn to develop alternative hypotheses and consider present evidence when trying to make a judgment about what caused something to happen.

LESSON

INTRODUCTION TO CONTENT AND PROCESS

- When things happen that we don't like, we often try to find out what is causing them. If we find out the cause, we can sometimes fix it. If the picture on your TV is fuzzy and you know it is because the antenna is pointing in the wrong direction, you can fix it by moving the antenna. If that's not the cause, you may not be able to fix the picture until you find out what the cause really is. Trying to find a cause requires some careful critical thinking.

- Finding out what causes something is called *causal explanation.* This involves thinking about possible causes and then deciding which is the real cause based on evidence. Scientists do this all the time. When we don't know a cure for a disease, scientists try to find out what causes the disease. That may help them find a cure. When there's a natural disaster like a flood, scientists try to find out why it occurred, in order to prevent it in the future. This lesson is going to give you a chance to learn how to think carefully about a situation in order to find a cause.

- Scientists are not just interested in things like floods that happen today. They are also interested in major changes that happened to the earth a long time ago. One thing that has puzzled scientists for a long time is what happened to the dinosaurs at the end of the Mesozoic Era. No one knows why they became extinct, but it's worth thinking about what could have caused their extinction and how we could find out. We might be able to learn something that will help us prevent other species from becoming extinct in the same way.

- Dinosaurs lived for a very long time. Even though there were lots of them and many were huge animals, not one survives today. Some were plant eaters only; others ate meat and hunted other animals. What other things do you know about what the world of dinosaurs was like?

THINKING CRITICALLY

- List different possible conditions that could cause the dinosaurs to become extinct. Work in collaborative learning groups to brainstorm as many possibilities as you can. Make sure you include different and unusual possibilities.

- Suppose you looked for clues about which of these possibilities was the likeliest explanation. What sorts of things might you find today that could give you evidence for or against each possibility? How could you go about finding these things out? Each group should pick one of these possibilities and make a list of the possible evidence using the graphic organizer for causal explanation.

CAUSAL EXPLANATION

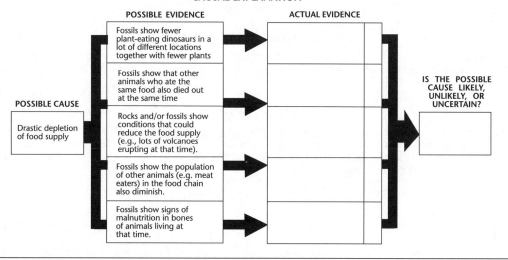

Figure 2   Causal Explanation

- Imagine that while looking for clues you find the following in various sedimentary rocks:
    - lots of dinosaur tracks at one level, fewer at another, and then none.
    - fossilized leaves and plants at one level, and then very few.
    - more mammal tracks and bones in some levels than in others.

When you bring these to a laboratory for Carbon 14 dating, you find that the plants and leaves coincide with a lot of dinosaur tracks. The layers with fewer plants came just before there were fewer, and then no other dinosaur tracks. The increase in mammal bones came as the dinosaur tracks were diminishing.

What possible explanations does this evidence count in favor of?

- Scientists shouldn't accept an explanation until they have sufficient evidence to be sure. Is this sufficient evidence? Why? What other evidence would you need to be sure that this was the best causal explanation?

- Do you know of any other evidence that has been found about the extinction of the dinosaurs either from your text or from other sources? What possible cause(s) does this evidence count in favor of? What possibilities does this evidence count against? Fill in the evidence on a graphic for those possible explanations.

THINKING ABOUT THINKING

- Map out the way you tried to figure what caused the extinction of the dinosaurs. What did you think about first, next, etc? How well does this map of causal explanation represent what you did?

- Compare what we considered to the way you ordinarily think about causes. Which do you think is the better way to try to find causes? Why?

- Think about a "causal" situations that comes up for you often, like causes of sickness or causes of problems around the house. Plan what you might think about the next time you don't know what caused something and want to find out.

> **CAUSAL EXPLANATION**
> 1. Possible causes?
> 2. Possible evidence?
> 3. Actual evidence?
> 4. Likely causes?

APPLYING YOUR THINKING

Immediate Transfer:

- We have studied other animals that are classified as endangered species. Make a list of these and then pick one you'd like to study further. Use your plan for causal explanation to determine what is causing them to be endangered. Do you have any ideas about what we might do to help these animals? Explain.

- There are a number of things that happen at school that many students and teachers are concerned about: lots of noise in the cafeteria, a great many library books get lost every year, etc. Select something that could be changed to make our school better. Try to find out the cause(s) of some of these things so we can recommend some remedies.

Reinforcement Later:

- We're going to be studying the increase in the population of mammals after the Mesozoic Era. When we do, we'll try to figure out why this happened using the same strategy for causal explanation.

WRITING/ART EXTENSION

After the students have brainstormed possible causes of the extinction of the dinosaurs, ask them to pick one of these and write a story about how this could have killed the dinosaurs. Ask them also to draw some pictures to go along with their stories.

LIBRARY RESEARCH EXTENSION

After the students have searched their textbooks for evidence about what caused the extinction of dinosaurs, ask them to use the school library and find books or articles in which people have discussed the extinction of dinosaurs. Have them record explanations for extinction that they find and the evidence that is offered to support them. They should report to the class on these different theories and discuss whether they are well supported.

Adapted from Swartz & Parks (1992a) and Barman, et al. (1989)

Figure 2 (continued)

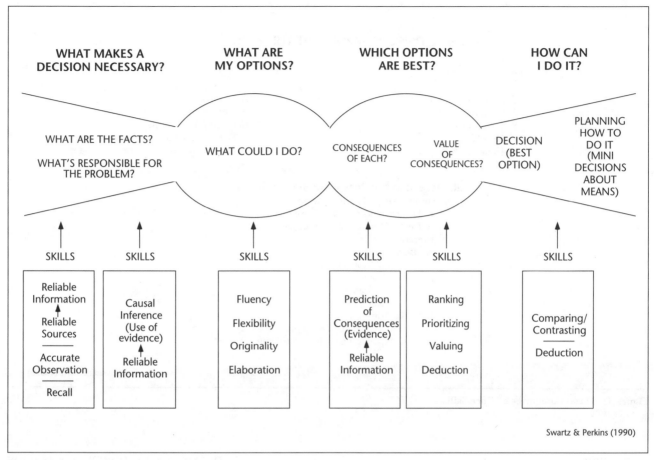

Figure 3   Relationships of Thinking Skills

skills of critical thinking related to making well-founded critical judgments. (See Figure 4).

Of course, the distinction between skills and processes is only rough. But it has some importance for pedagogy. Both thinking processes and the thinking skills they involve need attention. At each of the two levels we fall prey to the defaults of thinking.

Unfortunately, *many approaches to the teaching of thinking neglect one level or the other.* Some concentrate on skills only. They reflect an atomistic approach, all too common in other subjects such as mathematics, which breaks down the domain in question into small units isolated from one another and teaches them one at a time. Often, the units never come together in students' minds to empower them to undertake broader, more meaningful tasks. For instance, students may learn the *skill* of comparing and contrating but they should also learn to apply this skill in the context of the *process*

of making decisions, together with other skills important to good decision making.

While atomism is one threat, other approaches to teaching thinking focus only on overall processes like decision making and problem solving, with little attention to developing students' ability with contributing skills. Moreover, those who concentrate on skills only do not always attend to skills in each of the three important categories. Some emphasize analytical skills, some creative thinking skills, and some critical thinking skills. In our view, both skills and processes should show a strong presence in a well-rounded effort to teaching thinking. And the broader the range of skills, the better. If you are working with one of the more limited approaches, you may want to supplement it.

A third important dimension of thinking also needs instructional attention. Whereas processes and skills concern what you do to think well, dispositions

THREE TYPES OF IMPORTANT THINKING SKILLS

I. Generating Ideas

  1. **Alternative Possibilities**
     A. Multiplicity of Ideas
     B. Varied Ideas
     C. New Ideas
     D. Detailed Ideas

II. Clarifying Ideas
  1. **Analyzing Ideas**
     A. Comparing/Contrasting
     B. Classification/Definition
  2. **Analyzing Arguments**
     A. Finding Conclusions/ Reasons
     B. Uncovering Assumptions

III. Assessing the Reasonableness of Ideas
  1. **Support of Basic Information**
     A. Determining Accurate Observation
     B. Determining Reliable Secondary Sources
  2. **Inference**
     A. Use of Evidence
        1. Causal Explanation
        2. Prediction
        3. Generalization
        4. Reasoning by Analogy
     B. **Deduction**
        1. Conditional Reasoning (If … then …)
        2. Categorical Reasoning (All/Some …)

Swartz & Parks (1992a)

Figure 4   Three Categories of Core Skills

or attitudes concern your tendency actually to do it (cf. Ennis, 1986; Perkins, Jay, & Tishman, [in press]).

Students learn many things. However, often they do not use what they learn, except perhaps for passing the test. Why not? Perhaps they lack the motivation to use a particular skill or piece of knowledge. Or perhaps they lack the habit of putting it to work, even though they would like to. Or perhaps they do not detect occasions when it could be used. In other words, a disposition is a matter of motivation, but also of other factors such as habits and sensitivity to occasion—all these contribute to the actual deployment of better thinking. To teach thinking, we must go beyond developing skills and processes. We must also help students develop the dispositions they need to think well.

Dispositions come in all sizes. One can speak of very specific dispositions, such as the disposition to explore options carefully when you face a decision-making situation. But one can also speak of very broad dispositions, such as the disposition to hold off final judgment until you have thought carefully about all the factors—no matter whether you are making a decision, solving a problem, or engaging in some other thinking process.

Moreover, certain broad dispositions can be seen as direct counters to the four defaults of thinking—hasty, narrow, fuzzy, and sprawling. In some curriculum development work and writing, we and our colleagues Shari Tishman, Heidi Goodrich, and Eileen Jay have highlighted four dispositions. As can be seen in Figure 5, each in turn "takes on" one of the thinking defaults and recommends an opposite pattern of behavior. Of course, the bare statement of slogans does not instill dispositions in students. However, when one keeps coming back to them and elaborates the processes and skills that go with them, they will take hold and help organize students' behavior away from the defaults and toward better thinking.

How, in general, can we as teachers help students develop dispositions—whether overarching or more specific ones? We can model our own commitment to both as natural occasions come up in the classroom. We can show our open-mindedness, our attention to evidence, and our pursuit of op-

---

FOUR KEYS TO THINKING DISPOSITIONS

☞ Give your thinking time!

☞ Make your thinking adventurous and broad!

☞ Make your thinking clear and careful!

☞ Make your thinking organized!

Figure 5 Four Keys to Thinking Dispositions

tions, to inspire students' attention to them. We can also engage students in exploring when different skills and processes should be used, to build their sensitivity to appropriate occasions. And we can keep our students at the enterprise of thinking well in different content areas and on different occasions so that they develop habits of thinking well.

Basic #4. *The development of students' thinking calls for cultivating their (a) skills, (b) processes, and (c) dispositions concerning better thinking. A well-rounded approach addresses a diversity of all three.*

The Importance of Explicitness

Research suggests that thinking skills, processes, and dispositions are best treated explicitly in the classroom—spelled out, talked about, made conscious. This means that teachers should commit classroom time to focusing on thinking—defaults, better patterns of thinking, strategies, standards of judgment, ways to plan and direct thinking, and so on. Stand-alone courses, which involve the teaching of thinking, always have taken this approach. We urge that when teachers infuse thinking into their content instruction that they also attend to thinking with the same explicitness.

How? Lecturing students about thinking is the least desirable way. Rather, teachers should employ a common organizing vocabulary of thinking skills, processes, and dispositions (such as *making decisions,* and *considering options*). In the well-known article "Do You Speak Cogitare?" Arthur Costa shows how the ordinary language of the classroom can be transformed to elevate the level of students' thinking (1991). Such moves take advantage of the

verbal thinking organizers already a part of the English language. But one can go further. To what standards should we hold our predictions? What steps might we take to make a well-considered decision? Explicit verbal and graphic thinking organizers that go beyond the resources of everyday English answer such questions by expressing steps, standards, and other elements of a thinking skill, process, or disposition (Black & Black, 1990; Jones, Pierce, & Hunter, 1988-1989; McTighe & Lyman, 1988).

This does not mean that teachers must necessarily teach thinking organizers directly to students. An inductive approach is also possible. Teachers can guide students in developing their own thinking organizers. For example, teachers can engage students in thinking about decision making, identifying problematic aspects of decision making, and creating a graphic organizer for the process. Whether organizers are taught or drawn from students, explicitness is key.

For instance, the sample lesson on the extinction of dinosaurs makes explicit what skillful causal explanation involves. The teacher discusses causal explanation at the outset, using terms like *possible cause* and *looking for evidence*. Later in the lesson, the instructor guides the students through a well-organized process supported by a graphic organizer. As the students articulate a map for the thinking they did, they make aspects of causal reasoning explicit again to themselves.

Earlier, we contrasted infusion with teaching *for* thinking, which simply emphasizes experiences of better thinking during content instruction. Explicit attention is the key difference. It is good to ask challenging content-oriented questions that engage students in deeper thinking than they would otherwise display. But it is better to give thinking explicit attention. Only then can one reasonably expect students to understand and appreciate the enterprise of better thinking and make efforts to put to use what they have learned about better thinking in many settings.

Basic #5. *Explicit attention to thinking during content instruction (via verbal and graphic thinking organizers, discussion, reflection, and so on) makes the crucial difference between just giving students experiences of better thinking and empowering them as aware users of better thinking practices across diverse settings.*

Attention to Metacognition

Most of the power we human beings wield over our environment comes from our ability to *think about the world*—to invent, solve problems, make reflective decisions, and so on. By analogy, much of our power to direct our own thinking, the internal world of our minds, would flow from our ability to *think about our thinking*. Psychology has a word for this process: *metacognition.*

In the context of teaching thinking, *metacognition* simply means thinking about your own thinking (Swartz, 1989). (In some technical psychological contexts it takes on slightly broader meanings.) For instance, when you ask yourself, "How well did I really handle that decision?" you are asking yourself a metacognitive question. You are setting out to think about your own thinking. When you sit down to tackle an assignment and ask yourself, "Now just how am I going to approach these problems?" you are again asking yourself a metacognitive question. You are planning in advance what strategy to use with the assignment.

Many people mix up metacognition with other kinds of thinking. However, the query, "Am I thinking about my own thinking?" proves a reliable key to sorting out true metacognition. For example, suppose Mirabelle says to herself, "I don't like the way I ended that short story." Is she thinking about her own thinking? No. She's thinking about an external product, the short story. That is

not metacognition. In contrast, suppose Mirabelle says to herself: "I settled on the ending of my short story too quickly. I should have given it more thought." Is she thinking about her own thinking? Yes. She is noting how she reached a conclusion. That is metacognition.

Metacognition is supremely important to the cultivation of good thinking. Through metacognition, people become aware of their usual thinking practices and gain the perspective they need to fine-tune or even radically revise those practices. How this works becomes clearer if we distinguish four degrees of metacognition, a kind of ladder of metacognition with the most powerful variety at the top (Swartz & Perkins, 1990).

- *The bottom rung: Tacit use.* Most often, people make use of different kinds of thinking—seeking evidence, imagining options, criticizing arguments—without any awareness. They just do it. This involves no metacognition at all.

- *The second rung: Aware use.* Sometimes, people use different kinds of thinking with more awareness, especially if they have participated in some instruction about good thinking practices. They are sometimes aware: "Now I'm making a decision. Now I'm finding evidence. Now I'm inventing ideas." Such awareness is thinking about one's thinking to only a limited degree, just categorizing and labeling.

- *The third rung: Strategic use.* Sometimes people deliberately deploy thinking organizers to guide their thinking. For instance, they say: "This is an important decision. I'm going to brainstorm a pile of options to give me some real choices. And I'll have to think out the consequences for options that look good really carefully." Such deliberate, strategic self-instructions go beyond labeling and categorizing. They involve thinking about one's thinking in order to direct it.

- *The top rung: Reflective use.* Occasionally, people think about their own thinking and the thinking organizers they use to critically assess and creatively revise their practices: "You know, when I make decisions, I don't often stretch my mind far. Let me see if I can get beyond the obvious options and find some better ones." Such episodes involve thinking about thinking in the richest sense, not just labeling and categorizing, nor even just directing, but rather examining and reinventing how one thinks.

The ladder of metacognition provides a telling reminder that there are different degrees of metacognition. Many efforts to teach thinking pay some attention to metacognition. Often it is the second rung, simply a matter of categorizing and labeling, or even the third rung, emphasizing good choice and careful following of thinking organizers. But rarely does the top rung figure in instruction. Rarely are learners encouraged to think about their thinking critically in different contexts, to size it up, and to redesign it. In our view, a principal challenge in the teaching of thinking involves lifting students to the top rung, reflective use of different kinds of thinking.

What is this like? For example, earlier in the article we invited readers to think about some recent decisions they made that did not work out well and analyze what went wrong. This is top-rung metacognition, thinking about your own thinking in a critical way. The same activity can be done with youngsters in a classroom.

For another example, notice how metacognitive activities appear in the infusion lesson on the dinosaurs. The lesson asks students to map out explicitly how they thought about the causes of the extinction of the dinosaurs, what they did first, and what next. Perhaps with help they would say that first they thought about possible causes, then possible evidence, and so on. Next, students compare this way of thinking about causes to their ordinary practices. They can discuss which is better, why, and when. Such episodes of critically evaluating the way they think are top-rung or reflective instances of metacognition.

As these examples illustrate, building metacognition into the teaching of thinking can be done readily enough. It's mostly a matter of making time in a lesson and taking some pains so some of that time serves top-rung, reflective metacognition. The gains in students' awareness of and thoughtful con-

trol over their own thinking and learning are well worth the investment. In summary:

Basic #6. *Developing learners' metacognition is an important facet of teaching thinking. It is especially desirable to cultivate top-rung metacognition—critical examination and creative revision of one's own thinking practices.*

Teaching for Transfer

One of the most important but neglected general goals of education is transfer of learning. Transfer, a term from the psychology of learning, occurs when students learn something in one context and apply it in another significantly different context (for a more developed explanation, see Perkins & Salomon, 1987). For example, when moving from one to another house, you might rent a small truck. You find that you can drive it well enough because of your experience driving cars—transfer from car to truck driving. For another example, when you use math skills acquired in the classroom on your income tax form, that is transfer. For another, if you are a chess buff and find opportunities to apply principles of chess—like "take control of the center"—to politics or business, that is transfer. As these examples make plain, some transfers reach further than others. The truck situation is relatively close to the car situation, a case of "near transfer," but politics and business are quite different from chess, a case of "far transfer."

Why is transfer so important to educators? For two reasons. First of all, the impact of education depends on transfer. We do not instruct students in mathematics so they can perform well on math quizzes, but so that they can use mathematics on income tax forms, in the supermarket, for keeping household accounts, and for pursuing professions in accounting, engineering, or science. We do not instruct students in history so they can pass the history quiz, but rather so they will read about current events with more savvy, vote with a deeper sense of the democratic tradition, and display sensitivity to the social forces around them.

The second reason is this: Research shows that transfer cannot be taken for granted. Often, students do not display the kinds of transfer we would like to see. They do not apply their mathematical or historical knowledge to later studies or to situations outside the classroom. In most classroom settings, it is taken for granted that students make the appropriate transfer of what they are learning. But for many topics and skills, transfer does not occur.

This is a major problem for education in general and for the teaching of thinking specifically (Swartz, 1987). Just as students often do not transfer content knowledge, they often do not transfer ways of thinking that they have learned in a particular class. What can be done? Here, research is encouraging. Certain studies show that we can get the transfer we want if we teach for transfer. Although transfer does not happen automatically, if instruction includes specific components designed to foster transfer, then students display much more transfer of learning.

It's useful to characterize two general approaches to teaching for transfer: *hugging* and *bridging* (Perkins & Salomon, 1986; Fogarty, Perkins, & Barell, 1991). The basic idea of *hugging* is to make the instruction as much like the diverse potential applications as possible, including in the instruction samples or simulations of applications. Thus, the instruction "hugs" the envisioned applications as much as possible.

In contrast, *bridging* does not involve students' direct experience with possible applications. Rather, with the guidance of the teacher, students make generalizations about what they are learning, anticipate possible applications, and compare different circumstances analytically in a wide-ranging fashion. Thus, bridging is analytical and conceptual, while hugging is experiential. Both are useful ways of teaching for transfer, and both can be used together.

More concretely, what can be done to teach for the transfer of better ways of thinking? The first rule is: Set aside time to teach for transfer. As to using that time, notice how the dinosaur lesson handles transfer. It asks students to apply the same strategy to an endangered species; calls for them to analyze some school concern, such as noise in the cafeteria, to determine its causes; and plans ahead to employ the same strategy again later in the term to examine the causes of the increase in the population of mammals during the Mesozoic Era. All of these are examples of hug-

ging; in all cases the students directly practice other applications of the process.

For another example, suppose that your students learn something about decision making in the context of looking at Harry Truman's decision to use the atomic bomb to end World War II (Swartz & Parks, 1992). To teach for transfer, you might:

- *Do a similar exercise with a different example.* For instance, you might engage your students in working through the decision of Southern politicians to secede from the Union. Such an application helps students generalize the decision-making perspective introduced with the Truman example. It is a form of hugging, a direct experience with other examples.

- *Compare and contrast with personal decisions.* You might ask your students to choose personal decisions they have made and compare the process of making those decisions with how you all, in class, rethought Truman's decision. This is bridging, an analytical compare-and-contrast exercise.

- *Have your students keep decision diaries.* You might ask your students to keep "decision diaries" for three or four weeks. They work through some personal decisions in their diaries, keeping in mind some of the decision-making principles they are learning. In their diaries, they also compare and contrast those decisions with historical decisions you are studying at the same time. This involves both hugging and bridging—hugging in directly working through personal decisions and bridging through the analytical comparison and contrast.

Some teachers will find it comfortable to teach for transfer with tactics very like those in these examples. Others with different agendas can devise other hugging and bridging maneuvers to help youngsters transfer what they are learning. Most important is the principle involved:

Basic #7. *Teaching for transfer of better ways of thinking is an important part of the teaching of thinking. This means allocating specific time to engage learners in actually experiencing wider applications (hugging) and generalizing and thinking analytically about possible applications (bridging).*

BUILDING AN INFUSION PROGRAM

Beware Token Investment

Commonly, efforts to infuse thinking into subject matter instruction are sporadic. This is understandable, in that teachers' lives are horrendously busy, and they have all too many agendas to serve. At the same time, both common sense and some research suggest that a minimalist approach to infusing thinking into subject matter learning does not achieve very much, probably nothing. When teachers who teach a class four or five times a week only include a thinking activity once a week or once every two weeks for fifteen minutes or a half hour, there is likely to be no long-term impact whatsoever, although often the activity itself goes very well.

Probably, teachers should do something every day, even if briefly, for the initiative to be worthwhile. Something, but what? In our view, it is not necessary to focus on a key process, such as causal reasoning, with fully elaborated lesson after lesson, like the one about dinosaurs. One to three lessons with such step-by-step guidance are enough for a specific process or skill—provided that they are followed up with regular reinforcement through transfer examples. For instance, one would ask students to think through other issues requiring causal reasoning in a more self-guiding way. Such applications often have to begin with the students reminding themselves of the strategy they used before, the teacher helping only as necessary. It is important to replace teachers' external guidance with students' internal guidance as they gain more experience.

Besides frequency, diversity is important too. The same skills and processes should be introduced in a number of different subject areas and reinforced by teachers working from the same thinking frameworks across the curriculum and grade levels. This provides repeated practice and fosters transfer. And there is another reason as well: Part of the aim in teaching thinking is to modify student dispositions or attitudes so that they appreciate the value of good thinking. Showing that we value it enough to give it a prominent role across the whole curriculum supports the development of

these dispositions. This is a short but very important basic. To sum it up:

Basic #8. *Attention to thinking in content instruction needs to be fairly frequent to (a) build students' skills and insights and (b) systematically deepen content understanding. Don't shortchange it!*

The Need for Continuing Staff Development

Gaining facility in creating and teaching subject matter lessons infused with the teaching of thinking is not very difficult. However, it cannot be accomplished overnight. Four basic elements are involved:

- Work from a clear conception of the kind of thinking that you want to teach your students. Have skills, processes, dispositions, and relevant thinking organizers in mind.

- Find natural points of opportunity in the curriculum you teach, places that invite attention to the kind of thinking in question.

- Structure your lessons to introduce (or, in an inductive approach, elicit from students) the thinking skills, processes, and dispositions explicitly through thinking organizers.

- Help your students reflect on the thinking they are doing (metacognition) and give them plenty of practice in using that kind of thinking in diverse contexts and in reflecting on how it might apply elsewhere (transfer).

Each of these points is best accomplished in the context of ongoing staff development programs for groups of teachers. Although virtually all teachers already do some things to cultivate students' thinking, most have not received any formal introduction to the teaching of thinking. Time is needed to become familiar with the variety of thinking skills and processes that are important in good thinking and to find ways to work them into the curriculum. There is no "quick fix." Going to a single workshop will not impart facility in teaching thinking well. (For a general practical perspective on the problems of teacher development and school change, see Fullan, 1991.)

Multiple exposures are important. But, beyond that, effective staff development requires more direct learning opportunities, typically through individualized coaching sessions. Research on staff development strongly supports this. Coaching sessions should focus on specific lessons that teachers either have designed or are in the process of designing. The coach can sit in on a class and discuss what happens afterward with the teacher. Or the coach can meet with a teacher before the lesson is taught to help work through the lesson design. The coach need not be an outside consultant, but may well be a teacher in the same school with more background to draw on. Whatever the details, the coaching process should focus directly on classroom implementation of general ideas obtained through workshops or other means.

For instance, a workshop might introduce a group of teachers to causal reasoning, with the dinosaur lesson as an example. The teachers are asked to design causal reasoning lessons relevant to their own content. A few days later, the workshop presenter or a teacher with prior experience in such instruction might discuss the designs with each teacher individually. One teacher might have designed a causal explanation in social studies on the causes of the Civil War. Another might bring one on what caused feuding in "The Pushcart War." The discussion often yields major changes in the lesson and builds teachers' confidence in their efforts to infuse thinking into their content instruction.

There is no substitute for this kind of careful work on lesson design as you build an infusion program for a classroom or a whole school. We have many models of this process already. The best "thinking" schools utilize a variety of support structures for such ongoing staff development programs. These range from relief time for inservice programs to peer coaching arrangements. Teachers work collaboratively to ensure a common focus across classes and subject matter. Striving to cultivate students' thinking, they find themselves engaged in thinking and rethinking their approaches to teaching and their school's curriculum. The school becomes a setting that values and fosters both students' and teachers' thinking.

Basic #9. *The infusion of thinking into content area instruction is not a "quick fix" accomplishable by a single workshop. Schools and teachers need to commit themselves to a continuing process of thoughtful staff development (much of which may be handled internally by the school) to undertake successfully this profound and exciting qualitative change in the learning experiences of youngsters.*

Arthur Costa constantly reminds us that the better thinking practices we stress in classrooms for our students' sake should permeate the entire atmosphere of the school, inspiring teachers and administrators (1991). Schools like this are "homes for the mind." We believe that everyone in the long run can afford this sort of home. Indeed, we as a society cannot afford not to afford them. In the years to come, the expanding art and craft of infusion will help create such schools far and wide.

REFERENCES

Barman, C., DiSpezio, M., Guthrie, V., Leyden, M., Mercier, S., & Ostlund, K. (1989). *Addison-Wesley Science* Menlo Park, CA: Addison-Wesley.

Baron, J. B., & Sternberg, R. S. (Eds.). (1986). *Teaching thinking skills: Theory and practice.* New York: W. H. Freeman.

Black, H., & Black, S. P. (1990). *Organizing thinking.* Pacific Grove, CA: Midwest Publications.

Brandt, R. (1984). Editorial. *Educational Leadership, 41*(1), 3.

Costa, A. (1991a). Teaching, for, of, and about thinking. In A. Costa (Ed.), *Developing minds: A resource book for teaching thinking, revised edition* (Vol. 1) (p. 31-34). Alexandria, VA: Association for Supervision and Curriculum Development.

Costa, A. (1991b). *The school as a home for the mind.* Palatine, IL: Skylight Publishing.

Ennis, R. H. (1986). A taxonomy of critical thinking dispositions and abilities. In J. B. Baron & R. S. Sternberg (Eds.), *Teaching thinking skills: Theory and practice,* (p. 9-26). New York: W. H. Freeman.

Fogarty, R., Perkins, D. N., & Barell, J. (1991). *How to teach for transfer.* Palatine, IL: Skylight Publishing.

Fullan, M. G. (1991). *The new meaning of educational change.* New York: Teachers College Press.

Jones, B. F., Pierce, J., & Hunter, B. (1988-89). Teaching students to construct graphic representations. *Educational Leadership, 46*(4), 20-25.

McTighe, J., & Lyman, F. T. (1988). Cueing thinking in the classroom: The promise of theory-embedded tools. *Educational Leadership, 45*(7), 18-24.

Mirman, J., & Tishman, S. (1988). Infusing thinking through "connections." *Educational Leadership, 45*(7), 64-65.

Nickerson, R., Perkins, D. N., & Smith, E. (1985). *The teaching of thinking.* Hillsdale, NJ: Lawrence Erlbaum.

Perkins, D. N. (1992). *Smart schools.* New York: The Free Press.

Perkins, D. N. (1987). Myth and method in teaching thinking. *Teaching Thinking and Problem Solving, 9*(2), 1-2, 8-9.

Perkins, D. N. (1986a). *Knowledge as design.* Hillsdale, NJ: Lawrence Erlbaum.

Perkins, D. N. (1986b). Thinking frames. *Educational Leadership, 43*(8), 4-10.

Perkins, D. N. (1986c). Thinking frames: An integrative perspective on teaching cognitive skills. In J. B. Baron & R. S. Sternberg (Eds.), *Teaching thinking skills: Theory and practice,* (p. 41-61). New York: W. H. Freeman.

Perkins, D. N., Goodrich, H., Mirman, J., & Tishman, S. (in press). *Connections.* Menlo Park, CA: Addison-Wesley.

Perkins, D. N., & Salomon, G. (1989). Are cognitive skills context bound? *Educational Researcher 18*(1), 16-25.

Perkins, D. N., & Salomon, G. (1988). Teaching for transfer. *Educational Leadership, 46*(1), 22-32.

Perkins, D. N., Jay, E., & Tishman, S. (in press). *Beyond abilities: A dispositional theory of thinking.* Merill-Palmer Quarterly.

Swartz, R. (1991a). Structured teaching for critical thinking and reasoning in standard subject-area instruction. In J. Voss, D. Perkins & J. Segal (Eds.), *Informal reasoning and education,* (p. 414-450). Hillsdale, NJ: Erlbaum.

Swartz, R. (1991b). Infusing the teaching of critical thinking into content instruction. In A. Costa (Ed.), *Developing minds: A resource book for teaching thinking, revised edition* (Vol. 1), (p. 177-184). Alexandria, VA: Association for Supervision and Curriculum Development.

Swartz, R. (1989). Making good thinking stick: The role of metacognition, extended practice, and teacher modeling in the teaching of thinking. In D. Topping, D. Crowell, & V. Kobayashi (Eds.), *Thinking across cultures: The third international conference,* (p. 417-436). Hillsdale, NJ: Erlbaum.

Swartz, R. (1987). Critical thinking, the curriculum, and the problem of transfer. In D. Perkins, J. Bishop, & J. Lochhead (Eds.), (p. 261-284). *Thinking: The second international conference.* Hillsdale, NJ: Erlbaum.

Swartz, R., & Parks, S. (1992a). *Infusing critical and creative thinking into elementary instruction: A lesson design handbook.* Pacific Grove, CA: Midwest Publications.

Swartz, R., & Parks, S. (1992b). *Infusing critical and creative thinking into secondary instruction: A lesson design handbook.* Pacific Grove, CA: Midwest Publications.

Swartz, R. J., & Perkins, D. N. (1990). *Teaching thinking: Issues and approaches.* Pacific Grove, CA: Midwest Publications.

Tishman, S. (1991). Connections. In A. Costa (Ed.), *Developing minds: Programs for teaching thinking, revised edition* (Vol. 2), (p. 69-72). Alexandria, VA: Association for Supervision and Curriculum Development.

MIND TOOLS FOR MATTERS OF THE MIND

—

Jay McTighe and Frank T. Lyman

With feigned earnestness, the first grade teacher informs the class that today will be an "exactly right day" during which no one will make any mistakes. Noting that the children accept this plan as reasonable, she proceeds to write a story on the board, writing down only the words "I" and "the." When asked what they think of this story, the children are baffled and amused. The teacher explains that "I" and "the" are the only two words she knows how to spell correctly. They end up telling the teacher it is better to make mistakes than to write only two words down. The teacher then asks them whether there are other times when it is O.K. to make a mistake, and writes on the board: What is good about making a mistake? She then tells them that they will make a theory about the good effects of making mistakes. As she does this, she gives hand signal cues for cause/effect and evaluation, and sets thinking wheel arrows on the symbols for these two basic types of thinking.

Setting a wall chart indicator on "think" she asks the children to think of a time when they made a mistake. After ten seconds, she sets the indicator on "pair" and the children tell each other about their mistakes. Volunteers then "share" examples of mistakes with the whole class and the teacher lists them on a memory chart for reference later. Following "think" and "share" cues, the children recall other mistakes made by familiar literary characters, such as Pinnochio and the three little pigs, and discuss what these characters learned from their mistakes. Going through the think-pair-share cycle again, the students *pick certain listed mistakes and discuss in pairs how making these mistakes might help the children in some way.*

After the second pairing, the teacher again moves the indicator to "share" and places the students' answers on a web-shaped graphic organizer. The students are amazed at the ways a mistake can help them. Later, the teacher creates a wheel-shaped organizer that illustrates general ways mistakes can be helpful and specific examples to match these effects. The wheel is then laminated and placed on the wall as a reference. (See Figure 1.)

* * *

*B*oth teacher and students are visibly bothered by the incessant squabbles inside and outside the seventh grade social studies classroom. The teacher decides to enlist the students' help in restoring peace and places three web-shaped graphic organizers on chart paper: one for causes, one for effects, and one for prevention/resolution of conflict. Before working on these maps, students, individually and with a partner, generate all the examples of conflict they can. To help with this recall, the teacher posts a list of contexts, such as book titles, movie titles, historical events, and life settings.

Individually, students then list and share examples of conflict with the class. Once a list is compiled, the teacher asks each student to choose at least five examples and place the causes of each conflict on a personal web-shaped organizer. After the students have generated causes and sought common ones with a partner, they share the most frequently identified causes with the class. The teacher places the most common of these on the first graphic organizer, titled "causes."

The process is repeated for effects of conflicts and for possible prevention measures or resolutions. By the end of two class periods, the students have formed a theory of cause, effect, prevention, and resolution of conflict. They have also investigated the relationship between certain causes of conflict and measures for prevention or resolution. The teacher takes the information and, with the help of four students, designs a large concentric wheel organizer. The organizer is laminated and placed on the wall as a guide for prevention and resolution of classroom conflict. The graphic organizer also serves as a theory template to help students examine and understand the historical conflicts studied in class.

When the wheel is first displayed, the teacher uses think-pair-share and asks the students to identify the types of thinking they used to create their theory. For this identification they refer to the question-response cues on the "thinking matrix" (thinktrix). Symbols for each type of thinking are then attached to the appropriate parts of the wheel. The teacher refers to this analytical and labeling process as "shared metacognition."

* * *

At the beginning of the period, the high school literature teacher targets the objective of the day – to analyze Willie Loman, the play's central character. He then distributes copies of the character map, giving each student approximately five minutes to develop a preliminary character sketch by making notes on the graphic organizer. Students work on this activity individually while referring to their anthologies.

Following their individual thinking time, the students shift to pre-assigned cooperative learning groups of four students each. Using their individual maps as a starting point, the group members engage in a discussion of the character traits of Willie Loman with the goal of producing a group character map. For the next twenty minutes, the classroom is filled with lively conversation as groups reach consensus and prepare a large map on chart paper.

Upon completion, each group tapes its chart paper map to a chalkboard or wall. As a result of their own involvement in the character analysis, students are eager to see the ways in which others interpreted the character. The teacher capitalizes on this heightened interest by concluding the period with a "gallery walk" around the classroom to view the completed maps. This brief tour provides students with a glimpse of the analyses of other groups in preparation for tomorrow's group presentations. The students leave the room with Willie Loman on their minds.

What characteristics do the preceeding scenarios share? At least three common elements may be noted. First, in each situation, the teacher has consciously applied specific, research-based, instructional techniques for actively involving students in constructing meaning—for example, developing a theory of conflict or analyzing a literary character. Second, the learning activities are facilitated by cognitive tools, which are tangible devices that assist thinking in the classroom—for example, the thinking matrix and the character map. Finally, classroom actions and interactions are cued through a mutually understood system, such as thinking symbols and signals for think-pair-share. The focus for this chapter is on these "theory-embedded tools" and their associated cues.

Throughout history, human progress has been propelled by the development and utilization of tools. Tools such as the wheel, the bow and arrow, the windmill, the telegraph, the microscope, and the computer have greatly extended human physical and mental capabilities. Increasing knowledge provides a springboard for the development of new and more sophisticated tools.

How can this concept of tools be applied in education? A theory of tool-based instruction has been formulated by Nathaniel Gage (1974). Gage proposes that teachers use "tools of the trade" —tangible teaching/learning devices that are the material embodiment of theoretically valid teaching/learning ideas. According to Gage, such tools demonstrate four characteristics: psychological validity in which tools reflect what is known about teaching and learning; concreteness, or embodiment of the knowledge in materials and equipment; relevance, or practical value to teachers facing the daily pressures and challenges of the classroom; and differentiation by type of learning, a relationship between the type of tool and the way that a skill, concept, process, or attitude is best learned.

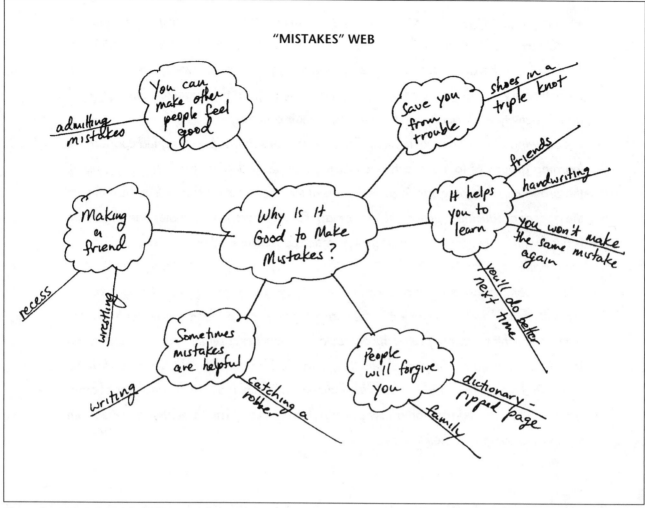

Figure 1   "Why it is Good to Make Mistakes" Web

THEORY-EMBEDDED TOOLS FOR THE "MINDS-ON" CLASSROOM

Successful classroom application demonstrates that cognitive tools provide a practical medium for blending theory and practice. The following are examples of nine theory-embedded tools and associated techniques conducive to a "minds-on" classroom, where active thinking leads to meaningful learning.

Think-Pair-Share

After the teacher asks a question, first-graders think for ten seconds and then talk in pairs as the teacher moves an arrow on a cue chart from "think" to "pair."

More than twenty years of research on "wait time" confirms the many benefits of allowing three or more seconds of silent thinking time after a question has been posed (wait time I) as well as after a student's response (wait time II). These benefits include longer and more elaborate answers, inferences supported by evidence and logical argument, greater incidence of speculative responses, increased student participation in discussion, and improved achievement (Rowe, 1986).

Additional research confirms the effectiveness of cooperative learning. The use of various cooperative structures promotes student involvement and increases verbal interaction, resulting in positive effects on attitude and achievement (Slavin, 1981; Johnson & Johnson, 1984). The think-pair-share method (Lyman, 1989, 1981) combines the benefits of wait time and cooperative learning (Dansereau, 1986).

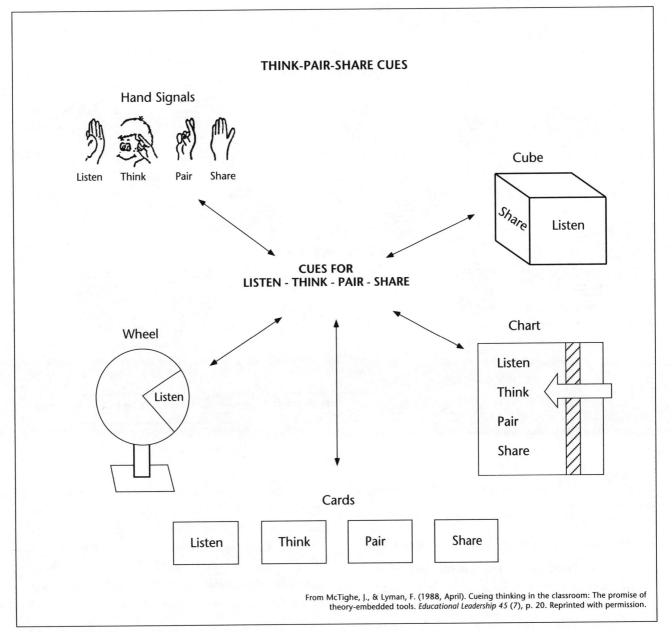

Figure 2   Think-Pair-Share Cues

Think-pair-share is a multimode discussion cycle in which students listen to a question or presentation, have time to *think* individually, talk with each other in *pairs*, and finally *share* responses with the larger group. The teacher signals students to switch from listening to *think, pair,* and *share* modes by using cues. (See Figure 2.)

Cueing enables teachers to manage students' thinking by combating the competitiveness, impulsivity, and passivity present in the time-worn recitation model. Both wait time I and wait time II can be consistently achieved with think-pair-share since students raise their hands only on signal, not directly after the question or a response. Students, individually and in pairs, may write or diagram their thoughts. Other cues give scripts or options for how students are to think or work in pairs. For instance, teachers may cue them to reach consensus, engage in problem solving, or assume the role of devil's advocate. (See Figure 3.)

The overall effect of these coordinated elements is a concrete, valid, and practical system made man-

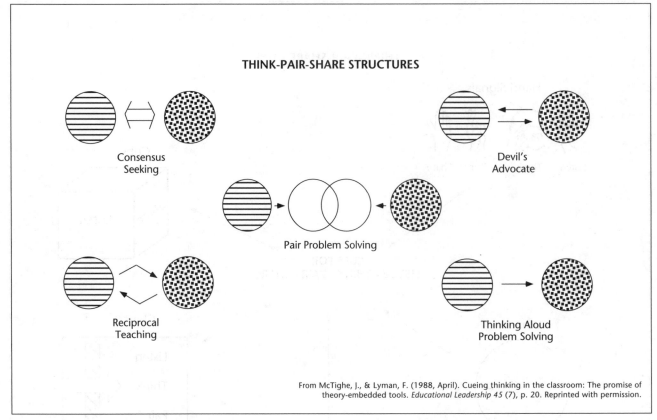

THINK-PAIR-SHARE STRUCTURES

Consensus Seeking

Devil's Advocate

Pair Problem Solving

Reciprocal Teaching

Thinking Aloud Problem Solving

From McTighe, J., & Lyman, F. (1988, April). Cueing thinking in the classroom: The promise of theory-embedded tools. *Educational Leadership 45* (7), p. 20. Reprinted with permission.

Figure 3   Think-Pair-Share Structures

ageable, and thereby acceptable to teachers, by cueing.

Questioning/Discussion Strategies Bookmark

During a classroom discussion of the limits of First Amendment rights, a high school social studies teacher glances at a laminated bookmark he's holding and assumes the role of devil's advocate in response to students' comments.

More than 2,000 years ago, Socrates demonstrated the power of questioning to stimulate student thinking about content. Educators today know that the way a teacher structures a question influences the nature of the thinking required to respond. We also know that follow-up strategies, such as asking for elaboration, influence the degree and quality of classroom discussion. Despite this knowledge, however, Goodlad (1985) reports that most classroom questions require only factual responses and that, in general, students are not involved in thought-provoking discussions.

Teachers can integrate effective questioning and discussion strategies into their daily repertoires by referring to a "cueing bookmark" (McTighe, 1985), which features question starters on one side and discussion strategies on the other. (See Figure 4.) During classroom discussion, the bookmark reminds teachers to use these advantageous strategies.

Thinking Matrix

After looking at a thinking matrix game board, a fifth grade boy asks his classmate, "What caused the hero's death ... I mean, what was there about his life that made you think he had to die that way?"

In addition to learning to ask questions that promote thinking (Gall, 1970; Hare & Pulliam, 1980), teachers are recognizing a need to help students generate their own questions. Generating their own questions facilitates students' comprehension (Davey & McBride, 1986) and encourages them to focus attention, make predictions, identify relevant information, and think creatively about content.

CUEING BOOKMARK

STRATEGIES TO EXTEND STUDENT THINKING

- **Remember wait time I and II**
  Provide at least three seconds of thinking time after a question and after a response.

- **Utilize think-pair-share**
  Allow individual thinking time, discussion with a partner, and then open up for class discussion.

- **Ask follow-up questions**
  "Why? Do you agree? Can you elaborate? Tell me more. Can you give an example?"

- **Withhold judgment**
  Respond to student answers in a nonevaluative fashion.

- **Ask for summary to promote active listening**
  "Could you please summarize John's point?"

- **Survey the class**
  "How many people agree with the author's point of view?" (thumbs up, thumbs down)

- **Allow for student calling**
  "Richard, will you please call on someone else to respond?"

- **Play devil's advocate**
  Require students to defend their reasoning against different points of view.

- **Ask students to unpack their thinking**
  "Describe how you arrived at your answer." (think aloud)

- **Call on students randomly**
  Avoid the pattern of only calling on those students with raised hands.

- **Encourage student questioning**
  Let the students develop their own questions.

- **Cue student responses**
  "There is not a single correct answer for this question. I want to consider alternatives."

**Language and Learning Improvement Branch
Division of Instruction
Maryland State Department of Education**

QUESTIONING FOR QUALITY THINKING

Knowledge – *Identification and recall of information*
Who, what, when, where, how____?
Describe_____.

Comprehension – *Organization and selection of facts and ideas*
Retell _____ in your own words.
What is the main idea of _____?

Application – *Use of facts, rules, principles*
How is ____ an example of _____?
How is ____ related to _____?
Why is ____ significant?

Analysis – *Separation of a whole into component parts*
What are the parts or features of __?
Classify ____ according to _____.
Outline/diagram/web _____.
How does _____ compare/contrast with _____?
What evidence can you present for _____?

Synthesis – *Combination of ideas to form a new whole*
What would you predict/infer from _____?
What ideas can you add to _____?
How would you create/design a new _____?
What might happen if you combined ____ with _____?
What solutions would you suggest for _____?

Evaluation – *Development of opinions, judgments, or decisions*
Do you agree _____?
What do you think about _____?
What is most important _____?
Prioritize ____ according to _____.
How would you decide about ____?
What criteria would you use to assess _____?

From Language and Learning Improvement Branch Division of Instruction, Maryland State Department of Education. In McTighe, J., & Lyman, F. (1988, April). Cueing thinking in the classroom: The promise of theory-embedded tools. *Educational Leadership 45* (7), p. 20. Reprinted with permission.

Figure 4   Cueing Bookmark

The thinking matrix, or "thinktrix," is a device to aid teachers and students in generating questions and responses (Lyman, 1987). The vertical axis of the matrix contains symbols of types of thought. The horizontal axis lists categories that give points of departure for inquiry, which vary according to the subject area. For example, using the matrix in language arts (Figure 5), teachers or students point

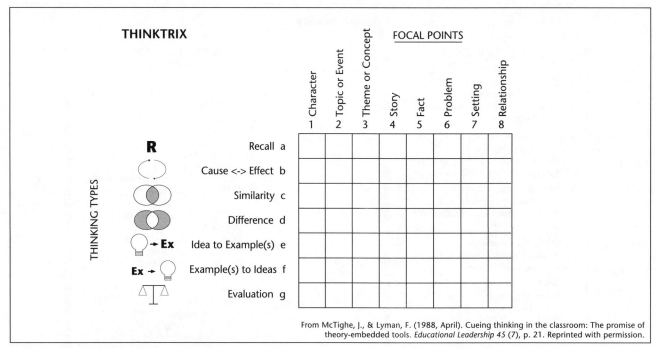

Figure 5   Thinktrix: Reading/Literature

to an intersection such as *cause/effect* and *event* or *character* and ask a question about the cause of the hero's death. In social studies (Figure 6), they could point to the intersection of *idea to example* and *concept or theory* and ask for historical examples of balance of power.

The thinktrix has many uses in the classroom. Students can analyze classroom questions or discourse, or they can create, analyze, and answer their own questions using a desk-size matrix as a game board. (See Figure 7.)

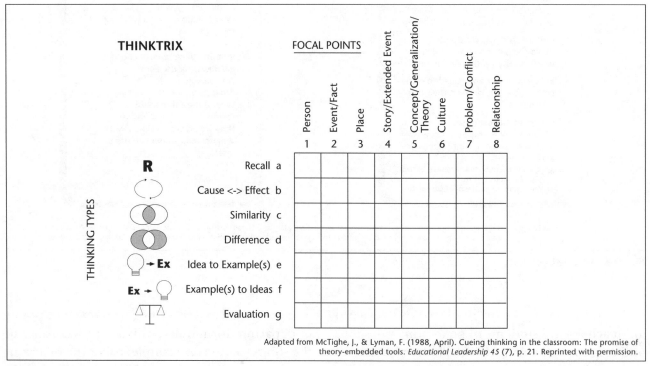

Figure 6   Thinktrix: Social Studies

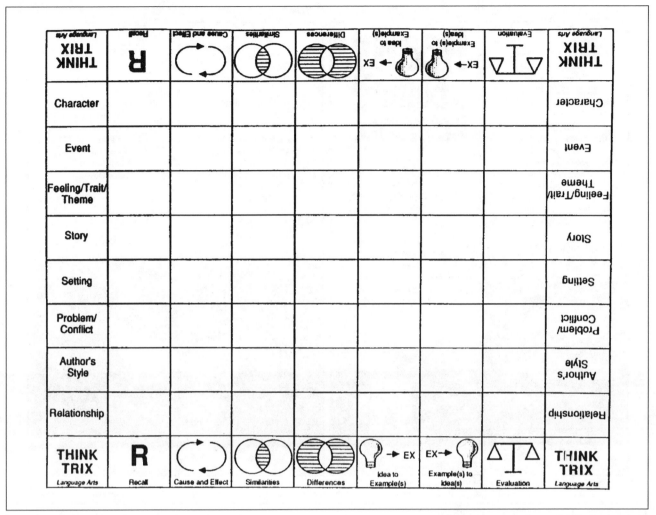

Figure 7 Thinktrix Gameboard

Using a poster-size matrix or wheel, teachers can make up their own questions, teach students how to design questions, show students how to respond to information using different thinking types, and point out the possible visual representations of each thinking type. In essence, the thinking matrix allows for shared metacognition in which teacher and students have a common framework for generating and organizing thought, as well as for reflecting on it.

Ready Reading Reference

While reading an article about sea lions in a children's magazine, a fifth-grader looks at his bookmark and creates a visual image of what he has just read.

Analysis of the differences between good and poor readers points out the importance of the strategic behaviors that good readers spontaneously employ before, during, and after their reading. For example, they concentrate on their purpose for reading, make predictions about the text, monitor their comprehension, and adjust their approach when necessary. Poor readers, on the other hand, are less mindful of such effective strategies. In fact, they tend to perceive reading as "decoding" rather than as the construction of meaning (Garner, 1980; Garner & Reis, 1981).

The ready reading reference bookmark (Kapinus, 1986) was developed to summarize knowledge about "good reader" strategies (Paris & Jacobs, 1984). The bookmark serves as a tangible instructional tool for teachers and as a concrete

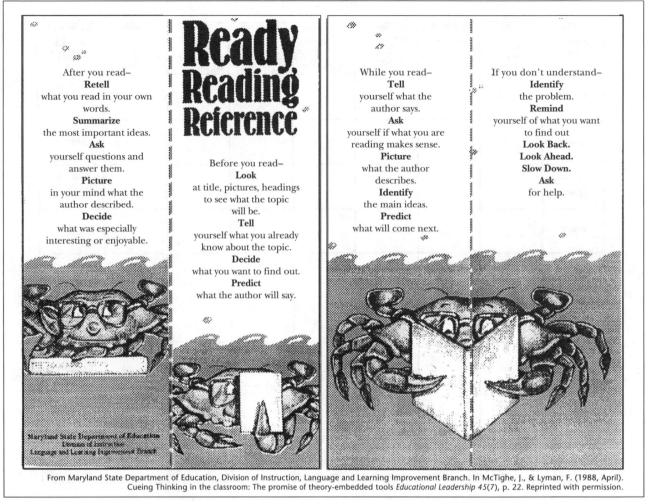

From Maryland State Department of Education, Division of Instruction, Language and Learning Improvement Branch. In McTighe, J., & Lyman, F. (1988, April). Cueing Thinking in the classroom: The promise of theory-embedded tools *Educational Leadership 45*(7), p. 22. Reprinted with permission.

Figure 8   Ready Reading Reference Bookmark

cue for students during independent reading. (See Figure 8.)

Problem-solving Strategies Wheel

As students in an algebra II class struggle to solve a word problem, their teacher points to a poster of problem-solving strategies and suggests that they consider strategy #5 – "draw a diagram."

Math and science teachers often experience frustration when students who demonstrate an understanding of basic facts and concepts cannot apply this knowledge to word problems. Fortunately, inquiry into the problem-solving behaviors of experts and novices has revealed important strategic distinctions for problem-solving instruction. Effective problem solvers spend time understanding a problem before attacking it. To this end, they

may create various representations or models. Expert problem solvers also report using problem-solving strategies, or heuristics, such as breaking the problem into subproblems. They also engage in metacognitive behaviors, including monitoring progress and checking the final solution (Mayer, 1983; Schoenfeld, 1979, 1980; Suydam, 1980).

Teachers who wish to improve students' problem-solving skills can spend classroom time examining the solution *process* along with the final answer; modeling their own strategic reasoning by "thinking aloud"; and providing explicit instruction in problem-solving heuristics using a tool such as the problem-solving strategies wheel (see Figure 9). Frequently found in the form of a large classroom poster, such an instructional tool is a visible cue that reminds teachers and students of the strategies of experts.

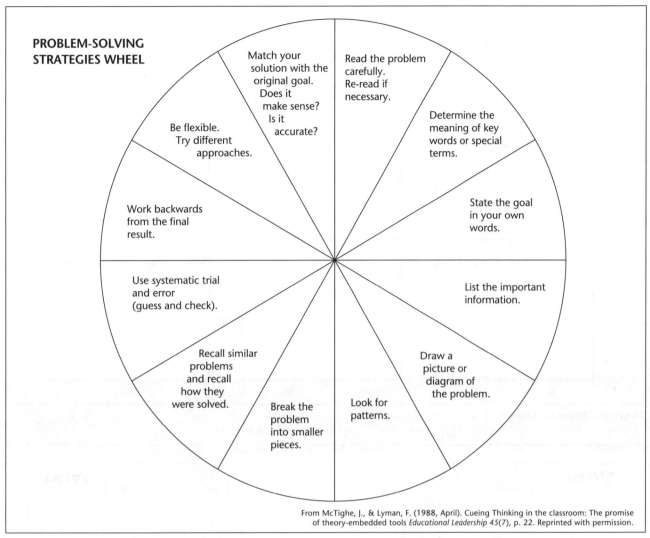

PROBLEM-SOLVING STRATEGIES WHEEL

Match your solution with the original goal. Does it make sense? Is it accurate?

Read the problem carefully. Re-read if necessary.

Be flexible. Try different approaches.

Determine the meaning of key words or special terms.

Work backwards from the final result.

State the goal in your own words.

Use systematic trial and error (guess and check).

List the important information.

Recall similar problems and recall how they were solved.

Draw a picture or diagram of the problem.

Break the problem into smaller pieces.

Look for patterns.

From McTighe, J., & Lyman, F. (1988, April). Cueing Thinking in the classroom: The promise of theory-embedded tools *Educational Leadership 45*(7), p. 22. Reprinted with permission.

Figure 9   Problem-solving Strategies Wheel

Graphic Organizers

Upon completing a character analysis map as part of a "prewriting" activity, an eighth grader comments, "I like graphic organizers because they help me see what I'm thinking."

The ability to generate and organize ideas and information is fundamental to effective thinking and learning (Armbruster & Anderson, 1980; Jones, Amiran, & Katims, 1985). Graphic organizers provide a visual, holistic representation of facts and concepts and their relationships. They serve as effective tools for helping students and teachers

- represent abstract or implicit information in a more concrete form,
- depict relationships between facts and concepts,
- generate and organize ideas for writing,
- relate new information to prior knowledge,
- store and retrieve information, and
- assess student thinking and learning.

Graphic organizers, also called cognitive maps, are used in classrooms from kindergarten through university levels. Perhaps the most widely used design is the web. Other designs include sequence steps or chains (Figure 10), vector charts for cause and effect, story maps, analogy links, concentric wheels, flow charts for decision making and problem solving, and character maps (Figure 11). Such graphic organizers become blueprints for oral discourse and written composition, particularly when used in conjunction with think-pair-share and

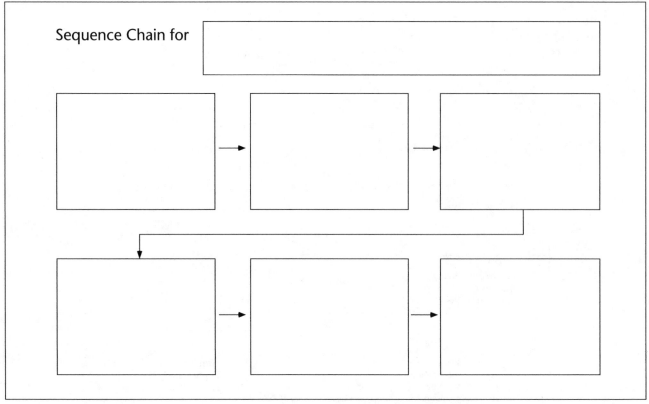

Figure 10   Sequence Chain

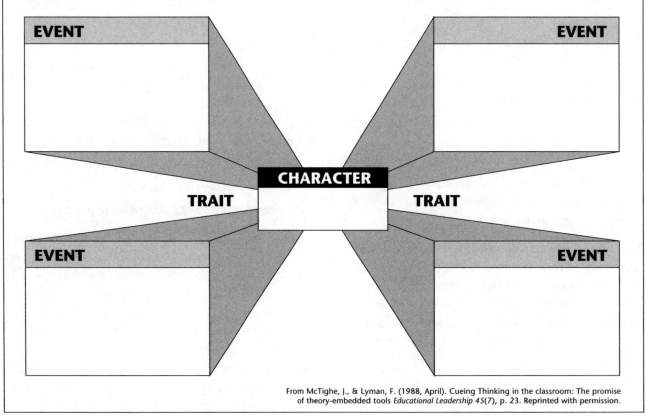

From McTighe, J., & Lyman, F. (1988, April). Cueing Thinking in the classroom: The promise of theory-embedded tools *Educational Leadership 45*(7), p. 23. Reprinted with permission.

Figure 11   Character Map

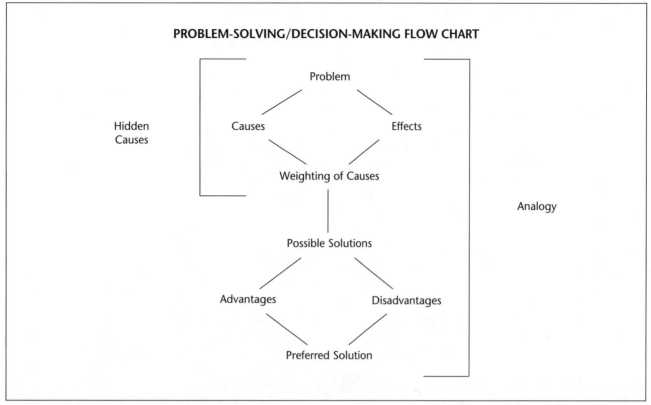

PROBLEM-SOLVING/DECISION-MAKING FLOW CHART

Problem

Causes   Effects

Hidden
Causes

Weighting of Causes

Analogy

Possible Solutions

Advantages   Disadvantages

Preferred Solution

Figure 12   Problem-solving/Decision-making Flow Chart

metacognitive cues, such as those on the thinktrix, the bookmarks, and the reading wheel.

Through their regular use of graphic organizers, students come to recognize that thought can be shaped, teachers discover a set of powerful tools for rendering the invisible process of thinking visible, and both students and teachers experience the benefits of shared metacognition.

The Problem-solving/Decision-making Flow Chart

A middle school teacher sits at home considering a frequent problem in the classroom: many students do not follow directions. As he thinks along a path suggested by a problem-solving flow chart, he discovers the hidden cause and decides on a solution.

A proven cognitive tool for enhancing student and teacher problem solving and decision making has been rendered as a flow chart. The problem-solving/decision-making flow chart (Figure 12) includes a behaviorally stated problem, analyzing cause and effect, weighting causes, seeking hidden causes, deriving solutions related to the key causes, evaluating solutions according to predicted effects, selecting a solution, deriving a principle underlying the solution, and testing the solution formally or informally. In addition to this logical sequence, the user may also apply analogical thinking at any point in the problem-solving process.

This flow chart (Eley & Lyman, 1987) has evolved from work with beginning teachers to help them with the often overwhelming tangle of classroom problems and decisions. In its present form it has been proven sufficiently useful and flexible to relieve the teacher of considerable anxiety.

Both teachers and students seem to recognize the strength of this particular problem-solving, decision-making process more when they first try to solve problems without it. In this fashion, they realize how close the heuristic is to the way most people work at problem solving. They also realize that not having a guide to the process makes it more likely that they will skip crucial steps and thereby make an ill-considered decision.

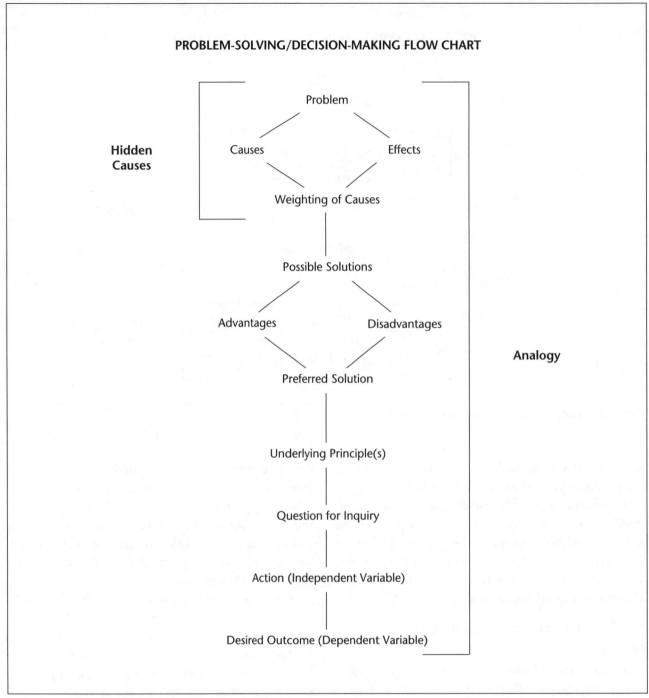

Figure 13   Problem-solving/Decision-making Flow Chart

Teachers also discover that this process, once cued and practiced, makes an indelible imprint on their minds and is even helpful in solving problems outside of the classroom. In addition, children find the flow chart understandable and useful.

The flow chart serves as an ideal format for classroom-based action research (de Pinto, 1988). Once the problem has been identified, the solution emerges as the independent variable for a formal study of effects (Figure 13). As teachers recognize the similarities between the type of thinking called for in problem solving and the research process, they will see educational research as more relevant and connected to their day-to-day work.

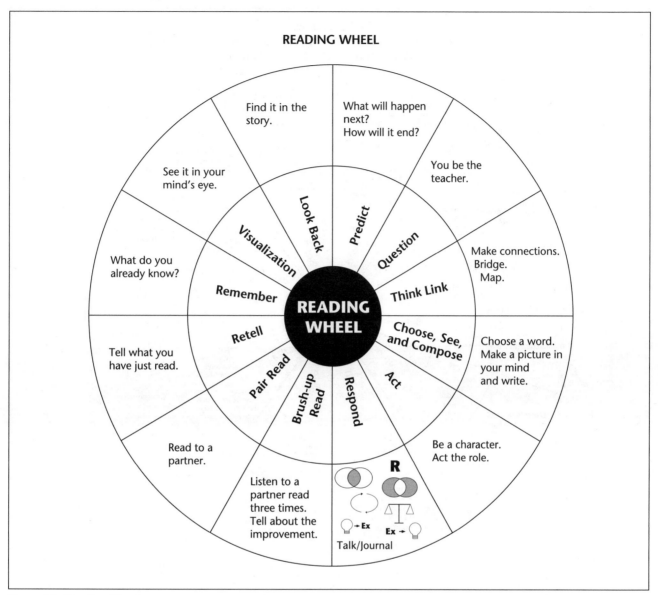

Figure 14   Reading Wheel

The Reading Wheel

As the fourth graders conclude silent reading, they look at the reading wheel poster mounted on the classroom wall to remember their next task. The wheel indicators are set on question, predict, and think link.

In reading and literature groups teachers tend to neglect all but a few learning or comprehension strategies, relying instead on what Delores Durkin (1978 - 79) calls interrogation. Even though it is current to include prediction, and in enlightened situations the reciprocal teaching sequence, most elementary teachers do not employ other proven strategies. To the extent that forgetting within the complexity of classroom events is a major cause of this omission, a solution is the reading wheel (Figure 14), a tool containing numerous reading response strategies.

With such a tool teachers can teach children how to comprehend text and derive meaning. The students learn how to learn as they regularly apply proven comprehension strategies. The wheel, or another shape, reminds teacher and students of research-tested mental activities. Used with indicator arrows, the wheel can be set to remind all

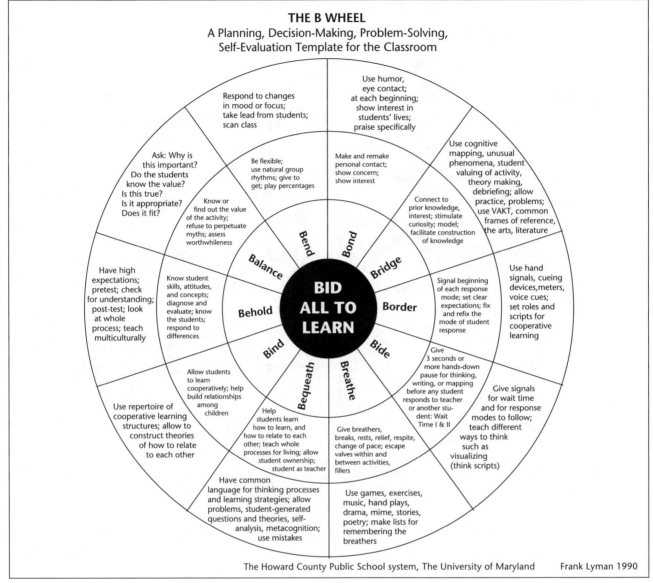

Figure 15   The "B" Wheel

participants where they are and what is expected at any given moment. The strategies can be named cleverly to appeal to the particular age and development levels of the students. The reading wheel is similar to the ready reading reference bookmark, though it is more inclusive and is used as a wall cue.

The "B" Wheel

The eleventh grade physics teacher is frustrated by the apathy of her students. In search of an idea to improve classroom attitudes toward her subject, she looks at a wall chart—the B wheel—chooses bridge,

and asks the students to think about how the newly introduced concept will be useful in their lives.

As a stimulus to unfortuitous amnesia the classroom can't be beat. In a swirl of events, teacher and students have difficulty recalling content, processes, and concepts. The result is stilted dialogue and halting action unrepresentative of what the participants know or can do. This inability to remember is particularly damaging when the teacher has to make on-the-spot pedagogical decisions. Given this phenomenon of the classroom, a visible cue serves as a valuable aid by reminding the teacher of key concepts and principles of teaching and learning.

It is possible to display such cues as individual principles as well as in an integrated format. The "B Wheel" (Figure 15) offers such an integrated design. Constructed from numerous theory-making sessions with teachers and student teachers, this theory-practice template serves as a reminder of critical attributes of effective teaching/learning interactions. The teacher can use the laminated tool in desk size or as a display poster to be seen across the room.

The proposition underlying the use of tools such as the B Wheel is that teachers will use the accessible theory to make better decisions than they would if they had no reminder. When the concepts are coined and patterned as on the B Wheel, there is also the likelihood that the teacher will eventually think of the elements without looking at the cue.

THE BENEFITS OF THEORY-EMBEDDED TOOLS

The aforementioned cognitive tools serve as catalysts for creating an active, responsive, "thinking" classroom. Teachers and students who reside in such classrooms have pointed to at least five benefits realized from the use of these tools.

An Aid to Memory

Thinking tools serve as tangible cues for teachers and students. They provide immediate access to theoretical knowledge when it is needed most—at the point of decision making. In the complex and distracting dynamics of school, the concreteness and stability of these tools remind teachers and students to use what they know to enhance their thinking and learning. The permanence of the tools frequently leads to "mental templating." This is evidenced by reports from teachers and students who remember the message embedded in the tool even when the tool itself is not present. As a result, memories of ways to think and act persist beyond the classroom.

Common Frame of Reference

Thinking tools provide a mutually understood frame of reference for teachers and students by of-

fering common terminology, such as the thinking types on the thinktrix, and specific cues for action, such as the signals associated with think-pair-share. The tools provide congruence that facilitates carryover from one classroom and subject area to others, resulting in a consistent approach within the school. This common frame of reference also contributes to the ability of students and teachers to reflect on their own thinking and learning, or shared metacognition.

Bridging In/Bridging Out

Current understanding of the learning process points to the importance of mobilizing relevant prior knowledge associated with new concepts to be learned. By taking time to "bridge in" and "bridge out," teachers help students activate a conceptual pegboard in their minds on which they can hang or integrate new concepts. Theory-embedded tools such as graphic organizers serve as tangible representations of this prior knowledge and as a medium for connecting it to new knowledge. Cued learning strategies such as visualizing aid students in assimilating new information.

Cognitive tools also facilitate transfer by "bridging out" from the initial learning context. For example, the use of a graphic organizer, such as the character map, not only serves as an aid for analyzing literary characters. It may also be applied to historical figures studied in a social studies class. The social studies teacher who mounts a character map poster on the wall facilitates cross-disciplinary application through the use of this cognitive tool.

Theory Making and Theory Use in the Classroom

Ready-made devices such as those described in this chapter offer one set of examples of theory-embedded tools. Another application emerges from the constructivist view of learning (Brooks, 1990). As illustrated in the first two classroom scenarios at the beginning of this chapter, students can be involved in actually creating their own theories and inventing associated tools. Such an approach to instruction turns the educational process away from the passivity of the lecture/recitation model; it actively involves students in constructing knowledge.

By serving as an epistemic reminder that all knowledge was created, rather than being passed down intact, this constructivist approach encourages children's ownership of their own learning.

The same process of theory building offers equal benefits when applied within teacher education courses or staff development programs. As teachers become actively involved in constructing theories regarding significant variables such as motivation, instruction, and classroom management, more mindful and reflective teaching occurs. In addition, such professional theory making leads to the development and refinement of even more effective classroom tools. The B Wheel is a product of such theorizing.

Theory making spawns theory using. Once a theory template is developed and made available in the classroom—in such forms as a wall chart, game board, and bookmark—the teachers and students have a common frame of reference to serve as a reminder and guide for the lesson's depicted strategies, rationale, contexts, or dispositions.

Teacher Education/Staff Development

Innovations are difficult to maintain in schools. These thinking tools, visible and concrete, may help hold an innovation in place. Although teachers are bombarded by advice and mandates, many of which appear to complicate their work, they welcome new ideas and materials that have a proven value. The theory-embedded tools described here have been enthusiastically received because they have practical value and are ready for immediate use. These tools enable teacher educators to send both novice and experienced teachers into the field with practical embodiments of theory. Staff developers who encourage the invention and use of instructional tools will see the elusive theory-into-practice connection made and maintained. Furthermore, as Gage (1974) suggests, research on tools will test theory in practice and expand the knowledge base for teaching.

An interesting phenomenon has been observed as a result of the expanded use of theory-embedded tools. Teachers who observe such tools as bookmarks, wheels, and posters in the classrooms of their colleagues inevitably inquire as to their use. This inquiry leads to a discussion of their benefits, frequently culminating in a request for the tool. Thus, the tool serves as a stimulus for collegial interactions, and a catalyst for a "natural curiosity" approach to peer-to-peer staff development.

THE PROMISE OF THEORY-EMBEDDED TOOLS: IMPLICATIONS FOR THE CLASSROOM

Instructional tools present a valid, concrete, relevant, and practical system for involving students from nursery school through graduate school in the active processing of ideas. These tools are an essential part of the vision of the active, minds-on, cooperative, responsive, and constructivist classroom. Their use ensures the embedding of theory in practice. The restraining forces which over time have prevented state-of-the-art teaching and learning can be partially overcome through these tools. It is important to realize, however, that the formula for creating a community of learners includes more than the use of tools. Cooperative learning (the sharing of thought), wait time (the time for thought), metacognition (the awareness of thought), cognitive incongruity or problematics (the fuel for thought), theory making (the ownership of thought), and cognitive mapping (the shaping of thought) are all essential, overlapping, and interactive with the tools and each other. The classroom is an econiche of crucial variables dependent upon each other and enhanced by theory-embedded tools. Theory-embedded cueing devices promise to bring classroom teaching into closer harmony with known principles of effective instruction, thereby improving the quality of thinking and learning for all students.

REFERENCES

Armbruster, B. B., & Anderson, T. H. (1980). *The effect of mapping on the free recall of expository text.* (Tech. Rep.160). Urbana-Champaign: University of Illinois, Center for the Study of Reading.

Brooks, J. (1990). Teachers and students: Constructivists forging new connections. *Educational Leadership, 47*(5), 68 - 71.

Dansereau, D. H. (1986). Cooperative learning strategies. In C. Weinstein, et al. (Eds.), *Learning and study strategies: Issues in assessment, instruction, and evaluation* (pp. 103-120). New York: Academic Press.

Davey, B., & McBride, S. (1986). Effects of question-generation training on reading comprehension. *Journal of Educational Psychology, 78*(4), 256-262.

Davidson, J. L. (1982, October). The group mapping activity for instruction in reading and thinking. *Journal of Reading, 27*(7), 53-56.

de Pinto, T. (1988). Action research: A teacher's perspective. *Reading Issues and Practices, 5*(3), 52-56.

Durkin, D. (1978-79). What classroom observations reveal about comprehension instruction. *Reading Research Quarterly, 14*, 481-533.

Eley, G., & Lyman, F. (1987, Spring). Problem solving and action research for beginning teachers. *Maryland A.T.E. Journal, 2*(2), 16-19.

Gage, N. L. (1974). *Teacher effectiveness and teacher education: The search for a scientific basis.* Palo Alto, CA: Pacific Books.

Gall, M. (1970). The use of questions in teaching. *Review of Educational Research, 40*, 707-721.

Garner, R. (1980, Spring). Monitoring of understanding: An investigation of good and poor readers. *Journal of Reading Behavior, 12*, 55-64.

Garner, R., & Reis, R. (1981). Monitoring and resolving comprehension obstacles: An investigation of spontaneous text lookbacks among upper-grade good and poor comprehenders. *Reading Research Quarterly, XVI*(4), 569-582.

Gemake, J., & Sinatra, R. (1986, November-December). Using maps to improve writing. *Early Years, 17*, 52-65.

Goodlad, J. (1985). *A place called school.* New York: McGraw-Hill.

Hare, V., & Pulliam, C. (1980, Spring). Teacher questioning: A verification and an extension. *Journal of Reading Behavior, 12*, 69-72.

Johnson, D., & Johnson, R. (1984). Cooperative small-group learning. *Curriculum Report, 14*(1), 1-6.

Jones, B. F., Amiran, M., & Katims, M. (1985). Teaching cognitive strategies and text structures within language arts programs. In J. Segal, S. Chipman, & R. Glaser (Eds.), *Thinking and learning skills (Vol. 1): Relating instruction to research,* (pp. 259-290). Hillsdale, NJ: Lawrence Erlbaum.

Kapinus, B. (1986). *Ready reading readiness,* (bookmark). Baltimore: Maryland State Department of Education.

Lyman, F. T., Jr. (1989). Rechoreographing: The middle-level minuet. *The Early Adolescent Magazine, 4*(1), 22-24.

Lyman, F. T., Jr. (1987). The think-trix: A classroom tool for thinking in response to reading. In L. Gambrell (Ed.), *Reading: Issues and practices, yearbook of the State of Maryland International Reading Association Council* (pp. 15-18). College Park: Univ. of Maryland.

Lyman, F. T., Jr. (1985). The reading wheel: Response cues for comprehension. In L. Grambrell (Ed.), *New directions in reading: Research and practice, 1985 yearbook of MD International Reading Association* (pp. 30-35). College Park: Univ. of Maryland.

Lyman, F. T., Jr. (1981, Spring). The development of tools. *Maryland A.T.E. Journal, 1*(1), 20-21.

Lyman, F. T., Jr. (1981). The responsive classroom discussion: The inclusion of all students. *Mainstreaming Digest, 1*(1), 109-114.

Lyman, F. T., Jr., Lopez, C., & Mindus, A. (1986). Thinklinks: The shaping of thought in response to reading. Unpublished manuscript.

Mayer, R. (1983). *Implications of cognitive psychology for instruction in mathematic problem solving.* San Diego: San Diego State University.

McTighe, J. (1985). *Questioning for quality thinking: Strategies for extending student thinking,* (bookmark). Baltimore: Maryland State Department of Education.

McTighe, J., & Lyman, F. (1988, April). Cueing thinking in the classroom: The promise of theory-embedded tools. *Educational Leadership, 45*(7), 18-24.

Paris, S., & Jacobs, J. (1984). The benefits of informed instruction for children's reading awareness and comprehension skills. *Child Development, 55*, 2083-2084.

Rowe, M. B. (1986). Wait time: Slowing down may be a way of speeding up! *The Journal of Teacher Education, 31*(1), 43-50.

Schoenfeld, A. (1980). Heuristics in the classroom. In S. Krulik & R. Reys (Eds.), *Problem solving in school mathematics* (pp. 9-22). Reston, VA: National Council of Teachers of Mathematics.

Schoenfeld, A. (1979). Can heuristics be taught? In J. Lochhead & J. Clement (Eds.), *Cognitive process instruction* (pp. 315-338). Philadelphia: Franklin Institute Press.

Slavin, R. E. (1981). Synthesis of research on cooperative learning. *Educational Leadership, 38*(8), 655-660.

Suydam, M. (1980). Untangling clues from research on problem solving. In S. Krulik & R. Reys (Eds.), *Problem solving in school mathematics* (pp. 34-50). Reston, VA: National Council of Teachers of Mathematics.

Vaughn, L., Jr. (1982, February). Use the construct procedure to foster active reading and learning. *Journal of Reading, 25*(5), 412-422.

MEANING IS THE METHOD: WHOLE LANGUAGE IN THE THOUGHTFUL CLASSROOM

—

Laura Lipton

It is the teacher who can open the book, unfold the story, and invite the reader. It is the teacher who can create the safe harbor where students can share their lives and their literacy. And it is the teacher, above all, who can join hands with the learners.—Dorothy J. Watson

Whole language is about the joy of teachers and students holding hands and engaging together in making meaning of the world. It defies definition because it is an expression of the way in which teachers create learning opportunities for their students and themselves. As Lois Bird said, "Whole language is a way of thinking, a way of living and learning with children in classrooms" (1987).

The curriculum in the whole language classroom is organic. It exists as a natural outgrowth of the interaction among the teacher, the students, and the environment. It is supported and nurtured by the ongoing discoveries of learners as they explore the world around them and strive to make sense of it. Whole language instruction is built on learners' questions, reflections, trials, and errors as they engage in purposeful, relevant activities of

their own choice. In fact, language users learn as much from their errors as they do from their successes, and often more. Whole language teachers strive to create an environment in which students have lots of opportunities for language use, where they can grow as a result of experimentation, and where error reduction—not error elimination—is the aim of instruction.

The whole language teacher is a co-learner in a classroom community of learners. Every day, the teacher provides models of printed conventions by reading to and with the class and by writing for and with the students. Every day, too, the teacher responds to students in ways which encourage risk taking and demonstrate the expectation that everyone is an able learner.

Whole language instruction is a developmental, holistic, meaning-making approach to literacy and learning. Students learn through purposeful, contextual experiences rather than through instruction of isolated skills. This chapter presents classroom climates, teacher behaviors, instructional activities, and curriculum from the whole language perspective. The following sections explore the teaching/learning relationship. They focus on providing positive learning experiences in developing literacy, viewing reading as a problem-solving strategy, and helping students cultivate the joy of reading as a lifelong pursuit.

DEVELOPING MEANING: DEVELOPMENTALLY APPROPRIATE INSTRUCTION

Thoughts are our way of connecting things up for ourselves. If somebody tells us about the connections he has made, we can only understand him to the extent that we do the work of making those connections ourselves.—Eleanor Duckworth

Spoken language develops as a result of function and social interaction. The need to communicate creates a purpose for language. Consider the first words uttered by most toddlers, "Ma-ma, Da-da, ba-ba, bye-bye." These words convey the clearest meaning in the most efficient way. We use language to make sense of the world, to have our needs met, and to maintain some control of our environment. Toddlers gauge the responses to their initial efforts and begin to refine and expand their ability to communicate in a meaningful way. When the baby says "ba-ba" and is given a bottle, the communication has been successful. Over time, children experiment with more sophisticated constructs, exploring new sounds and word combinations and stringing several words together to make sentences. Always, though, meaning is the primary goal.

Literacy develops just as naturally as language does. It would never occur to parents of a normal toddler that their child will not learn to speak. Nor would it be likely that the parents would respond to these initial attempts at language by saying, "No, not ba-ba, *bottle*. Now try again." And yet, in many traditional classrooms, teachers respond to children's initial attempts at literacy in just such a way. On the path to learning, children approximate language conventions. They combine a smattering of letters with other symbols and squiggles to convey meaning in print. They "read aloud" a story they've heard repeatedly using picture cues and their memory. By attempting to eliminate errors, rather than celebrate them as a child's experimental ef-

forts at learning, teachers can easily squelch a student's motivation to continue to engage in language learning without the certainty of being correct.

Children come to school with a tremendous amount of knowledge about the conventions of language. They are aware of the variety of the print they find in the environment, such as stop signs and store names, as well as elements of stories and books (Pearson & Dole, 1987). They can make distinctions between different types and purposes of writing—for example, a letter as opposed to a story. Most children entering kindergarten understand about 5,000 words, speak in complex sentences, and are curious about the appearance of their language in writing (Norton, 1983). Whole language instruction begins with what each student already knows. In the whole language classroom, children are provided additional models of speech and print. They are read to every day from a literature base that includes poems, songs, plays, non-fiction, a variety of genre of fiction, and any other appropriate and authentic material. The story sounds, content, and form expand students' knowledge base about literature, add to the shared experience base of the class, and serve as the departure point from which students can launch their adventures in reading and writing.

Opportunities abound for students to engage in purposeful activities that help them exercise their developing skills and work out the kinks—for it is by reading that one learns to read, and by writing that one learns to write. In these learning endeavors, experimentation and error reduction are the norm. And just as the natural response to the request for *ba-ba* would be to provide the bottle and say, "Here is your *bottle*," the natural response to initial attempts at spelling, grammar, or form might be a compliment of the effort and a response in print that models the convention, gently shapes growth, and fosters self-esteem.

As children are given a voice in selecting their learning options, they begin to develop a greater level of responsibility for their work and a greater level of commitment to their learning. Within given parameters, students should be able to choose some of the things they want to learn about and when they will learn them. These "curricular invitations" are carefully planned by whole language teachers (Watson, 1989, p. 136). These teachers use their knowledge of student needs and interests and appreciate the importance of cultivating students' ownership in their reading and writing. Choices can include which ten spelling words a student wants to learn this week, which book to read, or at which centers to work.

Whole language instruction relies on relevant materials that are authentic—not materials contrived to provide drill for isolated skills. Such authentic reading and writing materials are plentiful and accessible. The whole language classroom is filled with trade books, newspapers, magazines, resource materials, restaurant menus, flyers, posters, student-produced books, written directions, message boards, and so on. In the early grades, books such as Eric Carle's *The Very Hungry Caterpillar*, Bill Martin Jr.'s *Brown Bear, Brown Bear*, and Margaret Wise Brown's *Good Night Moon* provide repetitious or patterned language to help give emergent readers confidence and experience in anticipating text.

Examples of student-generated language are also apparent. Experience charts and stories provide teachers with an opportunity to demonstrate writing conventions, and they give students relevant text to read. In one second grade classroom in Rochester, New York, one wall is devoted to a "living" bulletin board. The students create large scenes based on the topic or theme being studied. They put words and labels, signs, and speech in bubbles connected to the various characters in the scene. As the unit progresses, new information is added, words are changed, and concepts are more clearly expressed through the written dialogue between the bulletin board figures. In a fourth grade classroom in Decatur, Indiana, students create word mobiles, four sided figures suspended from the classroom ceiling. Each week, students fill in one side of their mobiles with words that are meaningful or interesting to them, or relevant to a topic being studied. Weekly, on mobile-hanging day, students ceremoniously read aloud their word list to the class before adding it to the mobile. The classroom is filled with print in an ever-changing display. Each month, students take home their mobiles and begin new ones.

Writing is a celebrated activity. Most whole language classrooms have writing centers, publishing possibilities, and special opportunities for student authors to share their work. Students need experience writing for 'real' reasons and for 'real' audiences. As part of the daily routine, students are encouraged to generate lists, write notes, send messages, compose riddles, produce plays, and keep journals. A first grade classroom in White Plains, New York, has a wonderful yard-sale relic, a plushy taffeta-covered armchair. It has become the "author's throne." Each week, a student author who has recently "published" a piece of work in class has a chance to sit on the throne and read the work aloud to the class. The work is then shared with others in the school. Often the published piece is returned to the author with special messages from those who have enjoyed the chance to read it. In another school district in Westchester, New York, library cards are pasted in the back of each student's published book, and the book is placed in the school library. At the end of the year, the authors can see how many people have checked out their work.

Language is central to learning. Halliday (1984) suggests three types of language learning— learning language, learning through language, learning about language—all of which develop through using language in meaningful contexts. Fundamental to whole language instruction is the principle that meaning is always the goal of language use. Learners construct meaning while reading and listening, and they express meaning while speaking and writing. In a whole language classroom, instruction builds on students' experiences by providing authentic, functional activities through which students engage in language learning. Children learn language conventions by employing them purposefully.

MAKING MEANING: PURPOSEFUL INSTRUCTION

Can we really believe that a child is going to develop a sense of self doing reading skills for forty minutes a day, five days a week, thirty weeks a year? Does an

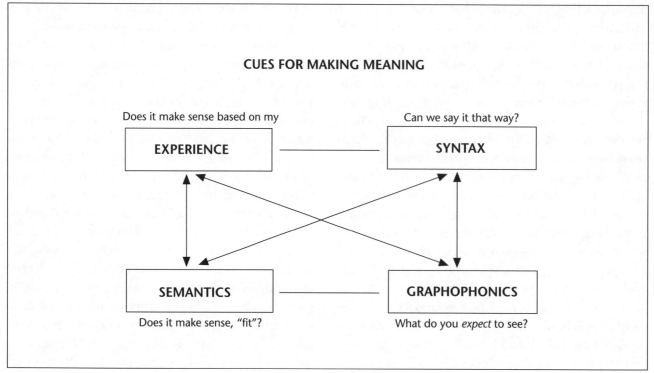

Figure 1   Cues for Making Meaning

uninterrupted diet of skill and drill make a child want to escape into the world of books or away from it? —Jim Trelease

Reading comprehension is what readers do to make sense of printed information (Harste, 1989). Ken Goodman calls reading a "psycholinguistic guessing game" (1967). It is a constant stream of predicting, confirming, and integrating information. Text offers three primary sources of information, or cueing systems: semantic, syntactic, and graphophonic. Here is an illustration. Choose a word to fill the blank in the following sentence: The little girl rode her_____. You might have chosen *horse*, *pony*, or *bicycle*. You used semantic cues to choose a word that makes sense. Chances are that you also chose a noun. Your knowledge of English syntax supported that choice. If a phonetic clue, such as an initial consonant, were available, there would be another method for confirming or refining your hunch. For example: The little girl rode her m_____. Now, you might have chosen *motorcycle*, or *mare*.

These cueing systems provide students important sources of information for making meaning from text. Fluent readers rely on these cueing systems—combined with their own experience—to make and confirm their best guesses during reading. (See Figure 1.) They use their semantic sense, drawn from their own life experience and picture clues; their syntactic sense, drawn from knowledge of spoken language and of book language; and their graphophonic sense, based on their knowledge of spelling patterns and word structure. Skilled readers use these cues interactively when reading. They use these cueing systems to cross-reference their predictions and the meaning they are making from the text. This cross-checking can raise discrepancies and facilitate self-correction. Thus, it is important that students can flexibly use all three sources of information and not overly rely on any one.

As we read, we use the language cueing systems and our own experience to anticipate what is coming next and to make inferences. Read the following passage:

Vanessa heard the gravel crunch on the driveway. She quickly said good-bye and slammed down the receiver. She scanned her room for the most obvious mess, grabbed for the clothing scattered on the floor and began stuffing it under the bed. Five o'clock already!

What was Vanessa doing? What was she supposed to have been doing? What guesses might you make about Vanessa and about her home? Although the reader is not told explicitly, it can be inferred that Vanessa was on the phone (slammed down the receiver), that she was supposed to clean her room (scans and stuffs), and that someone has arrived to whom she is probably accountable (crunch on the driveway, five o'clock already!). Further, you might infer that she is a teenager (home alone, on the phone, room a mess), and that she comes from a suburban home (phone in her room, gravel drive).

In the whole language classroom, learners are provided opportunities to develop strategies that build on their experience and support their ability to use their experience to make meaning. In addition, instruction is organized to enable learners to connect new information to prior experience. Thus, learners are better able to integrate new knowledge into existing schema and to 'own' that which is now known.

INTEGRATING MEANING: STRATEGIC INSTRUCTION

The more meaningful, the more deeply or elaborately processed, the more situated in context, and the more rooted in cultural, background, metacognitive, and personal knowledge an event is, the more readily it is understood, learned, and remembered.

—Iran-Nejad, McKeachie, & Berliner

Meaningful learning is an active, constructive, and cumulative process (Shuell, 1990). "Fluency is not a state which is finally attained; one is continually arriving" (Newman, 1985, p. 31). Learning to read and write develops from the continual process of interaction with print and language.

Reading is the interaction between the reader and the text. The experience of the learner is a critical component in this interaction. There is a clear correlation between success in reading and the reader's level of background knowledge. Therefore, ensuring that students bring some background knowledge to a reading task can be crucial to the students' success. While all students have some experience and prior knowledge to bring to a learning situation, some do not have the ability to link it to new information or even to retrieve it. For these students, their prior knowledge remains "inert" (Bransford, et al., 1986). These students must be taught strategies that will help them access what they already know, as well as strategies for organizing new information into patterns that will help them make connections and integrate new understandings. Brainstorming is an excellent method for generating and enriching students' knowledge base before reading. The term *brainstorming* was coined by advertising executive Alex Osborn in the late 1940s. The acronym **DOVE** helps students remember the brainstorming rules:

Defer judgment (no praise or criticism)

Opt for originality

Variety and volume are desired

Expand by piggybacking

(Bellanca & Fogarty, 1991, p. 57)

The idea-generation process surfaces students' inert knowledge for their active use. Also, setting time limits for the process helps keep groups focused. One extension of brainstorming is to group the ideas into categories after they have been generated. Then, create titles for each group. Charts listing each category can be posted and additional ideas can be recorded as the unit progresses. The charts give the class a picture of their current working knowledge and demonstrate that learning is a process.

Another structured strategy for brainstorming is the *what I know, think I know, want to know* chart adapted from a strategy developed by Donna Ogle at the National College of Education in Evanston, Illinois. For this strategy, students work in small groups with a recorder in each group. The groups brainstorm all of the things they either know, think they know, or want to know about the topic they will be studying. They record their ideas on a three-column chart. As students offer ideas, they tell the recorder in which column to place them. The "Think I Know" column serves as a pressure release valve. Those students who are unsure but would like to contribute can direct their ideas to this column. The questions in the "Want to Know" column create a purpose for reading about the new topic. As with all brainstorming, the goal is to generate as many ideas as possible. It is not a time for debate or discussion about the ideas. These charts can be saved or posted for students to reference as they study the material. Posting the charts also serves to immerse students in their own language.

Other ways of building background knowledge include providing input through a film, a field trip, a discussion, a simulation, an experiment, or a demonstration. Sometimes a simple reading passage can provide a foundation for students to understand a more complex piece of reading. Clearly, however, we know that background knowledge is necessary for understanding. When teachers take the time to elicit from students what they already know; surface and clarify any misconceptions; provide concrete and foundational experiences prior to new learning; and discuss previously learned concepts and make predictions as to where they might lead, they are greatly increasing the likelihood of students gaining successful new learning experiences.

Characteristics of effective readers have been identified in varied literature. Successful learners are strategic (Paris, Lipson, & Wixson, 1983). They have a repertoire of cognitive and metacognitive strategies, which they can employ before, during, and after reading to construct meaning and retain information. They actively adopt a problem-solving approach to learning (Bereiter, 1989). Through self-regulation during reading, they monitor their understanding and recognize when meaning has been lost (Garner, 1990). They use their "conditional knowledge" to know when to invoke the appropriate strategies for solving the meaning-making problem (Paris, Lipson, & Wixson, 1983). Further, successful learners know when to disband use of an unsuccessful strategy and choose another.

Judith Newman (1985) described three basic types of reading strategies: predicting, confirming,

and integrating. When readers use predicting strategies, they generate expectations of what will come next based on information from one or a combination of the cueing systems available. Confirming strategies are comprised of self-questioning or self-monitoring to see whether the prediction was correct, and whether what is being read makes sense. Integrating strategies incorporate new information and newly constructed meaning with prior knowledge. We integrate new definitions, unfamiliar concepts, and complex ideas and relationships. These three strategies rely on making meaning from the text as a whole and monitoring our meaning making. Students need to internalize the questions that support metacognition: "How am I doing?" "Does this make sense?" "What should/might I do differently?" "What resources do I have/need?" Fluent readers continually confirm predictions and generate new ones. They confirm or refine tentative understandings based on additional information and integrate new information as a basis for further prediction. These strategies work continuously and in concert as readers engage with text.

Consider your own strategies for making meaning. Take a moment to think about what you do when you lose meaning while reading, or when you encounter something unfamiliar in the text. Most fluent readers choose from a number of alternatives: they can continue reading to see if information is offered later in the passage; they can generate a substitute that makes sense to temporarily hold the place of an unknown term or concept and go on; they can refer back to what they already read to see if they missed something that would give some clues; or they can do nothing to see whether not knowing a particular term will matter in terms of understanding the whole passage. If we ask our students that same question, "What do you do when you come to something you don't understand?" the fluent readers will describe one or more of the above. Our less able readers will usually say that they "sound it out," "look it up," or "ask someone."

In the whole language classroom, finding and conveying meaning is the only reason for reading, writing, listening, and speaking. This message cannot just be told; it must be modeled constantly and conveyed instructionally. Students need practice in dealing effectively with unfamiliar words or ideas while reading. Whole language classrooms provide these opportunities in a variety of ways. By moving from skills lessons to strategy lessons, we help students become fluent readers while understanding that the meaning of the whole is not necessarily dependent on being able to identify and understand every word. The following examples illustrate strategy lessons that help students develop predicting, confirming, and integrating strategies. These activities also encourage dialogue among students.

The *word splash*, developed by Dorsey Hammond of Oakland University in Rochester, Michigan, is a motivating and interesting method for generating predictions. Students are given a page with a group of eight to ten words "splashed" across it. The words are taken from a reading selection. Students work in groups to predict what the reading will be about. They can be directed to generate best guesses or even outline their hunches about the storyline. The selection could be a piece of literature, an article on a current event, or content-based text material. Directed reading and thinking activities such as this one are appropriate with any coherent text.

Synonym substitution, developed by Yetta Goodman and Carolyn Burke, teaches students to use the place-holding strategy to maintain meaning and not interrupt the flow of their reading. Students work in small groups. First, students silently read a passage, underlining any unfamiliar words. Then, each group reads the same passage together, trying to supply a minimum of two substitutions for each underlined word. The substitutions, which can be words or short phrases, are recorded and later discussed. A good method for introducing this activity is to use familiar stories or fairy tales, which are less threatening to less proficient readers.

Reader-selected miscues, developed by Dorothy Watson at the University of Missouri, demonstrates that one does not have to understand every word to make meaning from text and that what is familiar can be used to understand what is not. For this activity, students silently read a selection, highlighting anything that is not clear or that they have

questions about. Then, with their small group, they take turns discussing what they have marked. They are asked to consider which items affected their understanding of the selection and which did not. During the discussion, students are encouraged to refer to the text for clarification. Either factual or fictitious passages can be used.

For *say something,* developed by Jerome Harste of the University of Indiana, students choose partners. Before reading their copy of a selection, partners decide how they will read—silently or orally, and in unison or alternately—and how much they will read before stopping to 'say something.' Students read until they reach their predetermined points to stop. Then they ask questions, react to information, seek clarification, discuss other information that is confirming or contradictory, or say something else. After each pair has completed reading and discussing the selection, they share their reactions with other student pairs. This activity promotes the connection of new information to that which was previously known. The sharing enables students to see how others make meaning, expands the students' shared experience base, and facilitates integration.

Reading is an interpretive process that incorporates much more than the visual material on a printed page. Efficient readers supply important nonvisual information to make meaning from print. Therefore, interpretations are individual and distinct. The whole language teacher provides frequent and varied opportunities for students to construct their own meaning while engaging with many types of printed material. The opportunity for verbal interaction with other students allows for a richer understanding of the process. The focus of these interactions should help students articulate their own interpretations, consider those of others, and relate all of this back to the text.

Students need not be their own curriculum coordinators (Lincoln, 1990). Whole language shifts curriculum control from "teachers' manuals to teachers" (Goodman, 1989, p. 215). The whole language curriculum integrates the language arts as well as the content areas. Content information provides a substantial forum for exercising literacy.

The challenge is to develop strategies to help individuals in the process of creating a unity of knowledge (Taba, 1962). Meaning must be made from the information of content areas. In their subject areas, students engage in such strategies as questioning, predicting, organizing, interpreting, and summarizing.

Students need explicit instruction in context-based planning and monitoring (Garner, 1990; Ceci & Liker, 1986). In addition, for successful transfer across contexts, students need extensive practice in a variety of settings (Brown, Campione, & Day, 1981). Whole language instruction, by offering relevant, authentic experiences that integrate curricular areas, provides such experience. When students research environmental issues, for example, and work on problem-framing/solution-finding projects, they are integrating science and social studies. When they conduct surveys, collect and graph data, write letters for information or in support of certain legislation, or suggest creative solutions for environmental problems, they are integrating the language arts as well.

ENHANCING MEANING: JOYFUL INSTRUCTION

Amidst all the workbook pages and academic jargon, we daily overlook the very purpose of literature: to provide meaning in our lives.—Jim Trelease

The ability to find meaning in our lives is both the greatest need and perhaps the most difficult achievement that we face as human beings. It is the function of literature, particularly fiction, to present life's meaning, to arouse our emotions, and to show us how to understand conflict. Literature provides an escape from our everyday existence into the lives of others. It allows us to vent life's pressures through laughter, tears, hate, and love. We look to books to give us insight into our own life story (Trelease, 1982).

In his widely recognized work, *The Uses of Enchantment*, Bruno Bettleheim (1976) credits three factors as being primarily responsible for instilling in children the beliefs that their lives are mean-

ingful, and that they are capable of making a significant contribution. These factors are parents, teachers, and literature.

What greater gift can a teacher give than that of a lifelong love for literature? Reading informs us, entertains us, and connects us to the world by reminding us that we are not alone (Boorstin, 1987). Yet, the unspoken message communicated in many classrooms is not that reading is purposeful and pleasant, or that it can bind us to a deeper universal experience, but that reading is boring work. It is associated with dull dittos, redundant worksheets, endless homework assignments, and end-of-unit tests. For many poor readers, "meaningless texts, contrived tasks, and competitive contexts can combine to distort [their] perceptions about reading, destroy their self-confidence and curiosity, and confound their efforts at becoming literate" (Winograd, 1989, p.240).

In the whole language classroom, several factors help students discover the delights of reading: reading aloud; uninterrupted, sustained, silent reading (USSR); many choices in learning activities; and a classroom culture that provides a risk-free environment in which reading is the norm.

Reading aloud to children is an important way to arouse their desire to read to themselves. Reading aloud can stir the imagination and introduce students to the different sounds of language and the different forms of literature. Reading aloud expands vocabulary. It can stretch and challenge thinking because, especially in the early grades, most children's listening comprehension far exceeds their reading comprehension. It can help children develop a taste for quality literature and an understanding of the ways in which it can connect them to the human experience. As Jim Trelease described:

My children and I have sat in a one-room schoolhouse with Carol Ryrie Brink's *Caddie Woodlawn*, chased monsters with Maurice Sendak and Mercer Mayer, . . . and swallowed magic potions with Judy Blume in *Freckle Juice*. With *James and the Giant Peach* by Ronald Dahl, we crossed the shark infested waters of the North Atlantic; we battled a Caribbean hurricane in Theodore Taylor's *The Cay*. We have searched for wayward brothers and sisters, evaded wolves, lost friends, and learned how to make new ones. We have laughed, cried, shaken with fright, and shivered with delight. And best of all, we did it together. Along the way we discovered something about the universality of human experience—that we, too, have many of the hopes and fears of the people we read about. (1984, p.22)

In addition to reading aloud as a daily activity, time should be preserved each day for students to engage in USSR—uninterrupted, sustained, silent reading. USSR demonstrates that reading is a valued activity in which everyone participates. Students and teachers alike take the opportunity to sit comfortably with a book of their choice.

Both reading aloud and USSR increase children's involvement with books for the sheer pleasure of it. Neither activity should require assigned responses or enforced follow-up activities. However, providing children with a chance to share their reading experiences with each other is another powerful way to encourage a positive attitude toward reading. Class time should be devoted to special interest groups (SIGs). These allow students who enjoy mysteries, adventure stories, or science fiction to gather and talk about their current reading in separate SIG groups. Opportunities to discuss literature help develop and maintain classroom norms that value and celebrate reading.

In a whole language classroom, time is spent on activities that demonstrate the value of reading. In one sixth grade classroom in Salem, Massachusetts, the students generate the ten greatest reading hits each month. The titles, authors, and publishers are posted on banners in the classroom. Minireviews are then published in a newsletter that is shared with the entire sixth grade. There is a great deal of discussion about which books should be included and why. The newsletter is a class project and the reviews are written cooperatively by student trios.

Another sixth grade classroom proudly displays a fish net on one wall with the motto "Get Hooked on a Book." Ensnared in the net are tagboard fish. Each fish has a book title, author, and the name of the student who read the book. The fish are guppies, groupers, and barracudas. Students work to become members of the "Barracuda Club." Ten guppies equal one grouper, and five groupers equal one barracuda. Barracuda club members are part of an oral reading project with the kindergarten and first grade.

Both of these sixth grade classrooms are examples of literate environments, where reading is celebrated, and where positive peer pressure preserves reading as the norm.

Literacy learning is a process. Language learning is a joy when it occurs in a risk-free environment, where children are invited to play with language, to experiment, and to experience. Language is a social activity. Experimenting with language requires opportunities for students to engage with each other. We can't learn language by watching it; we have to be willing participants. We can't expect perfection in form; we have to accept variety and approximation. If students are afraid to make mistakes, they may become nonparticipants. "When the cost of making mistakes becomes too great, children cease to take risks" (Newman, 1985).

The whole language classroom provides a fertile ground where learners can explore and expand, express and engage, experience and experiment with their blossoming literacy.

The whole language future? Our potential lies in the individual, the personal, 'the this is me.' Our potential lies in the partnership, the collaboration, the team support and effort, the 'this is us.' Our potential lies in the stories, those stories lovingly and carefully crafted by authors of literature for children and youth. Our potential lies in the parent, in the administrator, in the researcher, in the theorist . . . but our potential will be realized through the efforts of the teacher with the student.—Dorothy Watson

REFERENCES

Bellanca, J., & Fogarty, R. (1991). *Blueprints for thinking in the cooperative classroom* (2nd ed.). Palatine, IL: Skylight Publishing.

Bereiter, C. (1989, March). The role of an educational learning theory: Explaining difficult learning. In W. McKeachie (Chair), *Toward a unified approach to learning as a multi-source phenomenon*, Symposium at the American Educational Research Association, San Francisco.

Bettleheim, B. (1976). *The uses of enchantment: The meaning and importance of fairy tales.* New York: Knopf.

Bird, L. (1987). What is whole language? In D. Jacobs (Ed.), *Teachers networking: The whole language newsletter, 1*(1), 1-3.

Boorstin, D. (1987). Foreword. In O. Bettmann (Ed.), *The delights of reading* (p. xi-xiii). Boston: David R. Godine.

Bransford, J., Sherwood, R., Vye, N., & Rieser, J. (1986). Teaching thinking and problem solving. *American Psychologist, 41*, 1078-1089.

Brown, A. L., Campione, J. C., & Day, J. D. (1981). Learning to learn: On training students to learn from text. *Educational Researcher, 10*(2), 14-21.

Butler, A., & Turbill, J. (1984). *Towards a reading-writing classroom.* Portsmouth, NH: Heinemann.

Ceci, S., & Liker, J. (1986). Academic and nonacademic intelligence: An experimental separation. In R. Sternberg (Ed.), *Practical intelligence: Nature and origins of competence in the everyday world* (p. 119-142). Cambridge, England: Cambridge University Press.

Garner, R. (1990). When children and adults do not use learning strategies: Toward a theory of settings. *Review of Educational Research, 60*(4), 517-529.

Goodman, K. (1989). Whole-language research: Foundations and development. *The Elementary School Journal, 90*(2), 207-223.

Goodman, K. (1967, May). Reading: A psycholinguistic guessing game. *Journal of the Reading Specialist, 6*(4), 126-135.

Goodman, Y., & Burke, C. (1980). *Reading strategies: Focus on comprehension.* New York: Holt, Rinehart & Winston.

Halliday, M. (1984). Three aspects of children's language development: Learning language, learning through language, and learning about language. In Y. Goodman, M. Haussler, & D. Strickland (Eds.), *Oral and written language development research: Impact on the schools* (p. 165-192). Urbana, IL: National Council of Teachers of English.

Harste, J. (1989). The basalization of American reading instruction: One researcher responds. *Theory Into Practice, 28*(4), 265-273.

Iran-Nejad, A., McKeachie, W., & Berliner, D. (1990). The multisource nature of learning: An introduction. *Review of Educational Research, 60*(4), 509-513.

Lincoln, W. (1990, December 8). *Whole language: Getting your students to love reading and writing.* General Session Address, Learning Institute Course, Philadelphia, PA.

Newman, J. (1985). *Whole language: Theory in use.* Portsmouth, NH: Heinemann.

Norton, D. (1983). *Through the eyes of a child.* Columbus, OH: Charles E. Merrill.

Paris, S., Lipson, M., & Wixson. K. (1983). Becoming a strategic reader. *Contemporary Educational Psychology, 8*(3), 293-316.

Pearson, P. D., & Dole, J. (1987). Explicit comprehension instruction: A review of research and a new conceptualization of instruction. *Elementary School Journal, 88*(2), 151-165.

Shuell, T. (1990). Phases of meaningful learning. *Review of Educational Research, 60*(4), 530-547.

Taba, H. (1962). *Curriculum development.* New York: Harcourt, Brace & World.

Trelease, J. (1982). *The read-aloud handbook.* New York: Penguin Press.

Watson, D. (1989). Defining and describing whole language. *Elementary School Journal, 90*(2), 129-142.

Winograd, P. (1989). Improving basal reading instruction: Beyond the carrot and the stick. *Theory Into Practice, 28*(4), 240-247.

INTERACTIVE STRATEGIES FOR ENHANCING THINKING AND WRITING

—

Carol Booth Olson

When I first began teaching literature as a graduate student at UCLA, I thought it was my job to guide students toward an "accepted" consensus interpretation of each text. So, with yellow highlighter in hand, I went back through each line or page of the poem, story, play, or novel, carefully framing questions that would enable us to arrive at a place and a reading determined by my previous experience with the text, the readings of my professors—culled from old class notes—and the insights of literary critics. I will even admit to taking a look on a few occasions at that old standby *Cliffs Notes* for an annotation of some obscure textual reference or to see what their interpretation was of something I was feeling rather murky about myself. I did a lot of fishing in those days, fishing for the right answers to what were sometimes ill-framed questions. When the class didn't bite, I would often just answer the question myself so that we could "move on."

In his article "Dialogue with a Text," Bob Probst (1988) tells a story about a battle of wills he once observed between a teacher and her students in a secondary English class. It seems that the students were so troubled by a story they were reading called "So Much Unfairness of Things" (Bryan, 1979) which deals with a student who succumbs to the temptation to cheat on an exam, that they evaded the teacher's repeated question, "What techniques does the author use to reveal character in this story?" The students talked instead about the moral complexities of the story and its relationship to their own lives. The teacher "tolerated the outpouring for a few brief moments." But, bound and determined to steer the class back toward her own agenda, the teacher finally ordered the class to answer her question: "What techniques does the author use to reveal character in this story? We've had them before," she taunted. "You studied them last year, you know what they are, there are only three—now *what are they?*" When Probst later inquired about why the teacher had felt so compelled to focus on her question rather than on the students' genuine responses, she explained that she had to move on:

> There were other stories to cover, other skills and techniques to be learned, and there was to be a test that Friday. They had to be ready for the test. It had to do with the techniques of characterization and it was important. Those kids . . . would be under a

great deal of pressure to pass it, one way or another. They might even be tempted to cheat. (p. 33)

Like the teacher in Probst's story, moving on was very important to me in those early days of teaching, although I can't recall precisely why. It was often, although not always, a laborious journey. But, as I think back, the journey may have been more laborious for me than for my students. After all, I was the one who was painstakingly trudging through each text, giving the guided tour, as it were. Like the teacher in Probst's story, I also did not trust the students' own instinctive responses to texts, nor did I see student collaboration on a shared interpretation of a text as a legitimate goal of the literature classroom. In fact, on more than one occasion I assigned the paper on a work of literature to be due the day before the class discussion so no one could "borrow" any of their classmates' ideas. And, like the teacher in Probst's story, I didn't understand that clinging to one's own agenda and one's own reasonings prevents students from interacting with and thinking deeply about what they read. As Dan Kirby (1992) said, "If you're presenting the central tenets of your content as issues already settled, as truth already known and uncontested, then your students aren't going to be inclined to interact with that content and raise questions of their own. They're going to feel locked away from that content."

Since I've been exposed to all of the wonderful strategies shared within the National and California Writing Projects, I am much more willing and better able to let students embark on their own journeys through texts and arrive at diverse destinations. I say much more willing because key thinkers in the field of composition and English education, such as Probst, Kirby, and Ann Berthoff, have helped me to redefine learning and literacy and to respect and acknowledge the power of students' responses. I feel better able because the innovative ideas of Gabriele Rico, Jenee Gossard, Rebekah Caplan, my UCI Writing Project colleagues, and others, have expanded my repertoire of strategies beyond the traditional question-and-answer approach so I can help facilitate students' interactions with texts.

INTERACTIVE STRATEGIES

Below are just a few interactive strategies for enhancing student thinking and writing about literature. Although some of these strategies were originally popularized as tools to facilitate the writing process, teachers have naturally and easily adapted them to enhance the reading process as well. For the purpose of illustrating that these strategies are applicable at all grade levels, the examples feature a wide range of literary works.

As Rico (1992) says, "**Clustering** is a nonlinear brainstorming activity that generates ideas, images, and feelings around a stimulus word until a pattern becomes discernible." As students cluster around a stimulus word, "the encircled words rapidly radiate outward until a sudden shift takes place, a sort of 'Aha!' that signals a sudden awareness of that tentative whole which allows students to begin writing." Once an exciting "aha," in and of itself, clustering is now an essential and frequently used prewriting strategy for teachers and students alike. But it is also a stimulating idea-generating strategy for thinking, talking, and writing about literature before, during, and after the reading process. Clustering and freewriting about a book title, as in Figure 1, can bring out important themes, issues, questions, and feelings about the text. Clustering characters, settings, events, and symbols can offer students a chance to take a closer and deeper look at a text and to experience some of their own "Ahas."

As described by Berthoff in *The Making of Meaning*, the **dialectical journal** is a double-entry note-taking/note-making process the student can keep while reading literature. It provides the student with two columns that are in dialogue with one another, not only encouraging cognitive responses such as analysis, interpretation, and reflective questioning, but also eliciting affective reactions as well. "The reason for the double-entry format," says Berthoff (1981), "is that it provides a way for the student to conduct the continual 'audit of meaning' that is at the heart of learning to read and write critically." Figure 2 illustrates a note-taking/note-making response to a passage preselected by the teacher from *The Velveteen Rabbit* .

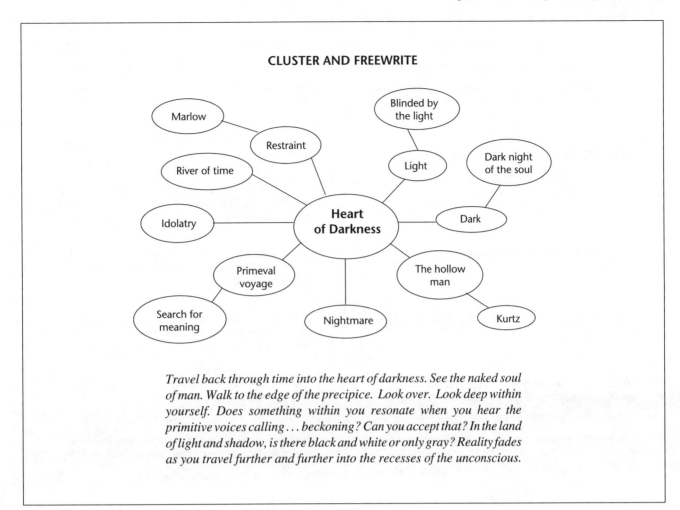

CLUSTER AND FREEWRITE

Travel back through time into the heart of darkness. See the naked soul of man. Walk to the edge of the precipice. Look over. Look deep within yourself. Does something within you resonate when you hear the primitive voices calling . . . beckoning? Can you accept that? In the land of light and shadow, is there black and white or only gray? Reality fades as you travel further and further into the recesses of the unconscious.

Figure 1   **Cluster and Freewrite on** *Heart of Darkness*

Note-Taking	Note-Making
"What is real?" asked the rabbit one day. "Real isn't how you are made, it's a thing that happens to you. When a child loves you for a long time, not just to play with but really loves you then you become real!"	Real doesn't come from within; "it isn't how you are made." Real comes from without. It is a gift someone gives to you...They affect the very essence of who you are because of the love they have for you. Real isn't automatic. It happens to you as a result of a process of being loved by another.

From C. Olson, (1992). Strategies for interacting with text. In C. Olson (Ed.), *Practical ideas for teaching writing as a process*, Sacramento: California State Department of Education. Reprinted with permission.

Figure 2   **The Velveteen Rabbit**

NOTE-TAKING/FACTS	NOTE-MAKING/FEELINGS AND RESPONSES
"I stood there with my hand in a box of Hi-Ho crackers, trying to remember if I rang it up or not." (p. 12)	The sight of the three bathing suited girls is *enough* to make Sammy lose his concentration?!
"I know it made her day to trip me up." (p. 12)	Negative attitude! He thinks everybody is out to get him?
"Not this queen." (p. 12)	He's singled out one girl—placed her on a pedestal by calling her Queenie. He places her on a pedestal from appearance alone.
"The sheep pushing their carts down the aisle." (p. 13)	What makes him refer to people as sheep? Is he bored with people, seeing them day after day shopping? Is he mad at them?
"I bet you could set off dynamite and all the people would keep checking off oatmeal." (p. 13)	He sees the A & P as a real boring place, boring people making a statement that a bomb wouldn't wake them up.
"Stoksie's married with two babies chalked up on his fuselage already." (p. 13)	Sammy sees Stoksie as already tied up, in this town, this job, this life. He's already caught.
"He thinks he's going to be manager some sunny day." (p. 13)	Is Sammy jealous? Or does he know that Stoksie will never make manager in this place? That nothing happens in this job.

From S. Koff (1992). What the text says: What the text means to me. In C. B. Olson (Ed.), *Practical ideas for teaching writing as a process.* Sacramento: California State Department of Education. Reprinted with permission.

Figure 3   John Updike's "A&P" Dialectical Journal

Figure 3 demonstrates the same process with student-selected entries for John Updike's short story "A & P".

For students who have not had much previous practice responding to literature through a dialectical journal, Gossard suggests reading passages aloud to the class and having students respond in a two to three minute "quickwrite." To facilitate the quickwrite, she puts up a poster with some possible sentence starters as shown below.[1]

I wonder . . .
I began to think of . . .
I like the idea . . .
I know the feeling . . .
I noticed . . .
I was surprised . . .

If I had been . . .
I was reminded of . . .

Once students have had practice writing to the teacher's preselected passage and sharing their individual responses with a partner or the whole class, they are better able to begin interacting with a text through the dialectical journal. Gossard provides students with the following information about the kinds of responses readers often have to texts:[2]

Common Reader Responses

- Feelings (boring, sad, exciting, weird)
- Reactions to characters or events (That Templeton is such a rat!—Ha, Ha.)

- Questions (I wonder why the author put in the boring parts?)
- Images (pictures in the mind, with full sensory response)
- Favorite (or detested) words or parts
- Echoes (of other books, movies, TV shows)
- Memories (people, events, places you've known)
- Connections (to other ideas, people)

These categories can become a springboard for the students' responses to whatever texts they are reading.

Found Poetry

One way to help students examine the language of a work of literature is to ask them to translate what they read into another genre. According to Susan Starbuck, many pieces of good prose are actually "poems" waiting to be "discovered."[3] In found poetry students are asked to "find" a poem that is embedded in a piece of professional or student prose. Freed from the constraints of creating the content, students can play with the words and format on the page and rearrange the images that resonate for them. As Starbuck says in the handout she compiled for teacher training workshops, "The result is a new insider's feeling for poetry as you talk about the poetic choices you make and the serendipity you experience as organic forms emerge from the words themselves."

Starbuck suggests that teachers model finding a poem in a prose piece before asking the students to work on their own. You may find her guidelines (also from the handout) helpful:

- Select a piece of prose that you particularly like. It should contain several strong images and some parallel structures. A passage with several prepositions works especially well. (For your students' first experience, select a passage from a work they are reading or with which they are familiar.)

- Underline the words and images that are strongest for you, that are emotionally charged or most essential to the feeling of the passage.

- Now, begin to play with these words and images. Find a satisfying order for them. For example,

  - use the lines for emphasis—separate the images so that you have one strong image per line.

  - place the words you think are most important at the ends of the lines.

  - set off powerful single words on lines by themselves.

  - indent lines that give details for other lines.

  - make a "picture" on the page for the eye to follow as it reads the meaning.

  - use whatever parallel constructions you find in parallel forms in your poem—for instance, start all your lines with prepositions, "-ing" words, or infinitives.

- Allow yourself to add new words or to change the words if they seem cumbersome or if a new idea begins to emerge for you. Your poem may begin to have a life of its own separate from the initial intention of the text. Let the poem set itself free. Letting go is an important aspect of writing poetry—as is the continuous process you will find yourself doing as you begin playing with form.

Figure 4 illustrates a poem I found in Edgar Allen Poe's "Ligeia." Although I have never experimented with having students transform poems into other genres, it seems to me that the process would work equally well in the reverse. Consider, for example, asking students, after reading Edward Arlington Robinson's poem "Richard Cory," to write a dialogue between two townspeople who heard the news of Richard Cory's suicide. Or after reading Alfred Lord Tennyson's poem "Mariana," ask students to draw the setting and to write a sensory/descriptive prose passage describing the exterior and interior/psychological landscapes in the poem. In all these instances, students must think critically about what they read and make what they read their own by casting the language in another form.

Guided imagery is a technique that enables students to tap their creative imagination and visual thinking skills. While the teacher slowly describes a setting or narrates a story using vivid sensory detail to elicit impressions or images, the students watch

FOUND POETRY—"LIGEIA"

There is one <u>dear topic</u>, however, on which my memory fails me not. It is the *person* of Ligeia. In <u>stature</u> she was tall, somewhat slender, and, in her latter days, even <u>emaciated</u>. I would in vain attempt to portray the <u>majesty</u>, the <u>quiet ease of her demeanor</u>, or the <u>incomprehensible lightness and elasticity of her footfall</u>. She came and departed as a <u>shadow</u>. I was never made aware of her entrance into my closed study save by the <u>dear music</u> of her low sweet voice, as she placed her <u>marble hand</u> upon my shoulder. In beauty of face no maiden ever equalled her. It was the <u>radiance of an opium dream</u>—an airy and <u>spirit-lifting</u> vision more <u>vividly divine</u> than the phantasies which hovered about the <u>slumbering souls of the daughters of Delos</u>. Yet her features were not of that regular mould which we have been falsely taught to <u>worship</u> in the classical labors of the heathen. "There is no <u>exquisite beauty</u>," says Bacon, Lord Verulam, speaking truly of all the forms and *genera* of beauty, "without some *strangeness* in the proportion."

Edgar Allan Poe
"Ligeia"

Found Poem
Ligeia

You strange, exquisite beauty
You came and departed
As a shadow
Wildly divine, spirit-lifting
You shimmered in the radiance of an opium dream
Ligeia
He worshipped you
You placed your marble hand
Upon his heart
Awakened his slumbering soul
Became his dear topic
His work of art
Frozen in his memory
An emaciated statue

Figure 4 **Found Poetry**

the "movie screens" in their minds—using visualization to develop their own mental pictures of the words they are hearing. While most guided imagery exercises are written by teachers or other professionals and are expressly designed to evoke certain impressions, literature is a rich and often untapped source of visualization. One might say that all literature is a form of guided imagery. However, as Dan Fader points out, many of today's students, conditioned by the pictures already manufactured for them by the television industry, often have difficulty creating their own mental pictures to accompany the text they need.[4] Ongoing practice visualizing vivid passages from works of literature, such as the one below from *The Velveteen Rabbit*, can help free the imagination and make literature come alive.

And while the Boy was asleep, dreaming of the seaside, the little Rabbit lay among the old picture books in the corner behind the fowl-house, and he felt very lonely . . . . He thought of those long sunlit hours in the garden—how happy they were—and a great sadness came over him. He seemed to see them

From C. B. Olson's Strategies for interacting with a text, in C. B. Olson (Ed.), *Practical ideas for teaching writing as a process*. Sacramento: California State Department of Education, 1992. Reprinted with permission.

Figure 5   Guided Imagery Drawing

all pass before him, each more beautiful than the other, the fairy huts in the flower bed, the quiet evenings in the wood when he lay in the bracken and the little ants ran over his paws; the wonderful day when he first knew that he was Real. He thought of the Skin Horse, so wise and gentle, and all that he had told him. Of what use was it to be loved and lose one's beauty and become Real if it all ended like this? And a tear, a real tear, trickled down his little shabby velvet nose and fell to the ground.

And then a strange thing happened. For where the tear had fallen a flower grew out of the ground, a mysterious flower, not at all like any that grew in the garden. It had slender green leaves the color of emeralds, and in the center of the leaves a blossom like a golden cup. It was so beautiful that the little Rabbit forgot to cry, and just lay there watching it. And presently the blossom opened, and out of it there stepped a fairy.

She was quite the loveliest fairy in the whole world. Her dress was of pearl and dewdrops, and there were flowers round her neck and in her hair,

and her face was like the most perfect flower of all. And she came close to the little Rabbit and gathered him up in her arms and kissed him on his velveteen nose that was all damp from crying.[5]

Moreover, asking students to respond to a guided imagery experience by drawing what they saw, as in Figure 5, will often bring to the surface important images that can be discussed.

Reader's Theater

Reader's theater is a way of dramatically rendering a text as if it were a play, thus bringing it to life in the classroom. The text can be scripted for the students, as Julie Simpson has done with Richard Wilbur's short story "A Game of Catch" in Figure 6, or students can choose the roles and write out the lines themselves. The same passage can be read or performed by more than one group of students. This allows the class to see how the lines have been interpreted and, therefore, read with more or less feeling, delivered in different tones of voice, and accompanied by different movements, by different groups.

A GAME OF CATCH
by Richard Wilbur

READERS

ON: Omniscient Narrator
G: Glennie
GN: Glennie's Narrator
S: Scho
SN: Scho's Narrator
M: Monk
MN: Monk's Narrator

ON: Monk and Glennie were playing catch on the side lawn of the firehouse when Scho caught sight of them. They were good at it, for seventh-graders, as anyone could see right away. Monk, wearing a catcher's mitt, would lean easily sidewise and back, with one leg lifted and his throwing hand almost down to the grass, and then lob the white ball straight up into the sunlight. Glennie would shield his eyes with his left hand and, just as the ball fell past him, snag it with a little dart of his glove. Then he would burn the ball straight toward Monk, and it would spank into the round mitt and sit, like a still-life apple on a plate, until Monk flipped it over into his right hand and, with a negligent flick of his hanging arm, gave Glennie a fast grounder.

They were going on and on like that, in a kind of slow, mannered, luxurious dance in the sun, their faces perfectly blank and entranced, when Glennie noticed Scho dawdling along the other side of the street and called hello to him. Scho crossed over and stood at the front edge of the lawn, near an apple tree, watching.

G: "Got your glove?"

GN: asked Glennie after a time. Scho obviously hadn't.

S: "You could give me some easy grounders,"

SN: said Scho.

S: "But don't burn 'em."

G: "All right,"

GN: Glennie said. He moved off a little, so the three of them formed a triangle, and they passed the ball around for about five minutes, Monk tossing easy grounders to Scho, Scho throwing to Glennie, and Glennie burning them into Monk. After a while, Monk began to throw them back to Glennie once or twice before he let Scho have his grounder, and finally Monk gave Scho a fast, bumpy grounder that hopped over his shoulder and went into the brake on the other side of the street.

S: "Not so hard,"

SN: called Scho as he ran across to get it.

M: "You should've had it,"

MN: Monk shouted.

From J. Simpson's reader's theater adaptation, University of California at Irvine Writing Project.

Figure 6   A Game of Catch

Showing, Not Telling

Like clustering, the concept of "showing, not telling," is well known to most teachers. As Caplan (1987) explains, the assumption behind showing, not telling, is that most students have not been trained to show what they mean. Showing, not telling, encourages students to dramatize their writing with specific details that paint pictures in the reader's mind. It involves giving students a "telling sentence" such as: *The room was vacant* or *The lunch period was too short.* The teacher then asks students to expand the thought into an entire paragraph. Students are challenged not to use the original statement in the paragraph. Rather, they must show that the room was vacant without making the claim directly. Giving students telling sentences about plot, setting, characters, and symbols in works of literature is a great way to prompt them to reflect on and interact with the text. For example, see the telling sentence in Figure 7 on the charac-

---

TELLING SENTENCE: "LENNIE'S MIND IS NOT RIGHT."

Towering over all like a giant, ignorant of his strength, Lennie crushes the life out of the objects of his affection like so many paper dolls. And then he looks at George, helplessly, questioningly, burning with shame because he has done another bad thing and terrified that there will be no more soft, fuzzy creatures to fondle. He's kind of like those puppies he smothers with love—filled with need, anxious to please, obedient to his master. George just shakes his head and wonders what's to become of them. "Tell me again about the rabbits!" The broken record is stuck on the same groove. Lennie smiles dreamily as the nightmare unfolds—oblivious to all but the pretty picture in his head.

From: C. B. Olson (Ed.) (1992). A Lesson on Point of View That Works. In *Practical ideas for teaching writing as a process*, p. 115, California State Department of Education. Reprinted with permission.

Figure 7   Telling Sentence

ter Lennie from John Steinbeck's *Of Mice and Men.* Asking cooperative learning groups to generate their own telling sentences about a work of literature for another group to "show" is also an excellent way to stimulate discussion.

Time Line

A time line is a graphic representation of a sequence of events or activities. In the study of literature, developing time lines often helps students reconstruct and reflect on what happened in the text. I got this idea from Joni Chancer, a teacher/consultant from the South Coast Writing Project at the University of California at Santa Barbara. Ask students to write positive (+) events above the time line and to write negative or problematic (-) events below the time line. For example, see the portion of a time line from "The Moon Lady" chapter of Amy Tan's *The Joy Luck Club* represented in Figure 8. This task causes a great deal of animated discussion and sends students back to the text as they discuss their varying interpretations of events. Students may also wish to illustrate their time lines with pictures and symbols.

Venn Diagram

Venn diagrams are overlapping circles often used in mathematics to show relationships between sets.

In language arts instruction, Venn diagrams are useful for examining similarities and differences. In responding to literature, Venn diagrams can be especially helpful for comparing and contrasting such items as characters, themes, and settings. For example, see Figure 9 for an analysis of Roger and Mrs. Louella Bates Washington Jones in Langston Hughes' short story "Thank You, Ma'am."

Creating Venn diagrams can help students understand not only the similarities and differences between characters, but also the nature of their relationships. Characters who at first glance seem to be polar opposites, may have more in common when explored in this manner. Relationships that appear to be "give" on one side and "take" on the other also may be viewed as more mutual upon closer inspection.

These are just a few of the strategies students might use to interact with a text. The nature of that interaction can be between an individual student and a text, between student partners and a text, between small groups and a text, between any of the aforementioned student groups, a text, and a teacher facilitating large-group discussion, and so forth. I would suggest using these strategies sparingly, allowing enough time for the students to discuss their responses fully. As Probst said, if one of our goals is to help students "make their own

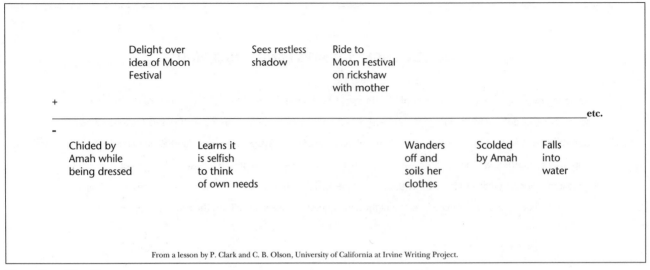

From a lesson by P. Clark and C. B. Olson, University of California at Irvine Writing Project.

Figure 8   Timeline

sense of texts," we must give students time to articulate their thoughts and help them find links between their reactions (1988, p. 35). I have had success with assigning small groups a strategy and with allowing each group to choose the technique that most interests them. Each group also had an opportunity to share its reflections with the whole class.

A PROCESS APPROACH

The strategies I have described for interacting with texts can be used independently as relatively brief, expressive reading/thinking/writing activities that help students make their own meaning from texts. Or they can be combined into a set of guided invitations to help students experience the text from

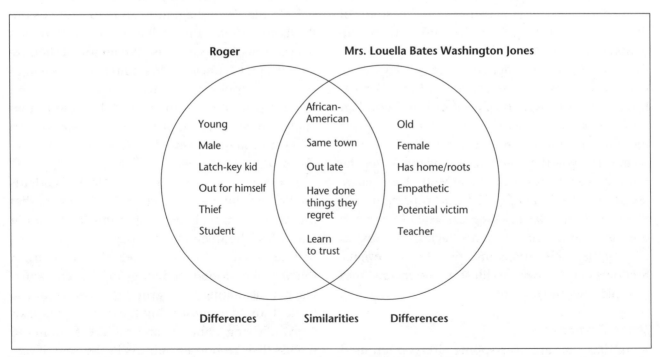

Figure 9   Venn Diagram

different perspectives as they work through a more sustained writing process. For example, the piece of writing may be intended to have multiple drafts and to be turned in and/or "published" in the class as a finished product.

The following discussion on Lynne Cherry's book *The Great Kapok Tree: A Tale of the Amazon Rain Forest* illustrates how one might sequence a number of interactive strategies as students work toward a particular writing goal. While the sequence provided here is teacher guided, students who are given opportunities to practice and internalize these strategies can easily determine which ones will assist them as they work with self-selected topics.

The Great Kapok Tree

The Great Kapok Tree may not be as familiar to readers as the other titles I have referred to in this chapter. Beautifully written and illustrated by Cherry, it is the tale of a man who enters the rain forest with orders to chop down the great Kapok tree. While the animals silently watch him from their hiding places among the branches, the man begins to chip away at the massive tree trunk: "Whack! Chop! Whack! Chop!" Soon, overcome with the heat and humidity of the forest and the hard labor of his task, he puts down his ax, sits beneath the tree for a short rest, and quickly falls asleep. While he slumbers, the animals who live in the tree come down, one by one, and present their case, as it were—whispering arguments into the sleeping man's ear about why the great Kapok tree should be spared. When he awakes, the man sees his surroundings in a new light, drops his ax, and walks out of the rain forest. Although his book was written for children—probably most suitable for grades four and up, but if read, understandable to younger students—I have used it successfully with adults. I believe it touches that sense of wonder, that child, in all of us.

Before reading the book, ask the students to cluster and freewrite what they know about rain forests. A sample cluster and freewrite might look like the web in Figure 10. Asking students what they already know about the rain forest—which may diverge greatly from one student to the next—helps the teacher assess the prior knowledge of the class. But also, it is a good opportunity for students, sharing their clusters in pairs or small groups, to add to each other's knowledge bank. The class also can come up with a list of questions that could be used to form their own agendas for a unit of study on the rain forest.

Reader's Theater

The Great Kapok Tree is ideal for a reader's theater because the whole class can participate. There are thirty parts overall—one omniscient narrator, two pantomine parts for the two men in the story who do not speak, and twenty-seven parts for the omniscient narrators of the animals and the animals themselves. The numerous roles allow participants to be up, out of their seats, performing the story and experiencing the impact of the words firsthand. With small children, I suggest numbering a set of cards one to thirty and numbering the text accordingly. Then hand out the cards to the students. For example, a child assigned to number nine can turn to the place where number nine occurs in the story and assume the part of the macaw. The teacher may wish to play the part of the omniscient narrator or assign it to a strong reader since that part has the most text. An excerpt from the reader's theater follows:

> **Omniscient Narrator:** *Soon the man grew tired. He sat down to rest at the foot of the great Kapok tree. Before he knew it, the heat and the hum of the forest had lulled him to sleep.*

> **Boa Constrictor's Narrator:** *A boa constrictor lived in the Kapok tree. He slithered down its trunk to where the man was sleeping. He looked at the gash the ax had made in the tree. Then the huge snake slid very close to the man and hissed in his ear.*

> **Boa Constrictor:** *Senior, this tree is a tree of miracles. It is my home, where generations of my ancestors have lived. Do not chop it down.*

> **Bee's Narrator:** *A bee buzzed in the sleeping man's ear.*

> **Bee:** *Senior, my hive is in the Kapok tree, and I fly from tree to tree and flower to flower collecting pol-*

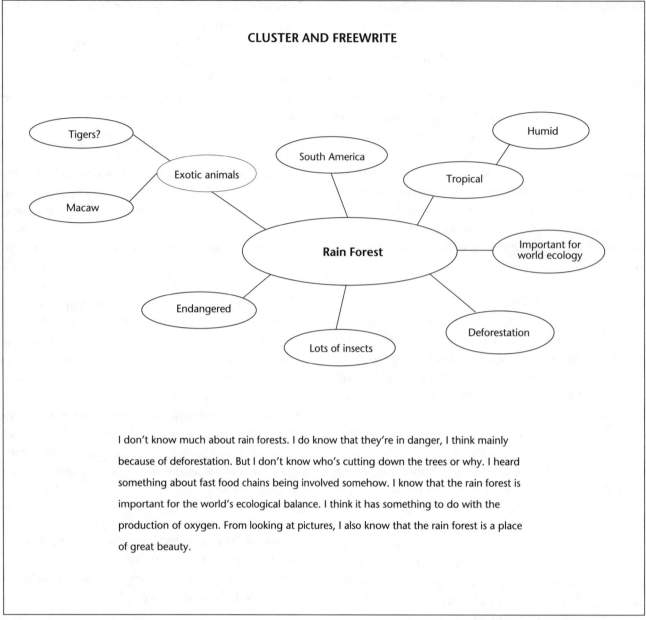

I don't know much about rain forests. I do know that they're in danger, I think mainly because of deforestation. But I don't know who's cutting down the trees or why. I heard something about fast food chains being involved somehow. I know that the rain forest is important for the world's ecological balance. I think it has something to do with the production of oxygen. From looking at pictures, I also know that the rain forest is a place of great beauty.

Figure 10   Rain Forest Cluster and Freewrite

len. In this way I pollinate the trees and flowers throughout the rain forest. You see, all living things depend upon one another.

Prewriting: Clustering

After students have completed the reader's theater, ask them to use a different color of ink to add information to their rain forest cluster. Encourage them to use the text as a resource to add to the cluster what they learned from the reader's theater. A cluster might look like the one in Figure 11.

Prewriting: Showing, not Telling

After students add to their original cluster, ask them to do a ten-minute quickwrite to the following telling sentence: *When the sleeping man awoke, he saw the rain forest with new eyes.* Here is my sample showing, not telling, paragraph:

He slowly disentangled himself from the embrace of the deep sleep that the hum and the heat of the forest had lulled him into and began his journey through the layers of consciousness toward awaken-

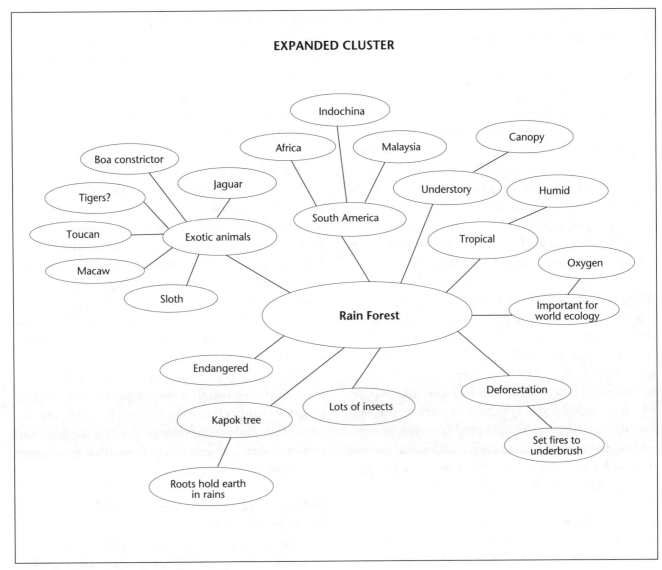

Figure 11   Rain Forest Cluster Expanded

ing. Strange whispers and murmurs echoed in his mind: "Senior, how much is beauty worth? Can you live without it?" He rubbed his eyes and shooed away the thought. Suddenly, the fragrant perfume of the crimson flowers that had been his pillow caught his attention. He breathed in and savored their sweetness for a moment before opening his eyes and gazing upon the sunlight, which was streaming in through the canopy. He had never noticed how the sunlight mingled with the darkness, causing a dance of light and shadow upon the thick verdant vines and colorful flowers that hung from the limbs of the great tree, which he was in the midst of chopping down. Quiet . . . It seemed oddly quiet. As he

lowered his gaze, he understood why. All the wondrous creatures of the rain forest were watching and waiting, talking to him with their eyes. The thought echoed again: "Senior, how much is beauty worth? Can you live without it?" And a response welled up inside his body, "No I can't," he said to himself, "I can't live without beauty."

WRITING

Although the showing, not telling, prewriting activity can be revised and shared as a finished product, it can also lead to a number of different writing options the students can choose from. A few of these options are provided below.

Sensory/Descriptive Writing

Students can "find" a poem in *The Great Kapok Tree* or in their showing, not telling, piece. One pre-composing strategy to assist with this writing task is to give students a yellow highlighter and ask them to underline the "golden lines" in the book or in each other's paragraphs. These lines can then be rearranged into a found poem. Students also enjoy finding a group poem composed of a golden line from the work of each writer which they can then transfer onto poster board and illustrate.

Imaginative/Narrative Writing

Students can speculate about what happens when the sleeping man leaves the rain forest and encounters the man who ordered him to cut down the great Kapok tree. They can then write a dialogue between the two men. The wood cutter can explain why he decided not to complete the task he was sent into the rain forest to do. As a precomposing strategy, you might want students to keep a dialectical journal in which they collect and reflect on the creatures' various arguments for sparing the tree.

Practical/Informative Writing

Students can write a report about some aspect of *The Great Kapok Tree* that sparked their interest. As a precomposing strategy, students might want to cluster the questions that arose for them while reading the story. Here are some sample questions students might choose to research.

- Who is Chico Mendes, and how did he give his life in order to preserve the rain forest?
- What is a Kapok tree, and is it native only to the rain forest?
- How does the rain forest produce oxygen?
- What animals live in the rain forest, and how does their habitat contribute to their survival?
- Does the sloth live only in the rain forest? What are its characteristics?
- What is the Yanomano tribe, and how does it depend on the rain forest?

Analytical/Expository Writing

Students can compose an essay about what they learned from the animals in *The Great Kapok Tree*, including why the tree is essential to all the creatures living in or around it. Again, as a precomposing strategy, students might turn either to clustering or to a dialectical journal.

Writer's Choice

Students can self-select a topic to write about. They might even choose to do a project, such as a mobile, sculpture, game board, or diorama, with a written description of what they created and why. For example, to show the interdependence of the animals in the rain forest, one student in the elementary language arts methods class at the University of California at Irvine created a puzzle out of the great Kapok tree, showing how all the pieces fit together.

All of the writing tasks described above can be shared at the rough-draft stage, revised, edited, possibly evaluated, and published in some way. Because the students have experienced the text and responded to it in a variety of ways, their investment will, most likely, be greater and their writing richer.

Letting Go of Leading the Guided Tour Through Literature

According to Kirby and Kuykendall (1991), "Reforming your teaching to nurture thinking involves more than dreaming up new activities or offering students more freedom." This new view of knowledge, "doesn't mean you have nothing to teach students or that textbooks are no longer important or that old knowledge is no longer valuable." What it does mean "is that we have to plan for and structure our classes in such a way that students construct their own versions of knowledge in new and personal ways." And allowing students to construct their own versions of knowledge in more personal ways means that you, as a teacher, have to allow students to embark on their own journeys through texts and possibly arrive at destinations that may be unfamiliar to you.

As I watch students interacting with the literature and with each other, I find their own, fresh questions and concerns replacing my prepackaged ones. I no longer lead the guided tour through the text. My students' own responses lead the way.

NOTES

1. Jenee Gossard's list of sentence starters comes from the handout she uses while conducting workshops on reader response logs. It was influenced by Audre Allison's work with reading logs as described in *Through Teachers' Eyes: Portraits of Writing Teachers at Work* (Portsmouth, NH: Heinemann, 1986).

2. Gossard's common reader response categories come from her article "Reader Response Logs," which appears in C. B. Olson (Ed.), *Practical Ideas for Teaching Writing as a Process* (Sacramento: California State Department of Education, 1991 edition).

3. Susan Starbuck is an English teacher at Polytechnic High School in Long Beach, California, and is a teacher/consultant for the UCI Writing Project. Several of Susan's articles appear in C. B. Olson (Ed.), *Practical Ideas for Teaching Writing as a Process*, (California State Department of Education, 1987). Although Susan has popularized found poetry among Writing Project teachers in our area, we were introduced to the concept by Marian Mohr, a teacher/consultant from the Northern Virginia Writing Project and author of *Revision: The Rhythm of Meaning* (Boynton/Cook Publishers, 1984).

4. Dan Fader made the point about the imaging problems of children who have grown up as part of the television generation at a workshop at the Univeristy of California at Irvine in 1984. He is a professor of English at the University of Michigan and the author of *Hooked on Books* (Berkeley Publishing corporation, 1966).

5. M. Williams, *The Velveteen Rabbit* (Philadelphia, PA: Running Press, 1981). Alfred A. Knopf Publishers has an audio version of *The Velveteen Rabbit* that is narrated by Meryl Streep. The audiotape of Streep's narration and George Winston's piano accompaniment is also especially effective for this guided imagery exercise.

REFERENCES

Berthoff, A. (1981). *The making of meaning: Metaphors, models and maxims for writing teachers.* Montclair, NJ: Boynton/Cook.

Bryan, C. D. (1979). So much unfairness of things. In H. McDonnell, et al. (Eds.), *Literature and life* (pp. 342-367). Glenview, IL: Scott Foresman.

Caplan, R. (1987). Showing, not telling: A training program for student writers. In C. B. Olson (Ed.), *Practical ideas for teaching writing as a process* (pp. 51-56). Sacramento, CA: California State Department of Education.

Caplan, R. (1984). *Writers in training: A guide to developing a composition program.* Palo Alto, CA: Dale Seymour Publications.

Cherry, L. (1990). *The great Kapok tree: A tale of the Amazon rain forest.* San Diego: Harcourt, Brace, Jovanovich.

Gossard, J. (1992). Reader response logs. In C. B. Olson (Ed.), *Practical ideas for teaching writing as a process.* Sacramento: California State Department of Education.

Kirby, D. (1992). Reforming your teaching for thinking. In C. B. Olson (Ed.), *Practical ideas for teaching writing as a process.* Sacramento: California State Department of Education.

Kirby, D., & Kuykendall, C. (1991). *Mind matters: Teaching for thinking.* Portsmouth, NH: Boynton/Cook Publishers, Heinemann Educational Books.

Koff, S. (1992). What the text says: What the text means to me. In C. B. Olson (Ed.), *Practical ideas for teaching writing as a process.* Sacramento: California State Department of Education.

Olson, C. B. (Ed.). (1992). *Practical ideas for teaching writing as a process.* Sacramento: California State Department of Education.

Olson, C. B. (1992). *Thinking/Writing: Fostering critical thinking through writing.* New York: Harper Collins.

Poe, E. A. (1967). Ligeia. In E. Carlson (Ed.), *An introduction to Poe: A thematic reader* (pp. 210). Glenview, IL: Scott Foresman.

Probst, R. (1988, January). Dialogue with a text. *English Journal, 77*(1), 32-38.

Probst, R. (1987). *Response and analysis: Teaching literature in junior and senior high school.* Portsmouth, NH: Boynton/Cook Publishers, Heinemann Educational Books.

Rico, G. L. (1992). Clustering: A prewriting process. In C. B. Olson (Ed.), *Practical ideas for teaching writing as a process.* Sacramento: California Statement Department of Education.

Rico, G. L. (1983). *Writing the natural way: Using right brain techniques to release your expressive powers.* New York: J. P. Tarcher.

Updike, J. (1962). *Pigeon feathers and other stories.* New York: Alfred A. Knopf.

Williams, M. (1981). *The velveteen rabbit.* Philadelphia: Running Press.

CONVERTING AT-RISK STUDENTS INTO REFLECTIVE LEARNERS

—

Stanley Pogrow

Education is at a critical turning point. The current concern with the development of more advanced skills can either be a boon or a disaster for the students who have been placed at risk. It is easy to provide thinking-in-content activities to these students. It is another matter to get them to the point where they can succeed in these activities to the full extent of their true intellectual capability—which is extensive. Furthermore, a common approach for developing students' thinking skills may result in a widening of learning gaps between at-risk and "regular" students. Developing the thinking skills of at-risk students to the point where they can be successful in thinking-in-content activities requires a different approach than for other students.

The purpose of this article is to share the conclusions I have reached about the development of thinking skills in students who have been placed at risk. These conclusions are based on my large-scale work with such students over the past ten years. Many of these conclusions are counter-intuitive, and most contradict conventional wisdom. However, interventions based on these conclusions have proven to be very effective.

THE KEYS TO CONVERTING AT-RISK STUDENTS INTO ACADEMIC LEARNERS

Converting at-risk students, many of whom read two to three years below grade level, into reflective academic learners is a formidable task. My research suggests that this goal can be achieved with a substantial number of these students if the following three key components can be brought together: an outstanding curriculum, outstanding teaching, and students with a predisposition to being reflective. Indeed, this combination is so powerful that it is effective even if it is provided for only a small part of the day. Unfortunately, putting this combination together is not as easy as it sounds—particularly since the criteria for the first two keys are not just "good," but "outstanding."

In order to understand the issues involved in bringing the three keys together, it is important to define what is meant by each of them.

Outstanding Curriculum

An outstanding curriculum is one which is consistently interesting to students and which uses a more discovery/Socratic approach to teaching and learning that effectively teaches content. With this type of curriculum, students are intrigued and are consequently stimulated to explore the content under study. Students learn partly as a result of their own curiosity. Instead of telling students what to do, teachers inquire about what has been found.

It is not clear what percentage of a given curriculum should have these characteristics. Those who say that all learning should involve thinking are misguided. The learning of facts is still important, and the best way to learn many series of facts is still rote memory. The best way to get students to learn the numbers table is still to provide an incentive for students to endure the repetitive practice necessary to learn it. However, there is probably an optimal way to combine thinking and rote learning so that even the thinking activities contribute to the learning of formal content facts. For example, I am currently developing a mathematics curriculum for grades six through eight. It will be designed in such a way that students discover many of the mathematical algorithms through experiments conducted on computers. Once the students have discovered key procedures they will then go through a drill on how to apply them. (It is not determined what the ratio of experimentation to drill should be. That will be determined by experimentation.) Rather than substituting thinking activities for content coverage, the goal for this curriculum (to be called HOTS-math) is to use discovery techniques to increase content learning.

It is far more difficult to design outstanding curricula than most realize. While it is easy to design thinking activities, it is much harder to design thinking activities that lead to systematic knowledge acquisition. It is also hard to design thinking activities that captivate students on an ongoing basis—particularly at-risk students, who are often difficult to motivate. Indeed, it is so difficult to develop outstanding curricula that the thousands of articles and speeches advocating a child-centered approach for middle schools and calling for thinking curricula have resulted in many efforts to develop those new curricula. It is easier to advocate the use of outstanding curricula than to develop

them or to deal with the reality of whether or not they exist. Indeed, there are very few middle school curricula available which are both creative and oriented to the development of thinking, and whose effectiveness has been validated. I have just started a survey of available middle school curricula to identify the exemplary ones. There are very few, and in some fields none at all. To indicate how few outstanding curricula have been developed in recent years, the highest rated mathematics curriculum in my survey is seventeen years old. None of the new curricula were as good.

It is so difficult to develop appropriate forms of curricula that it is not reasonable to expect teachers to do it. While teachers can, of course, develop specific occasional units, they cannot be expected to develop curricula that maintain intensive and interesting thinking environments consistent with key developmental and cognitive development theories. Good teachers are performers whose job it is to teach—not to develop curricula. The quality of a good actor and actress is their ability to perform Shakespeare—a previously written work. They are not expected to write a play of equivalent quality first.

Unfortunately, most curriculum specialists continue, unrealistically in my view, to advocate that teachers develop their own curricula. I suspect, however, that anyone who has ever set out to develop an outstanding curriculum will quickly come to the same conclusion that I have.

Outstanding Teaching

The near absence of adequate curricula is the first stumbling block in converting the at-risk student into a reflective learner. But even if there were appropriate types of curricula, there would be problems in providing appropriate forms of supporting teaching techniques. Seeing a Shakespeare play can either be a dull or a scintillating experience, depending on whether the actors are skillful enough to capture the nuances and the passions of the characters they portray. It is the same thing with a thinking environment. The most creative and reflective curriculum can be turned into rote learning by inadequate teaching. There is much talk that teachers should "teach as a process" and that they should "use a discovery mode." But what specifically do those things mean? What specific teaching behaviors are involved in such teaching? Can these behaviors be taught? Can they be learned—and if so by what kind of teachers?

Given an appropriate curriculum, the key to creating a reflective environment is in the way teachers talk and listen to their students. In most classrooms, the way teachers talk and listen to students follows a specific scenario: Teacher speaks many words, asks a question, gets a series of one-word answers, and acknowledges the correct one—and then the cycle starts over again. Teachers generally acknowledge the correct answer by repeating it and elaborating it. The amount of student talk, and understanding, is minimal.

The conversation taking place in the typical classroom is a ritual geared to getting students to accept what the teacher says is the correct answer rather than a process that promotes understanding. The ritual is particularly unhelpful for at-risk students, who generally do not have a good understanding of abstract concepts. (This matter will be discussed in more detail in the section on the students' predisposition to think.) Indeed, it is striking how little classroom dialogue promotes understanding. At-risk students frequently tell me that they are stupid, because the answers they are thinking of are not the ones that the teacher says is correct. These students have no notion why the supposedly correct answer is correct; why their answer is wrong—or even if it is wrong; that there can be more than one right answer; or how one arrives at answers which are judged "right" by teachers. To them it is a magic game, the rules of which they do not understand.

It is far more difficult to produce understanding in students than most realize. It requires a shift from a directive mode of teaching to a more Socratic one. The former is characterized by high levels of teacher talk, much of it devoted to telling students what to do, while the latter involves teaching by asking questions. In a Socratic environment the teacher is quizzical rather than authoritative. The goal is to ask the types of follow-up questions that lead the students to construct understanding on their own. It is only through extensive experience in constructing their own un-

derstanding under adult prodding that students can even come to develop a sense of what understanding is.

Developing the ability of even the best teachers to teach in a Socratic manner is a far more difficult process than is generally realized. Why it is so difficult, however, is something that I still find hard to put into words. You have to see someone try to teach Socratically to realize how hard it is to ask appropriate probing follow-up questions. The question must follow logically from the student's prior response, but it cannot be too specific (as that will provide an obvious clue), nor can it be too general (as to provide no stimulus to the student to rethink the initial answer). It is only when you watch a teacher trying to teach this way that you truly come to realize how hard it is.

After ten years' experience in training teachers to be Socratic, it is clear to me that it is possible to train Socratic instincts in teachers—but only under specific conditions. Training consisting primarily of philosophic advocacy about the importance of teaching Socratically is useless. A detailed system of specific techniques must be developed. (An example of such a system is contained in Pogrow, 1990b.) This system must be taught and practiced in the context of an exemplary curriculum. Teaching Socratically is so difficult that weak, or even average, teachers cannot be consistently Socratic.

Additionally, there has to be follow-up observation of the trained teacher. There is a world of difference between most teachers' perceptions of whether they are being Socratic and the reality. Self-reporting is a poor indicator of the degree of Socratic technique being employed by a given teacher. Indeed, the more sure teachers are that they are being Socratic, the higher the probability that they are being overly directive. A really good Socratic teacher understands that there is a very fine line between being directive and being Socratic. It is a matter of a few words said at the wrong time or in the wrong way. He or she also understands that it is as hard to tell which side of the fine line her words come out on as it is to tell how one's voice truly sounds to one's audience. You need a tape recorder for the former, and a trained observer for the latter.

Finally, it is impossible for even the best teacher to maintain a Socratic environment in a regular size class, particularly one in which a high percentage of students do not have a predisposition to think through ideas.

Students With a Predisposition to Think

With that last observation we have come full circle. It is probably impossible to convert at-risk students into successful academic learners without extensive experience in a Socratic environment, and at the same time it is nearly impossible to maintain the needed Socratic environment in regular size classes with a high percentage of at-risk students. So what can be done?

Even if you do provide exemplary teaching and content to at-risk students, that will not be sufficient to convert them into successful academic learners. The evidence for the inadequacy of good curricula and good teaching by themselves is the failure of the discovery-oriented curricula of the 1960s and early 1970s. Many good discovery-oriented science curricula were developed by the National Science Foundation (NSF) during the period. One of the goals of these curricula was to develop the interest and skills in science of inner-city disadvantaged youth. That goal was largely a failure. While officials at NSF are convinced that these earlier attempts failed largely because of inadequate teacher training, I do not think that was the case. I was teaching in an inner-city school at the time, and remember the frustration of the science teachers. These were good, well-trained, conscientious teachers. Yet, they would come back to the teacher room every day and say something like: "They (the students) are not responding. It's like I am talking a foreign language to them!"

Why did the inner city students not respond to a high-quality discovery curriculum and good teaching? After eight years of successful work with disadvantaged students, I refer to them as students who do not understand "understanding." At-risk students do not seem to know how to deal with unstructured types of learning, with generalizations, or with ambiguity. They seem incapable of dealing with more than one concept at a time, having a

conversation about ideas, thinking in terms of general principles instead of specific examples, and thinking ideas through. They view each piece of information as a discrete entity that only applies to the context in which it was learned. They do not seem to understand how to generalize, or that they are even supposed to generalize. They simply do not know how to work with ideas, and do not know what understanding is.

To teachers, this phenomenon manifest itself as students' inability to even begin the process of internalizing abstract ideas. When faced with this phenomenon, teachers are reduced to making the age-old request: "Please think!" This request usually elicits blank stares. The failure to communicate is all the more tragic, because each party desperately wants to communicate with the other—yet neither is capable. From the students' perspective, the teacher is in fact speaking a foreign language—the language of symbolic understanding.

It is only after the curriculum becomes more complex—after the third grade—that this understanding deficit manifests itself. Basic techniques help the at-risk student up to the third grade, and are then unable to stop a precipitous plunge of their scores thereafter. Once the curriculum becomes more complex, the only way to enhance learning is to deal with this understanding deficit. Overcoming this deficit requires an understanding of the causes of the problem.

That at-risk students do not understand "understanding" is not their fault. Nor is it an indicator of a problem with their intellect, or a function of their race, ethnicity, or economic class. It probably results from the failure of the adults in their lives to model the thinking process for them. Such modeling has typically been done through sophisticated conversation at the dinner table and in school. Conversation of this kind, however, is increasingly rare. Given the growing number of students coming from poor single-parent households, there is almost no conversation in the homes of most at-risk children—let alone conversations about constructing meaning. It is not so much that no one is teaching them how to think, but rather that no adult is asking them to develop and explain ideas and rationales. No one is asking them questions, and then asking "why?" when the child responds. Most at-risk students have literally never had opportunities to construct meaning on their own—not at home, nor in school. In school these students are generally told what to do. In my observations of classroom processes, one is struck by how little conversation exists in classrooms—even in small-group settings.

The absence of adequate interaction with adults leads to a profound understanding deficit. So what is the solution? Conventional wisdom is to provide thinking-in-content activities. Unfortunately, students who have major problems in constructing meaning will not be able to succeed in sophisticated thinking-in-content activities. Individuals who watch tapes of HOTS students are amazed at how primitive their reasoning skills are. There is simply no way that these students can successfully engage in sophisticated thinking-in-content activities at that stage of development. Even the best classroom teachers cannot cope with a substantial number of students who have understanding deficits in their classrooms.

Research by Charles Brainerd and Valery Reyna at the University of Arizona has led to the conclusion that rote learning and thinking are independent (Reyna & Brainerd, 1991) and antagonistic (Brainerd & Reyna, 1991) learning processes. Thus, energy devoted to one of the forms of learning detracts from the other. If this research is valid, it makes sense, at some point, to provide specific help in automating the basic thinking processes assumed by content learning. It is only when such processes have been automated that they do not interfere with acquiring content knowledge.

Providing thinking-in-content activities to at-risk students is the wrong approach and will widen learning gaps. Those students who understand understanding will do better, and those who do not will continue to stare at teachers. This fact not only explains why disadvantaged students did not respond to the science initiatives of the 1960s and 1970s, but also why they do not seem to be responding to more recent reforms. Middle schools have adopted many innovations over the past ten years. Yet, none really seem to reduce the at-risk problem. It is not that techniques such as cooperative learning and whole language are bad. It is just that they are not powerful enough to overcome this deficit. Nor can occasional thinking experiences overcome the understanding deficit. Producing the major cognitive change needed requires an intensive process:

- **35-minute Principle** Overcoming the understanding deficit requires two years of sophisticated general thinking activities in small group settings at least four days a week for at least thirty-five minutes a day.

- **Theory of Cognitive Underpinnings** At-risk students must first be placed in general thinking activities for one to two years before being put into sophisticated thinking-in-content activities.

Nor will any general thinking program have such effects. For example, "teaching" general thinking strategies will not work. These strategies will, like all the other information in the student's mind, be stored as disjointed ideas. A social process approach to thinking is needed. The curriculum must create situations where the students come to experience the need to think, and begin to share their perceptions of the thinking process with each other. While it is much harder to create this type of curriculum, it is believed that a social experiential approach to thinking is more appropriate for students who do not understand understanding. This type of curriculum is consistent with the theories of L. S. Vygotsky, who concluded that problem solving must first be practiced in a social setting before it can be integrated into the cognitive structure of the mind. The best approach is to recreate the social process of dinner table conversation. Recreating dinner table conversation in curricular form requires directed and mediated conversation. In such conversation, how the adult talks and responds to the child's ideas serves as an indicator of how adults use information. A major component of this conversation is to create situations around which problems can be posed and student efforts to respond can be critiqued in a coaching, nurturing way. It is important that the situations be such that students come to realize *on their own* the need to clarify a particular process or some information in order to respond to a problem posed by an adult.

The goal is to create an ongoing, powerful learning environment in which students begin to discover thinking through the social process of having adults react to their ideas. It is not a process of adults teaching something, but rather of reacting to students' ideas and students' attempts to construct meaning. By experiencing adults reacting to their ideas in a consistent way, students slowly begin to get a sense of what it means to understand something.

These conversations should not be linked to regular classroom content. These conversations mirror the ad hoc style in which parents use general events as an opportunity to query their children. The questions at a dinner table revolve around what happened that day. These questions and subsequent discussions develop a sense of what understanding is. Instead of a dinner table, and discussions about events of the day, HOTS uses computers, and discussions about what happened on the computer screen the previous day.

While overcoming the understanding deficit requires an extensive dose of general thinking experiences, our research demonstrates extensive benefits. Not only do thinking skills and social confidence improve, basic skill gains are double the national rate. In addition, 10-15% of the at-risk students start to make the honor roll. Once the powerful engines in their minds start to turn over, they can be successful in thinking-in-content activities. The key is to combine this knowledge into a practical plan.

PUTTING THE KEY COMPONENTS TOGETHER

Given the problems of providing any one of the three key components of outstanding curricula, outstanding teaching, and at-risk students predisposed to thinking, providing all three at the same time requires a carefully designed plan. It is not feasible to provide all three under conventional approaches to school improvement. Conventional wisdom advocates overall school improvement—that is, an effort to improve all teachers and courses. While such a diluted thrust will in fact improve some teachers and courses, it is too much of a hit or miss proposition for the at-risk student. Under such an improvement plan, at-risk students could go through three years of middle school without ever having all three components at the same time—let alone having them come together for a sufficient period of time to convert them into successful thinking-in-content learners.

The planning technique that has been devised for having all the components come together in a substantive way is called "Focused Centers of Excellence." Instead of trying for overall improvement, this planning technique creates pockets of excellence in a phased-in approach. The first component of the plan is to provide the students with sufficient and appropriate general thinking activities to develop students' sense of understanding and the predisposition to think. The second component is to have follow-up exemplary thinking-in-content courses available that are as good as can be created under existing knowledge—as good as any that can be found in an outstanding private school. The first component is provided using a general thinking program such as HOTS, in accordance with the 35-minute principle and the theory of cognitive underpinnings, to get at-risk students ready to benefit from the second component. In other words, the general thinking activities should be provided in small-group settings for as much as two years prior to the students being placed in the second component.

IMPLEMENTATION PROBLEMS

Implementing the Focused Centers of Excellence model is not as easy as it seems. The first problem is fiscal. Providing two years of small group general thinking activities to all at-risk students in a school is an expensive process. Ideally, class size should be limited to nine students per teacher or fifteen per teacher and aide. The smaller class size is generally funded through federal compensatory funds such as Chapter 1 and Special Education funds. A key problem arises in the middle school model in districts that spend all the federal funds at the elementary level. At that point, there probably are not sufficient district funds to cover the cost of providing intensive general thinking training to middle school at-risk students.

The other key problem in implementing the first phase is in obtaining top-quality teachers for the general thinking program. Not all principals can identify who the top-quality teachers are, and not all are willing to allocate them to such programs. As one principal of a large, embattled, urban middle school told me, "I only have four outstanding teachers in my school; how can I allocate two to the general thinking effort without creating problems elsewhere?" That is a valid concern. At the same time, however, a dynamic principal can use the development of the general thinking program as a carrot to recruit more good teachers to the school.

The biggest problem in establishing exemplary content courses is in picking the content area and teachers wisely. It must be a content area that has a core of excellent teachers who willingly agree to offer a new type of course, and who all agree to teach in a Socratic fashion. Depending on the size of the middle school, each exemplary course at a given grade level can require one to four excellent teachers. It requires a principal who knows and cares about good teaching, and is willing to be honest in deciding which teachers to approach about participating in the exemplary course. Average teachers will simply not be successful.

Identifying the right content area and teachers is not as easy as it sounds. It requires that a school has a core of excellent teachers in a given content area. It also requires a willingness to have them focus on offering consistent quality in one course. That will of necessity weaken other courses. However, once the success of at-risk students in the exemplary courses is demonstrated, there will be a greater receptivity to change on the part of the other teachers, which will then lead to greater opportunity for a more broad-based improvement.

The biggest problem with implementing the Focused Centers of Excellence approach may be tradition. This systematic proposal goes against the grain of tendencies to seek across-the-board solutions. The notions of a general thinking phase applied to one group of students, followed by a limited set of exemplary content courses is very counter-intuitive to a field brought up on the rhetoric of overall improvement, treating everyone equally, improving the entire school at once, and integrating thinking into all content.

The HOTS program has successfully countered the political instincts of the field to remedy the at-risk student, and to link such remediation to the classroom curriculum by first demonstrating success on a limited scale before attempting to network the ideas on a large scale. The experience with the HOTS program has demonstrated that there is a large group of educators who are willing to implement nontraditional approaches once evidence is available that the approach works. The same approach can work with the Focused Centers of Excellence model.

The bottom line is that most educators recognize that conventional approaches are not working and are eagerly seeking better solutions. It is possible to get novel ideas adopted if developers do the hard work of designing better solutions and then carefully demonstrate their advantage.

Why Just One Exemplary Course Per Grade Level?

The most widely asked question about the thinking-in-content component is: "Why limit the exemplary thinking-in-content courses to just one per grade level? Why not have more?" The answer is that it would be nice to have more, but realistically it is so hard to do one substantively that it doesn't make sense to try and do more. In addition, it may not be necessary to have more. One *great* course per day is enough to inspire and sustain the intellectual process. When asked: "How many of your middle or junior high teachers do you remember as having inspired an interest in learning?" most adults will remember only one or two teachers. In other words, it only takes a few outstanding educational experiences to inspire a student to chart a lifelong course of learning. The Focused Centers of Excellence plan insures that there is one such course per day in every student's schedule.

In addition, an excellent educational experience has tremendous cognitive impact on the at-risk student—even if it is sustained for only a small part of the day. The effects of an excellent curriculum combined with excellent teaching is enormous. Given my findings that general thinking for 35 minutes per day has a large effect on overall student learning, it is anticipated that just one exemplary thinking-in-content course can also have significant effects (Pogrow, 1990a). (The extent of such effects will be analyzed in future research with the urban middle schools project.)

The most important end goal is the stimulation of the intellectual ability of the at-risk student. If that can be done better with a few excellent courses than with many mediocre courses, then that is what schools should do. It is time to go beyond rhetoric and focus the limited available resources of good curriculum and good teaching into a few exemplary educational experiences that are carefully phased in over three or four years.

CONCLUSION

At-risk students have tremendous problems along with tremendous potential. It is possible to turn their problems around by the end of the middle school years. The at-risk student can become successful in exemplary academic courses. Yet, the problem of the at-risk student will not be solved with general rhetoric and advocacy. General proposals to eliminate tracking, improve all teaching, integrate thinking into all content, restructure, and spend more money are either not sufficient, not necessary, or harmful. A more systematic, and focused, approach is needed.

Bringing about substantial change for students who do not understand understanding requires a carefully orchestrated intervention. At-risk students cannot benefit from occasional, ad hoc exposure to thinking activities, as the student who already understands understanding can. Helping the at-risk student requires bringing together exemplary teaching, exemplary curricula, and students who have had several years of appropriate general thinking development. Unfortunately, while it is practical to bring this combination together, a realistic appraisal of schools as they exist (as opposed to a romanticized view) suggests that it is difficult.

The simple reality is that the typical urban middle school has a significant percentage of teachers who are not capable of successfully teaching exemplary curricula, and a small percentage who are. It is also very hard to find and develop exemplary curricula. The only possible solution is to bring the available kernels of excellence together and distribute them judiciously as opposed to letting them float around in a haphazard manner. If we can carefully bring together enough kernels to provide two years of general thinking activities, followed by one exemplary thinking-in-content course per year, we can convert at-risk students into successful academic learners.

REFERENCES

Adey, P. (1989, July). *Cognitive acceleration through science education.* Paper presented to the Learning to Think/Thinking to Learn conference sponsored by the Organization for Economic Development, Paris.

Baron, J., & Sternberg, R. (1987). *Teaching thinking skills: Theory and practice.* New York: W. H. Freeman.

Brainerd, C. J., & Reyna, V. F. (1991). *Memory independence and memory inference in cognitive development.* Manuscript submitted for publication.

Gagne, E. D. (1985). *The cognitive psychology of school learning.* Boston: Little, Brown.

Pogrow, S. (in press). What to do about Chapter 1: An alternative view from the street. *Phi Delta Kappan.*

Pogrow, S. (1991). A validated approach to thinking development for at-risk populations. In C. Collins & J. Mangieri (Eds.), *Building the quality of thinking in and out of schools.* Hillsdale, NJ: Lawrence Erlbaum Associates.

Pogrow, S. (1990a). Challenging at-risk students: Findings from the HOTS program. *Phi Delta Kappan, 71*(5), 389-397.

Pogrow, S. (1990b). *HOTS (Higher-Order Thinking Skills): Using computers to develop the thinking skills of students at risk.* New York: Scholastic.

Pogrow, S. (1990c). A learning drama approach to using computers with at-risk students. In C. Wagner (Ed.), *Current Issues in Technology.* Alexandria, VA: Association for Supervision and Curriculum Development.

Reyna, V. F., & Brainerd, C. J. (1991). Fuzzy trace theory and children's acquisition of scientific and mathematical concepts. *Learning and Individual Differences, 3,* 27-60.

Vygotsky, L. S. (1989). *Mind in society: The development of higher psychological processes.* Cambridge, MA: Harvard University Press.

MULTIPLE INTELLIGENCES THEORY: CREATING THE THOUGHTFUL CLASSROOM

Noel White, Tina Blythe, and Howard Gardner

Sophia roams around her kindergarten classroom, teasing classmates and disrupting games until it's her turn during story time. Then she becomes quickly absorbed in long and intricate tales of her own making. Rui, shy and inarticulate in his seventh grade English class, performs gracefully and compellingly in the school play. Lynn can't focus on any math problem for more than thirty seconds, but practices basketball for hours with methodical concentration, discipline, and dedication. They are puzzling, these students—and classrooms teem with them. Their inconsistent performances defy easy labels such as "under-achiever," "slow," and "learning disabled." Their strengths belie the less-than-satisfactory grades that cover their report cards. As these students become older and their schools more departmentalized, the chances that their teachers will see and value their particular strengths decrease dramatically. Even if he or she doesn't "catch" a student in some moment of greatness, a teacher who has to give a failing mark often does so with the nagging sense that the student is smarter than the grade indicates.

How do we begin to make sense of the peaks and valleys in these students' abilities? How do we address their failures in the classroom? Is there a

way—or even a reason—to recognize and reward their strengths? Can such recognition further the cause of the traditional goals of public schooling, namely reading, writing, and arithmetic?

For their appealing answers to such difficult questions, the alternative theories of intelligence espoused by Robert Sternberg (1985), Stephen Ceci (1990), David Feldman (1986), and others have been gaining popularity in educational circles. Despite their differences, these theories all assert that humans exhibit intelligent behavior in a wide variety of ways. People are not simply "smart" or "dumb." They vary in their intellectual strength depending on the context in which they are working. In the cases of Sophia, Rui, and Lynn, these theories might suggest that nothing is wrong with the students, but rather they have talents that traditional classrooms seldom tap. Educational standards do not have to be lowered for them, but should be expanded to offer a wider variety of opportunities for success. Teachers have not failed, but they may need to direct their talents to a diversified curriculum. At the same time, these students' strengths, once identified, could be used in the service of more traditional goals. This chapter explores some of the ways the theory of "multiple intelligences," developed by Howard Gardner and colleagues, has been used to approach traditional schooling from a more complex and, we argue, a more fruitful perspective.

MULTIPLE INTELLIGENCES THEORY

Gardner's theory of multiple intelligences maintains that we all possess several different and independent capacities for solving problems and creating products (Gardner, 1983, 1991a). Gardner and his colleagues gleaned the evidence for these capacities, or "intelligences," from many varied sources: empirical work with normal and gifted children; investigations of brain-damaged adults; and studies of idiot savants, prodigies, and other special populations. These data yield evidence for at least seven discrete domains of human achievement.

Linguistic intelligence involves not only ease in producing language, but also sensitivity to the nuances, order, and rhythm of words. Poets exemplify this intelligence in its mature form. Students who enjoy playing with rhymes, who pun, who always have a funny story to tell, who quickly acquire other languages — including sign language — and who write copious notes to their friends in class all exhibit linguistic intelligence.

Logical-mathematical intelligence entails the ability to reason either deductively or inductively, and to recognize and manipulate abstract patterns and relationships. Scientists, mathematicians, and philosophers all rely on this intelligence. So do the students who "live" baseball statistics or who carefully analyze the components of problems—either personal or school-related—before systematically testing solutions.

Musical intelligence includes sensitivity to pitch, timbre, and rhythm of sounds, as well as responsiveness to the emotional implications of these elements. While composers and instrumentalists clearly exhibit this intelligence, so do the students who seem particularly caught by the birds singing outside the classroom window, or who constantly tap out intricate—if irritating—rhythms on the desk with their pencils.

Spatial intelligence is the ability to create visual-spatial representations of the world and to transfer those representations either mentally or concretely. Well-developed spatial capacities are needed for the work of architects, sculptors, and engineers. The students who turn first to the graphs, charts, and pictures in their textbooks, who like to "web" their ideas before writing a paper, and who fill the blank space around their notes with intricate patterns are also using their spatial intelligence.

Bodily-kinesthetic intelligence involves using the body to solve problems, to create products, and to convey ideas and emotions. Athletes, surgeons, dancers, choreographers, and crafts people all use bodily-kinesthetic intelligence. The capacity is also evident in students who relish gym class and school dances, who prefer to carry out class projects by making models rather than writing reports, and who pitch their crumbled papers with annoying accuracy and frequency into wastebaskets across the room.

Interpersonal intelligence is the ability to understand other people, to notice their goals, motivations, intentions, and to work effectively with them. Teachers, parents, politicians, psychologists, and salespeople rely on interpersonal intelligence to carry out their work. Students exhibit this intelligence when they thrive on small-group work, when they notice and react to the moods of their friends and classmates, and when they tactfully convince the teacher of their need for extra time to complete the homework assignment.

Intrapersonal intelligence is personal knowledge turned inward to the self. This form of intellect entails the ability to understand one's own emotions, goals, and intentions. Although it is difficult to assess who has this capacity and to what degree, evidence can be sought in students' uses of their other intelligences—how well they seem to be capitalizing on their strengths, how cognizant they are of their weaknesses, and how thoughtful they are about the decisions and choices they make. The two personal intelligences are, perhaps, the hardest to observe and, at the same time, are the most important to success in any societal domain.

Along with positing these seven capacities, Multiple Intellgiences theory makes some important assertions about the way these intelligences develop and manifest themselves.

First, every normal individual possesses all seven intelligences, but in varying degrees of strengths. Each person exhibits a unique intellectual profile with preferred methods of approaching and solving problems. Thus, a standardized approach to education faces the serious problem of inevitably neglecting many students. Sophia, Rui, and Lynn, for example, would have scant opportunity to make use of their strengths in a traditional classroom, where certain aspects of linguistic and logical-mathematical intelligence are regnant while other forms of intelligence are largely ignored.

Second, intelligences are educable. Although determined to some extent by genetic predisposition, the development of intelligences is also a matter of culture and education. Traditionally, our culture has valued language and logic skills, so it has developed educational curricula and methods that favor students gifted in these two domains. According to Multiple Intelligences theory, even students not gifted in these domains can improve, but they may need to begin by drawing on their stronger intelligences. Lynn, for example, might sit easier in math class if the work involved opportunities to play with physical representations of problems or the manipulation of basketball statistics rather than isolated numbers. And if we decide to value other skills, they too can be accommodated and educated within our schools.

Third, each intelligence can be mobilized for a variety of tasks and goals. For example, Sophia's linguistic intelligence enables her to tell stories and to invent the rhyming nicknames with which she teases classmates. Furthermore, intelligences almost never operate in isolation; most goals and tasks involve a number of intelligences working together. For example, Sophia's storytelling reveals her linguistic abilities as well as her bodily-kinesthetic and logical intelligences. This is evidenced in her manipulation of the toy figures she uses to represent a story's characters and in her creation of a cause-and-effect plot for her stories.

Fourth, intelligences manifest themselves in specific domains with particular types of materials and problems. A person cannot develop fully or assess accurately one intelligence through the medium of another. For instance, a student's musical intelligence cannot be developed merely by discussing music—although, if the student is linguistically gifted, talking could be a good place to start. At some point, the student will need to experiment with the tools of the domain—for example, by playing an instrument, composing a melody, or beating a rhythm. By the same token, assessing the student's progress in music cannot be done solely through pencil-and-paper short-answer tests.

THEORY INTO PRACTICE

The particulars of Multiple Intelligences theory are not set in stone. Further research may modify our description of intelligences, may suggest different labels, or may identify altogether new intelligences. But these particulars are not as important as the basic implication that intellectual development involves more than a single, genetically determined capacity. This basic understanding complicates our picture of the factors at play in any educational setting. If we examine school through the lens of Multiple Intelligences theory, the typical classroom becomes a complex web of numerous strengths, weaknesses, opportunities, and dead ends. Students do not simply vary from one to another; they vary along several different dimensions. Teachers, too, are strong in some intelligences but not others, and they need to engage students who, for the most part, bear intelligence profiles different from theirs. When viewed through Multiple Intelligences theory, the standard curriculum itself has fortes, such as language and logic, and deficiencies—for example, many capacities receive only cursory acknowledgment in the form of gym, art, and music classes. All of these—students, teachers, and curriculum—interact in ways that are complicated, sometimes productive, and sometimes not.

Given this complex picture of school, Multiple Intelligences theory suggests educational practices that diverge considerably from the current push toward standardization of curriculum, pedagogy, and assessment. In particular, Multiple Intelligences theory calls for broadening the school curriculum to emphasize the divergent paths students can take toward understanding and for diversifying assessment. The following pages describe some examples of how these ideas might play out in the classroom.

BROADENING THE SCHOOL CURRICULUM

If students are to develop the full range of their potential, they need to be exposed early and often to a wide variety of activities and materials. Only the most gifted prodigies can develop their talents to any extent in the absence of external encouragement. One suspects, for example, that Mozart would have found a way to make music even if his father hadn't himself been an ambitious musician. However, Sophia might never have discovered, much less developed, her ability to create stories had not her teacher given her the time and the encouragement to do so.

In order to create a model for enabling very young children to explore their various intelligences and interests, multiple intelligences researchers worked with teachers to develop Project Spectrum (Krechevsky & Gardner, 1990b). In a Spectrum classroom, students visit "learning centers," where they can choose freely from a variety of hands-on activities that permit them to experiment with the materials of each domain. For example, imaginative figures and story boards aid students in storytelling, engaging their linguistic abilities. Sorting and assembling simple mechanical devices allows for the development of spatial and bodily-kinesthetic skills. Throughout the year, the teacher makes notes about which activities students gravitate toward, as well as the progress they make in working with the various materials. At the year's end, the teacher produces a report that details each student's intellectual profile and offers suggestions for activities which would encourage a child's strengths and shore up that child's weaknesses.

Of course, it is important for students—not just their parents and teachers—to understand their own intellectual profiles. Toward this end, activities involving reflection need to accompany these explorations. In Spectrum classrooms, students as young as four years old are asked to identify the activities that they like most, as well as the ones they

think they do best. Older students write in journals, create charts, or discuss their strengths with other students. Such reflection fosters the development of intrapersonal intelligence, a capacity that enables students to draw more readily on their strengths when solving future problems.

Self-knowledge is not the only benefit of a more inclusive curriculum. Motivation is another important byproduct (Csikszentmihalyi, 1990). Students who are encouraged to develop their strengths are more likely to enjoy their work and to persevere when they encounter difficulties in these domains. Such perseverance and the attendant increase in the students' skill builds both confidence and competence for dealing with more complex problems as they arise.

MULTIPLE PATHS TO UNDERSTANDING

Broadening the curriculum does not imply that traditional goals need to be disregarded. However, Multiple Intelligences theory does suggest that there may be more than one way to achieve those goals. Because each student has different strengths for experiencing the world, a presentation of the curriculum which emphasizes only language and logic will not be equally successful for all students. Each student will thrive depending on how he or she experiences the new materials. Some students need visual and physical representations of concepts. Some students prefer abstract mind-work. Some need ideas explained verbally in several different ways. Some students benefit when a classmate explains materials. Some work best when given the opportunity to play for some time with materials, as in a science lab, before they discover the key information. Others want to be told the answer directly.

Making the match between the standard curriculum and each student's proclivities is not easy, but progress can be achieved with the efforts of teachers and students. Teachers can take an active role by shaping their presentations of the curriculum to fit the needs of a wider range of students. Experienced and successful teachers often cater to a range of students by teaching each part of the curriculum in many different ways. They tend to revisit a key concept or theme often and with variations to provide several opportunities for students to approach a concept from different perspectives. In Multiple Intelligences terms, this variety provides the multiple paths to understanding necessary to engage the multiple intelligences that students bring to the classroom.

A Project Approach

One of the most common and most effective ways to provide multiple opportunities for students to use their strengths is through working on projects (Gardner, 1991b). Projects can allow students to choose topics or approaches that fit their interests (Olson, 1988). Projects also provide opportunities for extended work with peers, which develops interpersonal skills. Given the opportunity to present their information in forms other than writing, students can develop and display musical, spatial, and kinesthetic skills.

Public elementary school teachers in Indianapolis, Indiana created The Key School around Gardner's Multiple Intelligences theory. It makes projects an important part of each student's experience. Students in the Key School learn about multiple intelligences and are required to take regular classes in physical education, computers, art, music, and a foreign language, as well as the standard reading, writing, and arithmetic. They draw on these diverse experiences to create three major projects each year. Several elements of the projects encourage students to draw on and to develop multiple intelligences: the Key School's general course-work, which feeds into the projects; the encouragement to be creative and personal in developing projects; working on projects for extended periods of time; cooperating with others; performing or presenting their projects to classmates; and documenting the process and product on videotape, which captures much more than written documentation. With its focus on extended projects that emphasize a range of skills, including linguistic, musical, and interpersonal, the Key School has a lively and productive atmosphere. It differs enormously from schools that emphasize practice for written, standardized tests of language and logic. Students at the Key School acquire the "basic skills" required of public education, but they do so through multiple paths that take advantage of their personal and creative energies.

Teachers, school curriculum, and administrators are not the only ones responsible for matching student intelligences with curricular goals. Students can be encouraged to take some of the responsibility for shaping their school experience. Students can learn to adapt the curriculum to their needs, and to use their own strengths to better serve the demands of school. Most students stumped by a writing assignment or dismayed by the prospect of failing yet another math exam might give up or might overcome the difficulty only if the teacher intervenes. The student who approaches an assignment as if there is only one way to go about the task has little hope once stuck. Students with the perspective of multiple intelligences have a better chance by understanding that there are many approaches to writing and a variety of ways to gain insight into math. If students have had the opportunity to learn something about their own intelligences, then they have a better chance to find approaches that will work for them when facing tough assignments.

Training Practical Intelligence

The difficulty is that not all students know they can take responsibility for their learning by drawing on their own strengths and interests, and not all students know how. Put another way, some students have "practical intelligence." That is, they understand themselves well enough to know how their own ways of working are unique, and they understand school well enough to recognize how they can best utilize personal abilities—and overcome disabilities—to fit the varying demands of school tasks. Many students, however, do not posses the practical intelligence that would allow them to maneuver successfully through their school careers. The Practical Intelligence For School project (PIFS) developed curricular materials to help students take more responsibility for their learning (Krechevsky & Gardner, 1990a; Walters, Blythe, & White, in press).

Many efforts—generally called study skills curricula—already exist to teach practical skills. The PIFS project differs from these efforts in several respects. Study skills curricula often help when and where students do not need it, disconnected from their daily schoolwork. Proceeding on Multiple Intelligences theory's assertion that intelligences manifest themselves in specific domains with particular types of materials and problems, PIFS lessons consider practical knowledge in the context of the academic problems students face daily. Practical intelligence is not something more to be learned on top of reading, writing, and arithmetic. Rather, practical skills such as being organized, managing time, understanding one's best work styles, and understanding the school system at large are integrally mixed with and complicated by the process of learning these subjects. Study skills curricula often present single or simple solutions to complex problems, thereby failing to serve the needs of many students. Following Multiple Intelligences theory, the PIFS curriculum gives students opportunities in the course of their regular lessons to recognize that they have unique ways of going about schoolwork. In this manner, PIFS lessons help students establish personal, workable solutions to their own difficulties.

DIVERSIFYING ASSESSMENT

An important part of any plan to encourage a variety of abilities and to provide multiple paths between those abilities and the standard curriculum, is the broadening of assessment conceptions (Gardner, 1990a). Even educators who appreciate their students' different needs and strengths often give grades that credit only a narrow range of skills, mainly those that exploit language and logic. The scope of assessment can be expanded without severely altering classroom culture. Common school experiences, such as science laboratories and social studies projects, can be supplemented with notebooks, journals, portfolios, review conferences, videos, or other kinds of records. These supplements broaden the focus of both teachers and students. The most common student products, such as tests, papers, and oral presentations, highlight mainly linguistic and logical skills. Such products leave out other important skills students

may have and which certainly are important for students' overall growth.

To examine how assessment can include a wider range of intelligences, the Arts PROPEL project, a collaboration among Harvard Project Zero, the Educational Testing Service, and Pittsburgh Public Schools, has done considerable work toward making portfolios a practical and educational part of the classroom (Gardner, 1990b). By building portfolios over time, PROPEL classes encourage an examination of the evolution and range of students' thinking. Documenting the process that students undertake when they write, paint, or prepare for tests, these assessments generate more opportunities to recognize and encourage strengths that may not be evidenced in the final product (Winner et al., in press).

Building on the notion of portfolios, but taking care to focus on more than polished final products, Arts PROPEL calls its assessment devices "process-folios." A processfolio is a record of learning that captures a student's process of creation. The activity of focus may be in any domain: music, drama, science, English, history, or the like. Processfolios can include pieces that represent different styles, mastery of specific skills, and examples of pivotal works in progress. Unlike tests, processfolios can preserve examinations of problems that students find important, that may have several answers, or that require original and sustained research (Wolf, 1988). The Arts PROPEL processfolios sample a wide range of skills, among them are craft, pursuit (revision and development over time) expressiveness, inventiveness, self-assessment, use of criticism, the capacity to make distinctions among works, awareness of physical properties of materials, ability to work independently or collaboratively, and use of resources. Students develop critical intrapersonal and interpersonal skills by reviewing their processfolios with the teacher and with one another. Classrooms involved with the Arts PROPEL project recognize and encourage a larger range of student talents than classrooms relying only on such assessments as standard written tests and papers.

On a smaller scale, classes that extensively feature the informal assessments naturally integrated into activities, such as class discussions, self-monitoring, small-group work, and peer reviewing, also tend to promote a more productive range of thinking in students. By interacting with people other than the teacher, students have the opportunity to see ideas from many different perspectives and to gauge their own learning. Similar to portfolios, devices such as journals and videotapes can record the process of these important learning experiences as well as their results. When students have opportunities to review their learning, especially with peers, they develop a wider range of skills and begin assuming more responsibility in shaping their own educational experiences.

CONCLUSION

Theories that expand our notions of intelligence have offered some hope for understanding the successes and the failures of students like Sophia, Rui, and Lynn. Gardner's theory of multiple intelligences argues that these students may have great potential, both in school and adult life. Drawing on the basic notion that students bring multiple abilities with them to school, and that school can offer a much richer range of opportunities than is commonly emphasized, several ongoing efforts have shown how the perspective of Multiple Intelligences theory can help more students capitalize on their skills. The ultimate goal of these efforts is to reach beyond the schools and into later life.

Even more than school success, performance in any vocation or avocation depends on a combination of intelligences. One has only to reflect on the disparate duties performed by teachers, lawyers, mechanics, artists, doctors, parents, engineers, and business people to see that much more than linguistic or logical-mathematical intelligence is needed for success in any of these occupations. If we declare our educational goal to be preparing children for productive adult lives, we have an obligation to help students develop all of their intelligences. By more closely mirroring the complexities of adult life, including its demand for multiple and intertwined skills, school can better prepare our youth to assume responsibility for our world—and, in the future, their world.

We would like to express our gratitude to the William T. Grant Foundation, the Lilly Endowment, the MacArthur Foundation, the James S. McDonnell Foundation, the Pew Charitable Trusts, the Rockefeller Brothers' Fund, the Rockefeller Foundation, and the Spencer Foundation for their generous support of the work described in this chapter. We would also like to thank the students, teachers, and administrators who have been invaluable sources of information and enthusiasm in our research.

___

REFERENCES

Ceci, S. (1990). *On intelligence, more or less.* Englewood Cliffs, NJ: Prentice Hall.

Csikszentmihalyi, M. (1990). *Flow: The psychology of optimal experience.* New York: Harper & Row.

Feldman, D. H. (1986). *Nature's gambit: Child prodigies and the development of human potential.* New York: Basic.

Gardner, H. (1991a). *Intelligence in seven phases.* Paper presented at the 100th Anniversary of Education at Harvard, Cambrige, MA.

Gardner, H. (1991b). *The unschooled mind: How children think and how schools should teach.* New York: Basic.

Gardner, H. (1990a). Assessment in context: The alternative to standardized testing. In B. R. Gifford & M. C. O'Connor (Eds.), *Changing assessments: Alternative views of aptitude, achievement, and instruction* (pp. 77-119). Boston: Kluwer.

Gardner, H. (1990b). *The assessment of student learning in the arts.* Paper presented at the Conference on Assessment in Arts Education, Bosschenhooft, the Netherlands.

Gardner, H. (1983). *Frames of mind: The theory of multiple intelligences.* New York: Basic.

Krechevsky, M., & Gardner, H. (1990a). Approaching school intelligently: An infusion approach. In D. Kuhn (Ed.), *Developmental perspectives on teaching and learning thinking skills* (pp. 79-94). Basel: Karger.

Krechevsky, M., & Gardner, H. (1990b). The emergence and nurturance of multiple intelligences. In M. J. A. Howe (Ed.), *Encouraging the development of exceptional abilities and talents* (pp. 222-245). Leicester, England: British Psychological Society.

Olson, L. (1988, January 27). Children "flourish" here. *Education Week,* pp. 1, 18-21.

Sternberg, R. J. (1985). Beyond I.Q.: *A triarchic theory of human intelligence.* New York: Cambridge University.

Walters, J., Blythe, T., & White, N. (in press). PIFS: Everyday cognition goes to school. In H. Reese & J. Puckett (Eds.), *Advances in lifespan development.* Hillsdale, NJ: Lawrence Erlbaum.

Winner, E. (in press). Arts PROPEL: An introductory handbook. In E. Winner (Ed.), *Arts PROPEL Handbook Series* (vol. 1). Princeton, NJ: Educational Testing Service; Cambridge, MA: Harvard Project Zero.

Wolf, D. P. (1988). Opening up assessment. *Educational Leadership, 45*(4), 24-29.

SEVEN WAYS OF KNOWING

—

David Lazear

I n 1985, Howard Gardner published ground-breaking research on multiple intelligences in his book *Frames of Mind.* His findings point to a complex of seven intelligences, seven ways of knowing, perceiving, and understanding life. And Gardner believes there are probably other intelligences that we have not yet been able to test. Figure 1 gives an overview of seven ways of knowing we possess.

The good news is that each of us has all of these intelligences. However, since not all of them are developed equally, we do not always know how to use them effectively. Usually, one or two intelligences are stronger and more fully developed than the others. But this need not be a permanent condition. We have within ourselves the capacity to activate all of our intelligences, and as a consequence, amplified worlds of sensing, feeling, knowing, and being are opened to us!

In this chapter, I suggest a variety of practical classroom and school applications for the theory of multiple intelligences. There are at least three different ways multiple intelligences can be integrated into the curriculum.

Intelligence as a subject focus unto itself (teaching FOR multiple intelligences). Each of the intelligences can be taught as a subject in its own

right, such as teaching music skills; language; art as a formal discipline; mathematical calculation and reasoning; skillful body movement, as in physical education, dance, and drama; and various social skills necessary for effective functioning in our society. This approach involves teaching the accumulated wisdom of one's culture on the subject, the formal knowledge base, and the practical methods, skills, and techniques of the intelligence.

Intelligence as a means to acquire knowledge (teaching WITH multiple intelligences). Each of the intelligences can likewise be used as a means to gain knowledge in areas beyond itself. This could involve such things as using body movement to learn vocabulary words; music to teach math concepts; art (drawing, painting, and sculpture) to imagine different periods of history or different cultures; language to debate various perspectives on current events; and logical reasoning to compare and contrast characters in a Shakespeare play.

"Meta-intelligence"—intelligence investigating itself (teaching ABOUT multiple intelligences). Lessons that deal with meta-intelligence processes teach students about their own multiple intelligences—how to access them, how to strengthen them, and how to actively use them in learning and in everyday life. This is the metacognitive aspect of

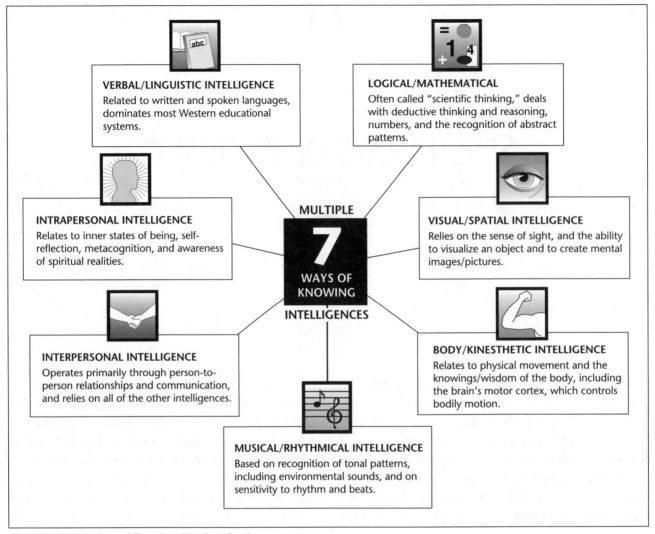

Figure 1 Seven Ways of Knowing, Not Just One!

using multiple intelligences in the classroom. The more students know about their different ways of knowing, the more skillful they can become in using them, both in the school situation and in their lives beyond the classroom.

SKILLS STUDENTS NEED TO ACCESS THEIR FULL INTELLECTUAL POTENTIAL (Teaching FOR Multiple Intelligences)

In my first book, *Seven Ways of Knowing*, I suggested a categorizing of different human capacities/potentials related to the seven intelligences. These have at times been called "sub-intelligences" by Gardner. A summary of these intelligence skills can be seen on the wheel in Figure 2.

It is also important to note that at different ages we have different capacities. This is crucial for designing curricula that teach students the full spectrum of intelligence skills in ways and at times appropriate to particular developmental stages of their growth as human beings.

The chart in Figure 3 represents an initial effort to list various skills for each of the intelligences that need to be taught and used by students at different stages of their developmental journey.

The first stage I have called **Basic Skill Development.** This development generally takes place during the early years of life and involves the "raw patterning" of the intelligence. This stage gives one the necessary building blocks of intelligence—those basic tools one will need later for more complex intellectual pro-

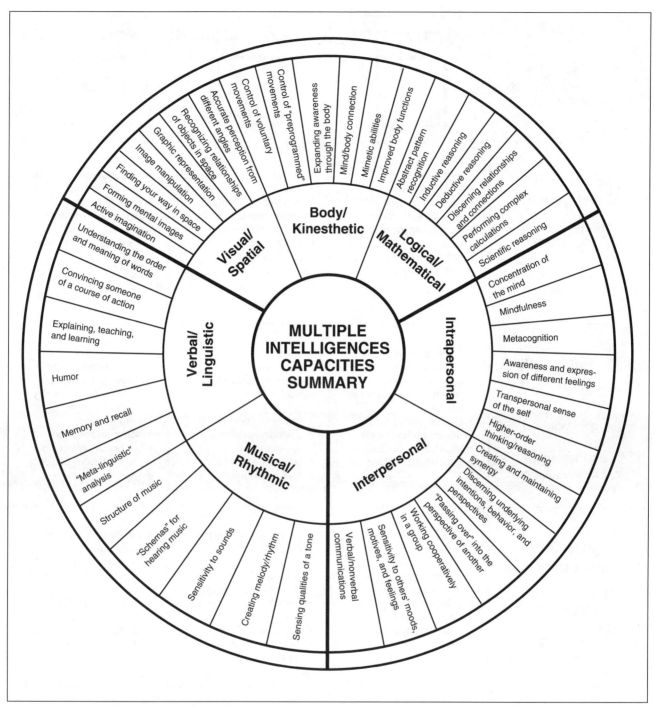

Figure 2   Multiple Intelligences Summary Wheel

cesses and operations. The acquisition of the skills appropriate to this stage is more or less "guaranteed" for most individuals, both by our neurobiological make-up and by the socialization processes of our culture. However, what happens to one's intellectual skill development beyond the early years is highly contingent on one's family, school, and social environment.

The second stage is **Complex Skill Development**. This stage involves several important elements, including an expansion of all intelligence skills —building on those basic patterns acquired during the first stage—based on instruction and experience in their effective use in problem-solving tasks. This is likewise the stage in which one begins to learn the

	VERBAL/LINGUISTIC	LOGICAL/MATHEMATICAL	VISUAL/SPATIAL
Basic Skill Development ("raw patterning" of intelligences) infancy/ pre-school levels	• infant babbling • single words • pairs of words/ meaningful phrases • simple sentences (poor syntax) • imitation writing (letters/name)	• object manipulation • counting • number recognition • simple abstraction • pattern recognition • cause/effect thought patterns	• sensori-motor explora- tion of the world • color discernment • shape discernment • drawing (simple) • getting from one place to another
Complex Skill Development (intelligences symbol systems) elementary/ middle school levels	• complex sentences (good syntax) • grasp of grammar • reading (stories & other narratives) • humor (telling & understanding jokes) • expanding vocabulary • self-initiated writing	• understanding math processes • performing standard math operations (+,-,x,) • problem-solving skills • thinking-patterns development • complex abstraction (math symbols)	• recognition of spatial depth & dimension • drawing, sculpting, painting (reproducing objects/scenes) • map reading • active imagination • decentration (seeing from different perspec- tives)
Higher-Order Intelligence (synthesis and integration) secondary school levels	• creative/expressive writing • story telling/inventing • poetry creation/ appreciation • debate/formal speaking • figures of speech • meta-linguistic conver- sation	• linking operations for complex problem solving • finding unknown quantities (algebra) • metacognitive process- ing • logic/math proofs • inductive/deductive reasoning processes	• building (blueprints) • map making • impressionistic/ expressionistic art form creation • abstract spatial imagery (e.g., geometry) • complex visual/spatial relationships (e.g., chess)
Vocational Pursuits (societal service/ career paths) college/ adulthood levels	• public speaking • writing (novelist, poet, journalist) • comedian • playwriting • newscasting • storytelling/writing	• scientific exploration • accounting/business • legal assistance • banking • computer program- ming • mathematician • medicine	• architecture • graphic design artistry • cartographer • drafting • painting (art) • sculpting • advertising

Figure 3   Growth and Development of the Seven Intelligences

BODY/KINESTHETIC	MUSICAL/RHYTHMIC	INTERPERSONAL	INTRAPERSONAL
• automatic reflexes • basic motor skills (crawling, standing, walking, sitting) • gaining physical independence • actions to control environment • goal-oriented actions	• the basic "Ur" song (universal song of babies) • tonal recognition • tonal reproduction • rhythm recognition • rhythm reproduction • sound association forming	• parental bonding • recognition/acceptance of familiar others • simple communication with others • imitation of sounds, words, and facial expressions	• expression of a range of body states • awareness/expression of personal feelings • correlation of certain emotions with specific experiences • awareness of separate self-identity
• folk/cultural dance • expressive gestures/ body language • gymnastics • role playing/charades • physical skills (e.g., typing, roller skating, riding a bike) • sports games	• melody/song production • reading music • production of varying rhythm/beats • music/rhythm technique development • enjoyment of certain music types	• establishment of peer relationships (beyond family) • development of social skills • empathy for others • being part of a team • social role playing	• concentration skills • "why" questioning (trying to make sense) • self-improvement skills attainment • defining personal likes/ dislikes • correlation of others' behavior with self
• inventing • creative/expressive dance (e.g., ballet) • dramatic enactment of complex scenes • complex physical exercise routines • sports (skilled execution)	• music composition • music performance • teaching music to others • understanding music theory • grasping the meaning of music symbols • music appreciation skills	• consensus building • understanding group processes • cooperative problem solving • recognition of cultural values and norms • recognition of various "social ideals"	• symbol creation/ understanding • conscious control of emotional states • identity search • personal beliefs/ philosophy • conscious use of higher-order thinking
• dramatic acting • athletics • professional dancing • inventing • mime • physical education instruction	• advertising • performance musician • composing music • music teaching • environmental sound engineering • film making • musical theatre • television	• counseling • professional teaching • politics • religious leader • therapist • sociologist • anthropologist	• philosopher • psychiatry • spiritual counseling • guru • cognitive patterns research • human potential exploration

Figure 3 (continued)

"language" and "symbol system" for each intelligence. For example, the language of musical/rhythmic intelligence includes tone frequencies, sound, rhythm, beat, and vibrational patterns, whereas its symbol system involves such things as notes on a musical staff, and various other markings and symbols that tell one how the notes are to be played. If one does not learn both the language and symbol system of the musical/rhythmic way of knowing at this stage, further development of the intelligence is thwarted. The same is true for each of the other intelligences.

The third stage I have called **Higher-Order Intelligence** (as in higher-order thinking). This involves a process of synthesizing information gained and skills learned in the previous stages, as well as learning how to integrate the intelligences into one's regular "repertoire of living." This stage involves learning how to skillfully use the different intelligences and to interpret or process the kinds of information one receives through the different ways of knowing.

The final stage is **Vocational Pursuits**. Generally, people will choose their career path(s) based on those intelligences that they best understand and with which they are most comfortable. If one has, however, learned how to use and appreciate the full spectrum of one's intellectual capacities, there will be increased work satisfaction, effectiveness, and creativity due to the ability to process information and engage in problem solving on many more levels simultaneously.

The divisions between these stages are not fixed, and there may be some overlap between aspects. However, this does give us a picture of how the intelligences develop, and how we can help students gain a full spectrum of knowing tools to amplify and enrich their education and their future lives.

One implication of this developmental approach to human intelligence is that we must take a new look at the curriculum we are teaching to make sure that students learn how to use each of the intelligences both in the classroom and in their lives beyond the school setting.

A New Look at the Curriculum: Taking the "Extra" out of "Extra-Curricular"

As I mentioned above, beyond the Basic Skill Development stage, intelligence development is greatly influenced by one's family and social environment. If we want our students to be more intelligent in more ways and at more levels, we must consciously and explicitly teach them! What this means is that the fine arts and so-called "extra-curricular" parts of the school curriculum should be the last to be cut when our schools are facing financial difficulties. It is often these "extra" parts of the curriculum that teach students to understand and use the full spectrum of their intelligence capacities. In light of current research on integrating the curriculum, we must find and teach the "fine arts" components that are present in every subject area. Following are four scenarios that illustrate what an integrated fine arts curriculum might look like.

SCENARIO 1: In history, students can learn the art, music, and dance of a particular period by performing them. They can study and enact the dramas that were popular or write their own in the style of the period using modern-day themes. They can read the great stories of the period. They can study science and perform the experiments that led to certain scientific discoveries and breakthroughs.

SCENARIO 2: In language arts, there are countless opportunities to teach the "fine arts," and thus, help students gain basic intelligence skills. In literature lessons, students can draw pictures or act out what they are reading. They can "role play" grammar or write a drama in which the characters are the parts of speech. In this way, students can be taught how to use the active imagination to fully appreciate and understand great literature.

SCENARIO 3: In math, students can learn math facts and concepts using manipulatives (e.g., sculpting with clay). They can write stories using verse and rhyme; study the mathematical patterns and concepts that are embedded in music and dance; and learn geometric formulas through role playing. The teacher may design "inventing projects" that require students to use a wide variety of math concepts and operations.

SCENARIO 4: In science, students can learn to draw accurately what they see under a microscope. Students can perform lab experiments in cooperative groups and keep a log of their findings. They can be encouraged to track and improve various thinking patterns, such as prediction, causal reasoning, comparisons and contrasts; or to study the science of sound and music and its effect on the body.

LESSONS THAT TAKE INTO ACCOUNT MULTIPLE INTELLIGENCES (Teaching WITH Multiple Intelligences)

There are three major presuppositions behind my thinking on teaching WITH multiple intelligences: (1) we can teach *all* students to be more intelligent in many more ways, and on more levels of their being than they (or we) ever dreamed of; (2) *anything* can (and should) be taught and learned through all of the intelligences; and (3) we as educators have some very important homework to do in order to learn how to use multiple intelligences in the teaching/learning process.

Generally speaking, there are four stages necessary to teach WITH multiple intelligences. The developmental sequence is something like the following:

Stage I: Awakening the Intelligences

We must first be aware that we do in fact possess multiple ways of knowing and learning, and we must learn various techniques and methods for "triggering" an intelligence within the brain/mind/body system. Each of the intelligences is anchored in the five senses so a particular intelligence can be activated through exercises and activities that use the sensory bases (sight, sound, taste, touch, smell, speech, and communication with others) as well as the "inner senses," such as intuition, metacognition, and spiritual insight.

Stage II: Amplifying the Intelligences

Second, we must learn how particular intelligences function. We must find out what capacities and/or skills are associated with them. We must find out how to access them, and how to use and understand different intelligence modalities. This involves practice in strengthening intelligence capacities as well as learning how to interpret and work with the different kinds of information we re-

ceive through each intelligence. We must learn to understand the unique language of each intelligence, that is, how each expresses itself. The language of body/kinesthetic intelligence, for example, is physical movement—not words, sentences, writing, or speech.

Stage III: Teaching With the Intelligences

We must learn how to teach content-based lessons that apply different ways of knowing to the specific content of a given lesson. This involves learning how to use and trust a given intelligence in knowing, learning, and understanding tasks. Teaching WITH intelligences is approached from the perspective of classroom lessons that emphasize and use the different intelligences in the teaching/learning process. Approximately ninety-five percent of the material we have to teach comes prepackaged in a verbal/linguistic or a logical/mathematical form. However, it is important to understand that in planning lessons to teach this material, we need not be bound by the packaging. We must learn how to design and implement lessons that emphasize all seven ways of knowing. In presenting lessons this way, we will reach more students more of the time.

Stage IV: Transferring the Intelligences

Finally, we must learn, and we must teach our students how to use, all of the intelligences to improve students' effectiveness in dealing with the issues, challenges, and problems they face in the task of daily living. This task is primarily a matter of approaching all problems on multiple levels, using a variety of problem-solving methods that tap the full spectrum of intelligences. The goal of this stage is to make multiple intelligences a regular part of one's cognitive, affective, and sensory responses to all of life's challenges. For a sample model lesson see Figure 4.

HOW STUDENTS BECOME AWARE OF THEIR OWN "SEVEN WAYS OF KNOWING" (Teaching ABOUT Multiple Intelligences)

As far as we know, human beings are the only creatures who are self-reflective; that is, who have the

PARTS OF SPEECH MODEL LESSON

1. *Discuss and understand the definition of your part of speech.*
   - Divide the class into eight teams with three to four students per team.
   - Give each team a card with the definition of one part of speech written on it (noun, pronoun, adjective, verb, adverb, preposition, conjunction, interjection).
   - Teams are to read and make sure that each member understands the definition.
   (NOTE: Be sure you check in with the teams to make sure they are clear on their assigned part of speech.)

2. *Write a song to teach your part of speech using a common tune.*
   - Decide on a common tune each team will use for their song (e.g., "Are You Sleeping, Brother John?")
   - Each team creates a song that communicates the definition of its assigned part of speech.

3. *Make up a physical gesture or body movement for your part of speech.*
   - Each team brainstorms a list of actions that "em-body" the definition of their assigned part of speech (something it might do or an action it might perform if it could!).
   - Teams decide on one (or a combination) of the actions/gestures on their list to teach their part of speech to the rest of the class.

4. *Create a flag and slogan for your part of speech.*
   - Pass out a large piece of paper and colored markers to each team.
   - Teams think of a symbol/picture/emblem for their assigned part of speech (something it might draw if it could!).
   - Each team is to create a slogan to go with their symbol/picture/emblem and to write it on the flag.

5. *List examples of your part of speech.*
   - Each team lists six to ten words that are examples of their assigned part of speech.
   (NOTE: The conjunction and interjection teams may need some special help from you to come up with six to ten examples.)
   - List the example words on the same piece of paper as the flag and the slogan.

6. *Present the team's report.*
   - Have each team present its definition, flag, slogan, song, gesture/physical movement, and list of examples to the class.
   - Check in with the class for understanding and/or questions.

7. *Combine words from each group to make sentences.*
   - In some random fashion, have each team select two words from each list of examples.
   - The sixteen words chosen are part of a pool from which each team is to make three separate sentences.
   (NOTE: Each of the sentences does not have to contain all of the words chosen, but each of the words must be used at least once in the three sentences. The sentences will most likely be somewhat bizarre! They may add articles as needed.)

8. *Reflect on the lesson.*
   - Have each group share one of its sentences with the rest of the class.
   - Discuss the lesson:
     - What struck you about this lesson? What did you notice?
     - What feelings did you have as you went through the various stages? What was fun? Surprising? Difficult?
     - What did you like about approaching the lesson in all these different ways? What did you dislike about it?
     - How did this way of learning about the parts of speech help you?
     - What did you learn about the parts of speech from the lesson?

Figure 4   Model Lesson

ability to step back and watch themselves, almost like an outside observer. Once we become aware of something in our lives, our self-consciousness gives us the power to change it if we so desire. This self-reflective dimension is at the heart of helping students understand their own multiple intelligences, how to improve them, and how to consciously use them to enhance their own and others' lives.

There are basically four levels of meta-intelligence lessons—lessons that can help students become aware of the seven ways of knowing and how to use them more effectively. These levels are modeled after research into the dynamic levels of metacognition.

TACIT ("I use the seven intelligences every day, I've just never called them that!"). The tacit level of learning about the intelligences involves exercises and activities that help students become aware of capacities and potentials that are part of their heritage as human beings. These are the generally taken-for-granted "intelligent" things we do in the normal course of living, such as parallel parking a car, listening to music while we work or exercise, using gestures and other body movement to express our ideas and feelings to others, telling jokes, and balancing a checkbook. Once a person is aware of the seven intelligences and how much they are a part of normal daily living, the possibility for improving them is established.

AWARE ("Now that I have a label for the different ways of knowing, I am more conscious of when and how I use them!") The aware level of learning about multiple intelligences involves exercises and practices for learning more about how the intelligences operate and how their functioning can be improved. In some ways, the use of the intelligences is like any skill we possess; the more we practice it, the greater our mastery of it. One of the tasks of lessons dealing with the aware use of the intelligences is to help students become conscious of their own intelligence strengths and weaknesses, understanding that weakness need not be a permanent condition. If a student discovers, for example, that she is not very good at using active imagination (a visual/spatial intelligence capacity), she may be made aware at the same time that this capacity is inherent in the brain and can thus be developed. The same is true for the capacities related to each of the other intelligences.

STRATEGIC ("Not only do I know about the seven intelligences, but I know when and how to use each one most effectively!") The strategic level of learning about the seven ways of knowing involves skill in the two previous levels of meta-intelligence I have outlined, plus a conscious decision to employ the different ways of knowing on a regular basis to enhance learning, expand creativity, and improve problem solving, both in one's self and others. In other words, the strategic use of the intelligences is a matter of using them with intention. For example, the student who suggests to his teacher particular intelligence strategies that could be used in a lesson to help students "get it" more quickly and thoroughly uses strategic metacog-

nition. A case in which a student assists another student with schoolwork by helping translate a lesson into a preferred or stronger intelligence modality may serve as another example.

REFLECTIVE ("I am learning how to use the seven intelligences to help me in my daily life!"). The reflective level of learning about the intelligences involves activities that help students integrate the seven ways of knowing into their "repertoire for living." They begin to understand that any problem or challenge can be approached through the seven intelligences, and that greater levels of creativity are available to them as a consequence. Likewise, with various learning tasks, the seven intelligences not only make learning more fun, but they also broaden one's knowledge base, for now it is known and understood in at least seven ways, not just one!

Figure 5 is a beginning list of ideas for teaching students ABOUT multiple intelligences. Figure 6 is a brief explanation of each tool.

AUTHENTIC ASSESSMENT OF LEARNING: TOWARD "MULTI-MODAL" GRADING AND TESTING

The idea of teaching FOR, WITH, and ABOUT multiple intelligences instantly raises concerns about grading, testing, and assessing students' academic progress and achievement. This is difficult given the verbal/linguistic and logical/mathematical bias of our current educational systems. Paper-and-pencil testing is fine as long as we recognize its limits, and if we understand the nature of the information about student achievement it provides us. However, we often try to make these kinds of test scores into an ultimate indicator of what students have or have not learned.

How do we assess students' intelligence capacities? We must first understand the relative strengths and weaknesses of students in the seven intelligence areas. This is important in light of the fact that current research indicates that intelligence is not as fixed or as static a phenomenon as we once thought (Gardner, 1985; Feuerstein, 1980; Houston, 1980, 1982; Harman & Rheingold, 1985; Machado, 1980; Sternberg, 1984; Guilford, 1979; Dickinson, 1987). In fact, intelligence appears to

---

TEACHING ABOUT MULTIPLE INTELLIGENCES: "META-INTELLIGENCE" LESSON IDEAS

I. TACIT: Tools for exploring intelligence capacities and potentials used daily but with little awareness or thought.
  • People Search
  • Self Report Card
  • "Wraparound" Processing
  • Recognizing Others' Capacities
  • Self Behavior Checklist

II. AWARE: Tools for creating awareness of how the intelligences work and for discovering one's own strengths and weaknesses.
  • Multiple Intelligence Activity Posters
  • Exploring Intelligence Capacities with a Partner
  • Self-Evaluation Techniques
  • Intelligence Games and Problem-Solving Activities
  • Intelligences "Think-Pair-Share"

III. STRATEGIC: Tools for using the intelligences to enhance learning, expand creativity, and improve problem solving.
  • Multiple Intelligences Coaching Teams/Activities
  • Multiple Intelligence Roles in Cooperative Groups
  • Multiple Intelligence Use and Improvement Planning Charts
  • Individual Intelligence Access Tracking (effective "trigger" techniques)
  • Kitbag of Favorite Intelligence Tools (paints, music, symbols, etc.)

IV. REFLECTIVE: Tools for reflecting on how to use the intelligences and for integrating them into one's "repertoire for living."
  • "7-in-1" Activities (all seven intelligences involved in a task)
  • "Each One Teach One" (an intelligence skill/capacity)
  • Intelligence Capacities Analysis with Graphic Organizers
      Venn Diagram (compare and contrast)
      Web (attributes)
      Matrix (classification by different characteristics)
      T-Chart (looks like, sounds like, feels like)
  • Reflective Journals and Logs
  • Daily Intelligence Focus

Figure 5 "Meta-intelligence" Lesson Ideas

be a dynamic, continually evolving process that changes throughout one's life. Thus, intelligence assessment and evaluation should change with an individual's age as well.

In *Seven Ways of Knowing* I suggest five techniques for beginning to get a picture or profile of students' intelligence strengths and weaknesses. This information is important from at least two perspectives: (1) helping students develop a fuller spectrum of intellectual abilities for use in the classroom and, hopefully, in their lives beyond the classroom; and, (2) finding new strategies for utilizing students' stronger intelligences to help more students succeed in school. These intelligence assessment techniques are built on the presupposition that we as educators need to develop new skills of carefully observing students involved in the learning process. We can learn an immense amount about our students if we watch them more carefully, using the seven intelligences as a

guideline! A summary of the techniques presented in *Seven Ways of Knowing* follows.

Multiple Intelligences Assessment I: Toward Evaluation of Intelligence Profiles

Student Intelligence Watch   Create a list of behaviors to watch for, which may give you clues as to how a student processes information in a lesson. For example, watch for the "doodler," the one who can't sit still, the incessant questioner, the peer relations fanatic, the silent/reflective one, etc. Keep an observation checklist in which you consciously log students' behavior patterns during knowing/learning tasks over a two-week period. Write down your reflections on what you learn about their ways of knowing.

Intelligence Skill Games   Watch students while involving them in a series of skill games. Let them choose which game(s) to play and then carefully

META-INTELLIGENCE TOOLS EXPLANATION

1. **PEOPLE SEARCH**: Create a list of questions about different skills and abilities related to the seven intelligences. Have students interview each other to find those who are good at performing the various skills.

2. **SELF REPORT CARD**: Give students large index cards and have them write information about themselves on the card related to the seven intelligences. For example, have them note a physical feat they can perform, draw a symbol of how they feel today, or note a favorite song. Have them share and discuss their report cards with two other students, noting similarities and differences.

3. **"WRAPAROUND" PROCESSING**: At the end of a lesson or activity have each student draw a visual symbol that represents how they feel about the lesson or activity. Each student then shows the symbol to the rest of the class but may not talk about it. Other variations include making a physical gesture or movement, making a sound, humming a few bars from a song, and writing a short poem.

4. **RECOGNIZING OTHERS' CAPACITIES**: Have students create a checklist of things to watch for in others that indicate they are using their seven intelligences, such as drawing, creative writing, using physical skills on the playground, or displaying social skills or problem-solving skills. Have students observe each other for one week, noting their differences and similarities.

5. **SELF BEHAVIOR CHECKLIST**: Start students on an intelligence tracking log or diary. Have them stop and analyze their behavior three times during the day using the seven intelligences as a guideline. List specific things they did with different intelligence capacities, for example, counting your change at the store, or giving or following instructions to go someplace.

6. **MULTIPLE INTELLIGENCE ACTIVITY POSTERS**: Design a poster (or workbook) that contains seven different activities for students to perform, each activity utilizing one of the intelligences. Writing humorous limericks on serious topics, creating a number pattern to stump someone else, and drawing a picture that symbolizes a goal are possible activities.

7. **EXPLORING INTELLIGENCE CAPACITIES WITH A PARTNER**: Make up a set of cards with different intelligence tasks written on each card—for example, make up a dance about the changing seasons, paint a mural about life in the year 2090, or create a rap song about an issue in your school or community. Pairs of students get a stack of cards and together perform the assigned tasks. Make sure the partners discuss their feelings about, and comfort level with, the different tasks.

8. **SELF-EVALUATION TECHNIQUES**: Design a variety of ways for students to evaluate their performance in using the seven intelligences. For example, have them rank themselves on a scale of one to ten on their comfort level with a particular intelligence, rank the intelligences by their own preferred modality, or do a "PMI" analysis of each intelligence (P=pluses for me, M=minuses for me, I=interesting to me).

9. **INTELLIGENCE GAMES AND PROBLEM-SOLVING ACTIVITIES**: Provide students with games to play that are related to the intelligences, such as "Scrabble," "Pictionary," "Twister," "Checkers," or "Name That Tune." Or, give them a problem to work on and ask them to find seven different ways to solve it.

10. **INTELLIGENCES "THINK-PAIR-SHARE"**: Have students work in pairs and tell each other about times they used each of the seven intelligences. One speaks and the other listens. Each pair then joins another pair. Each set of partners now tells the others about its experiences with the seven intelligences.

11. **MULTIPLE INTELLIGENCES COACHING TEAMS**: Group students to ensure heterogeneity in terms of different intelligence strengths. Create a series of activities that can potentially engage the full spectrum of intelligence capacities. For example, their task in the teams is to help all members of the team learn how to complete the activity and to practice approaching a given activity using several different intelligences.

12. **MULTIPLE INTELLIGENCE ROLES IN COOPERATIVE GROUPS**: When using cooperative techniques to enhance classroom learning, assign roles to students that are related to the intelligences. For example, assign a visual recorder (engages team in the creation of pictures to go along with the written record), a thinking tracker (keeps record of the logical thought processes the teams uses), or an inter/intra-encourager (ensures the support, identity, and trust of the team and makes sure that the feelings of individual members are honored).

13. **MULTIPLE INTELLIGENCE USE AND IMPROVEMENT PLANNING CHARTS**: For each intelligence create two lists: 1) When do I most like to and when do I most need to use this intelligence? and 2) What are things I can do to improve or strengthen this intelligence in my life?

14. **INDIVIDUAL INTELLIGENCE ACCESS TRACKING**: Have students brainstorm all of the different types of "triggers" they can think of for the different intelligences. Then have each individual rank the team's list from "the one that works best for me" to "the one that may work for others but does nothing for me."

15. **KITBAG OF FAVORITE INTELLIGENCE TOOLS**: Give each student a cigar box with the assignment that they are to put into the box something that represents one favorite tool or strategy for each intelligence, for example, a set of water colors, a favorite piece of poetry, or an audio-cassette tape of music. Encourage students to include things that remind them of the seven ways of knowing and how they can use them every day.

16. **"7-IN-1" ACTIVITIES**: Any activity can be approached in multiple ways. Have students figure out how to accomplish otherwise-taken-for-granted tasks on at least seven different levels, for example, the process of going to the lunch room, straightening up the classroom at the end of the day, or organizing the class for a game during recess.

17. **"EACH ONE TEACH ONE"**: Have all students rank themselves for strongest intelligence and weakest intelligence. Pair students, matching a strength with a weakness. Have the stronger students work with the weaker to improve their skill with the intelligence in question; for example, teaching the other how to "see with the mind's eye," how to tell directions outside, or how to play a simple tune on a piano.

Figure 6 Meta-Intelligence Tools Explanation

META-INTELLIGENCE TOOLS EXPLANATION
(continued)

18. INTELLIGENCE CAPACITIES ANALYSIS WITH GRAPHIC ORGANIZERS:

Venn diagram—List unique characteristics of an intelligence in each circle and the common characteristics in the overlap of the circles. Try working with a seven-way Venn eventually.

Web—List as many defining attributes of a given intelligence as you can think of on the rays of the web. Star the critical attributes, that is, the ones that are unique to the given intelligence.

Matrix—Make a chart that has seven columns across the top (one for each intelligence) and several rows down the side for such categories as "senses involved," "when most often used," "practice ideas," and "career examples." Have students fill in the chart with what they know about each of the intelligences according to the side categories.

T-Chart—Make three columns and label the first "looks like," the second "sounds like," and the third "feels like." Analyze each intelligence by listing appropriate information in the columns.

19. REFLECTIVE JOURNALS AND LOGS: Have students do a daily journal/log entry related to the seven intelligences using such lead-ins as: "The intelligence that I used most today was__," "I had most trouble using _____intelligence today because ...," or "A key insight I had about my intelligences today is..."

20. DAILY INTELLIGENCE FOCUS: At the beginning of a week, name each day of the week as an intelligence emphasis day. During the day do everything you can to use and learn about the intelligence focus for the day. For example, try an innovative approach to a mundane task using an intelligence not usually involved, or try expressing your thoughts and opinions in unique ways that take you beyond talking, writing, and logic.

Figure 6 (continued)

watch what they do as they are playing the game. Suggested games include "Pictionary" (visual/spatial), "Charades" (body/kinesthetic), and crossword puzzles or word jumbles (verbal/linguistic). Have at least one game per intelligence. Remember, how students play a game may be as instructive as which game(s) they choose. Do this a number of times and keep a log of your observations.

Intelligence Attention Foci Show students a film or a play in which the intelligences are dramatically portrayed; for example, one that involves great music, person-to-person relationships, lots of physical action or physical skills, clever problem solving, vibrant colors, symbolism, or great dialogue. Afterwards, lead a discussion on the performance, listening carefully to what students focused their attention on, what "captured their imagination," and what they liked or disliked. See if you can catch a glimpse of different intelligences in students as they watch the same movie or play.

Complex Problem Solving Expose students to a problem situation complex enough to stimulate several intelligences in the effort to find a solution. Make sure students know they can do anything they want to reach a solution, such as drawing, talking to each other, or getting out of their seats. Remember, from the perspective of building an intelligence profile of your students, how they approach the problem is far more important than whether they get the "right" answer. So watch carefully what they do as they work.

Inventing Provide students with an opportunity to design or create something. Around the room set up different kinds of "laboratories," each having the tools and materials of a different intelligence. For example, set paints, clays, colored marking pens at one station; drums, rattles, a guitar, and harmonica at another station; and so on. Give students time to create whatever and however they want. Watch them carefully as they work, noting both the "lab" to which they were naturally drawn and what they do once they are involved in the act of creation.

Multiple Intelligences Assessment II: Toward Evaluation of Academic Progress

Student Portfolios Have students create a portfolio that contains a selection of things they have produced during a term. These should be items that demonstrate progress toward their goals. Let them decide what to put in their portfolios, but encourage them to include items that give evidence of how their thinking has changed during the term, show an improvement of skills, demonstrate increased self-reflection or growth in self-knowledge, and show examples of their "best work."

Student Journals/Logs Provide students with a special notebook. At the end of a lesson or unit, give students time to write, draw, or paint their own thoughts and reflections. For example, have them think about what they have been studying and them have them write about its meaning for them today. Ask them to reflect on how they can use it beyond the classroom situation. Have them do an entry before and after the lesson to express their moods and feelings. Ask them to write about how their studies have been important in the past and how they will be important in the future.

"Multi-modal" Testing Instruments Experiment with nontraditional ways—ways which go beyond verbal/linguistic and logical/mathematical ways of knowing—for students to demonstrate their knowledge of a topic. For example, a test involving bodily/kinesthetic knowing could be couched in terms of body movement itself, including gestures, physical action, role play, dance, or inventing. A test using visual/spatial knowing could involve drawing, painting, active imagination, and sculpting as the primary means by which students demonstrate what they have learned.

Intelligence Transfer Strategies Create strategies to help students gain the knowledge of a lesson using many different ways of knowing. Use their stronger intelligences to train the weaker ones. For example, a child who is not strong in grasping math concepts may understand if they are put to music or rap, or one who is weak in language arts skills may be helped if invited to act things out or to draw them. Next, create strategies to help students translate their knowledge into the intelligence forms most valued by our culture, namely verbal/linguistic and logical/mathematical.

Metacognitive Evaluation of Strategies Provide occasions for students to explore their own multiple intelligences. Lead them in exercises in which they learn how to activate or "trigger" each intelligence. Teach them practices for strengthening and improving their weaker intelligences. Give them opportunities to use the intelligences in daily classroom work. Help them discover ways to use the intelligences in their everyday lives beyond the classroom. In short, do anything that will help them develop their full intellectual potential and to be intelligent in as many ways as possible!

	HISTORY	LANGUAGE ARTS	SCIENCE
VERBAL/LINGUISTIC	Debate key controversial historical decisions for today	Write a modern-day sequel to a classical piece of literature	Verbally tell how to perform an experiment so that others can do it
LOGICAL/MATHEMATICAL	Trace the patterns of historical development in the West	Predict what will happen next in a story	Apply the accepted steps of the scientific method
VISUAL/SPATIAL	Create murals that tell the story of an historical period	Illustrate a piece of literature with color, images, and patterns	Draw patterns/images to illustrate different natural processes
BODY/KINESTHETIC	Act out great moments from the past in a modern context	Play "Guess what author/ piece of literature I am?" (charades)	Act out scientific processes, such as planetary rotation
MUSICAL/RHYTHMIC	Learn about various periods of history by analyzing their music	Illustrate a piece of literature with music, sound, and rhythm	Make a music tape to accompany different scientific processes
INTERPERSONAL	Learn about part of a period and teach it to team members	Practice joint storytelling or writing with a partner	Assign teams to do lab experiments and to report them to the class
INTRAPERSONAL	Imagine having dialogues from the past	Write a reflection on what you learn from literature that applies to life today	Keep a diary on discoveries about the self in science

Figure 7   Multiple Intelligences Lesson Ideas Matrix

GLOBAL STUDIES	MATHEMATICS	PRACTICAL ARTS	FINE ARTS
Conduct a nations-of-the-world "spelling and finding bee"	Write story problems in teams for other teams to solve	Explain to others how to make something while they follow	Write descriptions of famous art, music, and drama
Analyze a culture's development deductively and inductively	Work with manipulatives to learn math operations	Follow a recipe to make baked goods from scratch	Do scene/character analyses of a play using graphic organizers
Study other cultures through their painting and sculpture	Play "Math Jeopardy"—find the operations for answers	Create posters that show steps of an exercise routine	Have imaginary conversations with classical pieces of art
Learn to play games that are popular in different cultures	Physically embody geometry formulas/fractions of a whole	Teach and play a series of noncompetitive games	Create "living paintings/sculptures" of an idea or feeling
Learn about cultures through their music and rhythm	Write math operations, formulas, and problem-solving rap songs	Use music to improve computer keyboard skills	Learn math concepts embedded in musical/dance pieces
Conduct interviews with people from different cultures	Teach a partner to process and apply problems	Invent something new and teach others how to use it	Choreograph a dance about human relating and caring
Brainstorm gifts of different cultures for the individual self	Think/write about how math concepts help in daily living	Note your moods/feelings when working on a computer	Write a reflection on personal tastes in art, music, dance, drama

Figure 7 (continued)

REFERENCES

Armstrong, T. (1987). *In their own way.* Los Angeles: J.P. Tarcher.

Bellanca, J., & Fogarty, R. (1991). *Blueprints for thinking in the cooperative classroom.* Palatine, IL: Skylight Publishing.

Buzan, T. (1977). *Using both sides of your brain.* New York: E.P. Dutton.

Costa, A. (1991). *The school as a home for the mind.* Palatine, IL: Skylight Publishing.

Costa, A. (Ed.). (1985). *Developing minds.* Alexandria, VA: Association for Supervision and Curriculum Development.

Dickinson, D. (1987). *New developments in cognitive research.* Seattle: New Horizons for Learning.

Feuerstein, R. (1980). *Instrumental enrichment.* Baltimore: University Park Press.

Fogarty, R., & Bellanca, J. (1989). *Patterns for thinking: Patterns for transfer.* Palatine, IL: Skylight Publishing.

Gardner, H. (1985). *Frames of mind.* New York: Basic Books.

Gardner, H., & Walters, J. M. (1985). The development and education of intelligences. In *Essays on the Intellect.* Alexandria, VA: Association for Supervision and Curriculum Development.

Guilford, J. P. (1979). *Way beyond I.Q.: A triarchic theory of human intelligence.* New York: Cambridge University Press.

Harman, W., & Rheingold, H. (1985). *Higher creativity.* Los Angeles: J. P. Tarcher.

Houston, J. (1982). *The possible human.* Los Angeles: J.P. Tarcher.

Houston, J. (1980). *Life force.* New York: Dell.

Lazear, D. (1991a). *Seven ways of knowing: Teaching for multiple intelligences.* Palatine, IL: Skylight Publishing.

Lazear, D. (1991b). *Seven ways of teaching: The artistry of teaching with multiple intelligences.* Palatine, IL: Skylight Publishing.

Machado, L. A. (1980). *The right to be intelligent.* New York: Pergamon.

Sternberg, R. G. (1984). *Beyond I.Q.: A triarchic theory of human intelligence.* New York: Cambridge University Press.

THE MINDFUL MIDDLE SCHOOL: A SHIFTING PARADIGM

—

Elliot Y. Merenbloom

Unique opportunities exist in the middle school classroom for teaching thinking, a continuing educational goal. Thinking is a prerequisite for success in the learning process as well as in life itself. Opportunities to develop students' thinking emanate from the unique needs of middle school students, an approach to middle school curriculum based on these needs, and a team approach to the delivery of curriculum and instruction. Appropriate teaching strategies offer additional options to address the teaching of thinking in grades six, seven, and eight.

DEVELOPMENTAL NEEDS

First and foremost, the milieu of the middle school classroom should be based on an awareness of the physical, intellectual, social, emotional, and moral developmental needs of students in grades six, seven, and eight. Early adolescence is a period of extensive physical growth, with one blueprint for girls and a separate plan for boys. Puberty is the major physical event of this growth period. Girls enter puberty as early as eight and a half years of age, while boys tend to lag two years behind the girls. Students' individual differences and variations in growth patterns perplex

middle school educators. The middle school concept or notion of flexibility evolves from this developmental variance.

As a result of research on physical development, home-base or teacher/advisory programs have emerged in an effort to help students better understand and cope with these changes. To fulfill the guidance function of the middle school, teachers develop activities to explore such critical areas as decision making, resolving conflict, communication, understanding self and others, and study skills. As teachers plan for instruction, they should also recognize the short attention span, restlessness, and fatigue factors of their students. Adults must be sensitive to the feelings of students in the various stages of development and be careful not to reinforce feelings of inadequacy. Students also undergo a wide range of mental development between the ages of ten and fourteen. Piaget described a period of concrete operations (ages seven to eleven), followed by a period of formal operations (ages eleven to fifteen). In the period of formal operations, students begin to hypothesize; they utilize logic and reasoning in decision making. Yet, at this stage, they still have difficulty with concepts such as government and religion. Again, individual growth patterns exist.

The Shoreham-Wading River Middle School project (1987) in New York state describes teachers' efforts to become sensitive to the developmental levels of students and correlates these with requirements implicit in curricular tasks. As a result, teachers have made their lessons more concrete, have become more conscious of the move from the concrete to the abstract, and have witnessed enhanced learning.

All middle-level educators are keenly aware of the intensity of social-emotional development in the classroom and the corridors. Major topics in this area include group membership, self-concept enhancement, the need for catharsis, the ethnic identification process, sex role identification, peer approval, independence from adults, and the search for sophistication. Each of these is a major issue for the young adolescent. Thus, each has a great impact not only on the learning process, but also on all daily interactions.

Moral development is another area. School systems are becoming more aware of the importance of developing morals and values in the classroom and throughout the school community. In increasingly more cases, parents support the school's efforts. A common core of values suggests a guide to the creation of a moral education program. Such values include courtesy, critical inquiry, equality of opportunity, human worth and dignity, loyalty, knowledge, order, patriotism, responsibility, and tolerance.

The middle school structure offers a unique approach for teaching moral development, values education topics, and/or the common core of values. Topics can be introduced through the home-base or teacher/advisory program and then reinforced in the context of each subject area in the existing curriculum. As students realize the importance of these topics, they integrate or assimilate them more quickly.

Developmental needs of the early adolescent learner have implications for teaching thinking in the middle school classroom. Following are examples.

- Relate the content of the curriculum to the development of the students. Content in English, social studies, science, home economics, and music must connect to independence from adults, the search for sophistication, group membership, and other social-emotional topics. In designing the motivational element of the lesson, teachers should use examples based on students' developmental needs. The home-base program also must relate directly to immediate, ongoing student development issues.

- Help students explore the world around them and the relationship between the pupil and the world. In social studies, for example, students must learn about various cultures in the world and the role of the early adolescent in each of these cultures. Through concrete examples, students must learn the meaning of the historical, governmental, economic, sociological, and geographical aspects of the world around them. Students must begin to see the relationship between these systems and career opportunities available to them.

- Be keenly aware of the individual timetables for growth. As in elementary education, teachers must see each student as an individual. Each student has a personal schedule for maturation. Instruction must be adjusted to this pace because all students may not necessarily be able to do the same assignment at the same time. Teachers must individualize their expectations of students to be realistic about each pupil's potential.

- Relate thinking processes and core thinking skills to the development of the individual. In concept formation, concrete examples play a major role. According to the mental development of individual students, there is a variance in the rate of moving from the concrete to the abstract, as well as in putting ceilings on the capacity for abstraction. In teaching analyzing skills, middle school teachers may have one expectation for grade six and another for grade eight. But, each middle school student is an individual, and instruction must be geared to that uniqueness.

The middle school classroom must be viewed as the link between elementary and high school from both the developmental and instructional perspectives. In many ways, the middle school serves as a transitional experience further complicated by the fact that students grow at varying rates. The student leaves the self-contained elementary school environment and begins to mature. Even at the point of entering high school, differences are profound and obvious. Instructional strategies in the middle school must help the pupil evolve from a dependent, highly directed learner to a more independent, self-reliant, curious student in a variety of required and elected courses.

A MODEL FOR CURRICULUM

In response to these early adolescent needs, models of a middle school curriculum have emerged that focus on three major components—organized knowledge or factual information, skill development, and personal development.

Organized knowledge or factual information refers to all content or subject matter in all courses in the curriculum for grades six, seven, and eight. Typically, middle school students enroll in English, social studies, mathematics, science, reading, foreign language, art, music, physical education, home economics, technology education, and health. There must be a clear emphasis on factual information in each of these sequences. The middle-level learner is ready for the emphasis on concept formation, principle formation, gathering of information, and remembering.

Middle-level teachers also have an obligation to continue the emphasis on skill development that was paramount at the elementary school level. A focus on skills is necessary to continue and to expand the learning process. In addition to factual information, pupils must be taught how to learn. Typically, basic skill development includes reading, vocabulary development, comprehension, study skills, writing, computing, and listening. Core thinking skills include focusing, information gathering, remembering, organizing, analyzing, generating, integrating, and evaluating. These elements must be evident on a daily, hourly basis to enhance instruction.

Because of the significance of the changes in their physical, intellectual, social-emotional, and moral development, middle school students need an opportunity to understand these changes—whether they have occurred or have yet to take place. More significantly, students need assistance in adjusting to those changes. Personal development topics typically include understanding one's self and others, group dynamics, decision making, resolving conflict, careers, and communication. These must be addressed on a daily basis through the home-base advisory program and then reinforced in the curriculum whenever possible.

There are two applications of this curriculum model. First, each subject must focus on organized knowledge or factual information, skill development, and personal development. Curriculum developed for English, social studies, music, or technology education must allow students to learn about content, skills, and personal development related to that segment of the course of study. A balanced curriculum for any subject in grades six, seven, and eight contains all three elements.

Secondly, the team approach to instruction is based on a fusion of organized knowledge, skills, and personal development. As an interdisciplinary team of English, social studies, mathematics, and science teachers work together, they find opportunities to integrate content, create a skill-of-the-week program, and correlate personal development topics.

This three-part model for middle school curriculum unifies the efforts of all teachers of all subjects of a grade level in the middle school. Thus, the students begin to see the interrelationship of all learning and the wholeness of curriculum. The early adolescent needs to see purpose and relationship on an ongoing basis. The team approach to content, skills, and personal development is far superior to the efforts of seven or eight teachers working in isolation.

The teaching of thinking is both manifested and reinforced by this curriculum model. Concept formation, for example, may well be a function of organized knowledge. But, it may also be viewed as an important skill for the early adolescent learner to master. Additionally, if the content relates to some aspect of early adolescent development, the personal development phase of the curriculum may be involved as well. For example, at first, remembering may appear to be a skill. But, as the unit or lesson unfolds, remembering may also relate to content and personal development. What is the content to be remembered? Why is it important to remember this content? How does the act of remembering this content relate to the unique developmental needs of a middle school student?

The use of this curriculum model enhances the teaching of thinking. Students become more effective thinkers as well as more effective learners when teachers utilize this holistic approach to curriculum geared toward the early adolescent. Effective learning must be related to the developmental aspects of the student. Critical and creative thinking emerge as students see the interrelationship of content, skills, and personal development.

TEAM APPROACH TO INSTRUCTION

Obviously, the responsibility rests with teachers to deliver this unified approach to curriculum in general, and to the teaching of thinking in particular. Teachers must begin by addressing the role and function of a team. They must define the team and begin to examine their identity as a team. They need to explore their commitment to the middle school concept, how they will share their responsibilities, and how they will work to support each other. They must be aware of the limits of local autonomy as part of a team, school, and school district. To what extent will the team members use flexibility as they attempt to address student needs? To what extent will they have confidence in themselves and their colleagues to develop a meaningful program for their students?

Interdisciplinary teams involve two or more teachers working together to coordinate instruction in two or more subject areas. In most cases, interdisciplinary teams consist of an English, social studies, mathematics, and science teacher—ideally, all teachers of the grade level work together in an interdisciplinary fashion. In many cases, this approach is part of a restructuring or site-based leadership process.

Teachers must see the relationship between planning periods and the instructional program.

Almost all that happens in a team teaching situation results from plans developed during planning periods. In organizing middle schools, adequate time must be provided for teachers to brainstorm instructional concerns. Again, ideally, these team planning periods are in addition to personal planning periods for each teacher.

To enhance teacher awareness of the relationship between planning periods and the instructional program, teachers should

- examine their own curriculum guide to identify opportunities for correlation of content, skills, and personal development.
- share with teachers of other subjects those topics and skills that can be correlated to enhance the learning experiences of students.
- prepare a calendar so these unified learning experiences can be scheduled throughout the year.
- utilize team planning periods to arrange for field trips, films, and guest speakers.

A team planning log is suggested to help the team monitor the daily, weekly, and/or monthly operation. The log provides an opportunity to record specific correlations of content, skill-of-the-week emphases, personal development topics with reinforcement in all content areas, pupil adjustments, and efforts to accomplish team goals. The log ensures a balanced focus on the needs of students and the delivery of instruction, including the integrated effort on teaching thinking throughout all content areas. The team has numerous opportunities to orchestrate the focus on thinking skills. The log can be used to guarantee a variety of strategies to meet the needs of all students in an interesting, ongoing, and spiraling basis. Logs can also be used for planning in future years.

To truly ensure a balance between content and focus on children as well as a comprehensive effort to teach core thinking skills and processes, the team must utilize modalities of flexibility. Such measures include rotating schedules, modular subdivisions of time, alternate day rotations, as well as grouping and regrouping pupils for instruction. Using a block-of-time schedule, there is no limit to the options available to the team once members understand their local options and the importance of the totality of the curriculum in the eyes of students. Flexibility is the key to delivering a meaningful program to students.

Teachers should also be responsible for evaluating the team process. Rather than bring in an external source, teachers get an opportunity to examine their role and function on a regular, systematic basis. Perhaps a peer can look at what works well for the team rather than an outsider who does not understand the uniqueness of that school or team, or the needs of that student body.

CURRICULUM AS A TEAM EFFORT

What emerges in the middle school is a team effort for delivering curriculum to students. In the elementary school, one teacher is responsible for all academic instruction. In the high school, subject matter teachers work in isolation. Thus, the middle school provides a transitional experience in which a team of teachers can present the total curriculum via a unified effort. Beyond the mechanical elements of teaming—such as agendas, modular subdivisions of time, conferences with parents, approaches to discipline, team-building activities, and subgroupings—the major focus of the teaming process should be the unification of the curricula.

Each subject routinely has its own curriculum guide with a scope and sequence for English 7, Algebra I, Science 6, or Technology Education 8. These guides are developed by experienced professionals who have mastery of content, pedagogy, and an awareness of student needs. Bulletins are developed to guide teachers in the current trends of addressing students in grades six, seven, and eight. If it were not for opportunities for correlation, the middle school experience might be more like the high school than it currently is.

To achieve a totality of curriculum, teachers must make day-to-day connections, correlations, and extensions of content, skills, and personal development issues, plus create interdisciplinary units. Correlations of content might include the English teacher teaching a novel set during the American Revolution while the social studies teacher is teaching that historical period; the

French and social studies teachers teaching the concept of revolution concurrently; or the art and music teachers working together to design scenery for a musical production.

In a unified fashion, teachers may address basic skills such as using manuscript form, setting up a notebook, following directions, and outlining. They may also address some of the thinking processes, such as problem solving, researching, and composing in a comprehensive way. All teachers of the grade level may address personal development topics, such as growing up in various cultures, resolving conflict, and helping the special needs person. In some schools, teachers work together to create and teach interdisciplinary units on space, water resources, United States history, telecommunications, and other topics.

Teachers who move beyond their responsibility to teach a specific subject in which they are certified can work together to create a total curriculum that addresses student needs. Within this arena, there are numerous opportunities for teaching thinking skills using content, a skills menu, and personal development elements that appear in the combined curriculum plan for all the subjects of that grade.

In addition to unique opportunities for curriculum development, implementation, and evaluation, teachers in the middle grades have unique opportunities to orchestrate the teaching of thinking throughout all courses. It is necessary, therefore, for teachers to recognize the potential of this comprehensive approach as they begin to identify appropriate teaching strategies with references for teaching thinking. No middle school teacher should approach the teaching of a specific strategy in isolation. Rather, there should be communication among all teachers to identify the most appropriate ways to teach these strategies concurrently.

APPROPRIATE STRATEGIES FOR TEACHING THINKING

A focus on teaching thinking skills via appropriate strategies for the early adolescent must be viewed in the context of student needs, an appropriate model for curriculum, and the team process. The

CREATING THE THOUGHTFUL CLASSROOM

following techniques are appropriate for routine instruction of the early adolescent as well as for specific emphasis on teaching thinking.

Provide Clear, Concise Structure for all Activities

The early adolescent learner has a great need for structure. It must be evident in every aspect of the instructional process because the student must know exactly what to do for each activity. A teacher planning a vocabulary activity must review the directions orally and write them on the chalkboard so students can refer to them later, should the need arise.

From this common beginning point, the teacher can then ask a number of questions to promote the thinking process. Questions can reflect material previously taught as well as material to be presented. Teachers must also anticipate the kinds of questions students will ask as they complete a particular activity. Instructions should be given on a step-by-step basis, and teachers should not assume that all students can see the interrelationship between the steps. To promote critical and creative thinking, flow charts are helpful when teachers present a series of tasks to students. With structure, the student can perform various dimensions of the thinking process.

Clarify Purposes for Each Activity

Pupils must know exactly why they are asked to complete a certain activity or answer a particular question within the scope of an activity. For example, in mathematics, pupils must realize the importance of studying percents as readiness to answer a verifying question about the accuracy of a response. In science, students must know the importance of safety as they work with the Bunsen burner in an information-gathering activity.

If students are aware of purposes for learning new information, they are more willing to participate in activities and assess their performance in relationship to these purposes. Without a stated purpose, pupils may not show the necessary enthusiasm for completing a meaningful activity. The teaching of thinking must be fully integrated with purposes for each activity. The sequence of thinking skills activities must be designed to help students become increasingly independent learners.

Provide Adequate Motivation, Readiness, and Goal Setting

Once purposes are clearly established, teachers must make an overt effort to provide motivation and readiness that guarantee students are prepared for the thinking process. A specific effort to get pupils interested in the topic is often needed; it should be a concrete activity drawn from the realities of the early adolescent experience.

Teachers must monitor students' responses to motivational activities before continuing with any thinking process or core thinking skill in a lesson plan. Teachers who preplan key questions to establish the relationship between the purposes of the lesson and the motivational activity enhance both thinking and learning.

Effective readiness in the middle grades includes preparation for content as well as skills. The student should receive separate motivation for content and skill. By the conclusion of the readiness portion of the lesson, the pupil should clearly see the relationship between the content and skill and be prepared to complete the activity with a high degree of enthusiasm.

Instruction for middle-level students must be goal oriented. Goals relate to content, skills, and/or the personal development phases of middle school curriculum. Teachers enhance goal setting by asking questions that enable the student to see the connections between content, skills, and personal development.

Utilize Recall Strategies

Without a carefully structured routine, students will not be able to recall the content of previous lessons. A student may attend social studies class during period one on Friday and return for the next meeting period seven on Monday. Much time passes between these class meetings, and many events may happen in the student's life in that time.

Recall, therefore, must provide a very careful link between the most recent instruction in a subject and the thrust of today's lesson. Recall questions, however, do not always have to be lower-order questions. Teachers can provide opportunities for students to recall previous instruction and identify implications concurrently. Recall is generally accomplished via a series of open-ended questions that help students see the connection between prior learning and the current lesson. The varying needs of students can be satisfied by altering the types of questions posed. Questions should require students to use various levels of thinking throughout the recall process. These questions should be individualized to the uniqueness of each student.

Provide Transitions to Connect Various Activities Within the Lesson

To satisfy the need for variety, an effective lesson for middle school students consists of several activities designed to accomplish one or more goals. Although the teacher may easily see the relationship between these activities, it is imperative that students recognize the relationships. Transitions make these connections.

An effective transition consists of a summary statement of the previous activity, a preview of the next activity, and an understanding of the relationship between the two parts. Knowledge, comprehension, application, analysis, synthesis, and evaluation questions may be used to facilitate transitions, which should be inductive whenever possible. A transition must be included to connect every activity in every lesson. Student thinking becomes focused as a function of these transitions.

Know the Cognitive Levels of Students

Middle school teachers must be as keenly aware of cognitive levels as they are of reading, mathematics, and IQ levels. Students in grades six, seven, and eight are typically at one of Piaget's stages of cognitive development. Piaget described a period of concrete operations in which students could comprehend concrete concepts or realities. This stage is followed by a period of formal operations in which students begin to hypothesize and use logic. All students do not enter these stages at the same time, and these stages can be subdivided as indicated by the terms *pre-operational, concrete onset, concrete mature, formal onset,* and *formal mature.*

Teachers should call on students at appropriate times in light of the students' cognitive levels. Meaningful questions about concrete material should be directed to students at pre-operational

or concrete onset. Questions that involve more abstract thinking should be reserved for those who are at formal onset or formal mature stages. Through critical and creative thinking, thinking processes, and core thinking skills, teachers have a responsibility to help expand students' cognitive levels. Although some students may never reach the formal mature status, middle school teachers should ask questions that are appropriate to the levels of their students' development and help students expand their thinking as much as possible.

Move from the Concrete to the Abstract in the Concept Development Process

Each activity should begin with a concrete example. Thus, lessons should move from the concrete or specific to the abstract or more general and theoretical. A simulation, picture, model, advertisement, or slide can be used to begin the thinking process. Whenever possible, teachers should permit students to see, feel, or touch these concrete examples. Knowledge and comprehension questions can be used to assess students' understanding of the concrete examples.

As the lesson unfolds, students should move their thinking to the abstract. Even though this may not be possible for every student, the teacher should facilitate movement in that direction but also keep in touch with students who may have difficulty going beyond the concrete. In exploring such abstract notions as democracy, photosynthesis, or irony, teachers must move slowly and assess student comprehension at regular intervals. Teachers should be able to assess cognitive levels of students, determine cognitive demands of curricula, and create a more appropriate match between the two.

Construct Effective Questions to Accomplish Objectives of the Lesson

Teachers must realize that the content of their questions affects how students process information. In preparing for instruction, teachers should plan key questions and include them in the formal lesson plan. To the greatest extent possible, questions should be open ended and designed to increase students' creative and critical thinking abilities.

Specifically, teachers should conduct a self-assessment of their questions by asking the following:

Are my questions clear and concise?

Do they help achieve the objective of the lesson?

Do I ask one question at a time?

Do I ask each question only once?

Do my questions elicit concepts as well as facts?

Do I call on a student after the question has been asked?

Questions are often the key to the success of the lesson. Teachers must critically evaluate their skills in asking questions according to specific objectives of a lesson or activity. Questions play a major factor in moving from concrete to abstract, facilitating learning, and encouraging students to think.

Use Wait Time Effectively

Wait time is defined as the length of the silent period following the presentation of a question and prior to the initial student response to that question. Wait time also includes the time between a student response and the next student response. Typically, the average teacher waits only one second for an answer. But, a longer wait time has been found to have a positive effect on the quality of teacher-pupil interactions and achievement in science lessons. Teachers should extend pauses before beginning explanations, giving directions, asking questions, or reacting to pupils' talk. These pauses give each student additional time to formulate an answer. Thus, there is a greater chance for all students to participate in the ensuing discussion.

By increasing wait time to five seconds, teachers may anticipate (1) lengthier student responses, (2) whole sentence replies, (3) more student questions, (4) revised teacher expectations of students, and (5) a greater variety of teacher questions. The correlation between wait time and encouraging thinking skills is significant for early adolescent learners. These students might be reluctant to even try to answer a question if they assume someone else will be ready to answer earlier. In addition, self-concept of the early adolescent is enhanced when all students receive a more reasonable amount of time to react to stimuli and participate in the learning process.

Provide a Summary or Assessment

Middle school students depend on a summary at the end of each activity or lesson to announce closure. Thinking and learning are enhanced when there is a definite starting and stopping point for lessons or segments of lessons. It is essential that students are fully aware of the starting and stopping points of each activity during the fifty minutes of an English or social studies class.

Assessment can be accomplished by way of a specific activity or a series of directed questions. Students state what they learned during the lesson as well as what they anticipate happening next in the learning process. Assessment can be on a group or an individual basis. Teachers should answer all students' questions and concerns prior to dismissing class.

By analyzing student responses in the summary, the teacher can be comfortable knowing that concerns are resolved. Teachers can determine changes in student thinking and learning behaviors as they assess responses in a portion of the lesson. Finally, teachers should be aware of the kinds of thinking they expect students to demonstrate at each point in the lesson.

Facilitate Student-to-Student Interaction

Traditional secondary teaching has been characterized by a pattern of a teacher's statement followed by a student's statement. The teacher asks a question, a student answers the question, and then the teacher asks the next question. However, the middle school classroom should feature many opportunities for student-to-student interaction. Cooperative learning strategies respond to the learning needs of the early adolescent. Students should interact with one another on mathematic problems, science laboratory experiments, charts and graphs in social studies, and the plot of a novel in English. In these cooperative activities, pupils have an opportunity to practice information gathering, organizing, analyzing, integrating, and evaluating skills.

Assign Team Tasks

Teams or small-group tasks extend student-to-student interaction and involve groups of students working on specific thinking skills. This approach responds to the social-emotional development of early adolescents, but it must be carefully supervised to keep competition in control. Team tasks are especially motivational for students who need peer pressure to expand their thinking horizons. Teachers of all subject areas are encouraged to find opportunities to teach thinking skills through small-group tasks. Time limits for these activities should then be clearly delineated.

Create Simulation and Game Techniques

Early adolescent students enjoy opportunities to enhance their thinking skills when teachers provide simulations and games within the structure of the classroom. Simulations and games provide all students the same readiness or prerequisites for thinking and learning. Social studies teachers have numerous opportunities to create simulations of topics in history, economics, or sociology. Technology education teachers utilize the assembly line process to encourage critical and creative thinking.

These simulations and games give all students a chance to experience an activity. After the simulation or game experience, the teacher may ask analysis, synthesis, and evaluation questions to help students comprehend and analyze what occurred. Beyond participation in the simulation, learning also takes place in the post-simulation thinking activities.

Anticipate and Prevent Problems

The successful middle school teacher anticipates problems that may occur in the classroom, on a field trip, or during any aspect of the learning process. By anticipating and preventing problems, the environment for learning is safer. Pupils are then willing to take the risks involved in learning. For example, pupils will try to answer a higher-order question when they feel the environment is secure and protected. Although initially leery of taking a risk, students will take a chance when student-teacher rapport is perceived to be positive. Thus, thinking is encouraged when the caring teacher provides the environment for students to take a risk.

Focus on Affective Issues

Thinking is enhanced when middle school teachers address affective or emotional topics that arise

in the course of the lesson. The science teacher may need to take a few minutes from the explanation of a scientific principle to resolve an altercation between two students in the classroom. A student who experienced abuse at home may feel comfortable sharing that information with the teacher. Thus, teachers should be concerned with affective issues, not just their subject matter. The more comfortable the student feels in a given classroom, the more likely it is the student will fully participate in the learning process.

Praise, Don't Criticize

Like adults, middle school students respond best to praise. All teachers must take the time to find ways to praise students in a manner that is accepted and respected by both the student receiving the praise and others in the classroom. Learning increases when teachers use a variety of terms to dispense praise, so as not to seem too mechanical. Although teachers are quick to point out shortcomings of students, they should find ways to inform parents of students' positive accomplishments. The appropriate use of praise reinforces and facilitates all aspects of the thinking and learning processes.

Appropriate strategies for teaching thinking are closely aligned with needs of the early adolescent learner. Some strategies can be utilized by every teacher in every classroom. Others may be utilized under certain conditions but in every content area. Some suggestions address the nature of the learning environment—a critical issue for the middle school student.

SUMMARY

Using the interdisciplinary team model, middle school teachers have unique opportunities to teach thinking skills in the context of the total curriculum. The early adolescent learner benefits when all teachers address common thinking skills within each subject. The development of these higher-level thinking skills enables all students to perform to their capacity in secondary education and beyond. Through team and faculty meetings, teachers can identify specific teaching strategies that respond to the physical, intellectual, social-emotional, and moral needs of this age group. Staff development should provide the entire faculty with the precise modalities of skill development and concept formation appropriate to the middle-level student.

———

REFERENCES

Alexander, W., Williams, E., Compton, M., Hines, V., Prescott, D., & Kealy, R. (1969). *The emergent middle school* (2nd ed.). New York: Holt, Rinehart and Winston.

Baltimore County (Maryland) Public Schools. (1983). *1984 and beyond: A reaffirmation of values.* Towson, MD: Author.

Baltimore County (Maryland) Public Schools. (1983). *Question power.* Towson, MD: Author.

Fusco, E. and Associates. (1987). *Cognitive matched instruction in action.* Columbus, OH: National Middle School Association.

Lomax, R. G., & Cooley, W. W. (1980). The student achievement instructional time relationship. Paper presented at the Annual Meeting of the American Educational Research Association, Boston, MA.

Marzano, R. J., Brandt, R. S., Hughes, C., Jones, B. F., Presseisen, B., Rankin, S., & Suhor, C. (1988). *Dimensions of thinking: A framework for curriculum and instruction.* Alexandria, VA: Association for Supervision and Curriculum Development.

Merenbloom, E. Y. (1991). *The team process: A handbook for teachers.* Columbus, OH: National Middle School Association.

Tobin, K. G. (1980). The effect of an extended teacher wait-time on science achievement. *Journal of Research in Science Teaching, 17,* 469-475.

CLASSROOM 2001:
EVOLUTION, NOT REVOLUTION

—

James Bellanca

How will students in the 21st century learn? What will they learn? When and where will they learn it? First, it is likely that 21st-century students will trudge off to the same school buildings, file into the same classrooms, and spend the same hours each day as their 20th-century counterparts. On the other hand, it is also likely that the 21st-century students will work more regularly with electronic technology, pose and solve more problems, collaborate in more decisions about how they learn, evaluate more purposefully their own progress, and cover far more content than they would have done in the previous century. They are likely to integrate such learning in their efforts to research, organize information, and reason.

Whatever meaningful changes that come in the next decade will start in the classroom. There, teachers, provided with a different curriculum and new technology, will integrate instructional approaches to accomplish complex and thoughtful outcomes. Teachers such as Virginia's Pat Taylor, Chicago's Linda Gaddis, and Palatine's Elsie Brownawell will challenge children to learn how to learn, and how to transfer that learning.

Pat Taylor teaches geometry in a multi-age, heterogeneous secondary classroom in Chesterfield County, Virginia. Unlike her colleagues, who teach a sequence of chapters from the text, Taylor integrates geometry concepts such as "circles" with the thinking skill "estimating," and cooperative learning strategies. Using manipulatives to help her multi-ability and multi-age students grasp the meanings of radius, circumference, and pi as these relate to estimation of circle size, Taylor guides her students through a variety of hands-on tasks. At the formal lesson's end, each of Taylor's students return to a computer terminal to demonstrate the ability to solve abstract algorithms and apply the new concepts with a variety of visual and abstract software-generated estimation problems, and assess the quality of their problem solving.

Linda Gaddis, a Chicago teacher, works in a seventh grade science classroom filled with forty-two high-risk students. Because her school's mission focuses on basic skill achievement, she integrates the science lesson with reading comprehension. In one lesson, teams of students work with graphic webs to identify keys to survival in space from their reading assignments. After discussing the pros and cons of their ideas, Gaddis moves among the student groups. At one station she helps students rethink problem-solving steps. At another she checks a print-out. At a third, she answers a question and redirects the students to a more appropriate application of their selection. The teams next move to four computer stations where they use a matrix to plan stories about their imaginary trips to space, help each other edit, and prepare all class presentations. After celebration of their accomplishments, she guides the groups in a thoughtful assessment of their work.

Elsie Brownawell teaches a kindergarten class with students from twelve cultures. This morning, she starts their science lesson with a review of yesterday's field trip. On a blackboard matrix, she writes the words her students use to describe the trees they examined on their walk. The matrix categorizes words that describe sights, sounds, smells, and touches. After the list is finished, Brownawell reviews pronunciation and meaning before she introduces a new word, "infer." She explains the word with several examples generated from her master terminal to an overhead screen. Next, she introduces their task. Because she has prepared them to work in cooperative groups, she is able to expedite their movement with a quick review of the task, the job each will do in group, and the cooperative rules. To each group, she hands a box, filled with mystery objects (leaves, bark), and a worksheet. The student teams go to work "inferring" what they find in each box. After the teams have worked with each box, ensuring that each member can pronounce the words, they return to their computer terminals to draw a picture that puts all the parts together. A touch screen enables them to label each part of the drawing. Brownawell works her way among the teams as she encourages, redirects their thinking with questions and comments, and helps them think about their thinking.

These vignettes describe engaged students guided by well- trained teachers skilled in a variety of instructional roles in their 1990s classrooms. The first half of each vignette describes a real lesson taught in the integrated instructional style the teacher uses throughout the year. Cooperative learning, integrated curricula, thinking skills, and concept development are practices familiar to all their students. What these classrooms lack are the electronic tools to extend and to simplify the instruction in the manner described on the second half of each vignette.

The shift from 1990s-style instruction to instruction for the 21st century will require two essential changes. First, each classroom will need the electronic tools to extend and simplify both curriculum and instruction. Second, each classroom will need a teacher trained with the skills to manage integrated instruction and integrated curricula for all students without regard to ability, race, talent, special need, or motivation.

The electronic classroom will contain at least four multimedia computer workstations. At each station, networked software will enable students to *gather* information from a school library of print and graphic video materials to access databases external to the schoolplace; to *process* information with a variety of mindware work tools; and *apply* information in a variety of media formats. To supplement each computer station, the classroom will have hands-on science, art, and mathematics labs, a library of social studies and language arts books, video and computer projection machines, and audio and video recorders. Teachers will have the opportunity to use computer and video projector equipment for large-group instruction, displays, and feedback on student work. They will assign students to work in cooperative groups at the electronic workstations, at lab stations, or in discussion clusters. Most importantly, teachers will have management software that enables them to guide and assess individual and group progress through the increasingly divergent electronics curricula; develop a personal log with feedback from teacher assessments, self-assessments, and peer assessments; and construct an electronic portfolio that maps completed work and conceptual and social development.

Second, every classroom in 2001 will need a teacher well trained to integrate instruction in the electronic classroom. This means she or he will need to know how to best access curricular content,

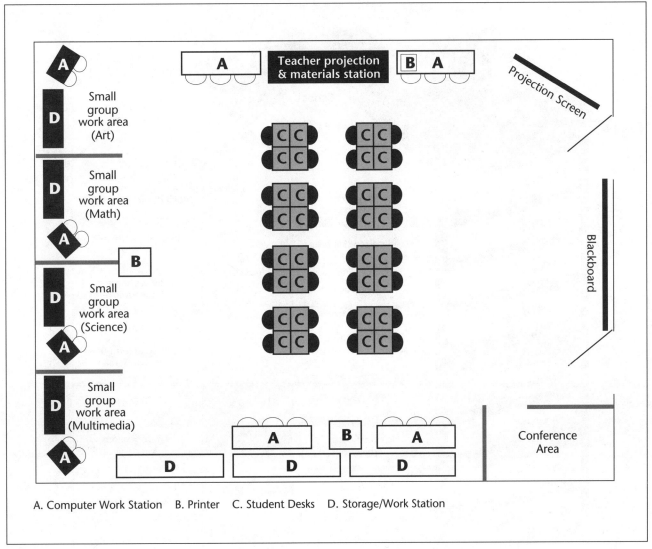

Figure 1   Classroom 2001

how to manipulate multi-media software, how to maintain a cooperative and creative work climate, how to structure computer-based inquiry across curricular areas, how to stimulate metacognitive transfer, and how to use the computer to assess and manage the individual progress of each student.

There are three predictable roadblocks that will slow this evolution: First, inadequate *hardware and software*; second, inadequate *staff development*; third, a prevailing *split view* of education.

The Software. The key to multimedia programs for the classroom is the CD/ROM. Current software and equipment is available, but at a high cost. As development of CD/ROM high-end graphics and video tools progresses, the availability of qual-

ity programs at lower cost will make it easier for schools to install electronic classrooms.

Staff Development. School districts will need to restructure how they think about staff development. In the best district staff development programs, there is an understanding that every teacher needs the opportunity to be a life-long learner. They know that the complexities of integrating cooperative learning, thinking, curricular areas, and technology require a financial commitment, time allocation, and a support system that go well beyond the scattered and unfocused development opportunities most 1990s teachers are provided. To foster the depth and extension of staff development needed for the electronic classroom,

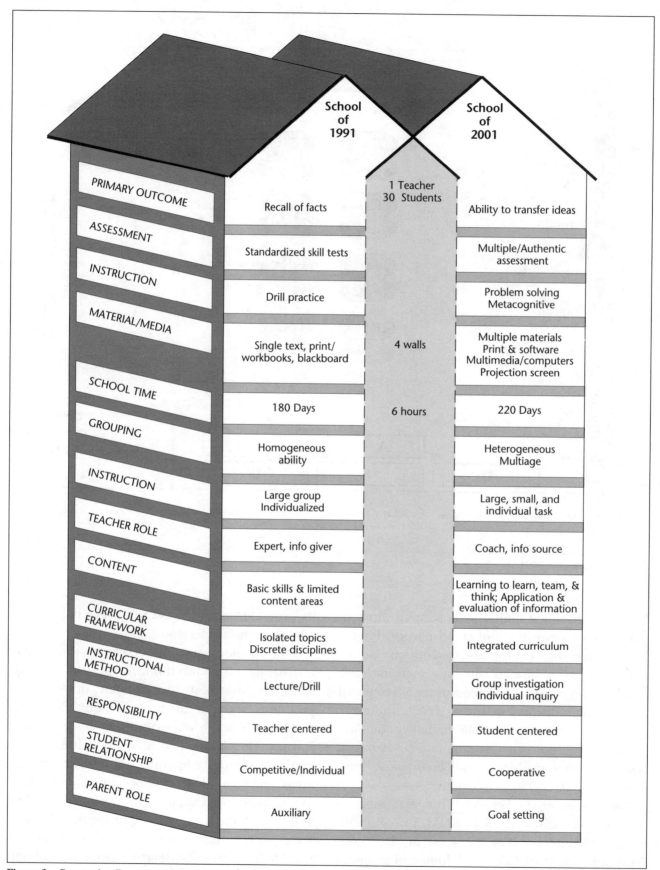

Figure 2   Comparing Present and Future

it is likely that districts will need to extend the school year by at least two weeks for no other purpose than staff development.

The Split View. This nation has a split view of education. On the one hand, some see the role of education as the mastery of basic skills. They want to use a battery of local, state, and national tests to ensure that "correct facts" and basic skills are acquired by all. Others argue that facts and skills, however necessary, are not sufficient for schooling in the 21st century. They argue for thinking, conceptualizing, cooperating, technology, and authentic assessment of the "whole" learner. If there is any chance for the electronic classroom to succeed, this either/or mindset must give way. It is important that basic skill development occur as students build toward more complex thinking tasks in all content areas.

This dual transformation is a process of evolution, not revolution. The three teacher examples described illustrate that a strong staff development program can move the theory into practice. As each of the teacher models attests, integrated instruction coupled with integrated curricula, electronic tools, and authentic assessment can result in students who are prepared for the 21st century. Step by step, instruction will change.

REFERENCES

Bellanca, J. (1991). *Building a caring, cooperative classroom.* Palatine, IL: Skylight Publishing.

Bellanca, J. (1990). *The cooperative think tank.* Palatine, IL: Skylight Publishing.

Bellanca, J., & Fogarty, R. (1991). *Blueprints for thinking in the cooperative classroom.* Palatine, IL: Skylight Publishing.

Brown, R. (1991). *Schools of thought: How the politics of literacy shape thinking in the classroom.* San Francisco: Jossey-Bass.

Brownlie, F., Close, S., & Wingren, L. (1990). *Tomorrow's classroom today: Strategies for creating active readers, writers, and thinkers.* Markham, Ontario: Pembroke.

Costa, A. L. (1991). *The school as a home for the mind.* Palatine, IL: Skylight Publishing.

Fogarty, R. (1991). *How to integrate the curricula.* Palatine, IL: Skylight Publishing.

Fullan, M. G. (1991). *The new meaning of educational change.* New York: Teachers College Press.

Hergert, L. F., Phlegar, J. M., & Pérez-Sellés, M. E. (1991). *Kindle the spark: An action guide for schools committed to the success of every child.* Andover, MA: The Regional Laboratory for Educational Improvement of the Northeast and Islands.

North Central Regional Educational Laboratory. (1990). *Restructuring to promote learning in America's schools* (nine-part video series). Oak Brook, IL: Author.

Sarason, S. B. (1990). *The predictable failure of educational reform: Can we change course before it's too late?* San Francisco: Jossey-Bass.

Spencer, L. S. (1989). *Winning through participation: Meeting the challenge of corporate change with the technology of participation.* Dubuque, IA: Kendall/Hunt.

CREATING COOPERATIVE LEARNERS

The ancient fable, "The Lion and the Mouse" provides insights about the value of living, working, and learning together. The mighty king of beasts captures a tiny mouse. The frightened mouse begs for her life. Moved by her pleas, her logic, and his own vanity, the lion roars with laughter, but sets the mouse free. Sometime later, while wandering through the forest, the mouse hears again the lion's mighty roar. This time, however, the mouse notices a cry laced with fear and pain. Investigating, the mouse finds the mighty lion trapped in a hunter's net. As human voices grow nearer, the mouse springs into action and gnaws through the ropes until the thankful lion springs free. Enlightened by his experience with the mouse's quiet courage, the mighty lion understands how caring can provide a special strength, a strength that in all his royalty he did not possess.

At first glance, the lion and the mouse seem to have little in common. Yet, the great king of beasts learns that his natural gifts are not the sole solution to every problem. Likewise, the tiny mouse, who appears so ineffectual and dependent, discovers she has mighty gifts that are indeed necessary for survival. Her quick thinking under pressure, her ability to chew, her size, her courage, and her willingness to sacrifice upstage the lion's "I can do it all myself" individualism.

When first introduced to cooperative learning, some students complain, "Why do we have to work with _____?" Like the lion, a significant number of students look superficially at their peers, make snap judgments, and strive to preserve their own self-centered, individualistic ways. Cooperative learning, when well-implemented in the classroom, enables these lion-like individualists to discover the value of accepting different talents and skills as valuable tools for learning. In essence, just as the mighty lion and the little mouse discovered the wonderment of collaboration, so too students in cooperative classrooms can learn the value of using their seemingly divergent talents and skills in constructive concert.

Cooperative learning has been cited as a means for developing intellectual skills. In this section, Johnson and Johnson support this contention. They note that there are strong positive effects on achievement as well as the ability to think critically, to perform higher-order thinking, to display more effective reasoning, and to think more creatively when working in a group. Other authors bear out the Johnsons' research with supportive descriptions from practice. They indicate that problem-solving and critical-thinking skills can best be experienced, practiced, analyzed, and applied in collaborative settings.

However, these behaviors should be considered more than mere by-products of teaching cooperative learning; they should become the intentions, goals, and outcomes of cooperative learning.

> *Every function in…cultural development appears twice: first, on the social level, and later on the individual level; first between people (interpsychological), and then inside (intrapsychological).*
>
> —Vygotsky, 1978

This capacity is called "co-cognition"—the capacity to think together. Co-cognition is a particularly fitting concept since the workplace our students will experience in the future will necessitate group problem-solving skills. The growth of intelligence of individuals and of organizations depends on their ability to think together: to resolve conflicts, empathize, value diversity of opinion, and seek consensus. As the articles in this section attest, the payoffs are powerful and far-removed from practices that simply "get students into groups."

COOPERATIVE LEARNING:
A THEORY BASE

—

David W. Johnson and Roger T. Johnson

R esearch on social interdependence began in the late 1800s when Triplett in the United States, Turner in England, and Mayer in Germany conducted a series of studies on the factors associated with competitive performance. Research on group versus individual performance dominated in the 1920s and 1930s, leading to a review of the research on cooperation and competition by May and Doob (1937). In the 1940s Morton Deutsch, building on the theorizing of Kurt Lewin, proposed a theory of cooperation and competition that has served as the primary foundation on which subsequent research and discussion of cooperative learning has been based. Our own theorizing and research is directly based on Deutsch's work. During the past ninety years over 550 experimental and 100 correlational studies have been conducted by a wide variety of researchers, with different age subjects, in different subject areas, and in different settings (see Johnson & Johnson, 1989a, for a complete listing and review of these studies). In our own research program at the Cooperative Learning Center at the University of Minnesota, over the past twenty-five years we have conducted over eighty-five studies to refine our understanding of how cooperation works. We know far more about the efficacy of cooperative learning than we know about lecturing, departmentalization, the use of technology, or almost any other facet of education. With the amount of research evidence available, it is surprising and even alarming that classroom practice is so oriented toward individualistic and competitive learning. It is time for the discrepancy to be reduced between what research indicates is effective and what students, teachers, and administrators actually do.

This chapter presents a broad overview of the theory and research on cooperative learning as a research-based school practice. Cooperation has been blessed with a well-formulated, strategic, and powerful theory and considerable research evidence verifying its effectiveness. The research has also identified a series of variables mediating the efficacy of cooperation. There have been numerous operationalizations of cooperative learning developed, which may be classified along a continuum of direct to conceptual approaches. Finally, what is good for students is even better for faculty. Cooperative learning is part of a basic change in organizational structure from a competitive-individualistic, "mass manufacturing" model of organizing to a high-performance, team-based organizational structure.

DEFINITION OF SOCIAL INTERDEPENDENCE

Together we stand, divided we fall.—Watchword of the American Revolution

Social interdependence exists when the outcomes of individuals are affected by each other's actions (Johnson & Johnson, 1989a). There are two types of social interdependence: cooperative, which is based on positive interdependence, and competitive, which is based on negative interdependence. Interdependence may be differentiated from dependence and independence. **Social dependence** exists when the outcomes of Person A are affected by Person B's actions, but the reverse is not true. **Social independence** exists when individuals' outcomes are unaffected by each other's actions. The absence of social interdependence and dependence results in individualistic efforts. **Cooperation** is working together to accomplish shared goals. In cooperative situations, the goal attainments of participants are positively correlated; individuals perceive that they can reach their goals if and only if the other group members also do so (Deutsch, 1949). Thus, an individual seeks an outcome that is personally beneficial and beneficial to all other individuals with whom the person is cooperatively linked. **Competition** is individuals working against each other to achieve a goal that only one or a few can attain. In competitive situations, the goals of the separate participants are so linked that there is a negative correlation among their goal attainments; each individual perceives that he or she can reach his or her goal if and only if the other participants cannot attain their goals (Deutsch, 1949). Thus, individuals seek an outcome that is personally beneficial but detrimental to all others in the situation. **Individualistic efforts** exist when individuals work by themselves to accomplish goals unrelated to those of others. In individualistic situations, there is no correlation among participants' goal attainments; each individual perceives that he or she can reach his or her goal regardless of whether other individuals attain their goals (Deutsch, 1962; Johnson & Johnson, 1975/1991). Thus individuals seek an outcome that is personally beneficial.

In the ideal classroom, all students would learn how to work cooperatively with others, compete for fun and enjoyment, and work autonomously on their own. The teacher decides which goal structure to implement within each lesson. Two interrelated questions are: (a) under what conditions will cooperative, competitive, and individualistic efforts affect desired instruction outcomes, and (b) what variables mediate the effectiveness of these efforts. In considering these two questions, only cooperation is dealt with in this chapter. The conditions under which competitive and individualistic learning may be productively used are discussed in Johnson and Johnson (1975/1991). This chapter focuses on the appropriate use of cooperation, as it is the most powerful and important, and least utilized, of the three.

WHAT DO WE KNOW ABOUT COOPERATIVE EFFORTS?

Everyone has to work together; if we can't get everybody working toward common goals, nothing is going to happen.—Harold K. Sperlich, President, Chrysler Corporation

Deutsch's original theory (1949) has served as a major conceptual structure for this area of inquiry for the past forty years. His pioneering theory and research evolved from Kurt Lewin's field theory (1935, 1948). Lewin stated that the essence of a group is the interdependence among members (created by common goals), which results in the group being a "dynamic whole" so that a change in the state of any member or subgroup changes the state of any other member or subgroup. He also noted that an intrinsic state of tension between group members motivates movement toward the accomplishment of the desired common goals.

Deutsch (1949, 1962), in his theory of how the tension systems of different people may be interrelated, conceptualized two types of social interdependence—cooperative and competitive. He defined individualistic efforts as the absence of interdependence. Deutsch's theory was based on two basic continua: one relating to the type of interdependence among the goals of the people involved in a given situation and one relating to the type of actions taken by the people involved. He identified as the ends of one continuum two basic types of goal interdependence. One is promotive: where the goals are positively linked in such a way that the probability of one person obtaining his or her goal is positively correlated with the probability of others' obtaining their goals. The other is contrient: where goals are negatively linked in such a way that the probability of one person obtaining his or her goal is negatively correlated with the probability of others' obtaining their goals. He identified as the ends of the second continuum two basic types of actions by an individual: effective (which improves the person's chances of obtaining a goal) and bungling (which decreases the person's chances of obtaining a goal).

He then combined the two continua to posit how they jointly affect three basic social psychological processes: substitutability, cathexis (i.e., the investment of psychological energy in objects and events outside of oneself), and inducibility (i.e., openness to influence). Essentially, in cooperative situations the actions of participants substitute for each other, participants positively cathect to each other's effective actions, and there is high inducibility among participants. In competitive situations the actions of participants do not substitute for each other, participants negatively cathect to each other's effective actions, and inducibility is low.

Building on Deutsch's theorizing, the premise may be made that the type of interdependence structured among students determines how they interact with each other. This, in turn, largely determines instructional outcomes (Johnson, 1979; Johnson & Johnson, 1974, 1989a). Structuring situations cooperatively results in promotive interaction; structuring situations competitively results in oppositional interaction; and structuring situations individualistically results in no interaction among students. These interaction patterns affect numerous variables, which may be subsumed

within the three broad and interrelated outcomes of effort exerted to achieve, quality of relationships among participants, and participants' psychological adjustment and social competence (see Figure 1).

INTERACTION PATTERNS

Two heads are better than one.

Simply placing students near each other and allowing interaction to take place does not mean that learning will be maximized; high-quality peer relationships will result; or student psychological adjustment, self-esteem, and social competencies will be maximized. Students can obstruct as well as facilitate each other's learning. Or they can ignore each other. The way students interact depends on how faculty members structure interdependence in the learning situation.

Positive interdependence results in students promoting each other's learning and achievement. Promotive interaction may be defined as individuals encouraging and facilitating each other's efforts to achieve, complete tasks, and produce in order to reach the group's goals. Positive interdependence in and of itself may have some effect on outcomes. However, it is the face-to-face promotive interaction among individuals, fostered by the positive interdependence, that most powerfully influences efforts to achieve, caring and committed relationships, and psychological adjustment and social competence. Students focus both on increasing their own achievement and on increasing the achievement of their fellow group members. Promotive interaction is characterized by individuals:

1. Providing each other with efficient and effective help and assistance.

2. Exchanging needed resources such as information and materials and processing information more efficiently and effectively.

3. Providing each other with feedback in order to improve the subsequent performance of their assigned tasks and responsibilities.

4. Challenging each other's conclusions and reasoning in order to promote higher quality

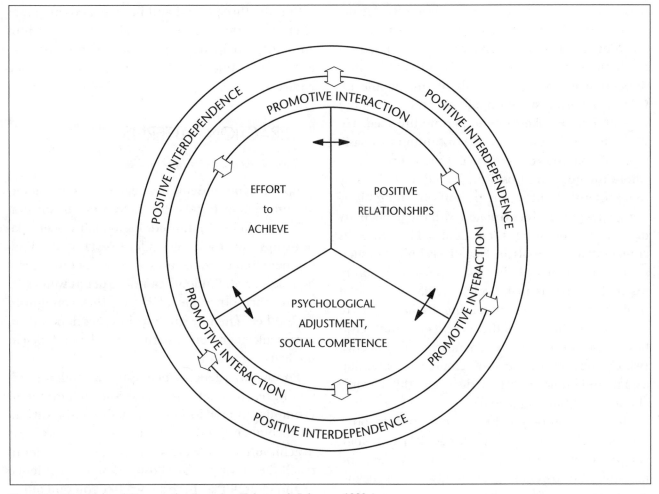

Figure 1 Outcomes of Cooperative Learning (Johnson & Johnson, 1989a).

decision making and greater insight into the problems being considered.

5. Advocating the exertion of effort to achieve mutual goals.

6. Influencing each other's efforts to achieve the group's goals.

7. Acting in trusting and trustworthy ways.

8. Being motivated to strive for mutual benefit.

9. Having a moderate level of arousal characterized by low anxiety and stress. (Johnson & Johnson, 1989a)

Negative interdependence typically results in students opposing and obstructing each other's learning. Oppositional interaction occurs as students discourage and obstruct each other's efforts to achieve. Students focus both on increasing their own achievement and on preventing any classmate from achieving more than they do. No interaction exists when students work independently without any interaction or interchange with each other. Students focus only on increasing their own achievement and ignore as irrelevant the efforts of others.

OUTCOMES

*A faithful friend is a strong defense, and he that hath found him, hath found a treasure.—*Ecclesiasties 6:14

Different learning outcomes result from the student-to-student interaction patterns promoted by the use of cooperative, competitive, and individualistic goal structures (Johnson & Johnson, 1989a). The numerous outcomes of cooperative efforts are broadly categorized into three groups: effort to

	mean	standard deviation	norm
TOTAL STUDIES			
Cooperative vs. Competitive	0.67	0.93	129
Cooperative vs. Individualistic	0.64	0.79	184
Competitive vs. Individualistic	0.30	0.77	38
HIGH QUALITY STUDIES			
Cooperative vs. Competitive	0.88	1.13	51
Cooperative vs. Individualistic	0.61	0.63	104
Competitive vs. Individualistic	0.07	0.61	24
MIXED OPERATIONALIZATIONS			
Cooperative vs. Competitive	0.40	0.62	23
Cooperative vs. Individualistic	0.42	0.65	12
PURE OPERATIONALIZATIONS			
Cooperative vs. Competitive	0.71	1.01	96
Cooperative vs. Individualistic	0.65	0.81	164

Table 1   Mean Effect Sizes for Social Interdependence and Achievement (Johnson & Johnson, 1989a).

achieve, positive interpersonal relationships, and psychological adjustment. Since research participants have varied as to economic class, age, sex, and cultural background, since a wide variety of research tasks and measures of the dependent variables have been used, and since the research has been conducted by many different researchers with markedly different orientations working in different settings and in different decades, the overall body of research on social interdependence has considerable generalizability.

Over 375 studies on achievement have been conducted over the past ninety years to give an answer to the question of how successful competitive, individualistic, and cooperative efforts are in promoting productivity and achievement (see Table 1). The results are expressed in effect sizes that show the strength of the relationship between social interdependence and achievement. The effect sizes shown in the tables are corrected for differences in variances, sample sizes, and number of findings per study.

Working together to achieve a common goal produces higher achievement and greater productivity than does working alone. This is so well confirmed by so much research that it stands as one of the strongest principles of social and organizational psychology. Not all the research, however, has been carefully conducted. The methodological shortcomings found within many research studies may significantly reduce the certainty of the conclusion that cooperative efforts produce higher achievement than do competitive or individualistic efforts. Thus, the results of well-conducted studies—in which individuals were randomly assigned to conditions, in which there was an unambiguous and well-defined control condition, in which teacher and curriculum effects were controlled for, and in which it was verified that the experimental and control conditions were successfully implemented—were analyzed together. When only the methodologically high-quality studies are included, the results are consistent with the overall findings. Cooperative learning, furthermore, results in more

	mean	standard deviation	norm
TOTAL STUDIES			
Cooperative vs. Competitive	0.67	0.49	93
Cooperative vs. Individualistic	0.60	0.58	60
Competitive vs. Individualistic	0.08	0.70	15
HIGH QUALITY STUDIES			
Cooperative vs. Competitive	0.82	0.40	37
Cooperative vs. Individualistic	0.62	0.53	44
Competitive vs. Individualistic	0.27	0.60	11
MIXED OPERATIONALIZATIONS			
Cooperative vs. Competitive	0.46	0.29	37
Cooperative vs. Individualistic	0.36	0.45	10
PURE OPERATIONALIZATIONS			
Cooperative vs. Competitive	0.79	0.56	54
Cooperative vs. Individualistic	0.66	0.60	49

Table 2   Mean Effect Sizes for Social Interdependence and Interpersonal Attraction (Johnson & Johnson, 1989a).

higher-level reasoning, more frequent generation of new ideas and solutions (i.e., process gain), and greater transfer of what is learned within one situation to another (i.e., group-to-individual transfer) than does competitive or individualistic learning. The superiority of cooperative learning over competitive and individualistic learning increases under the following conditions: when the task is more conceptual, when greater problem solving is required, when greater value is placed on higher-level reasoning and critical thinking, when creative answers are required, when long-term retention is desired, and when the application of what was learned is required.

Some cooperative learning procedures contain a mixture of cooperative, competitive, and individualistic efforts while others contain pure cooperation. The original jigsaw procedure (Aronson et al., 1978), for example, is a combination of resource interdependence (cooperative) and individual reward structure (individualistic). Teams-Games-Tournaments (DeVries & Edwards, 1974) and Student-Teams-Achievement-Divisions (Slavin,

1980) are mixtures of cooperation and intergroup competition. Team-Assisted-Instruction (Slavin, Leavey, & Madden, 1982) is a mixture of individualistic and cooperative learning. When the results of "pure" and "mixed" operationalizations of cooperative learning were compared, the pure operationalizations produced higher achievement.

Individuals care more about each other and are more committed to each other's success and well-being when they work together to get the job done than when they compete to see who is best or work independently from each other (see Table 2). This is true when individuals are homogeneous. It is also true when individuals differ in intellectual ability, handicapped conditions, ethnicity, social class, and gender. When individuals are heterogeneous, co-operating on a task results in more realistic and positive views of each other. It also results in more social support (see Table 3). Cooperative learning has been demonstrated to be an essential prerequisite for ethnic integration and mainstreaming. As relationships become more positive, absenteeism and turnover of membership decrease, member

	mean	standard deviation	norm
TOTAL STUDIES			
Cooperative vs. Competitive	0.62	0.44	84
Cooperative vs. Individualistic	0.70	0.45	72
Competitive vs. Individualistic	-0.13	0.36	19
HIGH QUALITY STUDIES			
Cooperative vs. Competitive	0.83	0.46	41
Cooperative vs. Individualistic	0.72	0.47	62
Competitive vs. Individualistic	-0.13	0.36	19
MIXED OPERATIONALIZATIONS			
Cooperative vs. Competitive	0.45	0.23	16
Cooperative vs. Individualistic	0.02	0.35	6
PURE OPERATIONALIZATIONS			
Cooperative vs. Competitive	0.73	0.46	58
Cooperative vs. Individualistic	0.77	0.40	65

Table 3   Mean Effect Sizes for Social Interdependence and Social Support (Johnson & Johnson, 1989a).

commitment to organizational goals increases, feelings of personal responsibility to the organization increase, willingness to take on difficult tasks increases, and motivation and persistence in working toward goal achievement increase. Also increased are satisfaction and morale, willingness to endure pain and frustration on behalf of the organization, willingness to defend the organization against external criticism or attack, willingness to listen to and be influenced by colleagues, commitment to each other's professional growth and success, and productivity (Johnson & F. Johnson, 1991; Johnson & Johnson, 1989a; Watson & Johnson, 1972).

Working cooperatively with peers and valuing cooperation result in greater psychological health and higher self-esteem than do competing with peers or working independently (see Table 4). Personal ego-strength, self-confidence, independence, and autonomy are all promoted by being involved in cooperative efforts with caring people who are committed to each other's success and well-being and who respect each other as separate and unique individuals. When individuals work together to

complete assignments, they interact (mastering social skills and competencies), they promote each other's success (gaining self-worth), and they form personal as well as professional relationships (creating the basis for healthy social development). Individuals' psychological adjustment and health tend to increase when schools are dominated by cooperative efforts. The more individuals work cooperatively with others, the more they see themselves as worthwhile and as having value. They also demonstrate greater productivity, greater acceptance and support of others, and greater autonomy and independence. Cooperative experiences are not a luxury. They are an absolute necessity for the healthy development of individuals who can function independently.

There are bidirectional relationships between efforts to achieve, quality of relationships, and psychological health (Johnson & Johnson, 1989a). Each influences the others. First, caring and committed friendships come from a sense of mutual accomplishment, mutual pride in joint work, and the bonding that results from joint efforts. The

TOTAL STUDIES	mean	standard deviation	norm
Cooperative vs. Competitive	0.58	0.56	56
Cooperative vs. Individualistic	0.44	0.40	38
Competitive vs. Individualistic	-0.23	0.42	19
HIGH QUALITY STUDIES			
Cooperative vs. Competitive	0.67	0.31	24
Cooperative vs. Individualistic	0.45	0.44	29
Competitive vs. Individualistic	-0.25	0.46	13
MIXED OPERATIONALIZATIONS			
Cooperative vs. Competitive	0.33	0.39	17
Cooperative vs. Individualistic	0.22	0.38	9
PURE OPERATIONALIZATIONS			
Cooperative vs. Competitive	0.74	0.59	36
Cooperative vs. Individualistic	0.51	0.40	27

Table 4   Mean Effect Sizes for Social Interdependence and Self-Esteem (Johnson & Johnson, 1989a).

more students care about each other, the harder they will work to achieve mutual learning goals. Second, joint efforts to achieve mutual goals promote higher self-esteem, self-efficacy, personal control, and confidence in individual competencies. The more psychologically healthy individuals are, the better able they are to work with others to achieve mutual goals. Third, psychological health is built on the internalization of the caring and respect received from loved ones.

Friendships are developmental advantages that promote self-esteem, self-efficacy, and general psychological adjustment. The healthier people are psychologically (i.e., free of such psychological pathologies as depression, paranoia, anxiety, fear of failure, repressed anger, hopelessness, and a sense of meaninglessness), the more caring and committed their relationships. Since each outcome can induce the others, they are likely to be found together. They are a package with each outcome a door into all three. Together they induce positive interdependence and promotive interaction.

WHAT MEDIATES?

The critical issue in understanding the relationship between cooperation and its outcomes is specifying the variables that mediate the relationship. Simply placing students in groups and telling them to work together does not in and of itself promote higher achievement. There are many ways in which group efforts may go wrong. Less able members sometimes "leave it to George" to complete the group's tasks, thus creating a free rider effect (Kerr & Bruun, 1981) whereby group members expend decreasing amounts of effort and just go through the team-work motions. At the same time, the more able group members may expend less effort to avoid the sucker effect of doing all the work (Kerr, 1983). High-ability group members may be deferred to and may take over the important leadership roles in ways that benefit them at the expense of the other group members (the rich-get-richer effect). In a learning group, for example, a more able group member may give all the explanations of what is being learned. Since the amount of time spent explaining correlates highly with the amount learned, a more able member learns a great deal while less able members flounder as a captive audience. The time spent listening in group brainstorming can reduce the amount of time in which any individual can state their ideas (Hill, 1982; Lamm & Trommsdorf, 1973). Group efforts can be characterized by self-induced helplessness (Langer & Benevento, 1978), diffusion of responsibility and social loafing (Latane, Williams, & Harkins, 1979), ganging up against a task, reactance (Salomon, 1981), dysfunctional divisions of labor ("I'm the thinkist and you're the typist"; Sheingold, Hawkins, & Char, 1984), inappropriate dependence on authority (Webb, Ender, & Lewis, 1986), destructive conflict (Collins, 1970; Johnson & Johnson, 1979), and other patterns of behavior that debilitate group performance.

It is only under certain conditions that group efforts may be expected to be more productive than individual efforts. Those conditions are:

- Clearly perceived positive interdependence.

- Considerable promotive (face-to-face) interaction.

- Acknowledged personal responsibility (individual accountability) to achieve the group's goals.

- Frequent use of relevant interpersonal and small group skills.

- Periodic and regular group processing.

POSITIVE INTERDEPENDENCE

The first step in promoting cooperation among students is to structure positive interdependence within the learning situation. Positive interdependence exists when one perceives that one is linked with others in a way so that one cannot succeed unless they do (and vice versa) or that one must coordinate one's efforts with the efforts of others to complete a task (Johnson & Johnson, 1989a). Positive interdependence is the most important factor in structuring learning situations cooperatively. If students do not believe that they "sink or swim together," then the lesson is not cooperative. When students are placed in learning groups but no positive interdependence is structured, the learning situation is not cooperative; it is either competitive or individualistic with talking. Under those conditions, there is no reason to expect groups to outperform individuals. In fact, the opposite may be true.

There are two major categories of interdependence: outcome interdependence and means interdependence (Deutsch, 1949; Johnson & Johnson, 1989a; Thomas, 1957). How students behave in a learning situation is largely determined by their perceptions of the outcomes desired and the means by which the desired goals may be reached. When persons are in a cooperative or competitive situation, they are oriented toward a desired **outcome**, end state, goal, or reward. If there is no outcome interdependence (goal and reward interdependence), there is no cooperation or competition. Outcome interdependence includes:

- **Goal interdependence**: individuals perceive that they can attain their goals if and only if the other individuals with whom they are cooperatively linked attain their goals. Goal interdependence subsumes **outside enemy interdependence**—striving to perform higher than other groups—and **fantasy interdependence**—striving to solve hypothetical problems such as how to deal with being shipwrecked on the moon.

- **Reward interdependence**: each group member receives the same reward for successfully completing a joint task.

The means through which the mutual goals or rewards are to be accomplished specify the actions required on the part of group members. Means interdependence includes:

- **Resource interdependence**: each member has only a portion of the information, materials, or resources necessary for the task to be completed, and members' resources have to be combined in order for the group to achieve its goal.

- **Role interdependence**: members are assigned complementary and interconnected roles.
- **Task interdependence**: a division of labor is created so that the actions of one group member have to be completed if the next group member is to complete his or her responsibilities.

Positive outcome interdependence results in group members realizing the following (Johnson & Johnson, 1989a):

- Members share a common fate where they all gain or lose on the basis of the overall performance of group members. One result is a sense of personal responsibility for the final outcome, and for doing their share of the work.
- They strive for mutual benefit so that all members of the group will gain. There is recognition that what helps other members benefits oneself and what promotes one's own productivity benefits the other group members.
- Group members have a long-term time perspective. Long-term joint productivity is perceived to be of greater value than short-term personal advantage.
- Individuals have a shared identity based on group membership. The shared identity binds members together emotionally and creates an expectation for a joint celebration based on mutual respect and appreciation for the success of group members. The experience creates a positive cathexis so that group members like each other. Feelings of success are shared and pride is taken in other members' accomplishments as well as one's own.

Positive means interdependence results in individuals realizing that the performance of group members is mutually caused. No member is on his or her own. Each member shares responsibility for other members' productivity (mutual responsibility) and is obligated to other members for their support and assistance (mutual obligation). As a result of the mutual causation, cooperative efforts are characterized by positive inducibility in that

group members are open to being influenced by each other and substitutability in that the actions of group members substitute for each other so that if one member of the group has taken the action there is no need for other members to do so. There is a mutual investment in each other.

Positive interdependence has numerous effects on individuals' motivation and productivity, not the least of which is that the efforts of all group members are needed for group success. When members of a group see their efforts as dispensable for the group's success, they may reduce their efforts (Kerr & Bruun, 1981; Kerr, 1983; Sweeney, 1973). When group members perceive their potential contribution to the group as being unique, they increase their efforts (Harkins & Petty, 1982). When goal, task, resource, and role interdependence are clearly understood, individuals realize that their efforts are required in order for the group to succeed and that their contributions are often unique. In addition, reward interdependence needs to be structured to ensure that one member's efforts do not make the efforts of other members unnecessary. If the highest score in the group determines the group grade, for example, low-ability members might see their efforts as unnecessary and thus contribute minimally. High-ability members might feel exploited and become demoralized and therefore decrease their efforts so as not to provide undeserved rewards for irresponsible and ungrateful "free-riders" (Kerr, 1983).

Finally, positive interdependence creates motives that enhance and complement each other. Affiliation needs and the desire to be involved in relations with others, for example, may operate directly to increase productivity and psychological health in cooperative situations.

Within the literature on positive interdependence, two controversies are: (a) whether goal or reward interdependence is the key to operationalizing outcome interdependence, and (b) whether resource interdependence is effective in the absence of outcome interdependence.

Goal vs. Reward Interdependence

There is a basic theoretical disagreement among researchers as to whether positive goal interdependence or positive reward interdependence mediate the relationship between cooperation and achievement. On the one side of the controversy are Deutsch (1962) and Johnson and Johnson (1974, 1989a) who state that positive goal interdependence results in a positive interaction pattern among individuals, which increases their productivity and interpersonal attraction. From this perspective, given the perception of positive interdependence, individuals will act to facilitate each other's goal accomplishment, and increased achievement results. On the other side of the controversy are researchers such as Hayes (1976) and Slavin (1983) who state that positive reward interdependence largely explains the relationship between cooperation and achievement. From this perspective, individuals will increase their achievement only if there is a specific academic group contingency reinforcing them for doing so.

Contrasting the two theoretical positions is complicated by the fact that, while it is possible to implement positive goal interdependence without positive reward interdependence, reward interdependence cannot be implemented without goal interdependence. In order for group members to be motivated by a group contingency, they must first perceive that their goal accomplishments are positively interdependent. To contrast the two theoretical positions, cooperative learning groups with only positive goal interdependence have to be contrasted with cooperative groups with both positive goal and reward interdependence. In a series of recent studies, Deborah Mesch and Marvin Lew contrasted individualistic learning, positive goal interdependence alone, positive goal interdependence with an academic reward contingency, and positive goal interdependence with both an academic and a social skills reward contingency (Lew, Mesch, Johnson, & Johnson, 1986a, 1986b; Mesch, Johnson, & Johnson, 1988; Mesch, Lew, Johnson, & Johnson, 1986). They used an A-B-A reversal design in studies that lasted over twenty-one weeks, carefully observing conditions each week to ensure that they were being implemented correctly. Their studies took place in elementary, junior high, and high schools. They found that, while positive goal interdependence is sufficient to produce higher

achievement than individualistic learning, the combination of goal and reward interdependence is even more effective. The impact of the two types of outcome interdependence seems to be additive.

Goal vs. Resource Interdependence

Although few research studies have attempted to differentiate between the effects of positive goal interdependence and positive resource interdependence, some distinction may be made theoretically. There are two basic positions, one represented by Deutsch and the authors of this chapter, and one represented by Aronson. From the theorizing of Deutsch (1962), it may be posited that when the cooperative situation is based on positive goal interdependence, individuals will act to promote each other's success out of recognition that they will benefit from doing so. When the cooperative situation is based on positive resource interdependence, however, there is mutual dependence on each other's resources, but individuals benefit only from obtaining resources from each other, not from giving their resources to each other. Aronson and his associates (1978) have conducted a set of studies in which they operationalized cooperation through a combination of positive resource interdependence and individual rewards, assuming that positive resource and goal interdependence were interchangeable and nonadditive. Their studies, and two major field evaluations by Eric Schaps and his associates (Moskowitz, Malvin, Schaeffer, & Schaps, 1981, 1985), indicate that positive resource interdependence with an individualistic reward structure does not increase achievement beyond what would be expected by a competitive or individualistic reward structure alone.

Theoretically, there are at least two reasons for hypothesizing that resource interdependence will not promote higher achievement than individualistic efforts in the absence of positive outcome interdependence. The first is that, while positive outcome interdependence creates a situation in which each person benefits from the achievement and productivity of fellow group members (and, therefore, exerts efforts to promote their success), resource interdependence creates a situation in which each person is dependent on receiving resources from other group members but does not gain from sharing his or her resources. When resource interdependence alone exists within a group, each person will be motivated to have others present what they know, but will be penalized by presenting what he or she has learned. Every minute a person presents his or her resources is a minute that he or she is not obtaining needed resources from others.

Second, positive goal interdependence may promote substitutability among the actions of group members, while resource interdependence may not. This may be seen in individuals' reactions to less able group members. Within a cooperative situation characterized by positive goal interdependence, when one member cannot do the work, group members will increase their motivation and effort in order to ensure joint success (because their actions can substitute for the actions of the less capable group member). Within a cooperative situation characterized by resource interdependence, when a member cannot provide his or her part of the required resources, the motivation and effort of the rest of the group members will decrease (because their actions cannot substitute for the actions of the less capable member).

To examine the relative impact of positive goal interdependence and positive resource interdependence on individual achievement and group productivity, Johnson, Johnson, Ortiz, and Stanne (in press) conducted a study directly comparing goal and resource interdependence. Sixty-three individuals enrolled in a U.S. Military History class participated in the study. The study lasted for five class sessions of forty-five minutes each. Achievement was measured by quizzes given at the end of the second, third, and fourth class sessions, and by a final test given at the end of the study. Students were randomly assigned to conditions and within conditions to groups of three. In the goal interdependence condition, individuals studied all the material and were graded on the basis of their total group score. In the resource interdependence condition, individuals were given one-third of the material to learn and teach to the other two members of their group, but were graded on their individual performance on the tests. Both on the quizzes and on the final examination, individuals in the goal interdependence condition performed better than did those in the resource interdependence condition.

To examine the relative impact of positive goal interdependence and positive resource interdependence on individual achievement and group productivity, Johnson, Johnson, Stanne, and Garibaldi (1990) conducted a study using a computer-assisted problem-solving task. Forty-four African-American high school seniors and college freshmen were randomly assigned to conditions, stratifying for ability, sex, and urban/rural background. Four conditions were included in the study: (1) both positive goal and resource interdependence, (2) positive goal interdependence only, (3) positive resource interdependence only, and (4) neither positive goal nor resource interdependence (i.e., individualistic). Positive goal interdependence promoted higher individual achievement and group productivity than did an absence of goal interdependence. The combination of positive goal and resource interdependence promoted higher individual achievement and group productivity than did any of the other conditions, indicating that two sources of positive interdependence are more powerful than one. When used in isolation from positive goal interdependence, positive resource interdependence produced the lowest individual achievement and problem-solving success. Students may achieve more under individualistic conditions than under a combination of resource interdependence and individual rewards.

PROMOTIVE (FACE-TO-FACE) INTERACTION

Promotive interaction was defined and discussed in the Interaction Patterns section of this chapter. The amount of research documenting the impact of promotive interaction on achievement is too voluminous to review here. Interested readers are referred to Johnson and Johnson (1989a).

Personal Responsibility/Individual Accountability

After positive interdependence and promotive interaction, a key variable mediating the effectiveness of cooperation is a sense of personal responsibility to the other group members. This involves being responsible for completing one's share of the work and facilitating the work of other group members; in other words, for doing as much as one can toward achieving the group's goals. There are a number of ways in which this personal commitment or responsibility may be inculcated. The first is through structuring positive interdependence among group members so that they will feel responsible for helping each other to achieve the group's goals. The second is through the teacher assessing each individual student's level of achievement, that is, holding each individual student accountable for completing assignments and learning the assigned material.

Students are not only accountable to the teacher in cooperative situations; they are also accountable to their peers. Learning groups should be provided with information about the level of mastery of the assigned material each student is achieving. Feedback mechanisms for determining the level of each person's achievement are necessary for members to provide support and assistance to each other. When groups work on tasks where it is difficult to identify members' contributions or when there is an increased likelihood of redundant efforts, a lack of group cohesiveness, or lessened responsibility for the final outcome, some members will try to contribute less to goal achievement (Harkins & Petty, 1982; Ingham, Levinger, Graves, & Peckham, 1974; Kerr & Bruun, 1981; Latane, Williams, & Harkins, 1979; Moede, 1927; Petty, Harkins, Williams, & Latane, 1977; Williams, 1981; Williams, Harkins, & Latane, 1981). If, however, there is high individual accountability and it is clear how much effort each member is contributing; if redundant efforts are avoided; if every member is responsible for the final outcome; and if the group is cohesive; then the social loafing effect vanishes. The smaller the size of the group; the greater the individual accountability may be.

SOCIAL SKILLS

Placing socially unskilled students in a learning group and simply telling them to cooperate will obviously not be successful. Students must be taught the interpersonal and small-group skills needed for high-quality cooperation and be motivated to use them. Furthermore, all group members must engage in them. If only the most socially skilled group members engage in all the needed leadership and communication skills, they will increase their skills at the expense of less active and less socially skilled group members—the "rich-get-richer" effect.

In their studies on the long-term implementation of cooperation learning, Lew and Mesch (Lew, Mesch, Johnson, & Johnson, 1986a, 1986b; Mesch, Johnson, & Johnson, 1988; Mesch, Lew, Johnson, & Johnson, 1986) investigated the impact of a reward contingency for using social skills, in combination with positive interdependence and a contingency for academic achievement, on performance within cooperative learning groups. In the cooperative skills conditions, students were trained weekly in four social skills, and each member of a cooperative group was given two bonus points toward the quiz grade if all group members were observed by the teacher to demonstrate three out of the four cooperative skills. The results indicated that the combination of positive interdependence, an academic contingency for high performance by all group members, and a social skills contingency, promoted the highest achievement. The more socially skillful students are, and the more attention teachers pay to teaching and rewarding the use of social skills, the higher the achievement that can be expected within cooperative learning groups.

There is only so much that structure can do. Students need to master and use interpersonal and small-group skills to capitalize on the opportunities presented by a cooperative learning situation. Especially when learning groups function on a long-term basis and engage in complex, free exploratory activities over a prolonged basis, the interpersonal and small-group skills of the members may determine the level of student achievement.

GROUP PROCESSING

In order to achieve, students in cooperative learning groups have to work together effectively. Effective group work is influenced by whether or not groups reflect on or process how well they are functioning. A process is an identifiable sequence of events taking place over time, and process goals refer to the sequences of events instrumental in achieving outcome goals. Group processing may be defined as reflecting on a group session to describe what member actions were helpful and unhelpful and make decisions about what actions to continue or change. The purpose of group processing is to clarify and improve the effectiveness of the members in contributing to the collaborative efforts to achieve the group's goals.

No direct evidence of the impact of group processing on achievement was available until a study was conducted by Stuart Yager (Yager, Johnson, & Johnson, 1985). He examined the impact on achievement of (a) cooperative learning in which members discussed how well their group was functioning and how they could improve its effectiveness, (b) cooperative learning without any group processing, and (c) individualistic learning. The results indicate that students at all levels of achievement in the cooperation-with-group-processing condition scored higher on daily achievement, post-instructional achievement, and retention measures than did the students in the other two conditions. Students in the cooperation-without-group-processing condition, furthermore, scored higher on all three measures than did the students in the individualistic condition.

Johnson, Johnson, Stanne, and Garibaldi (1990) conducted a follow-up study comparing (a) cooperative learning with no processing, (b) cooperative learning with teacher processing (the teacher specified cooperative skills to use, observed, and gave whole-class feedback as to how well students were using the skills), (c) cooperative learning with teacher and student processing (in addition to teacher processing, learning groups discussed how well they interacted as a group), and (d) individualistic learning. Forty-nine high-ability African-American high school seniors and entering college

freshmen at Xavier University participated in the study. A complex computer-assisted problem-solving assignment was given to all students. All three cooperative conditions performed higher than did the individualistic condition. The combination of teacher and student processing resulted in greater problem-solving success than did the other cooperative conditions.

These five essential elements—positive interdependence, promotive interaction, personal responsibility, social skills, and group processing—differentiate cooperative learning from traditional discussion groups and well-structured cooperative learning lessons from poorly structured ones. There are three broad types of cooperative learning groups that are structured through the use of the five basic elements.

TYPES OF COOPERATIVE LEARNING GROUPS

A cooperative structure consists of the integrated use of three types of cooperative learning groups. Cooperative learning groups may be used to teach specific content (formal cooperative learning groups), to ensure active cognitive processing of information during direct teaching (informal cooperative learning groups), and to provide students with long-term support and assistance for academic progress (cooperative base groups).

Formal Cooperative Learning Groups

Formal cooperative learning groups may last from one class period to several weeks, working to complete specific tasks and assignments (such as solving a set of problems, completing a curriculum unit, writing a report or theme, conducting an experiment, or reading a story, play, chapter, or book). Any course requirement or assignment may be reformulated to be cooperative. In formal cooperative learning groups the teacher:

- Specifies the objectives for the lesson (one academic and one social skill).

- Makes a series of decisions about how to structure the learning groups (such as what size groups, how students are assigned to groups, what roles to assign, how to arrange materials, and how to arrange the room).

- Teaches the academic concepts, principles, and strategies that the students are to master and apply, and explains the task to be completed, criteria for success, positive interdependence, individual accountability, and expected student behaviors.

- Monitors the functioning of the learning groups and intervenes to teach collaborative skills and provide assistance in academic learning when it is needed.

- Evaluates student performance against the preset criteria for excellence, and ensures that groups process how effectively members worked together.

Informal Cooperative Learning Groups

Informal cooperative learning groups are temporary, ad-hoc groups that last from a few minutes to one class period. During a lecture, demonstration, or film, they can be used to focus student attention on the material to be learned, help set a mood conducive to learning, and help set expectations as to what will be covered in a class session. They can also ensure that students cognitively process the material being taught and provide closure to an instructional session. During direct teaching, the instructional challenge for the teacher is to ensure that students do the intellectual work of organizing material, explaining it, summarizing it, and integrating it into existing conceptual structures. Informal cooperative learning groups are often organized so that students engage in three-to-five-minute, focused discussions before and after a lecture and three-to-five-minute, turn-to-your-partner discussions interspersed throughout a lecture. In this way the main problem of lectures—"The information passes from the notes of the professor to the notes of the student without passing through the mind of either one"—can be countered.

Cooperative Base Groups

Cooperative base groups are long-term, heterogeneous, cooperative learning groups with stable membership. The purposes of the base group are to give the support, help, encouragement, and assistance each member needs to make academic progress and develop cognitively and socially in healthy ways. Base groups meet daily (or whenever the class meets). They are permanent (lasting from one to several years) and provide the long-term caring peer relationships necessary to influence members consistently to work hard in school. They formally meet to discuss the academic progress of each member, provide help and assistance to each other, and verify that each member is completing assignments and progressing satisfactorily through the academic program. Base groups may also be responsible for letting absent group members know what went on in class when they miss a session. Informally, members interact every day within and between classes, discussing assignments and helping each other with homework. The use of base groups tends to improve attendance, personalizes the work required and the school experience, and improves the quality and quantity of learning. The larger the class or school and the more complex and difficult the subject matter, the more important it is to have base groups.

When used in combination, formal and informal cooperative groups and base groups provide an overall structure for school learning.

APPROACHES TO COOPERATIVE LEARNING

It is only when we develop others that we permanently succeed.—Harvey S. Firestone, Firestone Tires

Given the strong theoretical and research support for implementing cooperative learning in the classroom it is important to develop operationalizations that teachers can use. Approaches to implementing cooperative learning may be placed on a continuum with conceptual applications at one end and direct applications at the other (Johnson, Johnson, & Holubec, 1984/1990). Conceptual applications are based on an interaction between theory, research, and practice. Teachers are taught a general conceptual model of cooperative learning (based on positive interdependence, face-to-face interaction, individual accountability, social skills, and group processing—the essential elements approach) which they use to tailor cooperative learning specifically to their circumstances, students, and needs. Teachers are taught an expert system of how to implement cooperative learning that they use to create a unique adaptation to their specific circumstances. The resulting expertise is based on a metacognitive understanding of cooperative learning. The two conceptual approaches to cooperative learning have been developed by Elizabeth Cohen (1986) and the authors of this chapter (Johnson & Johnson, 1975/1991; Johnson, Johnson, & Holubec, 1984/1990). Cohen bases her conceptual principles on expectation-states theory, while we base our conceptual principles on the theory of cooperation and competition that Morton Deutsch derived from Kurt Lewin's field theory. Using the five basic elements of cooperation, faculty can analyze their current curricula, students, and instructional goals and design cooperative learning experiences specifically adapted for their instructional goals and the ages, abilities, and backgrounds of their students. Becoming competent in implementing the basic elements is a requirement for obtaining real expertise in cooperative learning.

Conceptual applications may be contrasted with direct applications that consist of packaged lessons, curricula, and strategies that are used in a prescribed manner. The direct approach can be divided into three subcategories.

- **The strategy approach**: Teachers can adopt a strategy (such as groups-of-four in intermediate math) that is aimed at using cooperative learning in a specific subject area for a certain age student.

- **The curriculum package approach**: They can adopt a curriculum package that is aimed at a specific subject area and grade level.

- **The lesson approach**: They can replicate a lesson they observed another teach. Faculty are trained to use a specific cooperative activity, lesson, strategy, or curriculum package without the necessity of any real understanding of cooperation. Some of the most powerful strategies include the jigsaw method, developed by Elliot Aronson and his colleagues (Aronson, et al., 1978), the coop/coop strategy developed by Spencer Kagan (Kagan, 1988), and the group project method developed by the Sharans (Sharan & Sharan, 1976).

While the two types of approaches are not contradictory, there are differences for the transfer of training from the workshop to the classroom and for the long-term implementation and survival of cooperative learning. Conceptual applications are theory-based while direct applications are based on materials and procedures. The conceptual approach trains teachers to be engineers who adapt cooperative learning to their specific circumstances and students. Direct approaches train teachers to be technicians who use the cooperative learning curriculum or strategy without necessarily understanding how it works. The conceptual approach promotes research that tests theory which generalizes to many different situations. Direct approaches promote evaluation studies that are, in essence, case studies demonstrating how well the curriculum or strategy was implemented in a specific instance, but the results do not generalize to other situations or implementations. Conceptual approaches are dynamic in that they are changed and modified on the basis of new research and refinements of the theory. Direct approaches are more static in that they tend to remain fixed no matter how the knowledge about cooperative learning changes.

When teachers gain expertise in cooperative learning through conceptual understanding, they can generate new lessons and strategies as the need arises. They can also transfer their use of cooperative learning to create more cooperative colleagial relationships, staff meetings, and relationships with parents and committees. Conceptual and direct approaches, however, complement each other. A carefully crafted training program requires a combination of a clear conceptual understanding of the essential elements of cooperative learning and concrete direct examples of lessons, strategies, and continued implementation in classrooms and schools.

THE COOPERATIVE SCHOOL

Take care of each other. Share your energies with the group. No one must feel alone, cut off, for that is when you do not make it.—Willi Unsoeld, mountain climber

For decades business and industrial organizations have functioned as "mass manufacturing" organizations that divided work into small component parts performed by individuals who work separately from and, in many cases, in competition with peers. Personnel were considered to be interchangeable parts in the organizational machine. Such an organizational structure no longer seems effective and many companies are turning to the high productivity generated by teams.

Most schools have also been structured as mass manufacturing organizations. Teachers work alone, in their own room, with their own set of students, and with their own set of curriculum materials. In this situation, students can be assigned to any teacher because teachers are interchangeable parts in the education machine, and, conversely, teachers can be given any student to teach. Schools need to change from a mass-manufacturing or competitive/individualistic organizational structure to a high performance, cooperative, team-based organizational structure (Johnson & Johnson, 1989b). The new organizational structure is generally known as "the cooperative school."

In a cooperative school, students work primarily in cooperative learning groups. Teachers and building staff work in cooperative teams, and district administrators work in cooperative teams. The organizational structure of the classroom, school, and district are then congruent. Each level of cooperative teams supports and enhances the other levels.

A cooperative school structure begins in the classroom with the use of cooperative learning the majority of the time. Cooperative learning is used to increase student achievement, create more positive relationships among students, and generally improve students' psychological well-being. A secondary effect is that using cooperative learning in the classroom affects teachers' attitudes and competencies concerning collaborating with colleagues. Teachers typically cannot promote isolation and competition among students all day and collaborate effectively with colleagues. What is promoted in the instructional situations tends to dominate relationships among staff members.

The second level in creating a cooperative school is to form colleagial support groups, task forces, and ad hoc decision-making groups within the school (Johnson & Johnson, 1989b). Just as the heart of the classroom is cooperative learning, the heart of the school is the colleagial support group. **Colleagial support groups** are small cooperative groups whose purpose is to increase teachers' instructional expertise and success, in particular by using cooperative learning. Participation in the colleagial support groups is aimed at increasing teachers' belief that they are engaged in a joint venture ("We are doing it!"); public commitment to peers to increase their instructional expertise ("I will try it!"); peer accountability ("They are counting on me!"); sense of social support ("They will help and assist me!"); sense of safety ("The risk is challenging but not excessive!"); and self-efficacy ("If I exert the effort, I will be successful!"). **Task force groups** plan and implement solutions to schoolwide issues and problems such as curriculum adoptions and lunchroom behavior. Task forces diagnose a problem, gather data about the causes and extent of the problem, consider a variety of alternative solutions, make conclusions, and present a recommendation to the faculty as a whole. **Ad hoc decision-making groups** are used during faculty meetings to involve all staff members in important school decisions. Ad hoc decision-making groups are part of a small-group/large-group procedure in which staff members listen to a recommendation, are assigned to small groups, meet to consider the recommendation, report their decision to the entire faculty, and then participate in a facultywide decision as to what the course of action should be. The use of these three types of faculty cooperative teams tends to increase teacher productivity, morale, and professional self-esteem.

The third level in creating a cooperative school is to implement administrative cooperative teams within the district (Johnson & Johnson, 1989b).

Administrators are organized into collegial support groups to increase their administrative expertise and success. Administrative task forces and ad hoc decision-making groups are also used. If administrators compete to see who is the best administrator in the district, they are unlikely able to promote cooperation among staff members of the school. The more the district and school personnel work in cooperative teams, the easier it will be for teachers to use cooperative learning and vice versa.

Cooperative learning is more than an instructional procedure. It is a basic shift in organizational structure that extends from the classroom up through the superintendent's office.

SUMMARY

Cooperative learning is the instructional use of small groups so that students work together to maximize their own and each other's learning. The effectiveness of cooperative efforts depends on how well positive interdependence, face-to-face promotive interaction, individual accountability, interpersonal and small group skills, and group processing are structured within the learning situation. These five essential elements may be structured within the learning situation, within the classroom, within the school, and within the school district. In a cooperative school, students work primarily in cooperative learning groups; teachers and building staff work in cooperative teams, as do the district administrators. The heart of the cooperative school is cooperative learning. Cooperative learning

groups may be used to teach specific content (formal cooperative learning groups), to ensure active cognitive processing of information during a lecture (informal cooperative learning groups), and to provide long-term support and assistance for academic progress (cooperative base groups). There are two general approaches to creating cooperative learning procedures, conceptual and direct. Long-term change in teaching practices depends on teachers' understanding conceptually what cooperation is as well as being able to conduct cooperative learning lessons. Within the school, staff members work in collegial support groups to increase teachers' instructional expertise and success. They also form task forces to plan and implement solutions to schoolwide problems and ad hoc decision-making groups to involve all staff members in important school decisions. At the district level administrators are also structured into teams.

Clear theory and abundant and consistent research support a change in school structure from their current competitive-individualistic organizational structure to a cooperative organization. The amount of research validating social interdependence theory and demonstrating the effectiveness of cooperative efforts is staggering. The amount of research demonstrating that cooperative efforts promote greater productivity, more positive relationships, and greater psychological health than do competitive or individualistic efforts places cooperation in a class by itself when considering how to make schools effective.

———

REFERENCES

Aronson, E., Blaney, N., Stephan, C., Sikes, J., & Snapp, M. (1978). *The jigsaw classroom.* Beverly Hills, CA; Sage.

Barker, R., Wright, B., Meyerson, L., & Gonick, M. (1953). *Adjustment to physical handicap and illness: A survey of the social psychology of physique and disability.* New York: Social Science Research Council.

Cohen, E. (1986). *Designing groupwork: Strategies for the heterogeneous classroom.* New York: Columbia University Teachers College Press.

Collins, B. (1970). *Social psychology.* Reading, MA: Addison-Wesley.

Deutsch, M. (1962). Cooperation and trust: Some theoretical notes. In M. R. Jones (Ed.), *Nebraska Symposium on Motivation* (pp. 275-319). Lincoln, NE: University of Nebraska Press.

Deutsch, M. (1949). A theory of cooperation and competition. *Human Relations, 2,* 129-152.

DeVries, D., & Edwards, K. (1974). *Cooperation in the classroom: Towards a theory of alternative reward-task classroom structures.* Paper presented at the annual meeting of the American Educational Research Association, Chicago.

Harkins, S., & Petty, R. (1982). The effects of task difficulty and task uniqueness on social loafing. *Journal of Personality and Social Psychology, 43,* 1214-1229.

Hayes, L. (1976). The use of group contingencies for behavioral control: A review. *Psychological Bulletin, 83,* 628-648.

Hill, G. (1982). Group versus individual performance: Are N + 1 heads better than one? *Psychological Bulletin, 91,* 517-539.

Ingham, A., Levinger, G., Graves, J., & Peckham, V. (1974). The Ringelmann effect: Studies of group size and group performance. *Journal of Personality and Social Psychology, 10,* 371-384.

Johnson, D. W. (1979). *Educational psychology.* Englewood Cliffs, NJ: Prentice-Hall.

Johnson, D. W. (1974). Communication and the inducement of cooperative behavior in conflicts: A critical review. *Speech Monographs, 41,* 64-78.

Johnson, D. W. (1970). *The social psychology of education.* New York: Holt, Rinehart & Winston.

Johnson, D. W., & Johnson, F. (1991). *Joining together: Group theory and group skills* (4th ed.). Englewood Cliffs, NJ: Prentice-Hall.

Johnson, D. W., & Johnson, R. T. (1989a). *Leading the cooperative school.* Edina, MN: Interaction Book Company.

Johnson, D. W., & Johnson, R. T. (1989b). *Cooperation and competition: Theory and research.* Edina, MN: Interaction Book Company.

Johnson, D. W., & Johnson, R. T. (1979). Conflict in the classroom: Controversy and learning. *Review of Educational Research, 49,* 51-70.

Johnson, D. W., & Johnson, R. T. (1974). Instructional goal structure: Cooperative, competition, or individualistic. *Review of Educational Research, 44,* 213-240.

Johnson, D. W., & Johnson, R. T. (1975/1991). *Learning together and alone: Cooperative, competitive, and individualistic learning* (2nd/3rd ed.). Englewood Cliffs, NJ: Prentice-Hall.

Johnson, D. W., Johnson, R. T., & Holubec, E. (1984/1990). *Circles of learning: Cooperation in the classroom* (2nd/3rd ed.). Edina, MN: Interaction Book Company.

Johnson, D. W., Johnson, R. T., Ortiz, A., & Stanne, M. (in press). Impact of positive goal and resource interdependence on achievement, interaction, and attitudes. *Journal of General Psychology.*

Johnson, D. W., Johnson, R. T., Stanne, M., & Garibaldi, A. (1990). Impact of group processing on achievement in cooperative groups. *Journal of Social Psychology, 130,* 507-516.

Kagan, S. (1988). *Cooperative learning: Resources for teachers.* San Juan Capistrano, CA: Resources for Teachers.

Kerr, N. (1983). The dispensability of member effort and group motivation losses: Free-rider effects. *Journal of Personality and Social Psychology, 44,* 78-94.

Kerr, N., & Bruun, S. (1981). Ringelmann revisited: Alternative explanations for the social loafing effect. *Personality and Social Psychology Bulletin, 7,* 224-231.

Lamm, H., & Trommsdorf, G. (1973). Group versus individual performance on tasks requiring ideational proficiency (brainstorming): A review. *European Journal of Social Psychology, 3,* 886-893.

Langer, E., & Benevento, A. (1978). Self-induced dependence. *Journal of Personality and Social Psychology, 36,* 886-893.

Latane, B., Williams, K., & Harkins, S. (1979). Many hands make light the work: The causes and consequences of social loafing. *Journal of Personality and Social Psychology, 37,* 822-832.

Lew, M., Mesch, D., Johnson, D. W., & Johnson, R. T. (1986a). Positive interdependence, academic and collaborative-skills group contingencies and isolated students. *American Educational Research Journal, 23,* 476-488.

Lew, M., Mesch, D., Johnson, D. W., & Johnson, R. T. (1986b). Components of cooperative learning: Effects of collaborative skills and academic group contingencies on achievement and mainstreaming. *Contemporary Educational Psychology, 11*, 229-239.

Lewin, K. (1948). *Resolving social conflicts.* New York: Harper.

Lewin, K. (1935). *A dynamic theory of personality.* New York: McGraw-Hill.

May, M., & Doob, L. (1937). Competition and cooperation [Special issue]. *Social Sciences Research Council Bulletin, 25,* New York: Social Sciences Research Council.

Mayer, A. (1903). Uber einzel-und-gesamtleistung des schulkindes. *Archiv fur die Gesamte Psychologie, 1,* 276-416.

Mesch, D., Johnson, D. W., & Johnson, R. T. (1988). Impact of positive interdependence and academic group contingencies on achievement. *Journal of Social Psychology, 128,* 345-352.

Mesch, D., Lew, M., Johnson, D. W., & Johnson, R. T. (1986). Isolated teenagers, cooperative learning and the training of social skills. *Journal of Psychology, 120,* 323-334.

Moede, W. (1927). Die richtinien der leistungs-psychologie. *Industrielle Psychotechnik, 4,* 193-207.

Moskowitz, J., Malvin, J., Schaeffer, G., & Schaps, E. (1985). Evaluation of jigsaw, a cooperative learning technique. *Contemporary Educational Psychology, 10,* 104-112.

Moskowitz, J., Malvin, J., Schaeffer, G., & Schaps, E. (1981). Process and outcome evaluation of a cooperative learning strategy. *American Journal of Educational Research, 20,* 687-696.

Petty, R., Harkins, S., Williams, K., & Latane, B. (1977). The effects of group size on cognitive effort and evaluation. *Personality and Social Psychology Bulletin, 3,* 575-578.

Salomon, G. (1981). Communication and education: Social and psychological interactions. *People and Communication, 13,* 269-271.

Sharan, S., & Sharan, Y. (1976). *Small group teaching.* Englewood Cliffs, NJ: Educational Technology Publications.

Sheingold, K., Hawkins, J., & Char, C. (1984). I'm the thinkist, you're the typist: The interaction of technology and the social life of classrooms. *Journal of Social Issues, 40*(3), 49-61.

Slavin, R. (1983). *Cooperative learning.* New York: Longman.

Slavin, R. (1980). Cooperative learning. *Review of Educational Research, 50,* 315-342.

Slavin, R., Leavey, M., & Madden, N. (1982). *Team-assisted individualization: Mathematics teacher's manual.* Baltimore: John Hopkins University, Center for Social Organization of Schools.

Sweeney, J. (1973). An experimental investigation of the free-rider problem. *Social Science Research, 2,* 277-292.

Thomas, D. (1957). Effects of facilitative role interdependence on group functioning. *Human Relations, 10,* 347-366.

Triplett, N. (1898). The dynamogenic factors in pacemaking and competition. *American Journal of Psychology, 9,* 507-533.

Watson, G., & Johnson, D. (1972). *Social psychology: Issues and insights.* Philadelphia: Lippincott.

Webb, N., Ender, P., & Lewis, S. (1986). Problem-solving strategies and group processes in small group learning computer programming. *American Educational Research Journal, 23*(2), 243-261.

Williams, K. (1981). *The effects of group cohesiveness on social loafing.* Paper presented at the annual meeting of the Midwestern Psychological Association, Detroit.

Williams, K., Harkins, S., & Latane, B. (1981). Identifiability as a deterrent to social loafing: Two cheering experiments. *Journal of Personality and Social Psychology, 40,* 303-311.

Yager, S., Johnson, D., & Johnson, R. (1985). Oral discussion, group-to-individual transfer, and achievement in cooperative learning groups. *Journal of Educational Psychology, 77*(1), 60-66.

BUILDING A RESEARCH SYNTHESIS

—

James Bellanca and Robin Fogarty

Any naysayer who says that cooperative learning is just a fad or another new wrinkle may find the following bit of history interesting. In the earliest settlements, the pioneer families knew the benefits of tutoring their children in groups. Very often, older students paired with the younger to "cipher the slates," read stories, and review their Bible lessons. In the pioneer schools, several families bunched their children into one room. The young teacher, very often one of the oldest students, relied heavily on the children to help each other with lessons. Well into the twentieth century in rural America, the one-room schoolhouse—with cross-age tutors, cooperative learning groups, and group investigations—was the norm. Not until the urban school emerged and the modern factory arrived did schools adopt the assembly line model of teaching and learning. Even at that time, educational leaders such as Francis Parker, superintendent of Quincy Public School (1875-80), John Dewey, Carlton Washborne, and Martin Deutsch were strong advocates of the cooperative learning model. As early as 1897, Triplett was conducting the first formal studies. Today, thanks to the work of Johnson and Johnson, Slavin, and others, numerous studies document the powerful effects of cooperative learning as well as the specific elements needed to make cooperation work in the classroom. No other instructional method used today can claim the quantity or quality of research highlighting its success.

In the 1970s, two major school issues gave birth to a concentrated focus on cooperative learning. The first was the mainstreaming issue; the second was the integration challenge. When Public Law 94-142 was passed by Congress in the 1970s, schools had to restructure classrooms to include the handicapped. Many students previously separated from regular classroom life were mainstreamed. Regular teachers, not knowing how to deal with students who had physical disabilities or learning or behavioral problems were concerned. The first concern focused on how the "regular" and the "special" students would get along. Many of the mainstreamed students lacked social skills and could easily antagonize their peers; many regular students, who were equally lacking in these social skills, estranged their new classmates.

Following the integration directions established by the Supreme Court in Brown vs. the Board of Education, 1954, schools across the nation were challenged to restructure student assignment patterns. "Separate but equal" schools were out. As students from different racial groups were mixed into unsegregated schools and classrooms, the concerns focused on how these young people would get along.

Roger and David Johnson, two brothers at the University of Minnesota, proposed a solution that applied to both challenges—direct instruction of social skills with guided classroom practice. They theorized that students who were taught to work cooperatively in small groups would develop positive social skills. This in turn, they speculated, would speed the integration of students who saw each other as different.

To everyone's pleasant surprise, the data gathered in these early programs not only showed that their methods worked as planned for improving student-to-student interaction, but also had two unpredicted side effects—dramatic increases in the academic achievement of students and improvement in students' self-esteem.

From these early studies sprang more than five hundred studies by Johnson and Johnson and other researchers. Over and over, with a consistency and reliability remarkable for a school methodology, the studies have demonstrated how and why cooperative learning is one of the most powerful teaching and learning tools available. In a research article on the various models of teaching, Joyce, Showers, and Rolheiser-Bennett (1987) wrote: "Research on cooperative learning is overwhelmingly positive, and the cooperative approaches are appropriate for all curriculum areas. The more complex the outcomes (higher-order processing of information, problem solving, social skills, and attitudes), the greater are the effects."

No instructional tool has held researchers' attention more than the cooperative model has. Johnson and Johnson, perhaps the most prolific researchers of cooperative learning, claim we know more about cooperative learning than any other instructional methodology. They further point out that the results of the research on cooperative learning hold true regardless of factors such as age, subject matter, race, nationality, and sex.

THE MAJOR FINDINGS

- Students who learn in the cooperative model perform better academically than students who learn in the individualistic or competitive models. Johnson et al.'s 1981 meta-analysis of 122 studies shows that cooperative learning tended to give higher achievement results than the other two methods, especially with such higher-level tasks as problem solving, concept attainment, and prediction. Further studies indicate why this superior success occurs.

- Because of the amount of "cognitive rehearsal," all students at all ability levels in cooperative learning groups enhance their short- and long-term memory as well as their critical thinking skills (Johnson and Johnson, 1983).

- Because cooperative experiences promote positive self-acceptance, students improve their learning, self-esteem, liking for school, and motivation to participate (Johnson and Johnson, 1983).

- Because cooperative learning leads to positive interaction between students, intrinsic learning motivation and emotional involvement in learning are developed to a high degree (Johnson and Johnson, 1989).

- Because cooperative learning nurtures positive peer relationships and structures positive interactions, students in cooperative learning classrooms develop stronger scholastic aspirations, more positive social behavior, and more positive peer relationships (Johnson, 1979).

There are a variety of successful approaches to cooperative learning. Although it is clear to the researchers that classrooms organized for cooperative learning produce superior academic, social, and personal results, they do debate which is the "best" approach—at least as measured by research standards. Because few practitioners have the luxury of isolating classroom practice to the "purity" desired by the researchers, most classroom teachers adopt a single approach or a combination of approaches that works best with their own teach-

COOPERATIVE LEARNING: FIVE MODELS				
MODEL	**CREATOR**	**DESCRIPTION**	**PLUSES**	**MINUSES**
CONCEPTUAL APPROACH	Johnson & Johnson Cohen	Theories of cooperation, competition, and expectation-state theory	+ creative teachers create + can easily enhance what experienced teacher already does	- time away from content - no recipes - extra planning time - not step-by-step - unskilled teachers - full commitment
CURRICULUM PACKAGES APPROACH	Slavin	Curriculum packages that have cooperative learning structured into the materials	+ easy to train + daily + pretested strategies + instructional variety + basic skills	- no direct teaching of social skill - discourages transfer - not a lot of curriculum packages available
STRUCTURES APPROACH	Kagan	A repertoire of interactive strategies	+ simplicity in structures + easy to use + builds repertoire of strategies	- cutesy - assumes transfer if restricted to low-level tasks
GROUP INVESTIGATION MODEL	Sharan & Sharan	The ultimate classroom jigsaw	+ inquiry + social skills + creative problem solving + facilitates skills + gives depth to content	- not good for curriculum coverage - if students have poor social skills - if parents want same assignment for all
COGNITIVE APPROACH	Bellanca & Fogarty	A synthesis of the four cooperative learning approaches with higher-order thinking focus	+ synthesis + creative application + transfer + blend graphic organizers + macro-thinking processes	- needs training - needs commitment from school & district

Figure 1   Cooperative Learning: Five Models

ing style and their students. Ironically, the research on staff development tells us that the most effective practitioners are more likely to pull the best from each approach and create their own approaches.

THE FIVE APPROACHES

A brief look at the major approaches will help teachers clarify the pluses and minuses of each and understand the tremendous wealth of successful cooperative tools that have been developed (see Figure 1).

Model One: The Conceptual Approach

Roger Johnson, a science educator, and his brother, David Johnson, a social psychology researcher, use their early studies of cooperative learning to frame the conceptual approach. The Johnsons argue that all effective cooperative learning is marked by five critical characteristics. If all five characteristics are present, there is cooperative learning; however, if any one attribute is missing, there may be group work, but not cooperative learning.

Johnsons' Five Elements of Cooperative Groups

1. *Face-to-Face Interaction.* The physical arrangement of students in small, heterogeneous groups encourages students to help, share, and support each other's learning.

2. *Individual Accountability.* Each student is responsible for the success and collaboration of the group and for mastering the assigned task.

3. *Cooperative Social Skills.* Students are taught, coached, and monitored in the use of cooperative social skills, which enhance the group work.

4. *Positive Interdependence.* A structure that includes a common goal, group rewards, and role assignments is used to encourage students to assist each other in completing the learning task.

5. *Group Processing.* Students reflect on how well they work as a group to complete the task and how they can improve their teamwork.

In any cooperative lesson, these characteristics overlap. They are identified to reinforce the notion that all groups are not cooperative groups. As mental "coat hooks," the characteristics provide a framework for designing strong and effective cooperative learning tasks. They also provide an umbrella under which a large variety of cooperative strategies, structures, and activities may be gathered. As the teacher designs a cooperative lesson, these characteristics are the checklist to ensure the greatest success.

Pluses and Minuses For teachers who dislike recipe and workbook teaching, the conceptual model is a delight. In effect, the Johnsons' research acts as a touchstone against which the experienced teacher can measure what he or she already does with groups and make quick, positive adjustments that result in greater student-to-student teamwork. For the teacher who has never used groups, the approach provides standards that point out some sure ways to start. The Johnsons recognize—as do adult learning researchers such as Fullan, Knowles, and Krupp—that a teacher is most likely to add to a repertoire of skills and strategies when there are street lights to guide the progress.

There are several minuses to the conceptual model. First, it requires extra time for planning lessons. Even when used only as guided lesson practice, this approach requires time to restructure lesson plans. When the teacher is taking a bolder step to prepare an inquiry or group investigation, even more time is needed.

Second, the conceptual approach doesn't work well for teachers who want a workbook, ditto masters for step-by-step procedure manuals, absolute quiet, or straight rows of desks. This approach requires a teacher who is most comfortable creating lessons in and around required concepts and skills. The teacher who cannot tolerate ambiguity and the chance that a lesson might go flat without a step-by-step procedure manual, workbooks, or blackline masters shouldn't start here.

Third, the conceptual model may end up as poison for the bright child. When a teacher restricts most of the cooperative learning to low-level recall tasks (vocabulary review, computational practice, etc.), the gifted child never gets the chance to soar. Instead, he or she ends up as a substitute teacher, doing work for the other children, never reaping any of the social or intellectual benefits.

Fourth, the conceptual model requires a full commitment to learning and transfer. The teacher needs time to learn the model, to develop the skills, strategies, and structures and to redesign the classroom. As Bruce Joyce has pointed out, this instructional change process requires not only well-taught demonstrations, but also a solid peer coaching program and administrative support for implementing the changes.

Fifth, because there is no prepared day-to-day cooperative learning curriculum, the conceptual model sometimes is used only as a filler for "What do we do on Friday afternoons?" and "Let's play a cooperative game."

Finally, the conceptual approach bumps against the "coverage" curriculum. It takes more time in the crowded day to teach lessons in the conceptual model of cooperative learning. Where does the social skill instruction fit in? Where is the time for group processing? The conceptual approach demands time away from content coverage to ensure successful learning by all students.

Model Two: The Curriculum Approach

Slavin's research (1980), conducted with colleagues at the Johns Hopkins University Center for Research on Elementary and Middle Schools, focuses on cooperative learning and basic skill instruction. Slavin and his colleagues have developed a series of cooperative curriculum programs in math and language arts. They have prescribed specific cooperative strategies that teachers can easily learn as they promote heterogeneous cooperation. Because they desire workable alternatives to tracking and ability grouping practices, especially where those practices are detrimental to poor and minority children, they stress packages that all teachers can easily use. Slavin's curriculum packages include:

- Team Accelerated Instruction (TAI)
- Cooperative Integrated Reading and Composition (CIRC)
- Teams, Games, Tournaments (TGT)
- Student Teams, Achievement Division (STAD)

Team Accelerated Instruction (TAI) is a mathematics program that combines cooperative learning with individualized instruction in a heterogeneous classroom. Designed for grades three to six, TAI utilizes the students to tutor each other, to encourage accurate work, to produce positive social effects, and to handle the record-keeping logistics of individualized instruction or program- med learning. Every eight weeks, teams of high, middle, and low achievers take achievement tests for placement in the individualized program. In the teams, students help each other through the material. Each day, the teacher pulls students from the heterogeneous groups for focused instruction. Students work in teams and across teams to progress through the material. Each week, progress scores are established for each team. Criteria are established in advance for the degrees of recognition each team receives.

TAI is most notable for dispelling the myth that math instruction must be done by track or ability group. One look at the results clearly shows how TAI students of all abilities do better at computation in concepts and at applications with supportive effects in math self-concept, math liking, behavior, relations, and acceptance of differences (Slavin, 1980).

Cooperative Integrated Reading and Composition (CIRC). In preparing a cooperative curriculum for language arts, grades three and four, Slavin's group used cooperative methods for reading groups (eight to fifteen students) and reading teams (two or three students). As students work in their teams, they earn points for their groups. Points based on scores from quizzes, essays, and book reports allow students to earn certificates. As some teams use a variety of strategies, the teacher monitors progress or instructs other teams in comprehension strategies (e.g., predicting, comparing, drawing conclusions). Included in the strategies are partner reading, story prediction, words-aloud practice, spelling review, partner checking, and team comprehension games. At times, students work individually doing independent reading, basal work, or book reports.

CIRC research results are most notable for showing the benefits of cooperative learning with mainstreamed handicapped students, without detriment to the highest-performing students. In the studies, high, medium, and low performers showed equal gains, although the mainstreamed handicapped gains were most impressive.

Teams, Games, Tournaments (TGT) This may be the most widely known of Slavin's curricular approaches and is adaptable to any curricular area, K-12. In this format, students work in groups to master content provided by the teacher. After practicing on worksheets, students demonstrate mastery of the content in weekly tournaments. Students compete in teams against other teams of equal ability (e.g., top achievers vs. top achievers).

STAD (Student Teams, Achievement Division). STAD was designed by Slavin and the Johns Hopkins Group in 1982. In these heterogeneous groups, four or five students of mixed ability, ethnicity, and gender work on worksheets that already have the answers provided. The common goal is to understand the answers, not fill in the blanks. The teams quiz each other until all members understand the answers. The task is completed when the teacher gives an individual quiz to each member. The team score is the sum of the improvement points earned by each individual. Special recognition is given to the teams with the greatest improvement.

Pluses and Minuses   There are seven pluses for the curriculum approach to cooperative learning: (1) It is easy to train teachers. The lessons and strategies are preset for a beginning level training program and show how to use the set curriculum. (2) The approach builds in daily cooperative learning that needs little pre-planning on the teacher's part. By setting out daily lessons, there is higher probability that they will be used. (3) The strategies are pretested as appropriate to each content. The teacher can worry less about "doing the right thing." (4) The curriculum has built-in instructional variety. Small-group, large-group, and individual activities are balanced with direct instruction by the teacher. (5) The programs take a higher-order thinking approach to direct instruction and guided practice of content. (6) Most of the critical attributes of cooperative learning outlined by the Johnsons are inherent within each curriculum. And, (7) it gets results in self-esteem as well as academic achievement.

The minuses most frequently discussed regarding the curriculum approach center on social skill instruction. In the model, social skills are developed indirectly. There is no room given for direct instruction to students on how to work cooperatively. While the approach works very well with skilled classroom managers and with students who are well-behaved, many teachers report that it breaks down when competition (as in TGT or CIRC) between groups becomes too intense, the teacher lacks strong management skills, or the students have little experience or valuing of cooperative learning.

The second minus derives from the first curriculum thrust. The detailed, step-by-step procedure for implementing cooperative learning within a set curriculum discourages transfer of the approach to other curricular areas. For instance, if the teacher is using CIRC for math, he or she may not see any way to use cooperative learning elements in reading social studies.

The third minus is the very small number of developed cooperative curricula available for the classroom. Although some major educational publishers are suggesting some cooperative activities within science and language arts texts, the scope of well-developed cooperative curricula is limited.

Model Three: The Structural Approach

Since 1967, Spencer Kagan has focused his research on the structural approach to cooperative learning. This approach is based on the creation, analysis, and application of content-free structures that cause students to interact in positive ways in the classrooms. Content-free structures, usable with any content, enable the teacher to make multiple applications of a single structure in a variety of subjects. (The debate about content-free structures and content-specific structures is heard, it seems, whenever skill theorists get together. Their debates on study skills, thinking skills, social skills, and reading skills have very similar dialogues. While there is clear evidence that both content-free and content-specific structures produce positive effects, there is little proof that one method is superior to the other.)

Kagan's structures fall into three groups:

- *In Turn.* The teacher structures a task in which individuals take a turn in a prescribed order. Included among these are "round robin" or "response in turn," "round table," "four corners," and "three-step interview."

- *Jigsaw.* The teacher structures the task so that each student in the group has part of the information to study. When all members teach each other their material, the whole is greater than the parts. "Level I jigsaw," "level II jigsaw," "co-op—co-op," and "think-pair-share" all follow this format.

- *Match-Ups.* The teacher structures student-to-student tasks, which formally and informally create cooperative situations. Included here are "match mine," "numbered heads together," "co-op cards" and "partners."

Pluses and Minuses   The pluses and minuses of the structural approach begin with its simplicity. Each structure is easy to use. This means it takes less than a staff development hour to master a single structure and to develop a variety of appropriate activities. The new structures blend quickly with lecture format and provide practical ways to develop "quick," informal student interactions and well-structured discussions.

Just as teachers easily switch to cooperative structures from more traditional classroom methods, students also easily adapt to the new methods. Because of the number of structure options, a teacher can introduce more variety into the daily regimen and thus boost motivation.

As the teacher builds a more extensive repertoire of cooperative structures, it is possible to find a number of ways to create multi-dimensional lessons. For example:

Anticipatory Set. The teacher calls a student to the front of the class and interviews the student. "Who are you? What is your age? Where were you born? When did you start school here? Why do you think I am asking you these questions?" The answer to the why question would be to model an interview that uses the basic five questions of who, what, when, where, and why.

Objective. The teacher shows the lesson objective on the overhead: "To develop interview questions in preparation for a news article."

Input. The teacher shows the newspaper model on the overhead, explains the key questions, and demonstrates how the parts of the graphic are used. She or he uses the questions asked in the anticipatory set to demonstrate.

Checking for Understanding. The teacher tells the students to turn to a neighbor. Next, one student in each pair explains to the partner how to use the newspaper model to generate the questions. After three minutes, the groups stop. Several different listeners from the pairs describe what they heard. Other students give corrective feedback as needed.

Guided Practice. The teacher distributes one copy of the model to each pair. A recorder and a checker are assigned. The pairs review

roles and cooperative guidelines as the teacher monitors and assists the pairs as needed. After this round, several pairs describe the questions they asked and explain why they made each selection. Again, corrective feedback is encouraged. A second round of models is given out for additional practice.

Unguided Practice. For homework, all students are given a sheet of instructions for interviewing a household member of their choice.

Closure. On the next day, each pair joins a second pair and they review and critique each other's interview questions. This is followed by an all-class discussion about interview questions. Which questions are most important? Why? What benefits the writer?

Another plus is that the structures readily lend themselves to problem solving and the application of thinking tasks. For example, partner structures can work at any level of thinking (see Figure 2).

The simplicity of the structural approach is a double-edged sword. Because the structures look "fun and cute," a teacher may save the structures for Friday afternoon fillers. Consequently, the students get the message that these are play activities, and they reap little value from the potential richness of the cooperative structure.

The second minus is that the structural approach assumes a great deal about student transfer of the cooperative ethic, cooperative skills, and cooperative behaviors. Much is left to the teacher's enthusiasm, assertiveness, and ability to design a variety of lessons for each content area—that is, if the teacher's classroom management skills and enthusiasm are to hook students into cooperative tasks. However, because the structural approach works best as a hook, the cooperative skills are transferred more by osmosis than by formal instruction. As with the curriculum approach, the lack of formal group processing and social-skill instruction limits the transfer of cooperative skills beyond the specific task to the super learners.

The third minus of the structural approach occurs when the teacher restricts the use of cooper-

THREE THINKING LEVELS

Thinking Level I: Gathering Information

1. Assign each pair in a team a list of vocabulary words. Have the pairs coach and quiz each other on the meanings of assigned words. If any pair is unsure of a definition, have it check with another pair for advice.
2. When all pairs are ready, have a final check for mastery in each team. Follow this with a quiz in which teams compete against each other.

Thinking Level II: Processing Information

1. Have each pair use the vocabulary words to create a story about the current season of the year. If any pair gets stuck, let it "travel" for help to another pair.
2. Have each pair share its story with the team. Encourage the team to explain why each story was done well.

Thinking Level III: Applying Information

1. Have each pair hypothesize changes that might occur to the current season of the year if global warming increases in the next decade.
2. Have pairs share their hypotheses in a team. Assign one person in a team to list the hypotheses on a sheet of newsprint. Encourage the teams to discuss and rank their hypotheses based on which effect would be most disastrous.

Figure 2   Three Thinking Levels

SHARAN AND SHARAN'S GROUP INVESTIGATION MODEL

Stage One: *Posing the Big Question and Forming Groups by Interest.* The teacher frames the broad topic, which the students investigate as a "big" question.

- What do you think will happen if the U.S. produces twice as much nuclear waste per year each year for the next decade?
- How would American society be different today if we had lost World War II?
- What can we learn from a study of plant life?

After the big question, students are encouraged to brainstorm what they want to know about the topic. If they need stimulation, the teacher provides a potpourri of print or video materials, a guest lecturer or a field trip. Generated questions are reviewed in teams, and then classified and synthesized into subtopics for small-group investigation.

Stage Two: *Identifying the Inquiry Problem and Planning How to Research.* Each student selects a subtopic to investigate. The subtopic teams formulate the problem statement and help each other discuss and plan the search process.

Stage Three: *Dividing Up the Work and Gathering Information.* The groups divide up the research. Members research their information, analyze it, and draw initial conclusions.

Stage Four: *Preparing the Report.* The groups translate their results into a class report. The teacher schedules the reports.

Stage Five: *Presenting and Evaluating the Report.* As the groups make formal presentations, the teacher guides discussions on their results. Finally, students evaluate their work.

Figure 3   Sharan and Sharan's Group Investigation Model

ative structures to low-level and routine classroom tasks (spelling words, worksheets, computation drill and practice, etc.). Students quickly perceive such limited used as a gambit to manipulate quick interest.

Model Four: The Group Investigation Approach

One classroom teacher who used both the conceptual approach and the structural approach called group investigation the "ultimate jigsaw." "For my classes," she says, "group investigation is the most powerful and empowering of the cooperative methods." In group investigation, students work together to plan how they will find answers to key questions about a topic of mutual interest. The group breaks the work down into individual or pair investigation tasks. Each person gathers the assigned information and brings it to the group for discussion, synthesis, and reporting to the class. The teacher plays the major facilitating role through each stage of this inquiry process (see Figure 3).

Pluses and Minuses   If the teacher wants the optimum structure for encouraging inquiry, student-to-student interaction, cooperative social-skill development, creative problem solving, and communication skills, this approach provides it. If the teacher wants the maximum opportunity to use his or her facilitation skills with students, group investigation provides it. If the teacher wants students to delve deeply into a concept in the curriculum, then he or she will find no better motivator.

On the other hand, if the teacher is concerned about curriculum coverage or a supervisor who expects quiet students seated in rows or needs to know what each student is doing every moment, then group investigation will not work. If students are not well prepared for positive interaction, question asking, problem solving, and consensus seeking, or if they cannot handle the open-ended tasks, the group investigation will fall flat. And if parents expect uniform assignments, daily quizzes, and grades, grades, grades, don't even think about group investigation. In short, the minuses of this approach focus on lack of order and recall; its pluses focus on abundant cognitive rehearsal.

Model Five: The Cognitive Approach

A study of these various approaches shows that no one approach is sufficient or superior. Cooperative learning in some form is a necessary tool for use in every effective classroom. It serves the practical teacher to use a design that borrows the best from each approach and builds a foundation for thoughtfulness.

As we have listened and worked with teachers in their classrooms, it has become more and more clear that a synthesized model that ties cooperative learning with a critical and creative thinking context of learning for transfer is needed. We look at cooperative learning as an essential ingredient for developing students who are better able to think critically and creatively. We sometimes sketch the picture of cooperative learning as a jet engine with critical and creative thinking skills being the fuel. When put together, they produce the power needed for soaring to new frontiers of discovery and adventure.

The Essential Concepts Plus One   The Johnson and Johnson model outlines the five essential ingredients that distinguish cooperative learning from other forms of group work and which are necessary for making cooperative learning succeed in the classroom. When combined with cognitive processing (lessons focus on higher-order thinking tasks) the additional element of thinking for transfer is also added. And when each and every lesson is structured from this transfer perspective, even more dynamic changes occur in the classroom.

What the Kagan model calls cooperative structures, trainers in other fields, such as Blanchard et al. (business training and development); Canfield and Wells (self-esteem); Raths (values clarification); and Goodman (creative problem solving) have called strategies. Whichever name is used, the common element is that the strategies approach to staff development encourages the quickest transfer and use without falling into the workbook mentality. In Bellanca and Fogarty's cognitive model, an inductive approach is used. First, teacher trainees begin with basic strategies that are easy to apply and use. This is the practical element. The integrated staff development program begins with participants working together to plan how to weave these

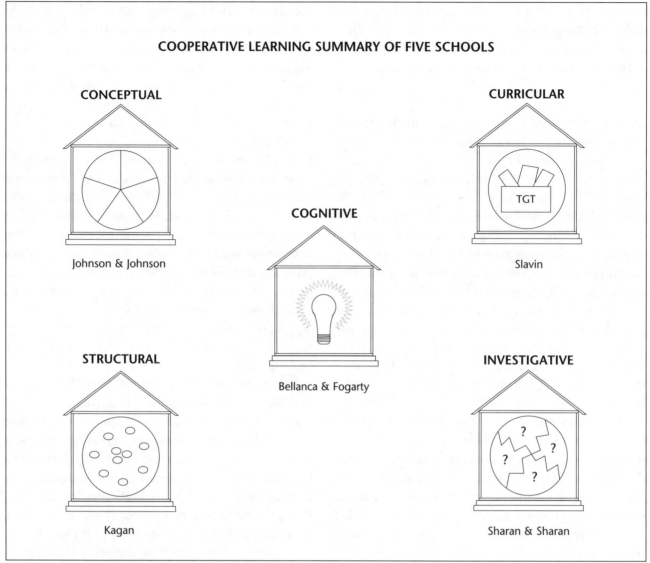

Figure 4 Five Schools of Cooperative Learning

basic strategies into the classroom. After the trainees have experienced strategies both as students and as teachers, they explore the conceptual framework; the concepts prevent the strategies from being isolated games. Later, in an advanced program, after intensive classroom application, the trainees focus on the more sophisticated strategies. These require students with higher-level social skills and concentration on inert cognition, problem solving, and reasoning in a variety of contents (e.g., math reasoning, language arts, science). In the final stage, trainees concentrate on two leaders for mentor coaching and curriculum renewal. Both extend the use of cooperative learning and cognitive instruction to teamwork and problem solving as key components for effective transfer.

Pluses and Minuses   The cognitive model asks for a long-term and intense commitment to staff development. Moreover, it expects that what happens in the training program, as well as what happens in the classroom, will be used. With this synthesis, teachers can begin switching from a focus on recall and quick-answer tests to a focus on transferring knowledge and skills across the curriculum, and into life outside the school walls.

This model takes time. In an already crowded curriculum, with more and more coverage being required, where is the time for group processing, metacognition, or social skills? To do these functions well, content coverage must give way.

The teacher who uses this model needs a high tolerance for ambiguity. If the classroom is a world of one right answer, the first precondition for developing intelligent behaviors and social skills is lacking. In this model, greater emphasis is placed on helping youngsters process and apply information than on having students memorize great quantities of detailed information. The teacher most often is asked to challenge and extend thinking and less often to inoculate students with information.

Teachers using the cognitive model also need strong planning skills and a creative beat. There is no page-by-page recipe or lock-step teacher's guide. Teachers must feel comfortable with their own ability to design lessons that incorporate not only cooperative learning, but also intelligent behavior and reasoning skills.

This model requires intense and supportive staff development for most implementors. This means the district will need to spend money not only for intensive training days, but also for coaching teams, administrative inservice, and opportunities to restructure curriculum.

The cognitive model is difficult to test with standardized instruments. This is especially true when trying to measure students' transfer of concepts, their ability to reason, and their acquisition of knowledge. To succeed, assessments other than scantron tests are needed. The cognitive model asks students to strive for intelligent behavior, not test results. This is well outside the norms imposed by the current interest in quick tests of isolated facts and skills.

The cognitive model will push a school on essential curricular change. Thinking and cooperating require more time for in-depth exploration of concepts and practice of skills and an emphasis on inquiry rather than answers. When the coverage of curriculum is the norm and isolated facts are king, there is no time for quality thinking or intense cooperation. Unless the school district is ready to challenge the restrictive time limits and coverage of materials, and unless it is ready to redesign curricula with transfer in mind, teachers can expect students to have a more difficult time with transfer.

The cognitive model does not necessitate total curricular changeover. But it does facilitate change by encouraging teachers to set new priorities in their curricula—i.e., "What are the most important concepts to establish firmly, and what are the facts to cover more quickly?"

It also encourages teachers to think about thinking skills as tools for unifying and integrating their curriculum. For instance, they can teach prediction in depth with language arts lessons and use science, math, and social studies materials for students to practice thinking skills in cooperative groups.

In effect, the combination of cooperative learning and cognitive development is not just equal to a math computation in addition (cooperation plus thinking is not the same as 3+3=6), but rather a multiplication of components (3x3=9) in the classroom. Add still another factor, a transfer-based staff-development program with structured coaching and support, and a powerful, exponential change process that produces effective, multi-dimensional results (3x3x3=27) is engaged.

REFERENCES

Bellanca, J., & Fogarty, R. (1991). *Blueprints for thinking in the cooperative classroom.* Palatine, IL: Skylight Publishing.

Canfield, J., & Wells, H. (1976). *100 ways to enhance self-concept in the classroom: A handbook for teachers and parents.* Englewood Cliffs, NJ: Prentice-Hall.

Deutsch, M. (1949). An experimental study of the effects of cooperation and competition upon group processes. *Human Relations, 2,* 199-232.

Fullan, M. (1982). *The meaning of educational change.* New York: Teachers College Press.

Johnson, D. W. (1979). *Educational psychology*. Englewood Cliffs, NJ: Prentice-Hall.

Johnson, D. W., & Johnson, R. (1989). *Cooperation and competition: Theory and research*. Edina, MN: Interaction Book Company.

Johnson, D. W., & Johnson, R. (1983). The socialization and achievement crises: Are cooperative learning experiences the solution? In L. Bickman (Ed.), *Applied social psychology annual 4*. Beverly Hills, CA: Sage Publications.

Johnson, D. W., Maruyama, G., Johnson, R., Nelson, D., & Skon, L. (1981). Effects of cooperative, competitive, and individualistic goal structures on achievement: A meta-analysis. *Psychological Bulletin, 89*, 47-62.

Joyce, B., Showers, B., Rolheiser-Bennett, C. (1987). Staff development and student learning: A synthesis of research on models of teaching. *Educational Leadership, 45*(2).

Slavin, R. E. (1980). *Using student team learning*. Baltimore, MD: Center for Social Organization of Schools, Johns Hopkins University.

Slavin, R., Leavey, M., & Madden, N. (1982). *Team-assisted individualization: Mathematics teacher's manual*. Baltimore: Johns Hopkins University, Center for Social Organization of Schools.

Triplett, N. (1897). The dynamic factors in pacemaking and competition. *American Journal of Psychology, 9*, 507-533.

BUILDING A CARING, COOPERATIVE CLASSROOM

—

James Bellanca

"A cooperative classroom? Students who respect and care for each other? My students only know how to put each other down."

"Teach students how to cooperate? Are you kidding? I don't have time to do everything else as it is. I've got test scores to raise."

"Social skills? Aren't they the job of the parents?"

"Come on now. You have to be kidding. What else do you want to add to the curriculum. Isn't it already an overstuffed sausage?"

"Isn't the school responsible for too much already? Why should we have to teach the social skills too?"

"These are just little children. Isn't this premature?"

Such are the legitimate questions that arise whenever the topic of building a caring, cooperative classroom erupts in the faculty lounge. Each deserves a thoughtful response.

Why build a caring, cooperative classroom? Why teach students how to cooperate? There are several valid answers. Each answer may not fit every school, but all describe contributing reasons.

The following three factors have contributed greatly to the increased number of students who have little idea about how to behave in a social organization, other than what they have learned from the negative social models that saturate their lives. As the number of these students increases, the amount of attention that a teacher can give to the academic work in school diminishes. More time is spent on correcting negative behavior, stopping for interruptions, and managing conflicts.

The Dissolution of the "Traditional" Family

Sociologists have documented the increasing number of children who come from single-parent, dual working-parent, and no-parent homes. We can now add the homeless child as well. They tell us that in today's world, these family structures are the norm, not the rare exception. These same sociologists have shown us the effects that the different family structures may have on student achievement and behavior in school (Comer, 1987). Most experienced teachers can corroborate those effects. And most parents, especially those who must raise children as the sole parent or as dual working parents, know the special challenges and unique child-rearing problems they experience. Probably nothing is more difficult than the lack of time these parents have for their youngsters. The time to support, assist, correct, model positive values, communicate expected behavior, and encourage social skills is often not there, not because the parents are bad, but because they are struggling to earn the dollars to keep the family fed and clothed. Add the decreased time and energy for proper supervision and the result is more students arriving at the schoolhouse door without the basic social skills in place.

TV Models

The change in family structure can account for only a small portion of the rationale for teaching social skills in the schoolhouse. However, when we combine the enormous number of hours that young people sit in front of the television each week with the decrease of adult supervision, support, and direction, we can readily see why the electronic baby-sitter has such a negative influence on young minds. Television, with its aptitude for modeling anti-social, anti-caring behaviors, has filled a void in the character formation of today's youth.

If a child wants to learn how adults learn to laugh, he or she needs only to copy the art of the put-down in today's situation comedies and cartoon shows. If a child wants to learn how adults solve problems, he or she needs only to watch the horror movies and the detective shows to master the arts of "shoot-em-down" or "beat-em-up." Love and kindness? Cooperation? Just review the soaps. Mutual support or caring? Try "family" shows such as "The Simpsons." Given the average student's four hours or more of television per day, it is a wonder that any positive behavior occurs on the playground or in the classroom (see Kubey and Czikszentmihalyi, 1990).

Unclear Value Focus in the School

In pursuit of our nation's desire to provide equal educational opportunity for all who come to the schoolhouse door, the desire to be free of religious influence inside the schoolhouse has caused our public schools to adopt a value-empty philosophy. This in turn has left most public schools without any focus on what is most important for students to learn. As so many studies on school excellence have argued, a school without a focus is like a ship without a rudder. In place of the traditional value focus, an "every man for himself" philosophy often dominates. In such an environment, young people become confused and unclear. In this state, they learn little about social responsibility, mutual caring, respect, or cooperation.

PARADIGM SHIFT

The long-range reasons for taking time to focus on cooperative social skills have to do with the paradigm shift our society is experiencing with more intensity each year. That shift has the world moving from a highly individualistic "me-first" social structure to a "we-sink-or-swim-together" structure.

We see the shift all around us. For instance, we see how many major corporations weave teamwork, quality circles, vertical decision teams, and other "we" approaches to participatory management into the fabric of their organizations. In several of the top MBA programs, students are assigned team projects, work for team grades, and are evaluated for their team contributions. The international economy requires business transactions with people of very diverse cultures. Success in the shrinking global economy depends very much on finely tuned "people skills."

If the American school is going to adhere to the ideal that every child be educated to the fullest of his or her potential, the problems and challenges created by the changing world in which both students and schools exist must be addressed. The school, and more specifically, the classroom teacher, can only do so much. Given this unique challenge and given the limited resources and the increasing pressures on education, the teacher and the school must start with what they can most control: instructional time and proven methods that address the problems which most regularly block quality instruction time.

The methods for teaching cooperative social skills have not only proven their worth (Johnson and Johnson, 1989; Cohen, 1986), but also provided a framework for intensifying academic achievement, fostering higher-order thinking, and extending learning into new dimensions for all learners (Joyce, Showers, and Rolheiser-Bennett, 1987).

What all this says to us is that tools do exist to counteract the problems and to move students to the high levels of learning that teachers desire. The task of moving students to higher levels of learning will require that we re-order instructional priorities, restructure curriculum, and reschedule time.

The answer to "why social skills," therefore, does not mean that a teacher has to cover less of his or her academic curriculum: it does mean that he or she will spend more time getting students ready for their academic work by taking some extra time in the beginning of the school year to change behaviors and attitudes. After the teacher takes the time at the start of the year to work on cooperative social skills, the students dig into the academic work more deeply with fewer interruptions and more time on task. Like the "little engine that could," the teacher puts a great deal more energy into getting the train to roll, but much less energy once the train is roaring down the tracks.

HOW CAN A TEACHER BUILD A CARING, COOPERATIVE CLASSROOM?

Creating a caring, cooperative classroom is a major teaching challenge. First, the attitudes promoted in the cooperative classroom run counter to the put-down, competitive culture in which most students live. Second, attitudes and beliefs don't change easily. Many students are deeply mired in negative, non-cooperative behaviors learned from their environment. Third, the effort and time needed to produce change is hard to find in the already full teaching day. But, it can be done! As Alfie Kohn (1986), Jeannie Oakes and Martin Lipton (1991), and other authors point out, there are a host of exemplary classroom models in which caring and cooperation are the rule. James Comer's work, IRI's Project Extend (Lewis, 1991), and classrooms in Washington, British Columbia, West Virginia, Oklahoma, California, and other states show that it is possible for even the most difficult and at-risk students to learn cooperative behaviors and develop caring attitudes.

One example of "best practices" in action was developed in Project Extend by a team of cooperative learning consultants. Project Extend, funded by the U.S. Department of Education's "Follow Through" Program, worked for three years in five school districts in northern Illinois. In that time, teachers and principals learned how to use cooperative learning as the critical instructional tool. Special emphasis was placed on teaching "at-risk" K-3 students how to work cooperatively, how to care about classmates, and how to respect themselves, their teachers, and their parents. Parents also learned to work with the cooperative framework and to reinforce the "we take care of each other" attitudes. As this project's research results show, a caring classroom focus can produce powerful academic results. Not only did students learn caring and cooperative behavior, they learned to read and do math at significantly higher levels than peers in the control groups (Lewis, 1991).

When is it Best to Start Social Skill Development?

A well-conceived early childhood program ought to be saturated with social skill instruction and opportunity for the young students to practice as they play together. Unfortunately, all such programs are not so well conceived. In some programs, more and more academic content is forced at earlier and earlier ages to such a degree that this rich opportunity for social skill formation is eliminated. In others, the students play randomly, sometimes alone and sometimes together. The ideal program, even at the pre-school stage, would provide some modeling, guided practice, and constructive feedback in cooperative social skills, along with language development and fun activities that make learning an active engagement for all students.

This social skill instruction cannot end with graduation into the primary grades. If anything, the primary grades can be the best opportunity for young students to fully develop the foundation of social skills which will ensure academic success and positive self-esteem in the later years. And, as students move into the middle grades where peer pressure is so strong, the encouragement and support must continue.

ENCOURAGEMENT

Sounds Like	Looks Like
"Keep at it."	thumbs up
"Atta girl!" "Atta boy!"	pat on back
"Way to go!"	smile
"Here's another way to look at it…"	head nodding
"Great idea."	beckoning hand
"Keep trying."	
"You're getting close."	

Figure 1   Encouragement T-Chart

Some upper-grade teachers argue that today's students didn't have this foundation. Thus, they say, it is a waste of time to start now. Nothing could be further from the truth. Although it may be more difficult to introduce students already formed with negative social skills to the values of cooperation, trust, and respect, it is never too late. In fact, it is probably all the more important to take the extra time and introduce social skills even in the twelfth grade if that is what the students most need.

What is the Best Way to Teach Social Skills?

In Project Extend, social skill instruction worked best in the direct instruction transfer model pioneered by the Johnsons. This model calls for six key steps in its recipe for success.

The hook or set. This is a "hands-on" classroom experience that engages students in what the cooperative social skill looks like and sounds like. The activity works best when it is content-free, fun, and engages all the students. Hands-on activities let children observe and assess their own use of the social skills they are learning. These in-class experiences provide a foundation that fills in the "prior knowledge" void with which these students enter the classroom. Once the void is filled, they can build their learning on a solid foundation.

The lesson. After each "hook" activity, the children reflect on what they did and said in the activity. Aided by the teacher's questions, the children develop one or two lists. List one identifies specific behaviors (words and actions) of the non-example (e.g., put-downs are the non-examples of giving encouragement). They may construct a second list of the exemplary behaviors (i.e., what words and actions encourage a person) (see Figure 1). Both lists are posted and labeled as acceptable or not acceptable. Whenever possible, companion lists that identify how someone might feel when treated with the O.K. and not O.K. behaviors can be posted.

Practice or follow-up. Massed practice (short, intense, and frequent) of the targeted behaviors follows the list-making. At least once a day for five to seven minutes, structured and explicit practice of the behaviors will cement the social skill and make it a normal behavior. Social skill practices work well as a daily sponge activity at the beginning of the elementary day. They also work as a sponge to close a day. The best massed practices are content-free, focused on the acceptable behaviors, and receive positive reinforcement for their display.

When it becomes evident that the students are becoming comfortable with the social skill in the artificial practice (this usually takes several weeks

Student \ Skill	CALLING EACH OTHER BY NAME	GIVING COMPLIMENTS	STAYING WITH GROUP	FOLLOWING INSTRUCTIONS
Sue	X	X	X	
José	X	X	XXX	X
Kyle	X		X	X
Maria	X	XX	X	X

Figure 2   Assessment Chart

with some reteaching and an occasional new "hook"), it is time to embed the skill practice into daily content lessons.

Reflection, discussion, or closure. As soon as the practices begin, it is best for students to also start their "look backs" and reflections on their practice of the social skills. At least once a week during the massed practice, it is best for students to spend time in structured reflections. At this time, they are asked to look back at their use of the targeted skills and discuss what they have learned about the social skill or its use, how much improvement they are making with the social skill, and how they might improve more. When the social skill is embedded in the lesson, it is helpful for them to reflect on how the use of the social skill is helping the small group, how the skill practice can be improved, other places to use the same skill, and how group members can help each other further develop the skill.

Feedback, recognition, and celebration. As the students demonstrate improvement in the use of the targeted social skill, private and public feedback on progress is the next step. The steps identified above create perfect opportunities for "catching students doing good things."

Some teachers keep a classroom chart, marking all instances of appropriate use of the targeted social skill by each student; others chart the progress of the class as a whole. (See Figure 2.) Some teachers use bean jars on each group's table to track each group's progress. Others hand out certificates when individuals or groups demonstrate marked improvement. Easiest of all, of course, is when the teacher stops by a group and affirms the positive behavior in very specific terms: "I like how this group is keeping its voices low by having only one person speak at a time."

To go along with the positive feedback, all-class recognition of social skill improvement and classroom celebrations for multiple successes are even more helpful for promoting transfer inside and outside the classroom. (Contrast the positive effect of writing a student's name or a group's name on the blackboard for demonstrating attentive use of a cooperative social skill to the destructive effect of publicly embarrassing the student by writing his or her name on the blackboard for disruptive behavior.) From simple "hurrahs" to certificates, popcorn parties, and earned time for every group that demonstrates growth in the day-to-day use of the targeted social skill, there are many options to let groups know that they deserve recognition for a job well done.

Transfer. To help students transfer the targeted social skill outside the classroom to the cafeteria, gym, playground, bus, and home, it helps if there is an all-school plan for recognizing classes that excel in using the skills throughout the school. It matters little whether classroom points are tabulated with precision or the staff votes on successful applications (this is not a competition; all classes that meet the application criteria outside the classroom walls deserve recognition). What matters is that the cooperative behavior is noticed, that recognition is made public to the rest of the students, faculty, and parents, and that students continue to reflect on their own positive behavior.

Within the classroom, transfer is much easier. By selecting one or two social skills per school year, the teacher can have ample time to reinforce and extend the use of each social skill into every lesson in the classroom. The behavior charts mentioned above are an easy means to encourage children to practice the social skills all day long. Thus, once the children show understanding of a social skill, the attendant behaviors, the skill's value inside and outside the classroom, and once they begin to use it automatically, it is imperative that the teacher embed the skill in every cooperative lesson. This is possible with little difficulty and no loss of time. At the beginning of each lesson, no matter what the content, the teacher can cue the class to attend to the practiced skill. By adding an incentive such as bonus points, a group reward, or the opportunity for the groups to assess the use of the skill, the teacher can heighten the students' attention to practice of that skill.

Which Social Skills Should be Stressed?

The possibilities are endless. However, there are several cooperative social skills that may be more helpful to students and teachers alike in starting the school experience. These "foundation" skills are calling each other by name, forming small groups, attending to instructions, and giving compliments. From a practical perspective, these are the skills that ensure basic management of the cooperative classroom. More importantly, however, they are the basic tools that enable students to discover the world of mutual respect.

With the foundation social skills in place, the teacher can move to the second level of skills that seem to have the most impact: encouragement and listening. While these are "big words" for young students, the direct instruction model makes concrete the abstract concepts of encouragement and listening. As students learn the specific behaviors associated with each social skill, they practice their use throughout each day, self-evaluate their progress, and experience the benefit of living in an environment where mutual listening and encouragement are the norm. As they give and receive positive encouragement, they empower themselves to think and believe that all learning is within their group. Caring becomes an authentic weave in the fabric of their school-life tapestry, not an isolated afterthought.

Once the students share their daily contacts with each other by listening and encouraging each other, other social skills are easily added: teamwork, collaboration, responsibility, friendship, conflict resolution, and problem solving.

What About Time?

Time is a question of priority. If caring and cooperation are an instructional priority, then the instruction will receive "time." For the direct model described here, a look at the lesson together requires thirty to forty minutes. To reinforce and review the students' applications, another ten to twenty minutes a day will suffice. If a teacher is teaching two or three social skills per year, the time is minimal. This is especially true if the teacher finds ways to integrate the practice into content lessons.

There are many opportunities to integrate social skill practices into lessons that are designed to develop reading, thinking, listening, and speaking skills through a variety of media.

- Social skills can provide a thematic bond for the reading of *literature*. Using video and print versions of classic myths, folk tales, and fables as models, children are exposed to literature as the springboard for learning about social skills. The children can be invited to examine the characters in the story and draw life lessons from the ways these literary characters solve problems and interact with others. Such video stories as "The Lion And The Mouse," "How The Elephant Got His Trunk" and "The Red Balloon" are a few examples.

- Throughout the social skill lessons, index cards can be used to label objects and to construct lists of words for *choral reading*. Overheads with simple instructions, bulletin boards with single-word procedures, and other easy-to-read methods extend oral reading opportunities throughout each lesson. In the choral reading, the teacher sounds out names attached to persons or objects and then leads the class as a chorus to practice saying the words.

- The teacher can group strong readers with readers who have lesser developed skills. The *readers are encouraged to read* as others in the small group follow along in a single text. In like manner, many social skills can be structured for the teacher to read aloud to the class. This does not mean that the weaker readers never read. It is advisable to rotate the reader and foster encouragement of fellow group members.

- Many activities invite student groups to *complete stories* or make parallel stories to enact in puppet shows or live drama for the class, other classes, or parents. If these are stories that exemplify the targeted social skill, the lesson provides a double opportunity.

- The teacher can structure group activities so that every student has the opportunity to *summarize ideas, stories, or decisions* and explain why the group decided as it did. By building in instructional strategies such as wait time, equal distribution of responses, the wraparound, fat questions, and all-student cueing (Bellanca and Fogarty, 1991), the likelihood that all students will become involved is increased. As they work on the content, they also practice the social skill.

Because students are learning these social skills to use for a lifetime, not for a test, the integration model has a unique capability for avoiding the time crunch. In addition to integration into language arts lessons, the teacher may elect to nest the social skills practice in cooperative math, social studies, science, physical education, and other subject lessons. To extend the practice, the teacher can join with other teachers to help students practice social skills in the cafeteria, the hallways, or recess.

When Do We See the Results?

At first, even the young students resist the shift in expectations from competition to caring. They feel uncomfortable. Many feel "phoney" before their peers. However, as the teacher reinforces expected cooperative behaviors, they see the changing norms. Once the "critical mass" is set, more students than not treat each other with care and respect.

What is the Best Way to Assess Student Development in Social Skills?

For the primary grades, use of the behavior T-charts will make it easiest to track individual progress. By outlining the specific behaviors the students need to develop, the teacher creates the format for behavior checklists and for evaluation.

When it comes time to report this progress to parents either on a formal report card or in an informal summary, the teacher can communicate progress on the basis of increased incidents of the desired behaviors or in comparison to standards. To set the standards, the teacher can decide how many instances of desired behaviors he or she would label as "outstanding," how many "steady," and how few "not yet." If the teacher must give a grade, he or she can write the name of the social skill that is the semester focus or use a more generic "cooperation" label on the report card (e.g., "Shows caring for classmates") and assign a letter or number grade appropriate to the number of incidents. For example:

	LETTER	NUMBER	SYMBOL
Listening	A	92	+
Encouraging	B	84	X
Doing Tasks	A	93	+
Caring	C	79	—

In addition to the behavior measure, it is helpful to make a portfolio of student work. This may include a "Cooperation Journal" with a weekly entry that focuses on what the child believes he or she has done well in using the social skills, copies of artifacts from the child's group work, and observation notes about the child's use of social skills in the classroom.

The student shift from competition and conflict to cooperation and caring requires a full commitment. In order to create a cooperative and caring classroom filled with students who demonstrate a genuine regard for each other, a paradigm shift at the most concrete level is required. It is a day-to-day, concerted teaching effort, led by teachers who model and teach what they expect and celebrate what their students accomplish.

———

REFERENCES

Bellanca, J., & Fogarty, R. (1991). *Blueprints for thinking in the cooperative classroom.* Palatine, IL: Skylight Publishing.

Cohen, E. G. (1986). *Designing groupwork: Strategies for the heterogeneous classroom.* New York: Teachers College Press.

Comer, J. (1987). Making schools work for underachieving minority students. Paper presented at a conference entitled *Our National Dilemma.*

Johnson, D., & Johnson, R. (1989). *Leading the cooperative school.* Edina, MN: Interaction Book Company.

Joyce, B., Showers, B., & Rolheiser-Bennett, C. (1987). Staff development and student learning: A synthesis of research and models of teaching. *Educational Leadership, 45*(2).

Kohn, A. (1986). *No contest: The case against competition.* Boston: Houghton-Mifflin.

Kubey, R. W., & Czikszentmihalyi, M. (1990). *Television and the quality of life: How viewing shapes everyday experience.* Hillsdale, NJ: Erlbaum.

Lewis, M. (1991). Unpublished report on *Project Extend.* Palatine, IL: The IRI Group.

Oakes, J., & Lipton, M. (1991). *Making the best of schools.* New Haven: Yale University Press.

DEVELOPING RESPONSIBILITY THROUGH COOPERATION

—

Margaret McCabe and Jacqueline Rhoades

If we expect our students to be responsible we must provide them with the opportunity to learn and practice responsibility. The objective of this chapter is to explain the relationship between cooperative learning and responsibility. To fulfill that objective we will offer a brief historical overview of the development of responsibility, how responsibility is defined and interpreted, and how specific components of cooperative learning enhance the development of personal and social responsibility.

RESPONSIBILITY—WHAT IS IT?

Historically, the characteristics associated with "being responsible" have changed as our society has changed; moving from an agricultural base to an industrial base to the information- and technology-driven world of today. At the turn of the last century, many individuals were born, lived, and died within a five-mile radius. Roles were clearly delineated. Expectations were clear. Although responsible behaviors differed somewhat from region to region and subculture to subculture, it was a rare child who did not know exactly what it meant to be responsible. Despite the changes brought by the industrial era, individual choices regarding behavior, career, schooling, and even the selection of a spouse were often limited to the expectations of the immediate society. The skills associated with being a responsible individual were mostly taught in the home and reflected the norms and values passed on from one generation to the next.

Today, the skills needed to function as a responsible adult have become more complex. We need a set of skills just to deal with the rapidity of changes occurring in our world. Technological developments have expanded our national and international awareness to the point that we know we must think and act globally; we can no longer limit our feelings of responsibility to our city or even to our state or country.

Since it is the role of our school system to prepare students for the world into which they will graduate, discussion about the school's role in any area of concern can be enhanced by knowing some of the changes we can expect in the next ten years. Conversations with Dr. Norman Feingold, an internationally known expert in the area of careers, indicate that half of the jobs that will be available to today's kindergartners when they enter the work force do not yet exist. Dr. Feingold also stated that individuals will change careers five to seven or more times in their lifetimes.[1]

Marvin Cetron in *The American Renaissance* wrote:

- In the next ten years the amount of raw knowledge will double and it will double again in the following ten years.

- By the turn of the century, 85 percent of employed adults will work in the service sector.

- Diversity will become valued.

- Within professions the body of knowledge that must be mastered to excel in a particular area precludes excellence across all areas (Cetron & Davies, 1989).

The fabric of the American society is changing. Families are on the move; the support system of the extended family is diminishing and the percentage of households with both parents working is increasing. Single-parent homes are also on the rise. The average amount of one-to-one contact time between parent and child is now approximately fifteen minutes per day.

While the skills required to become a responsible individual have increased, the traditional support system for transmitting these values, the family, has eroded.

The demands placed upon the education system to adjust to the requirements of the information age have been significant. A restructuring of curriculum content and of the process for disseminating that content has become an urgent task. While the "three Rs" remain essential components, the need to prepare our students for a rapidly changing world has become an imperative. The success and well-being of individuals and of our nation rest upon the school system's ability to produce responsible, thinking adults. But, what is responsibility and what characteristics are found in the responsible person?

The final report of the California Task Force to Promote Self-Esteem and Personal and Social Responsibility defined self-esteem as "appreciating my own worth and importance, and having the character to be accountable for myself, and to act responsibly toward others" (California Task Force, 1990, p.18).

The task force clearly affirmed the intricate interrelationship between self-esteem and responsibility by adopting as one of its premises: "Nurturing healthy self-esteem relates directly to and provides a solid foundation for developing personal and social responsibility" (California Task Force, 1990, p. 22).

The task force concluded that personal responsibility involves taking care of one's health; adopting a set of basic values that may include trust, honesty, truth, openness with self and others; making careful and informed decisions; and accepting the consequences of our actions rather than blaming others or circumstances if our decisions do not result in the outcome we wanted or expected. Citing the disposability of our current lifestyle, the task force also includes as an aspect of personal responsibility a willingness to make and honor a commitment.

We act responsibly toward others when we treat people with respect and dignity; when we experience a sense of competence; when we provide a feeling of belonging to others; and when we are involved in establishing rules and consequences of failing to follow those rules (California Task Force, 1990, p. 35).

Ernest Boyer suggests that civic education programs intended to help students become responsible should have several characteristics:

> *"Civic education is concerned, first, with communication. The work of a democracy is carried out through thoughtful discourse—town meetings, city councils, study groups, informal conversation, the television screen—and citizenship training, if it means anything at all, it means teaching students to think critically, listen with discernment and communicate with power and precision"* (Boyer, 1990, p. 5).

Boyer further comments that students in the civics classroom should not be passive, limited to writing papers or reading texts. Rather, the classroom should be an active place where students participate in mock trials and role play different governmental situations; students should be involved in the decisions made in the school as practice for what life will later require of them; and students should be helped to understand the relationship "between what they learn and how they live." Boyer believes that "education means devel-

---

ATTRIBUTES OF RESPONSIBILITY

- Being accountable for one's own actions: being answerable, acknowledging one's acts, not blaming others for one's own mistakes.

- Analyzing a situation and making careful decisions based on that analysis.

- Accepting the consequences of decisions and choices, i.e., not blaming circumstances or other people if choices yield undesired results.

- Ensuring one's own physical health.

- Having an awareness of the needs of a group and the ability to use this awareness to help the group work or live together more effectively.

- Getting along with others.

- Understanding other points of view.

- Having organizational skills.

- Knowing how to achieve consensus and make group decisions.

- Understanding how trust is developed.

- Being trustworthy.

- Growing toward independence—the ability to act on one's own, without being specifically directed by someone else.

- Growing toward interdependence—recognizing that no one lives in a vacuum; that what one person does affects others; and that working together results in greater success.

- Having the ability to make moral and rational decisions. Being capable of making these types of decisions presupposes a set of values within the mores of the society, knowledge of acceptable social behaviors, and an understanding of cause and effect.

- Being concerned with local and global issues.

- Having the ability to communicate with others.

- Understanding the economy well enough to handle personal finances.

Figure 1 Attributes of Responsibility

---

oping the capacity to make judgments, form convictions, and act boldly on values held" (Boyer, 1990, p. 7).

Sheldon Berman, president of Educators for Social Responsibility, notes: "Social responsibility is a personal investment in the well-being of others and of the planet" (1990, p. 75). Berman identified several aspects of social responsibility, including: developing a "consciousness of group," i.e., becoming aware of group needs, then using this consciousness to help the group more effectively work and live together; being able to understand another's point of view; having organizational skills; and having the ability to use consensus building and group problem-solving skills.

Berman (1990, p. 77) and Keister and Resnik (1990, p. 29) both suggest that in order to develop responsibility, students must be taught specific social skills such as effective communication, problem solving, and cooperation.

Finally, the American Heritage Dictionary defines responsibility as the act of being:

- Legally or ethically accountable for the care and welfare of another.

- Involving personal accountability or ability to act without guidance or superior authority.

- Capable of making moral or rational decisions on one's own and therefore answerable for one's behavior.

- Capable of being trusted…

- Having the means to pay debts or fulfill obligations" (DeVinne, 1985, p. 1053).

Clearly, responsibility is an abstract concept subject to different interpretations. There are, however, clear characteristics and attributes of responsibility that can be used when planning and developing specific educational goals or outcomes of instruction (see Figure 1).

Helping students develop responsibility means teaching:

- Critical thinking.

- Effective communication, including perceptive listening, and clear, precise speaking.

- Problem solving and conflict management.

- Cooperation.

We cannot expect our students to develop a sense of responsibility for themselves or for the society in which they live by simply talking about it. Developing responsibility is an active exercise. We need to provide instruction in the skills involved with responsibility but, perhaps more importantly, we must provide our young people the opportunity to learn about and develop a sense of responsibility through experience. In other words, we must provide them multiple opportunities to be responsible.

The final report of the California Task Force to Promote Self-Esteem and Personal and Social Responsibility suggests we act responsibly when we encourage people to grow beyond dependence toward independence and interdependence. Bringing this principle into the classroom requires a role change for many teachers. The traditional role of teacher as sole expert fosters dependence; the role of facilitator of learning fosters independence; and teachers and students becoming facilitators fosters interdependence.

One of the recommendations of this same task force was to encourage the use of cooperative learning strategies in all areas of instruction because these strategies "are among the best researched innovations within education. Hundreds of studies demonstrate academic, social, and psychological benefits from well-implemented cooperative learning programs, with improved self-esteem and a sense of shared responsibility being important outcomes" (California Task Force, 1990, p. 81).

COOPERATIVE MEETING MANAGEMENT TECHNIQUES

Cooperative learning as an instructional process inherently helps students develop responsibility because each student is not only accountable for her or his own performance, she or he is responsible for helping fellow group members know and understand the assignment.

Incorporating cooperative meeting management techniques further enhances individual responsibility. These techniques are based on the premise that every classroom is a meeting place. Students and teachers meet for the broad purpose of gaining knowledge and skills, to enhance abilities, to further develop strengths while improving areas of weakness, to explore novel ideas, and to revisit old ideas.

Our classrooms need to be safe environments where our students can take risks to reach and exceed their perceived ability levels and where each and every student feels important and valued. In other words, our classrooms should strive to become micro-communities. Introducing specific elements of the cooperative meeting management process into the classroom routine will promote these goals.

The first step in setting up a classroom based on meeting management theory is to recognize the factors inherent in group development. Whenever people assemble a group is formed. Some groups come together as a cohesive unit almost immediately. Others do not come together; they remain a collection of individuals in the same space, never seeming to agree on anything, never establishing supportive relationships, and usually failing to accomplish their goal.

Students in a cooperative classroom become a cohesive group with the teacher's guidance. A community is established with students caring, helping, and respecting each other. These students not only learn about responsibility, they gain social skills, enhance self-esteem, and increase their academic performance. To create the type of environment that fosters these characteristics takes time, effort, and energy but it is well worth it.

Teachers will need to guide their students through each of the following six stages in the group development process (Rhoades & McCabe, 1989) as shown in Figure 2.

Stage I—Setting Standards

Any group that meets on a regular basis will eventually develop a set of norms, behaviors that are expected or acceptable within that group setting. If the group is to be an effective one, meeting its objectives and accomplishing its goals in a timely manner, the first step is to establish these standards of behavior.

This is also true in classrooms. Unless the teacher establishes beginning norms, or standards of behavior, students are left in the untenable position of not knowing what is acceptable and what is not acceptable. Students are then forced to learn through trial and error and by observing the consequences their classmates face for certain behav-

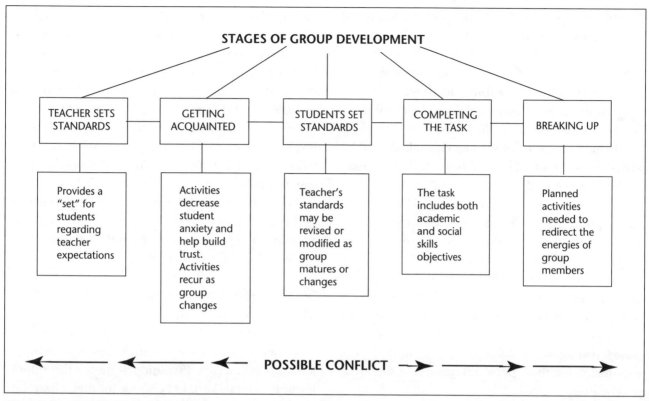

Figure 2 Stages of Group Development

iors. For example, Mark observes that nothing happens when Jack and Marie talk to each other while the teacher is explaining an assignment so Mark talks to Anne who is sitting next to him. A norm is beginning to become established that it's okay to talk to your neighbor while the teacher is giving directions. The likely result is that as soon as several students are talking to each other, the teacher will become angry and students will be reprimanded. The incident could have been avoided if initial standards had been set and explained.

So, the first step in developing a cohesive cooperative classroom is for the teacher to set standards in a conscious, directed manner and then to explain and model, if necessary, what is meant by each standard. To set standards, community norms and values as well as district and school rules must be considered because classroom rules cannot contradict the already established standards of community and school. Teachers need to think about what is really important, what behaviors are completely unacceptable and what behaviors are an absolute must. It is best to begin with no more than

five standards of behavior and each should be phrased in positive terms: e.g., "Raise your hand before speaking," rather than "Don't speak out."

Sample Standards:

Be on time. This means that students are responsible for being in their seats or work areas at the appointed time.

Be responsible for your own learning. This is a different approach than we usually see in our nation's classrooms. It means that the teacher will: do everything possible to provide a stimulating and exciting learning environment; share as much information, data, and materials as possible; offer as many experiences as possible; and be available to listen, discuss, or otherwise promote mutual learning. It is then the students' responsibility to avail themselves of the resources and to share their own ideas.

An addendum to this standard is that students must first request help from other members of their group. In other words, if students are confused, have questions, or miss something, they must first ask other group members for help. If no one in their group can help, the student then asks the teacher.

Students' questions should always be answered but students must take the initiative to clear up any confusions they may experience.

Be responsible for your own materials and assignments: Students have a responsibility to themselves and their cooperative group members to carry their share of the work load. A clear procedure outlining how to gain access to resource materials should be posted for students. This will help students actualize their responsibilities.

Only one person can speak at a time: This is one of the beginning steps in teaching communication and meeting management skills. It cannot be assumed that students of any age have internalized this basic socialization skill. This standard gives a strong message that what each student has to say is important and students are to show respect for each other's contribution to the group effort.

Keep your work and desk area clean: Students are responsible for their personal space and the areas used by everyone.

Stage 2—Getting Acquainted

The first time students enter a classroom in a small school they may already know all or most of the other students. In larger schools, however, they may recognize only one or two other students. Taking time to help students become acquainted with each other will develop group cohesiveness, or a sense of community, more quickly. This, in turn, promotes accelerated learning of both social skills and academic content.

There are numerous getting acquainted activities that can be completed within a few minutes. Examples include a variety of interview questions about information such as: name, number of brothers and sisters, favorite food, pets, favorite things to do, etc..

Two other types of activities closely related to getting acquainted activities are *openings* and *transitions*. Opening activities are used at the beginning of the school day; they help students get ready for their school work by developing a "mind-set" for the day. An example of an opening activity is the Focus Worksheet (see Figure 3), which is a prepared worksheet on which three to ten questions have been listed. The questions may be academic,

social, trivia, or a combination thereof. Each student receives a copy of the worksheet with instructions to complete it by interviewing fellow students. Give a specific amount of time to complete the activity, five to fifteen minutes depending on the complexity and number of questions. Be prepared for a lot of movement and a relatively high noise level. At the end of the time, the teacher can have students hand in their completed worksheets or discuss each question with the entire class.

The Focus Worksheet is excellent for reviewing and reinforcing material, preparing for a test, becoming better acquainted, and for preparing students for the school day.

Stage 3—Students Setting Standards

This stage of group development provides an opportunity for students to have a say in the class rules. It empowers them; it tells them their thoughts and opinions are important. Providing students the opportunity to set standards of behavior for their classroom is collaborative management. This step gives students the chance to become self-regulated which leads to sense of social responsibility. It also teaches them that by following specific procedures, they can make a difference. As a high school principal, one of the authors offered students the opportunity to challenge and change established school rules or to add others. By following a specific process that included gaining consensus of the student body, approval of local merchants, approval of faculty and finally of the school board, students successfully had the campus changed from a closed to an open one at lunchtime.

Each teacher must decide which initial standards may not be changed and when it is appropriate to offer students the opportunity to review standards. New standards can be set by students only with a consensus decision from the class as a whole.

Stage 4—Completing the Task

In this stage students work, individually and in cooperative groups, toward academic and social skills objectives. Some teachers will be able to involve their students in setting standards before any serious academic activity occurs. Other teachers will not involve students in setting standards until weeks into the term.

FOCUS WORKSHEET

INSTRUCTIONS:

(a) Find someone who can and does correctly answer the following questions or who fits the description.

(b) Have that person sign on the appropriate line.

(c) Each question or description should be signed by a different person.

(1) What are getting acquainted activities?_____

(2) Describe the major stages of group development: _____

(3) Someone wearing blue:_____

(4) What is one definition of "responsibility"?_____

(5) Someone who ate spinach last week: _____

Figure 3   Sample Focus Worksheet

Stage 5—Breaking Up

There comes a time for each group to end, to break up. This can be a difficult time for students in a cooperative classroom because the group has become a cohesive community. Students can work through their feelings of loss and anxiety if activities are carefully planned. These activities must help provide a living memory of their time together and also redirect their energy to the next phase of their lives. Activities such as exchanging photographs, planting trees, writing a letter to the next class, and visiting the next grade level help with a difficult transition.

Stage 6—Conflict

The sixth and last stage in the group development process is conflict. In actuality conflict is not a stage in the normal sense of the word. It does not occur at a specific time in a sequence; it can occur at any time in the group development process.

Conflict is a normal part of any relationship development process, whether between two people or among a group. As intimacy is gained, students will feel safe enough to express their opinions, thoughts and feelings and the teacher will be faced with conflict.

Strangely enough, conflict is most likely to occur during the last weeks of the school term. The reason for this is because students are suddenly faced with losing the group they have come to trust.

Anxiety and frustration accompany this feeling of loss which is similar to the grief cycle. Disagreements and conflict occur as ways of dealing with these feelings. (It's a lot easier to leave someone you like and trust if you have a fight—you can go away angry.)

Planning and implementing breaking up activities will diffuse much of the conflict that can occur at the end of the year. Knowing and using the process of group development is an important tool in instilling the concepts of responsibility in young people. The next step when incorporating meeting management techniques in the classroom is to integrate group roles into cooperative lessons.

Teaching and using group roles associated with meeting management will encourage shy students, students with low self-esteem, and low-performing students to participate. Roles will build their self-confidence, which will be reflected in greater academic achievement. At the same time, group roles will encourage verbose students to share some of the limelight with the quieter students.

Group roles help students become aware of how their actions affect the group's productivity. Students develop a sense of responsibility for their own behaviors. Group roles, however, do not occur spontaneously. Each needs to be introduced, explained, modeled, and practiced. Introduce one role at a time and give students sufficient time to practice and master each role before moving on to the next one. Roles should be rotated among students so that every student has the opportunity to develop the skills inherent in each role. Rotating roles also reinforces the concept that each student is of equal importance to the group.

You will notice that we do not include a role called "leader." We want students to share equally in the responsibility of the group's outcome, with leaders come followers. Groups tend to depend on the "leader" to take more responsibility for completing the assignment; we want each student to take this responsibility.

It's best if the teacher assigns the roles for each group, especially during the first several months. There are a couple of reasons for this: first, teacher-assigned roles eliminate the possibility of conflict that can arise when two students in the same group want to be the facilitator; second, the teacher can assure that each student will have the opportunity to perform each role multiple times during the school year; and third, knowing the skills of each student, the teacher can assure a successful experience—as an example, the teacher would not assign the role of recorder to a student who could not write.

Assign only the roles needed for each activity, i.e., if nothing needs to be written to complete the assignment, the recording role is not assigned.

In our experience, the roles that are beneficial in most classrooms are:

Group Member: Unfortunately, too many people think they know what it is to be a group member—you attend the meeting and perhaps even participate, but you wait for someone else to take the lead; it is also somebody else's responsibility to make certain everything runs smoothly. This attitude results in one or two students doing all the work for the group. This is not a cooperative effort. Clearly identifying the group member as a critical role with specific responsibilities will reinforce the concept of individual accountability.

When explaining the role of group member, point out that this is the most important role because we are always group members and the success of the group is dependent upon every member doing his or her share of the assignment.

The following list reflects the responsibilities of the group member and the reason each is important:

- Arrive on time because tardiness breaks the flow of work already in progress.

- Actively participate by contributing ideas and suggestions.

- Attend to the task and refrain from distracting the group with behavior unrelated to the task, because time is wasted and the quality of the product lowered unless every member gives undivided attention to the task at hand.

- Help the group complete its assignment; group members are collectively and individually responsible for the completion of the assignment.

- Follow through on assignments and agreements made in the group. If one member does not complete his or her part, the group product will be incomplete.

- Take turns speaking and listening to other members; this reinforces the concept of equal importance.

- Encourage other members of the group to share their ideas.

Facilitator-as-Monitor: This role is the same as the traditional monitor role. We refer to it as a facilitator because the title familiarizes students with the terminology, which prepares them for the more complex facilitator role.

Responsibilities of the facilitator-as-monitor are to:

- Get and distribute written assignments to group members.

- Quietly and quickly get the materials necessary for the completion of the assignment or project such as the dictionary, thesaurus, or other reference sources.

- Collect group work and turn it in to the teacher.

Beginning Recorder: This person's job is to keep a record of the group's discussion and ideas as they relate to the assignment and to write the group's responses for the assignment.

Praiser: The praiser's job is to give compliments and praise to members of the group for specific preselected behaviors such as: staying on task; completing assignments; returning quietly after a break; listening to others; paraphrasing, and so on.

More often than not, students do not know how to give and receive compliments or praise, yet giving and receiving praise gracefully and sincerely is a very special and important social skill. This is also a skill that requires direct instruction.

One activity that helps students learn how to give compliments or praise is to have the class brainstorm some praising statements and write them on the chalk or white board. Those that come up frequently include: "Good job;" "Good idea;" "You're really listening to others;" and whatever the current vernacular is among our youngsters; some examples from the past include: rad, bad, and awesome. Students tend to go overboard when first learning this skill; the praising sounds really phony but eventually students become more sincere and perceptive, and praising becomes a normal part of their communication and interaction process. The role of praiser helps students learn to focus on the positive rather than criticizing or finding fault with others.

Timekeeper: The role of timekeeper is a simple but important one in the group. The timekeeper helps the group pace itself by keeping track of how much time has been used for a task and how much is left to complete the task. It is important to give examples of when and how to give the group time alerts. With one class, one of the authors did not make it clear enough about when to give warnings; in one group the timekeeper interrupted the group every five minutes telling the number of minutes used and the number of minutes left.

To teach this role, explain and model the responsibilities:

- Periodically tell the group how much of the allotted time has been used and how much is left to complete the assignment. For example,

if forty-five minutes has been allocated to writing a paper, the timekeeper would say something like: "We have used twenty minutes and we have twenty-five minutes left."

- Give fifteen-, ten-, or five-minute warnings before the expiration of the time, as appropriate. The warning times depend upon the amount of time allocated. When a half-hour is provided, it's helpful for the group to have fifteen- and five-minute warnings; when only fifteen minutes are allotted for the assignment, five- and two-minute warnings are appropriate.

Checker: This role is used when students are reviewing or studying material that has a correct answer, such as spelling words, vocabulary, or math facts. The checker has the answer key and tells group members whether their answers are right or wrong. If the response was incorrect, the checker provides the correct answer.

The role of the checker may be rotated around the group by passing the answer key to the next student after each question.

Observer: The observer's role is descriptive only. Its purpose is to improve group interaction and increase the efficiency and effectiveness of the group by giving an objective report about how often a desired behavior is occurring.

The observer is assigned a specific behavior to observe. He or she sits just outside the group in a position that makes it possible to see and hear each member. Using paper and pencil, the observer counts and records the frequency of the specified target behaviors. At the end of the time period, the observer reports back to the group.

The observer's report recognizes and reinforces behaviors that enhance group success without condemning or judging the lack of those behaviors.

The key to understanding the observer role is knowing what a behavior is. It is something that can be seen or heard; it is tangible and it can be counted, i.e., it is quantifiable. A behavior is not an attitude, value, feeling, or judgment. "Jamie is nice" is not a behavior, it is a judgment. It doesn't say anything about Jamie because we each have different perceptions of what "nice" is. "Jamie invited me to play a game with him" is a behavior. It can be seen and it gives a clear statement of what Jamie did.

To teach the observer role, it is first necessary to conduct a lesson on the difference between behaviors and feelings and judgments. One way to lead this lesson is to write two columns on the chalk board; one column for behaviors, the other for feelings or judgments. Elicit from students words associated with each. For example, words in the behavior column might include: late to class; offers ideas; asks questions; makes noises. Words in the other column might include: rude; impolite; distracting; nice; courteous.

Assign the role of observer for only five to ten minutes at a time. The observer:

- Is objective, not evaluative or judgmental.

- Sits just outside the group but close enough to see and hear what is being done and said.

- Counts and records the frequency of a specified target behavior. (Students must have been taught and have practiced the behavior being observed.)

- Gives an oral report to the group at the end of the observation time. It is important that the report be given with neither emotion nor editorializing comments; this includes such subtle cues as: "Chuck praised four times, Lillian only praised two times." The interjection of the word "only" is a qualifier and denotes an evaluation. Tone of voice, raised eyebrows, smiles, frowns, and other nonverbal cues also act as powerful evaluations and detract from the purpose of observation.

Other points about the role of observer:

- Observe only behaviors that have been taught and practiced.

- Make positive observations about behaviors. For example, observe "taking turns speaking" rather than "did not interrupt others." Positive observations enhance the supportive atmosphere of the classroom and focus on what you are trying to have students learn.

- Primary-age children and nonreaders can be taught to observe. Symbols or pictures can identify the behavior, e.g., a picture of children engrossed in reading or writing to represent "on-task" behavior. Color codes can be used instead of names, with each student wearing a colored tag that matches a space on the observation form. The observer can then make a mark next to the appropriate colored space to count how many times each group member demonstrates the specific skill (McCabe & Rhoades, 1989).

As mentioned before, these are just a sample of the roles that can be used in the classroom. There are many others that can be introduced to help students to learn how to work within a group more effectively and to develop responsibility.

Teaching cooperative meeting management roles, effective communication techniques, problem solving, and conflict management leads to more responsible, community-conscious students. Students realize they are not lone entities; they learn that their actions or inactions affect others as well as themselves. Their learned social skills make them better prepared for future academic, social, and occupational endeavors.

CONCLUSION

What happens when students become responsible learners? Students become more enthusiastic learners, their learning and retention increase, and both students and teachers have more fun in school. Cooperative learning provides a research-based methodology for the classroom teacher to teach social skills. Cooperative learning is a vehicle through which personal and social responsibility can be developed and reinforced.

NOTES

1. Norman Feingold. National Careers Center. Washington, D.C. Continuing conversations 1982 to present.

REFERENCES

Berman, S. (1990, November). Educating for social responsibility. *Educational Leadership, 48,* 75-80.

Boyer, E. (1990, November). Civic education for responsible citizens. *Educational Leadership, 48,* 5-7.

Boyer, E. (1988, Fall). The future of American education: New realities, making connections. *Kappa Delta Phi Record,* pp. 6-12.

California State Department of Education. (1987). *History-Social Science Framework.* Sacramento, CA: author.

California Task Force to Promote Self-Esteem and Personal and Social Responsibility. (1990). *Toward a state of self-esteem.* Sacramento, CA: California State Department of Education.

Cetron, M., & Davies, O. (1989). *The American renaissance.* New York: St. Martin's Press.

DeVinne, P. (Ed.). (1985). *The American heritage dictionary.* (2nd college ed.). Boston: Houghton Mifflin.

Educational Leadership. (1989, December - 1991, January). Alexandria, VA: Association for Supervision and Curriculum Development.

Feuerstein, R. (1980). *Instrumental enrichment.* Baltimore, MD: University Park Press.

Goodlad, J. (1984). *A place called school.* New York: McGraw-Hill.

Keister, S., & Resnik, H. (1990, November). Responsibility is an active word. *Educational Leadership, 48,* 29.

McCabe, M. E., & Rhoades, J. (1989). *The nurturing classroom: Developing self-esteem, thinking skills, and responsibility through simple cooperation.* Willits, CA: ITA Publications.

McCabe, M. E., & Rhoades, J. (1986). *Cooperative meeting management.* Willits, CA: ITA Publications.

Meichenbaum, D. (1979). *Cognitive behavior modification.* New York: Plenum Press.

Reische, D. L. (1987). *Citizenship: Goal of education.* Arlington, VA: American Association of School Administrators.

Rhoades, J., & McCabe, M. E. (1985). *Simple cooperation in the classroom.* Willits, CA: ITA Publications.

United Way Strategic Institute. (1990, July-August). Nine forces reshaping America. *The futurist.* Bethesda, MD: World Future Society. pp. 9-16.

THE POWER AND THE PROMISE OF COOPERATIVE LEARNING

—

Marie Meyer

T he decade of the 1990s has ushered in an era in education with powerful research-based practices making it comparable to the decade of the 1950s in medicine with the advent of antibiotics. Teachers are coming to the realization that learning to teach takes a lifetime and that an education does not result from passive learning but from thinking actively, creatively, holistically, and collaboratively.

Cooperative learning has the power and the promise to transform teaching and learning beyond the classroom walls to the family, the community, the voting booth, and the workplace. It is more than just another method for instruction; the philosophy and conceptual model are preparation for a world characterized by interdependence, pluralism, conflict, and rapid change.

The factory model that has served as the structure for American education for decades is based on competitive rote learning and on the view that schooling is finished at some point, rather than on the concept that learning is a life-long process. Nowhere is there more reluctance to change this model than at the high school level. Finally, however, more and more risk-taking and confident high school teachers have begun the shift. The age

of cooperation is approaching, from Alaska to California to Florida to New York, from Australia to Norway to Israel to Britain, with increasing numbers of students in secondary schools having the opportunity to join a community of learners. There is growing substantial evidence that high school students who are working successfully in small cooperative groups master content better than students working on their own. One only has to interact with high school teachers practicing cooperative learning to experience the successful transformation that is taking place for both the students and the teachers.

IN THE SCHOOL

Glenbrook North High School

"I have been teaching high school mathematics for ten years and I used to be able to tell in the first three weeks of a semester which students would make it and which would not. Now, with few exceptions, everyone in my classroom is successful," reports Dan Workman, a math teacher at Glenbrook North High School, Northbrook, Illinois.

Dan Workman and Sonia Reardon, a special education teacher, both teach at Glenbrook North

High School, District #225, Northbrook, Illinois. They have been team teaching and using cooperative learning in basic track algebra classes for the past three years. They report that cooperative learning is not only good for the students but is good for the teachers as well; "Formerly, working with a lower-level algebra class was boring." In a cooperative learning classroom, the students concentrate and are more creative; they experience successes which they would not normally achieve in a non-cooperative classroom taught by one teacher."

Dan and Sonia compared traditional and cooperative classes in a study using quizzes, tests, homework, and individual student surveys. Special education students were included in both the experimental group and the control group. The experimental group was consistently more confident in its ability to master algebra and expressed a higher expectation that they would learn more in their algebra course than in their other courses. Identified handicapped learners also expressed higher confidence. A comparable percentage in both the experimental and control groups indicated a desire to learn algebra, but the experimental groups were significantly higher in valuing algebra. This included considering algebra as a way to see things from different perspectives, finding it enjoyable and viewing it as a means to learning new communication skills, as a vehicle for cooperating, and as a means to respect others' rights. These ways of valuing algebra indicate an ability to appreciate multiple perspectives and to use communication and cooperative skills.

In the data on relationship skills, the control group reported significantly higher incidents of *not* knowing their classmates. More experimental students expressed caring about others' failing; the control groups were convinced that someone has to fail. The data supported the conclusion that members of the experimental classes knew each other better, cared more about each other, and were more supportive of each other.

In comparing test scores, there was little noticeable difference on the variability in test one but by test three an interesting trend developed. The means for the two groups remained close; however,

the variability in the regular class increased. In the cooperative group, fifty percent of the scores fell in the 82-92 range, while in the regular class the range was from 72-90. Students in the cooperative group gravitated toward the mean, while the regular group became more divergent.

In comparing homework and six-week averages for first-semester classes, the experimental group averaged 83.2 while the regular class averaged 65.1. In the cooperative section peers helped peers complete homework so that it was finished on a regular basis. This was reflected in less variability of scores in this section. What makes the data even more remarkable is the failures had been removed from the regular class.

The teachers report that what happened in the cooperative learning classes didn't happen in the regular classes. As one teacher said, "It was interesting to see that [in the cooperative class] the brighter students didn't just want to work with the other brighter students and that their goal was not only to get through the work and get the right answer." Both teachers report incidents where students set aside time in study hall and after school to help each other, and even when they switched groups every six weeks, they would still continue to work with students that they had gotten to know in the former group. The students reported that this was a really different experience than they had in other classes and that "it almost felt like a family."

Sonia said the group experiences helped students who would formerly have been afraid to answer or ask questions, sometimes because they "would feel stupid." These students progressed to being willing to ask questions in front of the whole class. For them this was the biggest learning and growing experience. Several girls had indicated that they were intimidated by going to the board and working problems, so each group was given overhead transparencies and markers and allowed to prepare a problem. They drew visuals to present to the whole class. Then, instead of one person going to the overhead, the group of students would go there together and they would feel a lot more confident. During a grading period, a group's average on quizzes was used for a special prize from a "Treasure Chest" for the group whose average increased the most. Banding together gave them a certain spirit and they charged ahead and also encouraged other groups. Dan and Sonia found students giving each other "high fives" and congratulating one another. At the high school level it is strange even to hear a student say "thank you, you really helped me out." Having students giving one another a "high five" and saying "good job" was unusual; but even though the students felt odd, they continued to do it.

Dan reports he knows his students better because he doesn't stand in front of the room talking at them, but walks among them and talks with them. Now, when he meets these students in the hall, even after they are no longer in his classes, they let him know how they are doing in math.

Wilmington High School

Barbara Hansen, a high school English teacher in Wilmington High School, Wilmington, Illinois, graphically portrays "BC" (before cooperation) and "AC" (after cooperation).

"My desks were in neat rows. Students took notes as I lectured. I covered the curriculum. I called on students who raised hands. It was a classic picture of a well-managed high school English class. Like many classrooms across the country, mine was quiet, orderly, systematic, and nearly antiseptic. I was a traditional high school teacher who taught individualistically; that's how I had been taught to teach. Now dramatic changes are occurring in my classroom, and cooperative learning is the catalyst. Some of the changes are the kind that are measurable; for instance, student failure rate has dropped by 15 percent to 4 percent; but, more importantly, the student success rate has markedly increased, not through grade inflation but through student production.

What produced these results for Hansen? How firm was her data? Hansen reports: "On a vocabulary unit, I divided the mastery words into two sets. The first set I taught traditionally, i.e., individualistically, and the second set I taught cooperatively. Students took mastery tests on their own. A comparison of the two sets of test scores showed that only 24 percent of the students achieved results in the A/B grade range on the portion that was learned individualistically, while 76 percent scored in the A/B range when the cooperative structure was used. The class average increased from 71 percent to 92 percent, with more than two-thirds of the students showing improved test scores after using the cooperative method for learning. The whole process was repeated the following year on the same unit and had similar results. The conclusion was simple: student achievement on vocabulary work increased dramatically when students were engaged in cooperative learning strategies."

In addition, Hansen reports on other kinds of changes in her classroom that were not as easily measured but were present and valuable. "When my students work cooperatively they enjoy it," she says. "In small learning teams, they increase each other's chances for success by creating mnemonic devices to aid retention and by drilling, quizzing, and checking each other's understanding. Verbalization is required from each group member. It is the old 'cognitive rehearsal' game, but with a new twist: they are having a good time while doing vocabulary work."

While monitoring the groups, Mrs. Hansen observed that the students were staying on-task, smiling, laughing, and creating clever, humorous ways to help each other remember the material. Somehow, she noted, learning and enjoyment had become separated in her traditional classroom; in her cooperative classroom, learning and enjoyment are together where they belong.

Hansen took cooperative learning beyond vocabulary and regurgitation. In her American literature curriculum, high school juniors had perennially studied Thoreau's *Walden*. They seldom liked it. Hansen's standard, traditional lesson plan included having students take notes during a lecture, read from the text, answer some study questions, and take a test. How did her plan differ when she translated *Walden* into a cooperative lesson?

"First," she reports, "I divided an introductory lecture into small segments, ten minutes in length, with each segment ending by requiring students to make a prediction. Students form impromptu 'summary pairs' by turning to a partner; each partner summarizes a lecture segment for two minutes.

Then the pair comes to consensus on a response to questions. Pairing of two students gives the opportunity for immediate verbalization and for encountering the material twice during the class period—first as passive recipients during a lecture—then as active participants in their pairs. The following day, students work in their formal task groups, which are pre-assigned to insure mixed ability levels with the objective to help 'un-confuse' each other about the assignment. The next step is to apply what they have learned. Each group is given one sheet of thoughtful questions such as, 'Let's imagine that Thoreau is your contemporary. He is a teenager attending this high school right now; what would he think about the computer club? The social security system? The use of a charge card? If he wanted to make popcorn, would he use the microwave, the fireplace, or the stove top?' Each group member is given a special responsibility to perform for the group, and all are expected to work on the collaborative skill of 'elaboration.' Individuals are called on at random to determine whether the group has been successful."

I observed a *Walden* class in action. As the students dig through *Walden*, sifting out pertinent facts, and probing their way to conclusions, I think of the countless times I was "handed" a lesson to cover the material. Now these students are uncovering ideas and enjoying it. Hansen spends a few minutes at the end of class helping the groups reflect on their academic insights and collaborative skills. One student asks, "Will you let us do some more of this Thoreau stuff tomorrow?" Hansen beams. I infer her pride and her pleasure in a lesson in which she was not the sage on the stage. That is the cooperative difference.

Joliet West High School

Joliet West High School in Joliet, Illinois, received an Urban Education Partnership Grant to implement Project T.E.A.M. (Together Each Accomplishes More) in August 1988 to meet the needs of minority students. Project TEAM focuses on reducing high failure and referral rates among freshman in regular level classes. Heterogeneous homeroom-like settings, called freshman seminars, provide a mainstream setting for at-risk students.

Three years of intensive teacher training in cooperative learning provided the foundation for Project TEAM. Joliet West High School's program for at-risk students focuses upon Ouchi's *Theory Z* (1982): "Everything important in life happens as a result of teamwork or collective effort."

Maureen Dombrowski, Chapter I reading coordinator, directs the project at Joliet West High School. More than seventy faculty members trained in cooperative learning reinforce the collaborative and study skills during a daily twenty-five-minute seminar covering the curriculum and every content area. Results at Joliet West echo the findings of Johnson and Johnson's meta-analysis (1981) that "instruction that focused on cooperation and collaboration resulted in significant gains in the achievement, self-esteem, and social development." Since implementing the program in January 1988, Joliet West has seen a significant decrease in failure rate and referral rate; there has also been an improvement in grade point average for at-risk students.

Joliet West High School has data documenting improvement in grades and in reading attitudes, as well as a significant decrease in failure rate and referral rate. A compilation of student and teacher comments indicate the cooperative difference.

Among the students' comments were:

"I love to work in groups. It helps you to learn that your answers aren't always the best…"

"It gives you the feeling that you are safe and that whenever you are in need there will always be someone or somebody to help you. I learned that sharing was a big deal and we can learn to trust each other…"

"One skill I have developed is sharing—I never shared before…"

"Working in groups really changed me—I learned to connect with someone else and get along with them—I learned to disagree and to solve that disagreement…"

Among teachers' comments were:

"For the first time in more than twenty years of teaching, my freshmen didn't complain when I assigned them to softball teams."—a gym teacher

"After two students role-played a situation in study skills seminar, the rest of the class burst into spontaneous applause. Talk about encouraging one another to participate!"—an earth science teacher

"A student was to be moved from regular classes to special education classes. At the staffing, the father requested that his son remain in freshman seminar because for the first time in his high school career the young man felt he had made some friends because of his work in a cooperative learning group."—a guidance counselor

"In freshman seminar my students are forming their own groups to study before major tests. They quiz each other. They enjoy working together so much; they have even made up their own games and asked me to be part of their group."—a special education teacher

The more I see high school teachers using cooperative learning, the more I find that cooperative learning is resulting in higher achievement; greater use of higher-level reasoning; more positive heterogeneous relationships; better attitudes toward school and teachers; and true integration of cultures, minorities, and mainstreamed special education students. I also see, as in all the cases I have noted, that individual grades increase. This is not "grade inflation" as doubters often assert; it is an increase in the success rate. This is one more indication that cooperative learning is turning around the results in the high school classroom. Bs and As become the norm.

IN THE CLASSROOM: THE BASE GROUP PHENOMENON

Beyond the in-class successes reported, there is another application of cooperative learning that holds great promise at the secondary level. I call it the *base group phenomenon*. Base groups are skillfully applied at Joliet West High School to end the isolation experienced by secondary high school students. When base group structures are built into the high school play the impact is phenomenal.

In elementary schools, a child's sense of belonging is partially created by having one primary teacher, one set of classmates, and one classroom. In high school, that sense of belonging is threatened by the constant shifting from room to room and from teacher to teacher that departmentalization requires. The only place most students can call their own is the locker.

The president of the American Federation of Teachers, Albert Shanker, presents a vivid picture of how ludicrous it is to continue the factory-like, isolating practices that have dominated secondary education since 1900. Mr. Shanker (1990) says, "How many offices assign a worker to six different desks, in six different locations and to six different supervisors? Yet this portrays a day in the life of most secondary students. In an office you are expected to ask a co-worker for assistance; in a classroom it is called cheating."

Psychologists have demonstrated very clearly that long-term, caring, committed relationships are as important to a human being's psychological health as good nutrition and adequate sleep are to physical health. The research in this area is the oldest research in American education. There are ninety years of research and hundreds of studies that have shown conclusively that the students who are successful in life can point to at least one significant person who cared about them. *All* students need to know that there are people in the world who love them, are committed to them, and will provide help and assistance when needed (the need does not end with graduation from the eighth grade). In permanent relationships there are increased opportunities to transmit achievement-oriented values.

People who are not successful in life, who are in trouble with the law, or who live on the fringe of society say, "No one cared about me, not my parents, not my classmates, and certainly not my teachers." Prisons and mental institutions are packed, and the percentage of the population that is being incarcerated is growing. When the populations of these institutions are analyzed, it is found that the IQ of the inmates is usually above average. These groups were generally capable of learning when they were in school. The results of this body of research leave no doubt as to the importance of structuring a classroom for caring, interactive relationships.

Enter cooperative learning. The cooperative learning teacher creates activities that build group cohesion. By structuring base groups which stay together at least as long as the semester and sometimes the year, students have a place where they are needed and wanted. Receiving social support and being held accountable for appropriate behavior by peers who care and who have long-term commitment toward each other's success and well-being are important aspects of growing up and progressing successfully through school. The longer the group works together, the more cohesive and more powerful it becomes. *Everyone* "belongs" in his or her base group.

In an increasingly mobile society, one of the most traumatic experiences for an adolescent is to leave friends and transfer to a new school. Even in adulthood, the pain of remembering that experience from the high school years is vivid. The cooperative classroom provides for departing and for the new student by the care and concern expressed by base group members. Group members are taught social skills and are expected to take care of each other. The archaic values of working alone and not sharing are replaced with the positive interdependence which is so necessary for success in a workplace and in life itself. Students are taught how and are expected to take care of each other. Cooperative learning group members take care of absentees and even forgotten books and pencils are turned over to the group.

Base groups are a primary means of creating permanent relationships within the school. They are developed with the realization that students need each other's support and the skills to relate to each other in an honest and effective manner. These groups are long-term, heterogeneous, with stable membership whose primary responsibility is to provide encouragement, support, and assistance. They continue for at least a semester or a year and preferably for four years.

Beyond what base groups do to help students form stronger connections to the school, these same groups help high school students deal with increased cultural diversity, literacy, and workplace skills. The more rapidly these social pressures intensify, the more important it will be for secondary schools to use cooperative learning to prepare students for the world after school.

Cultural Diversity

Base groups structured to build on diversity can help students integrate cultures, races, and the disabled much more easily than any legislation. A three-year study of the base group phenomenon was conducted in a Los Angeles high school. Students who previously segregated themselves formed associations that integrated races and cultures as a result of cooperative learning classrooms. These students are recognizing that there are different viable ways of life and are being prepared to recognize the worth, the value, and the dignity of every human being. No longer are these high school students assuming that their own practices, beliefs, and standards are superior to those in other cultural and social structures.

Literacy

A quantum leap in expectation has ushered in a new age in American education. The standard used just a century ago to judge whether or not Americans were literate was a person's ability to sign his or her name. Fifty years ago, in the era of World War II, the measure was reading at a fourth grade level, and twenty-five years ago, the frequently used standard of the War on Poverty era was an eighth grade reading level. The 1986 assessment to profile young adult literacy defined it as the ability to "use printed and written information to function in society, to achieve one's goals, and to develop one's knowledge and potential." Formerly, everyone was subjected to an education where the standards for ultimate success would have best suited the achiever to be a college professor.

The amount of information in the world is doubling every eighteen months (Cook, 1988). A fully functioning person must face the enormous task of managing data and the learning environment. Technology has brought a knowledge explosion and an information-rich world. This is a new world—the world of technology, the post-industrial age, the information age. Problem solving and creativity are vital basics to accommodate and transform all this new information into meaningful knowledge and wisdom. Otherwise one becomes enslaved by the results of the technological advances. Product-oriented teaching and assessment must be replaced by process-oriented education. Although there is no made-to-order solution to these challenges, cooperative learning provides the foundation for maximizing student achievement, critical thinking, higher-level reasoning, and engagement in intellectual conflict.

THE WORKPLACE

Today the nation's concern with education appropriately encompasses all areas of learning with the glare of attention focusing on the workplace. The lines between workers, supervisors, and managers become blurred as "working in teams" or "quality circles" raise creativity and productivity. The team members put their hands together and solve problems.

In 1984, the National Academy of Science published *High Schools and the Changing Workplace: The Employers' View*. Composed primarily of employers, this study group concluded that the critical core competencies "include the ability to read, write, reason, and compute; an understanding of American social and economic life; a knowledge of the basic principles of the physical and biological sciences; *experience with cooperation and conflict resolution in groups*; and possession of attitudes and personal habits that make for a dependable, responsible, adaptable, and informed worker and citizen."

The basics in preparing students for the 1990s and beyond have become the collaborative and problem-solving skills of the workplace. In contacting local divisions of several major industries concerning what industries want from graduates, the response was that they consider the ability to work well in a team a top-priority job skill. It is not difficult to convince job-conscious teenagers that interpersonal skills can make the difference in surviving on the job. The transformation of the worker's role is indicative of the extraordinary changes in the workplace and has important consequences in the education of high school students.

Most employers today cannot compete successfully without a work force that has sound basic academic skills, but schools frequently teach isolated reading, writing, and computational skills. The use of these skills on the job will require additional proficiency in summarizing information, monitoring one's own work, and using analytical and critical thinking skills. Fifty-five percent of the time spent in communicating is spent listening, but schools offer scant instruction in oral communication and listening. Employers are "putting a premium on the ability to absorb, process, and apply new information quickly and effectively" (Barton & Kirsch, 1990). An organization's ability to succeed depends on the use of creative thinking to solve problems and overcome barriers. The ability to work cooperatively in teams is increasingly important for workplace success. Employers want employees to "have some sense of where the organization is headed and what they must do to make a contribution … and who can assume responsibility and motivate co-workers."

The workplace basics of collaboration and problem solving are so important that companies themselves are providing interpersonal skills training programs for their employees. The initial cost of such training, they feel, is more than offset by increases in quality and production.

There comes a time when every teacher asks, "What am I teaching for?" or "What do I really want for my students?" Preparing students for entry into the real world (the job market, the armed services, or marriage) is more critical on the high school level than anywhere else in education.

In 1987, the National Alliance of Business issued *The Fourth R: Work Force Readiness*. Work force readiness, the report said, "includes thinking, reasoning, analytical, creative and problem-solving skills, and behaviors such as reliability, responsibility, and responsiveness to change."

Training America: Strategies for the Nation (Carnevale & Johnston, 1989) concluded that team members will need "high levels of interpersonal teamwork, negotiation, and organizational skills—skills that enhance group effectiveness—as well as leadership skills."

Workplace Basics: The Skills Employers Want, (Carnevale et al., 1988) was issued by the U.S. Department of Labor. This document summarized the basic skills as Learning to Learn; Communication: Listening and Oral Communication; Creative Thinking/Problem Solving; Interpersonal Negotiation/Teamwork; Self-Esteem/Goal Setting; Motivation/Personal and Career Development; and Organizational Effectiveness/Leadership.

Formal education and literacy are important considerations, but most employers believe that there will be a deficiency in workplace functioning if a young person can deal well with print, but does not listen carefully to instruction, lacks personal discipline, and fails to function successfully in group efforts.

THORNTON FRACTIONAL EDUCATIONAL COOPERATIVE

There are no quick fixes for successful educational change. Any comprehensive program requires three to five years for staff development and implementation. Cooperative learning is no exception.

High School District 215 and the feeder elementary districts of Thornton Fractional Educational Cooperative adopted a five-year strategic plan beginning in 1989 to become cooperative schools. Year one focused on awareness sessions for administrators, teachers, and school board members at the annual Township Institute, administrators' monthly seminars and the annual summer Professional Development Institute. The focus was research-based basic elements of cooperative learning and classroom strategies. In year two, representative superintendents, teachers, and every elementary and secondary building administrator completed thirty hours of basic training in the Johnson model by participating in four-day sessions with certified trainers from the Illinois Renewal Institute. In the summer of year two, K-12 teachers and administrators completed thirty hours of advanced training. Every building administrator participated in a four-day workshop conducted by Roger and David Johnson on "Leading the Cooperative School."

Concurrent basic training is offered each year of the plan for untrained teachers. The fourth year of the plan will focus on the Illinois Renewal Institute model for *Blueprints for Thinking in the Cooperative Classroom* for teachers who have completed the basic and advanced Johnson training. Dr. Arthur Costa will present awareness sessions on metacognition and "Teaching for Intelligent Behaviors" for representative teachers and administrators.

CONCLUSION

Veteran teachers and administrators from Thornton Fractional, Wilmington, and Joliet high school districts are celebrating their successes and collaboration as teams. Cooperative learning in the classroom leads to a collaborative school. It becomes the norm for teachers to work as teams of professionals, modeling cooperative learning, using the very problem-solving strategies, positive interdependence, face-to-face interaction, group processing, and social skills which make education alive and real. Formerly, teachers in the high school taught independently of one another even when teaching the same subject area. Professional support groups are forming with positive interdependence and collaboration taking hold.

In District 215 and the feeder elementary schools, we believe there is no choice. The future is now for the high school classroom. We must have the cooperative learning model. Face-to-face interaction, heterogeneous interactive groups, the practice of collaborative and social skills, positive interdependence, higher-order thinking, and individual accountability must permeate the high school classroom and become its central focus.

REFERENCES

Barton, P., & Kirsch, I. (1990). *Workplace competencies: The need to improve literacy and employment readiness.* (Policy Perspective Series; Office of Education Research and Improvement) Washington, D.C.: U.S. Government Printing Office.

Bellanca, J., & Fogarty, R. (1990). *Blueprints for thinking in the cooperative classroom.* Palatine, IL: Skylight Publishing, Inc.

Bellanca, J., & Fogarty, R. (1986). *Future world, future school.* Palatine, IL: Skylight.

Carnevale, A., & Johnston, J. (1989). *Training America: Strategies for the nation.* Alexandria, VA: American Society for Training and Development.

Carnevale, A., Gainer, L., & Meltzer, A. (1988). *Workplace basics: The skills employers want.* Alexandria, VA: American Society for Training and Development.

Cook, B. (1988). *Video learner's guide for Bill Cook's strategic planning for America's schools.* Montgomery, AL: Cambridge Management Group.

Goodlad, J. I. (1984). *A place called school.* New York: McGraw Hill.

Johnson, D., & Johnson, R. (1989). *Leading the cooperative school.* Edina, MN: Interaction Book Company.

Johnson, D., & Johnson, R. (1989, December). Why use cooperative base groups? *The Cooperative Link,* p. 1.

Johnson, D., & Johnson, R. (1988). *Cooperative classrooms, cooperative schools.* Unpublished manuscript, University of Minnesota.

Johnson, D., Johnson, R., & Johnson Holubec, E. (1990). *Cooperation in the classroom.* Edina, MN: Interaction Book Company.

Johnson, D., Maruyama, G., Johnson, R., Nelson, D., & Skon, L. (1981). Effects of cooperative, competitive, and individualistic goal structures on achievement: A meta-analysis. *Psychological Bulletin, 89,* 47-62.

National Academy of Science. (1984). *High schools and the changing workplace: The employer's view.* Ann Arbor, MI: Books On Demand.

National Alliance of Business. (1987). *The fourth R: Work force readiness.* Washington, DC: Author.

Ouchi, W. (1982). *Theory Z: How American business can meet the Japanese challenge.* New York: Avon Books.

Shanker, A. (1990, February). Speech given at the Thornton Fractional Township Institute. Calumet City, IL.

Shanker, A. (1989, March). The case for restructuring our schools. Speech given for the Association for Supervision and Curriculum Development; San Antonio, TX.

Slavin, R. (1987, November). Cooperative learning and the cooperative school. *Educational Leadership.* pp. 7-13.

COOPERATIVE LEARNING: A NATURAL WAY TO LEARN

David Schumaker

—

It was early morning. The surf pounded a foggy beach near Monterey, California. Seventeen students stood shivering in the early morning, watching as a pick-up truck rumbled up and a somewhat grumpy professor stepped out. Even though it was his class and his field trip he seemed to us to be upset, as if it was a great inconvenience to be out so early. We gathered around him expecting instructions, a hand-out, perhaps a set of worksheets to guide us as we studied a sandy beach. As members of a marine ecology class we knew we were here to do a beach transect, to learn all we could about this small part of Monterey Bay. Much to our surprise, instead of instructions from the professor, we heard simply, "Well, get to work!"

We looked at each other. Some of us laughed. "What are we supposed to do?" someone asked.

He responded, "All of you know you are supposed to complete a transect of this beach. The instructions are in your books and we have discussed it in class. My problem was thinking up this assignment and getting all the stuff you need into the pick-up. Your problem is getting organized, figuring out what to do with it, and how you are going to help each other with the job before the tide comes in."

I was upset! He was being paid to "teach." We were paying to be taught! This man seemed to us to be derelict in his duties. We spent the next ten minutes complaining and whining while he strolled along the shore.

Eventually we realized that if we were going to get the job done we had better get to work. The professor obviously was not going to help. Soon we divided into teams, one for each beach zone, and assigned each team member a job. Some looked up the chapter on beach transects; another collected stakes, buckets, nets, and all the equipment the team needed for the job. Recorders took out notebooks and sharpened pencils while other people drove stakes in the sand and measured out plots to be studied. We worked quickly because we knew that the tide would soon turn and the beach would be covered with sea water.

All the time the professor strolled back and forth asking questions such as, "What do you suppose you have there?" and "Did that come from zone one or two?"

At the end of the day, as we gathered around the truck, compared notes, and discussed the experiment with the professor, I began to realize how much I had learned in a very short time and how deeply I was beginning to understand the zone we had examined.

I have often thought of that day. I never forgot that lesson. I have forgotten many others from less inspiring teachers—who based their teaching on having us memorize large collections of facts they spewed out from the lectern in the front of a room. There are, of course, some facts that I do not recall from that day, but all I have to do is wander back to the beach at low tide, poke around for a few moments, and it all comes back to me. It was my first experience with cooperative learning.

Years later, as a biology teacher, I often used the same method I participated in that day. Many of my students grumbled and complained that I was the teacher and I should teach them. They felt they were supposed to listen and learn. With patience they soon were working constructively as I strolled among them asking questions.

COOPERATIVE LEARNING — A NATURAL WAY TO LEARN

Humankind has most likely been working cooperatively ever since it became *Homo sapiens*. Still, even though almost every business has its employees working together and even though we look for ways to spend time together socially, we tend to force our students to work alone in the classroom. The only place where people are asked to work alone in a competitive atmosphere on a regular basis is in the classroom.

The brain likes to work on automatic pilot. This becomes a major problem that teachers must overcome. John H. Clarke states, "How much of the school day can be managed on automatic pilot? Paradoxically, the same school walls built to protect learning can also seal off students from compelling reasons to learn. Under normal conditions, students may see no need to direct the work of their minds to fit the purpose of schooling." (Clarke, 1990)

Cooperative learning is an effective method for jogging students off "autopilot." Research demonstrates that cooperative learning in non-competitive teams is a far superior method of learning for most students than either competitive or individualized methods (Johnson, Maruyama, Johnson, Nelson, & Skon, 1981). Most teaching today fails to take into account students' individual learning styles and multiple intelligences, or the damage done to those who lose in competitive classrooms.

Many teachers today know something about cooperative learning. Elizabeth Cohen, from Stanford University, says that cooperative learning is fairly widespread, a common method of teaching in many situations (Cohen, 1990). But many teachers have had little or no training in this method, or assume they know what it is just by hearing its name.

Recently I was confronted by a teacher who said, "I already know how to use cooperative learning. I have my students work in groups often." The teacher went on, "I don't think that it really works: usually the best student in the group does all the work while the others copy." Unfortunately, these people are missing the point and setting the stage for failure. Cooperative learning is much more than "group work." It is a highly structured and intricate process and—when used correctly—a powerful tool.

COOPERATIVE LEARNING MODEL

There are many successful models of cooperative learning developed or taught by people such as Roger and David Johnson, Spencer Kagan, Robert Slavin, Elizabeth Cohen, and Dee Dishon and Pat Wilson O'Leary. Most of their models, however, include similar components, as illustrated in Figure 1.

Positive interdependence refers to the group having a feeling that its members will "sink or swim together" as Roger and David Johnson would put it (Johnson & Johnson, 1988). **Individual responsibility** to the team is interwoven with the responsibilities of other members of the group, usually by assigned roles or duties. If one person fails to complete an assigned task, the entire group suffers in some way, usually by receiving a low team grade.

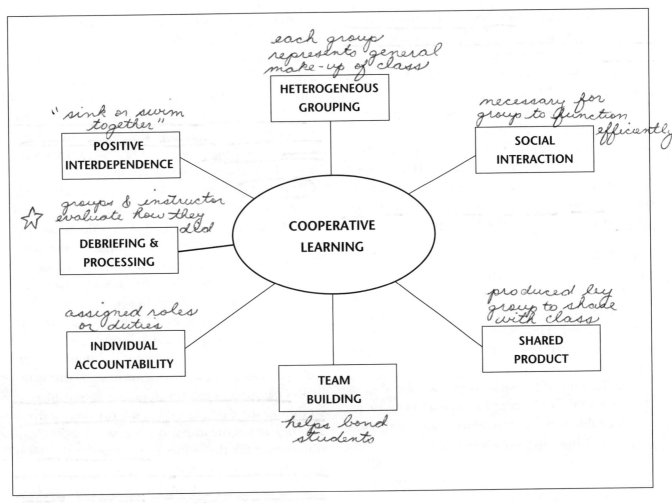

Figure 1   Cooperative Learning Model

The cooperative groups are built **heterogeneously**, with each group having students who represent the general make-up of the class. These groups then take part in **team-building** activities that help to bond the students together into a cohesive unit. At this point, depending on the experience of the group, the instructor may have to help the students develop the specific **social skills** that will be necessary for the group to function efficiently.

In most cases there should be some form of **shared product** produced by the group. This product is then shared with the other students in the class or turned in to the instructor.

Finally, when the work is completed, the entire class **debriefs and processes** the experience. This is a key component, in which the students and the instructor look closely at the entire process and evaluate how well they did. I find that at this point all participants learn how to improve the experience in the future and set the entire lesson in their minds. My classroom motto is, "None of us is as smart as all of us" and nowhere is this more evident than at this point, as my students solve problems and show me how to improve the methods of cooperative learning and the lesson next time.

LESSON DESIGN

Cooperative learning is not "kick-back" teaching, in which students work in groups while the teacher grades papers in the back of the room. It is a highly structured teaching method that requires careful planning and intense supervision by the teacher while it is in process. Success will depend on thorough preliminary planning just like any other method. After deciding on the basic structure of the lesson, the instructor must design the activity, keeping criteria for learning in mind.

The activity should follow good learning theory. Benjamin Bloom, Hilda Taba, and others have shown that we learn by processing information in stages (Costa, 1985). Art Costa breaks this learning process into four simple categories. These categories are: input, processing, output, and metacognition (Costa & Lowery, 1989).

Objective

The purpose of the activity must be clear in the mind of the instructor if it is ever to become clear to the student. This is often the most difficult part of the process. The objective should be written down and shared with the students at the beginning of the activity. For example:

- At the end of this activity you will be able to explain the difference between igneous, metamorphic, and sedimentary rocks and summarize how they are formed.
- By the end of this group activity you will demonstrate how to employ group problem-solving strategies by ...

Activity

Input If the brain is going to think about something, it must have the data to think with. This phase of learning uses all of the senses to take in the information that forms a knowledge base, a reference section of new information in the brain, for later use during more involved processes of learning. Research indicates that most instructors spend most of their teaching time on the input phase, typified by direct instruction which leaves the student in a passive learning phase. The student usually finds this time the most boring (Gall, 1984).

An example of an input activity about the three classes of rocks—igneous, metamorphic, and sedimentary—would be to assemble three piles of rocks on tables in the room, each pile containing rocks that represent one of the three classes of rocks and some books about rocks available for student use.

Teams of students would have to discover, by direct observation and the use of books, the qualities of each of the rocks in each of the piles and record their findings in their notebooks. The students would decide how this record would look.

Activities at this level are built around cognitive behaviors such as naming, describing, matching, listing, and recalling (Costa et al., 1989). This activity would be the foundation for the next.

Processing Once students have learned background knowledge, they can then begin to do something with the information in order to make it meaningful and commit it to long-term memory. First, for example, I would have students look for the similarities of the rocks in each pile and what makes them different from the rocks in the other piles. I would then ask the students to organize the rock types into a sequence that forms a cycle and to explain how one rock type could become another.

As you can see, the instructor designs this activity to encourage students to draw relationships or synthesize the data learned in the previous activity. This portion of the learning process becomes more stimulating for the student. Activities at this level are built around cognitive behaviors such as comparing and contrasting, explaining, making analogies, organizing, and inferring (Costa & Lowery, 1989).

Output The next activity allows students to apply the new knowledge and thus demonstrate that they truly understand the concept. I would have the team attempt to classify an unknown rock that had previously not been available to the students. I would ask them to make decisions about how it was formed and what it could become if it was treated to high pressure and intense heat. At this point, the student is working with such cognitive behaviors as generalizing, predicting, evaluating, hypothesizing, and speculating (Costa & Lowery, 1989).

Metacognition Along the way, I would encourage the students to stop and think about their answers. Students should attempt to see how they thought about the problems and decide if their reasoning is sound. The instructor should first model this behavior and structure it for the class. Having one student verbally recapitulate the pathway the group followed during the activity while others listen and react helps to focus the group on their reasoning.

As an example, here's how a student might "metacogitate" about a decision to place an unknown sample of rock with sedimentary rocks:

Let's see, we know from the book that sedimentary rocks are made up of particles that are cemented together. The unknown sample seems to be made of particles, although they are quite small. (We know because we looked at the rock with a hand lens.) We also know that sedimentary rocks often are softer than metamorphic or igneous rocks, and when we scratched the unknown rock with a coin or a fingernail, we could see small particles sprinkling off the sample. Therefore, we feel that the unknown sample is some kind of sedimentary rock. Does everyone agree?

If a team member does not follow the thinking or does not agree with the conclusion he or she may want to paraphrase the first student's statement and show where he or she thinks the thinking process strayed (Costa & Lowery, 1989).

This is not an easy process for many students. Because students usually are not asked to work in such a way, it takes time to bring them to a point where they can think about their thinking out loud.

Product As a final activity for the team I usually have them prepare some form of a product that may be shared with the rest of the class or each member of the team. These products might include briefing papers, posters, lab reports, oral reports, or individual writing assignments. Figure 2 is a guide that I have developed to help the teacher plan a cooperative learning activity. It is based on Arthur Costa's input, processing, and output design (Costa, 1985). The method can also be used to plan any lesson.

SETTING THE STAGE FOR COOPERATIVE LEARNING

Each year I start teaching by preparing my classes for cooperative learning from the very first day. As the students come into my classroom they must find their assigned seats by looking at a projected seating chart. The chart is written so that it represents the room from the teacher's viewpoint. Projected onto a screen it appears to be reversed, and, unless students are especially observant and examine the chart carefully, they inevitably sit in the wrong seats. I learned this technique from Harry Wong, a teacher trainer from the San Francisco Bay area.

As soon as the bell rings, I introduce myself and explain the process of "Think Aloud Problem Solving," or, as I prefer to call it, "Pairs Problem Solving" (Whimbey & Lochhead, 1982). Each student is a member of a two-person "thinking team." When approaching a problem that needs solving, one member becomes the problem solver and the other the listener. The rules are:

- The problem solver talks aloud about a problem and explains how he or she would solve it, step-by-step, verbally expressing all of the thoughts that come to mind during the process.

- The listener listens and makes certain that he or she understands the solver's reasoning. If the solver becomes quiet, then the listener reminds the solver that he or she must continue thinking aloud.

The members of each teacher-assigned pair think through the seating assignment—on the floor and on the chart—and then come to an agreement as to whether they are sitting in the correct seats. Then I provide time for the students to rearrange themselves. At this point I inform them that this team of two forms the basic cooperative unit for thinking. I say to them, "You are teamed with your thinking buddy. This is a person you will work with for the first grading period as a thinking partner."

Thinking buddies are an integral part of my classes. Many times during a period I ask questions or make statements and then direct the class to "turn to your thinking buddy and talk about this."

I often have students work on homework assignments as pairs of thinking buddy teams. For example, I rarely give a reading assignment from

COOPERATIVE LEARNING ACTIVITY PLANNER

Some basics to remember:

- Students must have time to develop **input** or basic information if they are to be able to work effectively.

- After the students have collected the basic facts, they must then manipulate those facts so as to make sense of them. They must have time to **process** the information.

- Finally the students must use the information to complete an **output** activity. At this point I find it important for the students to produce a product, such as a poster or paper.

Step I
State the topic of this activity.

Step II
Clearly state the basic concept or outcome that you want the student to understand as a result of this activity.

Step III
Design at least three input questions students should answer in order to build a body of background information for the activity, or design several input activities so students can investigate background information.

Step IV
Develop one or two processing activities that give the students time to work with the input information in order to truly understand it. During this activity students might find they need to seek more input information or that they need more time or more reference materials to complete the activity.

Step V
Define an output activity and a product the students will complete to use the new concept. This activity should allow the students to apply the information in some new way that is not just a repetition of previously learned material. A product of some kind should be made to share with the rest of the class.

Organization

Number of days needed to complete the activity:

Team size: _____ (2, 3, 4, 5, etc.)

Duties of each team member (e.g., timer, reporter, recorder, etc.):

Materials needed for each team (you may want the students to participate in the decision on materials needed):

Team-building activity:

Specific instructions for the students:

Debriefing questions:

Figure 2   Cooperative Learning Activity Planner

the textbook by page number. Instead I ask students to find out about a specific topic and mind-map all they can find out about the assigned subject (Buzan, 1976). A mind-map is a highly structured method of note taking or outlining. (Figure 1 is a simple example.) They may use any acceptable book. We previously agree on what "acceptable books" are, and on the requirement that they provide a bibliographic citation for the reference. This way a student can use either the textbook or any other reference.

The following day, as the students enter the room, they find large sheets of butcher paper and felt pens on the tables in the room. I ask them to sit with their thinking buddies and then to get together with one other thinking team. I then assign

---

SAMPLE COOPERATIVE LEARNING ACTIVITY

Lost In Mexico

This example I developed for a Spanish teacher who felt that there was no way that cooperative learning could be used in a foreign language class beyond practice teams.

A commercial airliner carrying a group of American tourists, none of whom can speak any Spanish, is flying over a remote portion of central Mexico. It has a problem and crash lands. All the people survive although some are injured.

In the airplane seat-pocket is a survival guide—with twenty-five Spanish words and their definitions—to be used in the event of an emergency. These words are all the survivors have to communicate with a group of native Mexican people who speak no English. The survivors must be able to communicate their own needs, the needs of the injured, and aid in the rescue using only the twenty-five words on the card. What words would you choose and why?

This activity is done in teams of five. Each team presents its list of words and its reasons for choosing them. The class then selects the final twenty-five words and acts out the situation.

Figure 3 "Lost in Mexico" Cooperative Learning Activity

them to compare their mind-maps and develop on the butcher paper a large mind-map that combines all the items discovered by each team member from their reading. After this activity is completed each team posts its large map on the wall and explains it to the class.

The teacher structures the activity of explaining the map to the class. All team members come to the front of the class and stand by their map. I then ask one student to explain a portion of the map that I select. This way each member of the team must understand the entire map and be able to demonstrate having learned what the other team members have discovered.

At the end of the activity we leave the maps up around the room for all to see during the time we are working with that subject. There is usually a tremendous amount of material, far beyond a simple "read from page 29-36 and take notes" style of assignment that many teachers give.

In order to support the process of cooperative learning, I have four class rules:

1. Everyone participates.
2. There is no such thing as the simple statement, "I don't know!" It is acceptable to say, "I don't know, but I will find out and here is how...!"

3. Follow directions.
4. Everyone deserves your respect until they earn your disrespect.

From the simple two-person teams I then develop larger teams, usually in small increments, for various learning activities. (See Figures 3 to 6 for sample cooperative learning activities.) I prefer to use teams of three, five, or seven. My favorites are a team of five for young students and a team of three for adults. There are many arguments among the experts about how many students should make up a team. Some, like Elizabeth Cohen of Stanford University, say five is the best number, while others prefer four to seven (Cohen, 1986).

At the end of the activity I call the student teams to the front of the room to present their findings to the class. I usually have them sit in chairs provided with their poster or overhead presented so the class can see it. At that time I begin to ask different students to explain various portions of assignment. I do not let them choose. This prevents a student from only learning one small part of the entire project. Everyone must understand all that the team accomplished and be able to explain it to the entire class.

I encourage students in the class to ask the team questions and challenge their findings. The team must try to find answers for the class questions.

SAMPLE COOPERATIVE LEARNING ACTIVITY

Rockets to Pluto

The following is an example of a culminating activity following a unit on the history of the development of navigation. The students had studied and experimented with the various methods of navigating on the earth. This example follows the planning outline explained previously.

You will work in teams of five or less today. The person with the longest first name will be the team leader. If a tie occurs, then the person with the longest first name and the longest pencil will be the leader.

Each team must agree on who will be the recorder (although everyone is responsible for keeping private notes), the procurer, the timer/prompter, the reporter, and the communicator. (The communicator is the only member of the group who can ask questions of the teacher.) The team must agree on each answer before the recorder writes the answer. Remember, you will be held to the time limits.

Task #1 (5 minutes)

Make a list of all the navigational aids that your group can think of and state the function of each.

Task #2 (3 minutes)

Organize your list from the oldest navigational aid to the newest.

Task #3 (10 minutes)

How could you use the navigational aids that you listed to determine latitude and longitude? Be precise. If you discover that you need more aids, add them to your list.

Task #4 (10 minutes)

Using the following format, make a list of five differences between navigation on earth and navigation in space.

Earth	Space
1. _____	_____
2. _____	_____

Task #5 (15 minutes)

What do you consider to be three major problems dealing with navigation between points in space? Why are they problems?

When you reach this point please inform the teacher. We will pause to discuss what each team has discovered with the entire class.

Task #6 (30 minutes)

Devise a method of space navigation to find your way from the Earth to the planet Pluto and back. Assume that all teams have the same rocket ship and the trip will take twenty years to complete, ten to get there and ten to return. Be sure to account for the many different problems of space navigation you have discovered and demonstrate how you would overcome them.

You must produce something to explain your team's solution to the class. Posters, handouts, or overhead transparencies are all examples of how this could be accomplished.

Task #7 (Homework)

How would you navigate between galaxies and what would be the major problems you would need to overcome?

Figure 4 "Rockets to Pluto" Cooperative Learning Activity

STUDENT SOLUTIONS TO "ROCKETS TO PLUTO" ACTIVITY

These diagrams are done by students and represent solutions to the problem of navigation to the planet Pluto and back. They were made from overhead transparencies that the students drew and presented in front of the class.

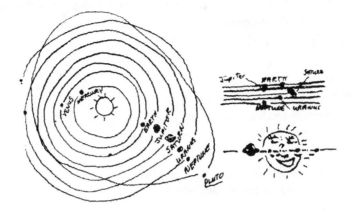

(I call this the rowboat method.) The spaceship would be guided by looking back at the configuration of the planets on any given day. A computer model would predict where the planets should be if the ship was on course for Pluto.

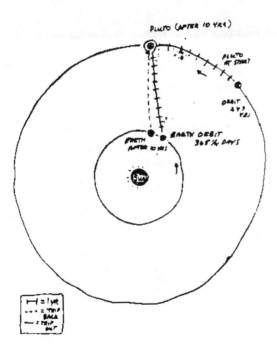

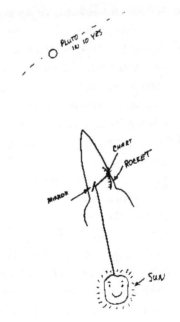

The sun would shine through a lens and reflect off a mirror projecting its image on a chart. The image would correspond to the rocket ship's location in the solar system and thus trace the ship's path along the chart toward the planet's predicted position at arrival time.

This method would be based on sighting the planet and determining the angle formed by a line drawn from the planet that intersected the path of the ship. The principle is that as the space ship moves along toward the predicted spot where the planet and the space ship will meet, the angle will become predictably smaller.

Figure 5 "Rockets to Pluto" Activity Solutions

SAMPLE COOPERATIVE LEARNING ACTIVITY

Capitola Beach Murder

It is often difficult to get students to listen to each other. The following activity is designed to encourage and demonstrate the importance of listening to others.

Students love to solve puzzles and I have found that students love to solve the following mystery written by three teachers (Peggy Marketello, Susan Nerton, and Joanne Roster) for use with cooperative teams of up to fifteen students.

Rules and instructions:

1. The team sits in a circle facing inward.
2. Each team member receives one or more clues.
3. One team member may not show written clues to another.
4. All clues must be communicated verbally.
5. The first team to accurately solve the crime wins.
6. You may organize your team any way you wish.

Mystery

A murder has been committed. Each of you has investigated the crime scene and has discovered one or more clues. You have been assigned to a team of detectives to solve the crime. You must determine who was the victim, who is the killer, and the motive.

Clues:

- Ben Allison owed Mrs. Singleton three months' back rent for a house in Soquel and planned to borrow a large sum of money from her.
- Charles Lentil was despondent over his girlfriend's dating of a married man.
- Mrs. Allison received a telephone call from a woman telling her of her husband's affair with another woman.
- Mrs. Singleton's gardener told her he would have the yard cleaned of debris, bagged, and taken away before the Clarkes arrived.
- Tuesday, Charles Lentil was arrested on the beach for littering. He decided to leave town the next morning.
- Tuesday, early, Mr. and Mrs. Clarke drove down from San Francisco to console their daughter who had called them.
- On the drive from San Francisco to Capitola, Mr. Clarke stopped at his son's shop eleven miles from Santa Cruz.
- Wednesday, 7:00 p.m., Mrs. Clarke drove her daughter to Dominican Hospital after she collapsed with a nervous breakdown.
- The hospital nurse gave Mrs. Allison a sedative for sleeping, while her worried mother sat in a chair by her bed for the evening. At midnight, the nurse gave Mrs. Allison and her mother another sedative.
- Ben Allison told his father-in-law he was filing for divorce.
- Mrs. Singleton rented a beach house on the cliffs overlooking Capitola Beach to Mrs. Allison's parents the day they arrived.

Figure 6 "Capitola Beach Murder" Cooperative Learning Activity

---

SAMPLE COOPERATIVE LEARNING ACTIVITY (continued)

Clues: (continued)

- The police pathologist reported that the body had been dead for twenty-four hours.
- No water was found in the dead man's lungs but there was a penetration above the left eye of the corpse and at the back of the head.
- Oct. 10th, 7:00 a.m. Mrs. Ben Allison reported to police that her husband was missing because his bed had not been slept in.
- 8:15 p.m., Thursday, Oct. 10th, a man's body was discovered on the shoreline of Capitola Beach.
- Martha Wood's neighbor, Lana Watch, told police she recognized the dead man from the newspaper picture as having been a frequent visitor to Martha's house on Old San Jose Road.
- Martha said Ben left her house at 7:45 to keep an 8:00 appointment.
- Ben Allison wanted to buy his brother-in-law's gunsmith shop in Davenport.
- A 22-caliber shell was found in the sand beneath the cliffs of Capitola Beach.
- Lana Watch, disabled in a recent car accident, was an ex-girlfriend of Ben Allison's.
- A surfer had seen a man dump a large bag in the water and called police.
- Martha admitted to police that she had had a quarrel with Ben on the evening of October 9th.

—Peggy Marketello, Susan M. Nerton, Joanne Roster

Figure 6 (continued)

The activity follows the input/process/output model and requires the students to understand what they know in order to predict possible answers to the final activity.

Test Taking

I often use cooperative teams to help students study for tests. I have the class brainstorm possible questions for the test and look at what we have been going over since the previous one. I give them some time to organize for the studying and I inform them that, beyond the individual grade they will earn on the test, they will receive a combined grade that is the average of the entire team's scores. On the day of the test I allow the team to discuss the test for ten minutes before the team members must work alone.

MISUSE OF COOPERATIVE LEARNING

In the movie *Teachers* there is a teacher named Ditto who sits in the back of the room reading the newspaper while his students face the other way and work quietly on their ditto sheets. He points out to anyone who criticizes him that he has received the award for the quietest classroom. One day he dies and no one notices his death for several periods.

Cooperative learning does not free you to be like Ditto. There are several things that cooperative learning is not. It is not a way to have students work while the teacher sits back and grades papers. Cooperative learning will fail if the teacher treats it as an activity that can run without direction and teacher involvement. During the time students are working, the teacher must move around and monitor the activity. He or she should be determining if the activity is achieving its goals and collecting data for feedback during the debriefing at the end of the activity.

Problems occur when the teacher does not design activities so that every group member has an active part which contributes to the whole. When this happens one person may end up doing all the work (usually the one most concerned about a grade). The others learn *nothing* yet earn the same credit for the activity.

Another common misunderstanding is that cooperative learning is easier to manage than other teaching methods. I find that planning and organizing a cooperative learning activity takes considerable time and effort. Without the proper preparation, cooperative learning will fail; the students will become frustrated and learn to hate the activity. With the proper planning, they will grow to see the value of the experience. Stanford University was hired by the Packard Foundation to evaluate a program I was teaching that depended heavily on cooperative learning as a teaching method. A team of evaluators interviewed my students at the beginning of the year and at the end. The students were asked their feelings about cooperative learning. They reported at the beginning that it was "stupid" and that "the teacher should teach." By the end of the year, however, they reported it was "exciting," that they could learn more about a subject, and that it is the "best way to learn." This would not have happened if they had not experienced success.

CONCLUSION

American education is good at adopting fads. As a high school teacher with over twenty-two years' experience in the classroom, I have seen many fads come and go, and, as a trainer introducing new ideas, I am often asked, "What did we used to call it?" In my experience, cooperative learning has taken hold and passed the point of being the latest fad in education. It has become a valuable tool, from the elementary school through the university—as well as in the business world.

The use of cooperative learning has greatly enhanced my teaching. Today, as a principal, cooperative learning is the main method that I use for faculty meetings and for teaching adults. I'm convinced that cooperative learning, when used properly, is a powerful tool for teaching real-life skills.

REFERENCES

Buzan, T. (1976). *Use both sides of your brain.* New York: E. P. Dutton & Co., Inc.

Clarke, J. H. (1990). *Patterns of thinking.* Boston: Allyn and Bacon.

Cohen, E. G. (1990). Continuing to cooperate: prerequisites for persistence. *Phi Delta Kappan, 72*(2), 134-138.

Cohen, E. G. (1986). *Designing groupwork, strategies for the heterogeneous classroom.* New York: Teachers College Press.

Costa, A. (1985). *Developing minds.* Alexandria, VA: Association for Supervision and Curriculum Development.

Costa, A. L., & Lowery, L. F. (1989). *Techniques for teaching thinking.* Pacific Grove, CA: Midwest Publications.

Dishon, D., & O'Leary, P. (1981). Teaching students to work in groups: Cooperative learning in the classroom. In *Structuring cooperative learning experiences in the classroom: The 1982 handbook.* Minneapolis, MN: Interaction Book Company.

Gall, M. (1984). Synthesis of research on teachers' questioning. *Educational Leadership, 42,* 40-47.

Johnson, D. W., & Johnson, R. T. (1988). *Cooperation in the classroom.* Edina, MN: Interaction Book Company.

Johnson, D. W., Maruyama, G., Johnson, R., Nelson, D., & Skon, L. (1981). Effects of cooperative, competitive, and individualistic goal structures on achievement: A meta-analysis. *Psychological Bulletin, 89*(1), 47-62.

Kagan, S. (1989). *Cooperative learning resources for teachers.* San Juan Capistrano, CA: Resources for Teachers.

Slavin, R. E. (1986). *Using student team learning* (3rd ed.). Baltimore: Johns Hopkins University, Center for Research on Elementary and Middle Schools.

Whimbey, A., & Lochhead, J. (1982). *Problem solving and comprehension* (3rd ed.). Philadelphia: The Franklin Institute.

LESSONS LEARNED IN A COOPERATIVE COLLEGE CLASSROOM

—

Martha E. Crosby and Dara Lee Howard

Great is the strength of feeble arms combined.—Homer

As we say in Hawaii, we are going to "talk story" about our first experience with cooperative learning in an undergraduate computer science course. We were invited to give a course on computer file design. This topic requires the mastery of technical concepts concerning the capacity of and retrieval from different types of files. In addition, this course includes an introduction to and use of a new programming language. Computer file design is practiced collaboratively and is learned best by hands-on experience. Thus, a traditional lecture presentation of the material may not be effective in assisting the students to master the material and develop the skills needed in a job environment. For this subject matter, a team approach in the classroom seemed a better way to implement the desired realistic environment.

We chose to try the cooperative learning format to foster the students' opportunities for success. Cooperative learning emphasizes participant interaction similar to what is required in many computer-related careers. It also offers an opportu-

nity for peers to motivate and assist each other with the challenge of a different programming language and with learning new technical concepts. Working together gives the students a chance to bring the learning situation closer to reality.

We were aware that results from research on learning suggested that people learn best when they are actively involved in the learning process. We thought that getting the students involved with each other would increase both their learning and their motivation. As peers are sometimes better able to understand and help each other with problems, we expected that they would benefit from having each other as friendly resources. Working together could also demonstrate that they were not the only ones having trouble with the course material—a reassuring fact for many students.

Our initial experience in cooperative classroom management was hectic but productive. We began with lots of enthusiasm and no practical knowledge about the mechanics of cooperative education. After our first cooperative learning attempt, we are still enthusiastic and would like to share some of the things we learned from our experience. We are excited about the cooperative format because it worked both for us and for our students. We plan

---

FIGURE 1: LESSONS LEARNED

Lesson 1: You don't have to be perfect.

Lesson 2: Adjustment time is needed.

Lesson 3: Interaction tempers the classroom.

Lesson 4: Cooperative rewards are needed.

Lesson 5: Dark clouds have silver linings.

Lesson 6: You can structure for success.

Lesson 7: Logistical nightmares do improve.

Lesson 8: Support is welcomed.

Figure 1   Lessons Learned

to continue using the cooperative format in future offerings of the course as well as in other appropriate learning situations. Hopefully this report will help others avoid some of the pitfalls we encountered. We encourage you to try this approach, as we think you will like it. The knowledge gained, by both us and our students, was well worth our effort.

For clarity we have organized our view of the experience into a series of lessons (Figure 1). We usually present them from the instructors' perspective, but frequently discuss student concerns also. We hope these lessons learned demonstrate to other neophytes that the cooperative classroom works despite the occasional problems we encountered. Figure 2 recaps the pros and cons that we found.

LESSON 1: YOU DON'T HAVE TO BE PERFECT

We put this first because, fearing failure, one may never begin. We certainly did not start out knowing much. Although we knew the meaning of cooperative learning, we learned as the course progressed. As we encountered barriers, we devised barrier bashers. Conditions may not be perfect. There

---

Barriers	Benefits
Students	*Students*
• trained to expect traditional formats	• committed to the class goals
• preferred working individually	• built rapport with each other
• employed so-so group skills	• participated in "win-win" learning
• conditioned as passive listeners	• wrestled with concrete problems
• devoted to crisis management	• helped each other with stumbling blocks
• suspected the equity of group evaluation	• asked probing questions
Instructors	• sampled "real work" environment
• required substantial preparation time	• opened up to instructors
• squeezed by too-short class period	*Instructors*
• hampered by unprepared students	• uncovered elusive information about learners' processes
	• savored students' achievements
	• quashed the "quiet" classroom

Figure 2   Barriers to and Benefits of Cooperative Learning

never seems to be enough time to develop a new skill; on the other hand, once developed, the skill is constantly put to use. Even though you may feel inadequately informed about cooperative learning theory, try it! Even if your colleagues are skeptical about the method, try it! The students are likely to reward you with more intelligent questions, better performance, and greater understanding of the topic.

LESSON 2: ADJUSTMENT TIME IS NEEDED

There are several facets to this adjustment. Some are related to the discipline, some to individual experience and preference.

Our first adjustment involved the learning preferences of our students. Many computer science students seem to prefer to work on their own. At the University of Hawaii, we have students who come from cultures in which educational practices are more traditional and formal than the approach we wanted to use in this class. Our Japanese and Chinese students in particular are not familiar with interactive classrooms, but typically come from educational institutions that use a formal, structured class format. In addition, computer science students have chosen to join a discipline which attracts introverted and self-sufficient people. Indeed, the results of the Myers-Briggs Type Indicator examination that we gave them showed that 70 percent of them were introverts, as compared to a 35 percent introvert to 65 percent extrovert split in the population as a whole. So we were definitely dealing with people who were conditioned by their past educational experiences and by their preferred learning styles for individual work.

Secondly, in cooperative learning, students need to use group skills. Some students may not have well-developed collaborative study or work skills. Competition had been the norm between students in a class. Cooperative learning teaches the lesson that one can win without someone else losing. This knowledge is valuable for both the educational and the professional environment.

The realization of the benefits of cooperation may develop slowly, but they do develop. From the first, we had almost universal acceptance of the social part of group work. As the semester progressed we saw the development of an appreciation for the benefits of learning together. When we asked for feedback we received favorable and illuminating comments. For example, one student said, "We get to see how other people do things (which is great if you're totally lost)." Another comments, "I especially like the group discussion times because it helps when you are working together—you don't just get your way of doing things but others' input too. It also allows the class to become a less 'hostile' environment because there's communication between the students."

A third adjustment was in the area of class format. Lectures are the usual instructional format for most computer science and other courses taught at the university level. As the only one using a non-lecture technique, our course didn't fit with the others the students were taking. The problem came from mismatched expectations. Lectures call for listening; cooperative learning calls for active involvement. We expected their participation; they expected to listen. Some students wanted traditional lectures by the instructor. They expressed a concern that they were not learning the material. For example, one student remarked, "I guess a lot more can be learned from teaching than group work;…though group assignments may be a good idea, the group work in class is definitely wasting time." Another student wrote, "I think perhaps it would be better to set up the class in a lecture style as usual—I seem to have an easier time learning since I have notes from the lecture and can review them at home."

Our approach to encouraging adjustment was to keep an open communication line. We explained what we were doing and why. We asked for feedback early in the semester and responded to their concerns. When it was possible, we followed their recommendations. Some concerns were voiced over things that we could not change, such as the system of group grades. In these cases we explained our rationale. Even though not all the students were entirely converted to the cooperative learning format, we think the group exercises were positive experiences for all of the participants.

LESSON 3: INTERACTION TEMPERS THE CLASSROOM

Both students and instructors gain from an environment that involves shared responsibility for the process of learning. In our class, several benefits accrue for the students. The improved socialization produced by constant interaction with different members of the class and with the instructors seems to loosen the students' tongues. They ask more questions of each other and of the instructors, both during designated question periods and during the instructor presentations. In a small group they can ask questions that were only partially formulated. Identifying unclear areas is vital to making sense of a new topic. Most people have difficulty in sharing these areas of ignorance even among friends. In our class, students met and grew to trust each other by working together.

Familiarity breeds confidence; because the instructors could be informally approached, students in our class began to ask those questions to which they secretly believed everyone else already knew the answer. We considered it an advantage that our former position as "the great authority" was gradually eroded to that of "a very knowledgeable, but still only one, possible source." Over the semester, we saw an increase in the number and quality of questions that were asked and answered within the groups and in the class. Our hitherto quiet classroom began to buzz. We consider this change to be a big achievement of the cooperative format.

Also the students saw the exercises as a way to help structure their information questions. Concrete exercises served as platforms for those detailed questions usually not formed until the instructor is long gone. We have all had the experience of watching someone solve a problem and being sure that we could do it because all the steps followed so "naturally," only to be stumped when we actually tried it by ourselves. But if students do these problems when there is someone to help overcome that bottleneck, they retain their enthusiasm and sense of progress. The cooperative format frees them to ask questions, gives them someone to address the questions to, and frequently helps them construct an answer as well.

For instructors, the cooperative format creates a wealth of information about the learning processes of individual students. We achieved insight into students' problems with the material. We knew when and where the problems were. We could immediately fine-tune the next lesson. This alone is worth the time and effort to learn how to create the cooperative classroom.

Typically, solid understanding of basic concepts and skills forms a better foundation for more advanced structures. The cooperative exercises created observable behavior in the struggling learners that opened a window to the internal cognitive processes for the watching instructors. Through this window, we were able to assess the condition of the foundation before we started to add the new floors. A delightful advantage in the classroom, don't you think?

LESSON 4: COOPERATIVE REWARDS ARE NEEDED

At first, we missed this important point about cooperative learning and relied on group grade activities. For learning and practicing basic skills, we envisioned that close collaboration, mutual support, and symbiotic development would automatically flow from working together. But it didn't happen. Group grades by themselves were not enough incentive. Even with group grades, the students still relied on individual effort for the group product and for their evaluation of how they were doing. Our grading scheme fostered this by rewarding the group based on the group product. We were encouraging the wrong thing: answers, not learning. We discovered the hard way that there has to be a positive inducement to overcome the entrenched traditional learning style.

We have experimented with creating a learning interdependence among the team members. Groups now earn their group scores as a function of the individually earned group members' scores, thus creating incentive for attending to the task and coaching other group members to improve their performance.

Not all students were enchanted with group evaluation. There was the expected concern: "Being graded as a group means that your grades are affected by others' ability to learn." The individual high achievers preferred to be on their own, without the responsibility of assisting other learners. A few of these students expressed a competitive outlook and voiced a resentment at sharing their talents and skills with someone else. We countered this argument with examples of how they were helped by the group. Then we pointed out that, in real jobs, group sharing of rewards and penalties was typical. Fortunately, this group represents a very small minority of our students.

There was another group that preferred not to be involved, although for a more altruistic reason. This consisted of the students who did not want to affect the grade of a fellow classmate. There are two different reasons for not participating offered by these students. One is that they chose the credit/no credit grading option. The other is that they think they might not do well and worry that they would unfavorably affect the group score by performing below some self-imposed standard level. We accommodated the ones who had chosen an ungraded option by not using their individual score toward their group's score. The second group began to relax as they saw that they were as much a contributor to as a benefactor of group averages.

LESSON 5: DARK CLOUDS HAVE SILVER LININGS

We began with some trepidation, expecting a Pandora's box of problems. Instead the box contained opportunities, not problems. The first opportunity concerned classroom interaction. Action in the classroom can be confused with loss of control. Our cooperative classroom looked unstructured and sounded noisy. There was an illusion of disorder. However, this hubbub signaled that something different was happening. As students and instructors were molding the learning milieu, the sound level rose. We saw the jumble as a blueprint in progress. We heard the noise as the music of enthusiastic learning.

We were reassured by our first few class meetings. The cooperative interaction did not signal a loss of control, but rather active participation by learners and instructors. We didn't feel a loss of authority; we felt a sense of community.

Frequently, what the instructor seems to give up becomes the basis for student commitment to the class. The students gain a vested interest in learning. The instructors trade the illusion of direct control for the reality of indirect influence. Two-way influence of small-group interaction replaces one-way influence from the podium. The exchange is rewarding; everybody wins.

Extroverted students, in particular, flourish. With this material, introverted students traditionally outperform the extroverts. In our class, both improved, but introverts not as dramatically as extroverts. Because their learning style favored active participation, extroverts not only improved their own performances but also served as leaders for their groups.

The second opportunity we find is the increase in the power of communication. Messages addressed to a small group have a greater impact on the listeners. The convenience of saying something once to the entire class is offset by the advantage of the rapport established in face-to-face dialogue. Conversation allows a student immediate feedback and even the opportunity to interrupt with a question. Two-way versus one-way communication prevails and fosters active learning.

The third opportunity emphasizes the value of adaptability. Initially, we planned class activities very thoroughly and in great detail. But our plan defined only one of many possible paths to our goal. Because our cooperative classroom had so many active participants, our plan tended to dissolve. Adhering to our objective depended on being open to alternatives. We had to pursue our goal rather than steer a set course. We learned to grasp opportunities as they occurred. For example, when we assigned a programming problem as a group project, we realized that we had created an opportunity to mirror the real world, one of our cooperative learning goals. For evaluation of this assignment, we chose to have the teams demonstrate the product rather than have the instructor read it. By seeing that their reward depended on each individual's ability to explain the team product, the students really internalized the goal of cooperative learning. After this experience, they seemed to value the underlying concept of group exercises. The group project personally fostered the understanding of cooperative learning in the students. The success we had in grasping this opportunity reinforced our goals.

LESSON 6: YOU CAN STRUCTURE FOR SUCCESS

This is one of our earliest concerns. How could we have the students productively use class exercise time if they had not done the assigned reading? A lecturer does not have to be concerned with whether the reading assignment was read. But, in a cooperative class, when exercise time rolls around, the instructor is concerned with whether the reading assignment has been read. Our expectation of the students' preparation differed from the actual facts. We could not depend upon individual students to be prepared. Many of them obviously relied upon the instructor's lecture to bring them up to speed. We realized that we could not change, almost overnight, the ingrained study habits of our entire class. Meeting our demand for preparation before each session seemed to conflict with the "crisis management" approach students used to schedule their workloads. We expected them to be prepared and they expected to have everything important explicitly pointed out during a class lecture. Positive outcome depended on their having something to work with. We found we needed to find some way to establish a foundation before the group exercises. We added a lecture and question period to the schedule. We structured the cooperative exercises so that the students could build on what they did know. Using their prior knowledge as a stepping-stone was the surest way to achieve active, productive group activity. It did not substitute for their preparation but it provided a constructive experience when they were not prepared, as was often the case. The students became more comfortable with the cooperative environment after we made these changes. Quality of participation in the group exercises improved. Their tests indicated that they learned more than they expected. The learning sneaked up on them. Now, when we present the class, we build a lecture/discussion component into the course from the beginning. This succeeds, we think, because the familiar approach reassures the students and gives them something to build on if they are not prepared.

Although we accommodated their lack of preparation, we did not give up on trying to encourage students to be prepared. For us, part of the problem seemed to be the short period of time between Tuesday and Thursday class sessions. It just didn't give the students enough time to juggle their obligations and prepare for the class. To alleviate this time crunch, we tried meeting weekly.

Feedback from the students suggested that this helped but was not universally appreciated. One student said, "I'm especially glad we meet only once a week for a couple of hours. (That's better than trying to squeeze in lectures and seat work in an hour and fifteen minutes.)" Another commented, "Meeting once a week means less pressure during the entire week." But there was an opposing view: "Since we only meet once a week, I tend to forget a lot of things. I can learn better if I hear things more often." You will note that once again there is an articulated preference for listening, as if learning is something that floats through the air and is gathered in.

By itself, the new schedule was not sufficient to motivate preparation before class. We are also using the tried-and-true technique of a weekly quiz. The quiz had two parts and was designed to test prior material and motivate reading the new material. The quizzes were simple, short, and lightly weighted in the overall grading scheme. In our opinion, the quizzes worked. Our students were better prepared. We expected some grumbling and got it. But to our surprise, a number of our students seemed to appreciate the chance to test what they knew in what they perceived to be a low-risk situation. One student said, "The quiz I think will help a lot in preparing for the test. It also gives students like me ... a sense of what to expect on the test." Another commented, "I like constant quizzes with 'little' weight toward the final grade. It keeps you on your toes but doesn't damage [your] feet much." A true win-win situation—we got better preparation and they got low-risk feedback on their progress.

LESSON 7: LOGISTICAL NIGHTMARES DO IMPROVE

We bring this up because it surprised, and, frankly, dismayed us. Perhaps we shouldn't have been surprised, but we were. Planning the materials for the cooperative exercises took more time and effort than preparing for a lecture-style class. Even though one of us was an experienced teacher well-versed in the subject and with a well-developed understanding of the students, it took concentrated effort to find appropriate exercises and problems to be done in class by a group. In addition to the usual problem of presenting material in digestible chunks, we were trying to insure that the groups' attention would be engaged. We solved this problem on a one-by-one basis for each class. We were constrained by the class time available for group exercises. The once-a-week format has removed this constraint by giving longer contiguous periods for student interaction. It also halves our set-up time (getting into groups, handing out exercises, etc.)

However, even though it took longer than we anticipated, we think that some of our best work for our students was done during this preparation time. It was during this time that we designed a facilitating environment. The results were positive. The frequent exercises enriched the students' understanding of concepts and improved their performance on specific tasks. The experience of doing the problems revealed the advantages of actively wrestling with concrete problems with other learners. Although we did not banish the stated preference for the most passive learning role of listener, students began to appreciate the advantages of cooperation as they experienced improvements in understanding and in examination scores.

LESSON 8: SUPPORT IS WELCOMED

The support we are talking about is the kind that helps you over the rough spots. You are trying new things, and it is extremely helpful to know you have not gotten totally off base. Colleagues, nearby or far away, are one support source. In our case, we had already made supporters in each other. A colleague who is also directly involved in the class is a welcome sounding board and a source of much-needed morale boosting. Planning the class and reviewing the results together made a world of difference to our personal confidence and to the class quality. Even if team teaching is not available, locate a kindred spirit, especially if this is as new to you as it was to us.

A convenient place to look for a friendly ear is within your immediate department. However, if you are a pioneer, this may not be a fruitful search. Our colleagues were not immediate converts to our project. Their philosophy continued to emphasize the topic and stick with the tried-and-true class format. Their attitude was that lectures were most efficient for presenting lots of material. Their attitude implied certain questions: Because instructor time with students is a scarce resource, why waste class time with students working together? How could uninformed students benefit each other? Given this attitude, they expected us to demonstrate success rather than to seek advice. Even early success met some skepticism.

If support is not available from your immediate neighbors, where else can you go? We found the Office of Faculty Development and Academic Support at our university a good source of articles and practical advice. They put us in touch with cooperative pioneers in other departments and campuses in our university system. It was reassuring to find we were not alone in trying this approach at the college level. If you have a similar instructor support center, try it.

Support can also come from farther away than your immediate campus. Fortunately for us, we knew an expert who was willing to be a long-distance mentor. She poured cold water on some of our ideas without dampening our enthusiasm. Her informed assurance that the students learn more when they are active relieved our anxiety about the possible bad effect of the new format on our students. Experienced mentors help you quickly evaluate your "brilliant ideas." If you find sources like this, latch onto them.

Besides a single mentor, individuals with similar interests tend to form networks. We recently discovered two networks concerned with cooperative learning. These are the Association for Supervision and Curriculum Development (ASCD) network[1] and the Professional and Organizational Development (POD) network.[2] In addition to linking you to other people, joining a network usually opens access to other sources of information, through newsletters, directories, and meetings at professional conferences.

If all other sources fail, "read the directions." That is, select from the abundant literature on cooperative learning. The literature can pick out some potholes in the road. We could have avoided some of our classic errors if we had used the available literature.

SUMMARY

This is only one experience with introducing cooperative learning into university-level courses. Others have ventured along a different but equally successful course. This is not the only way, or even the right way, to go about it. It's just one way that worked. Even with the problems we encountered, whether from our own ignorance or from external factors, we feel we succeeded. An adventure such as this calls upon a gambler's instincts, an explorer's skills, and a lion's heart. The rewards are worthy of the challenge.

NOTES

1. This network is called ASCD Network on Cooperative Learning. For information write Association for Supervision and Curriculum Development, 1250 N. Pitt Street, Alexandria, VA 22314-1403.

2. This network is called POD Network in Higher Education. For information write POD Network, Teaching and Learning Center, University of Nebraska, 121 Benton Hall, Lincoln, NE 68588.

REFERENCES

Bellanca, J., & Fogarty, R. (1990). *Blueprints for thinking in the cooperative classroom.* Palatine, IL: Skylight Publishing.

Fogarty, R. (1990). *Designs for cooperative interactions.* Palatine, IL: Skylight Publishing.

Gersting, J. (1989). The other two Rs in the discrete mathematics course. *Computer Science Education, 1,* 293-299.

Gibbs, J. (1987). *Tribes: A process for social development and cooperative learning.* Santa Rosa, CA: Center Source Publications.

Groves, N. B., & Groves, T. D. (1985). Creating a cooperative learning environment: An ecological approach. In R. Slavin, S. Sharan, S. Kagan, R. H. Lazarowitz, C. Webb, & R. Schmuck (Eds.), *Learning to cooperate, cooperating to learn.* New York: Plenum.

Myers, I., & Briggs, K. (1962). *The Myers–Briggs type indicator: Manual.* Princeton, NJ: Educational Testing Service.

Slavin, R. (1991). Synthesis of research on cooperative learning. *Educational Leadership, 48*(5), 77-82.

Webb, N. M. (1985). Student interaction and learning in small groups. In R. Slavin, S. Sharan, S. Kagan, R. H. Lazarowitz, C. Webb, & R. Schmuck (Eds.), *Learning to cooperate, cooperating to learn.* New York: Plenum.

COOPERATIVE LEARNING
WITH ADULT LEARNERS

—

Therese Bissen Bard

Cooperative learning is the best thing since bubble gum, or whatever that saying is.
        —Graduate student, School of Library and
            Information Studies, University of
            Hawaii at Manoa

My experience with cooperative learning at the University of Hawaii spans over seventeen years. More accurately, my experimentation with various cooperative learning activities covers that period of time. My method, regrettably, has been based on trial and error rather than a systematic approach.

My educational aims for cooperative learning during those first few years were vague at best. I thought sharing ideas in class discussions and small groups was a good thing. Exactly why it was a good thing, I wasn't sure. There was also a practical matter. Classes at the School of Library and Information Studies (SLIS) meet for three hours once a week, and at least one of my classes each semester would meet in the early evening. Many of the students in the evening classes had already worked all day. Three hours of lecturing to them would have

been ineffective. It might even have been called cruel and inhuman punishment—when the only crime committed had been to enroll in an evening course.

Cooperative learning is only one instructional method I use in my courses. I combine cooperative learning with lecturing, audiovisual presentations, guest speakers, field trips, and other instructional methods as appropriate for subject content and course objectives. During an academic term I spend approximately one-third of class time on cooperative learning, but the students may spend as much as one-half to three-fourths of their out-of-class time on these activities.

After a few years I dignified these class discussions with a name. I called them "peer learning," a term that does not describe what my students or I were doing. Peer learning, as I interpret the term, implies that one or more members of the group has knowledge to impart to others. The each-one-teach-one method of adult literacy instruction is an example. One or more children teaching others in a group how to play a new game is another. Peer learning as a formal instructional method normally means at least one member of the group already has the knowledge or skills that are to be taught. An instructor may be present to facilitate learning but is not a learner participant.

Cooperative learning expresses more accurately the instructional method my students and I were using. Unsystematic as my approach may have been, we were learning from one another. We learned about library and information studies, and we learned about learning. And, despite some resounding failures, the method has been successful.

In this chapter, based on my experience as a teacher at the school of Library and Information Studies[1], I will discuss planning a course for cooperative learning; instructional methods; teaching strategies and techniques; problems; and my conclusions and recommendations.

COOPERATIVE LEARNING METHODS

Different methods of cooperative learning are appropriate for different subject content, to meet different course objectives, and for different types of responses the instructor expects from students.

Small Group Discussions

People tend to respond more comfortably when in small group situations rather than large groups. Individuals are more attentive, supportive, and able to interject their own opinions with ease.

You are not only responsible for your own learning but also for the group's learning. You tend to prepare better because you want to be a contributing member of the group.

There are some drawbacks. There is a tendency in any group for one or two people to dominate the conversation unless firmly stomped upon. I speak from experience, as usually I am the one who needs to shut up and let other people talk for a change.

Group discussions often get sidetracked into areas that, while fascinating, have little relevance to the subject we are supposed to be discussing.

　　—Graduate students, School of Library and Information Studies

Small group discussions held during class time work well for:

- sharing responses to or criticism of literature written for children or young adults;
- in-depth discussion of assigned readings; or analysis and evaluation of journal articles, research articles, model projects for library services, and other types of professional literature.

The Socratic Method

I like the professor to lead a full class discussion on a book we have all read. I like probing questions, and I like to hear how other people see things. There are always people who see more than the rest of us.

　　—Graduate student, School of Library and Information Studies

The Socratic method used in a class discussion works well for:

- an assigned reading that raises profound and disturbing questions about the human experience; or
- a film, video, or other learning activity shared by the entire class that stimulates thinking about a topic relevant to the course for which there are no easy answers.

Informal Class Discussions

Class discussions are a useful learning method to share and synthesize material. It allows one the luxury of listening to others and learning from them. Muddy areas or convoluted thinking can be clarified. It enables one to go 'aha' even after an especially tedious session.

　　—Graduate student, School of Library and Information Studies

Informal class discussions work well for:

- a topic of general interest to the class that engages the students' feelings, e.g., censorship of library materials;
- response to a shared learning activity that presents new ideas and broadens students' perception of a subject, e.g., a video presentation or a guest speaker; or
- a topic for which there are answers that are generally acceptable to the profession and the

students, e.g., how to implement outreach programs for library services.

Dyad Discussions

When both persons are prepared with their own ideas and opinions, dyad discussions are fascinating and a great way of learning.
> —Graduate student, School of Library and Information Studies

Dyad, meaning two individuals forming a pair, is an unfamiliar word to most of our students, and a dyad discussion is an instructional method few SLIS students have used previously. I assign dyad discussions as an out-of-class course requirement. Dyad discussions work well for:

- substantive, dense readings that require students to analyze and evaluate what the author is saying; or

- readings on controversial topics that may require the student to do additional background reading as a preparation for their dyad discussion.

Group Term Projects

A group can cooperatively produce a superior product.
> —Graduate student, School of Library and Information Studies

Term projects that involve two or more students challenge their ability to work as as team over a period of time. This cooperative activity works well for:

- substantive projects that require time for research, preparation, organization, and presentation;

- complex projects that require students to achieve at all levels of Bloom's and Krathwohl's taxonomies (Bloom, 1956; Krathwohl, Bloom, & Masia, 1964); or

- projects that require a variety of knowledge and competencies so that individual students may make a unique contribution to the success of the completed project.

Writing Groups

For writing assignments, I had groups help each other from pre-writing to proofreading and found the students loved it as much as I did.
> —High School English teacher and graduate student, School of Library and Information Studies

Graduate students, like all writers, may suffer from paralyzing blocks. Two or four students working together in a group may help each other overcome their writing blocks and improve the quality of their work. This cooperative learning activity works well for any type of writing assignment if the participants believe in the idea of writing groups, set up simple rules for the group process, and follow these rules faithfully.

I introduced writing groups as a type of voluntary cooperative learning to one class this past semester. Unfortunately, I did not provide adequate guidance to the students. None of them had had experience with writing groups, so, except for two students working together, the activity just fizzled out. Next semester I plan to prepare guidelines and work with the students more closely. I have found a writing group invaluable in my own professional writing, and other instructors, like the English teacher quoted above, have had success with this method. It has the potential to raise the quality of students' writing at the graduate level.

Study Groups for Examinations

Everyone brings to the study group a culmination of all the wisdom gotten from other classes and from their own experiences.
> —Graduate student, School of Library and Information Studies

Studying together for examinations has, in my experience, improved the performance of students on midterm and final exams. Study groups work well in preparing for:

- both essay and objective exams;

- an exam for which the instructor has provided a study guide; or

- a situation in which the students know the instructor will adhere to the study guide and not surprise them with trick questions.

Learning Exercises

We need more cooperative learning exercises.

The exercises give us practice experience we can apply to real library situations.
— Graduate students, School of Library and Information Studies

Cooperative learning exercises can be done either in class or as an outside assignment. They can be graded or ungraded. This activity works well for:

- exercises that can be completed in a short time, perhaps twenty to thirty minutes in class or an hour or two outside of class; or

- exercises that present a problem that has a right answer or, at least, a plausible solution.

STRATEGIES AND TECHNIQUES FOR COOPERATIVE LEARNING

Basically, teaching strategies and techniques for cooperative learning do not differ from traditional university teaching. Planning, communicating, and evaluating remain the essential components of instruction.

Planning

The teacher's mind-set differs for cooperative learning activities. Therefore, the planning process differs. In developing a course and designing instructional units, the teacher no longer asks, "How can I present this subject so that each student can understand it?" Planning cooperative learning demands a more complex question, "What activities am I able to design that will help my students understand the content of this course better through cooperative learning than they would have been able to do through individual assignments?"

Effective and efficient cooperative learning depends upon the quality and appropriateness of the instructional materials the teacher prepares. Perhaps the key component to successful planning for cooperative learning is "over-organization." Organization of both the course and of each class meeting is vital. For example, organization for small group discussions may seem a simple matter, but it is not. Sometimes it is educationally effective to place students in different groups as frequently as possible. Other times it is more effective to have students work in the same group for a period of several weeks or even during the entire term.

Seemingly small matters affect the quality of learning. For example, does the teacher choose the group leader? If so, how? If not, how is the leader chosen? Choice of the discussion leader is an important decision because the leader is pivotal in group discussions.

Organization is essential for the first class meeting in which small groups are used. First, the teacher should prepare the discussion questions. All of the small groups may have the same question, or each group may have a different question. Then the teacher should decide who will be in each group. It is also advisable for the teacher to select the group leader and the member of the group who will report back to the class on the discussion. Finally, the teacher should prepare a handout that states the discussion question or questions, lists all the groups, and identifies the leader and the reporter for each group.

Later in the term, especially with relatively small classes, this level of organization for small group discussions is not necessary, but it is crucial at the beginning of the term for the students to have the security that detailed organization provides. Organization remains important throughout the term, however, even if it is not as controlled as at the beginning.

Communicating

Writing clear and comprehensible course materials; explaining performance expectations in adequate detail; being attentive to students' problems with cooperative learning; asking discussion questions that elicit thoughtful responses; listening to what the students are saying; attending to everything that occurs during a cooperative learning activity; reinforcing student contributions; creating a warm, supportive class environment—these and more are part of the communication process for cooperative learning. A class period is a time of "eternal vigilance" as the teacher encourages and monitors student expression and participation.

In an effort to communicate with students concerning cooperative learning as an instructional

---

GUIDELINES FOR COOPERATIVE LEARNING IN THE CLASS

Cooperative learning will be stressed in this class. Approximately one-third of class time will be devoted to cooperative learning activities, primarily small group discussions, class discussions, cooperative learning exercises, and student presentations of cooperative projects. In addition, much of your out-of-class time will involve cooperative learning. This amount of time will vary from student to student depending on our choice of assignments to meet course requirements.

These guidelines list objectives for cooperative learning in this course, identify my responsibilities as a teacher and yours as a student, and suggest steps to follow in preparing for cooperative learning activities.

Objectives

Cooperative learning will enable students to:

- enhance critical thinking and problem-solving skills,

- improve comprehension of course content,

- improve communication skills—listening, speaking, and writing,

- strengthen a positive attitude toward working on cooperative projects and activities,

- experience working as a member of a group toward a common goal, and

- simulate—within the limits of course content and the learning environment—the types of cooperative activities in which librarians are involved.

Responsibilities of the Teacher

- The instructor **plans** the course of the term, integrating cooperative learning activities as appropriate for course content and objectives.

- The instructor **prepares** for each class session so that cooperative learning activities are effective and efficient instructional methods.

- The instructor **monitors** in-class cooperative learning activities.

- The instructor **evaluates and re-evaluates** each class session by trying to answer the question, "How could I have done this better?"

Responsibilities of Students

- Students are **aware** that they are responsible not only for their own learning but for others who are participating in cooperative learning activities.

- Students **prepare** thoroughly by making sure they understand the content and are able to express themselves intelligibly.

How to Prepare for a Cooperative Learning Activity

- Analyze the reading, book, presentation task, project, or "whatever." Identify the thesis statement for a reading, especially a journal article, and the purpose or objective of a book or other library item, presentation, or project.

- Even if you are in inveterate highlighter, jot down the thesis or purpose. I don't know if any research studies show writing brief notes in addition to highlighting to be an effective learning device, but I do know teachers who are convinced highlighting by itself is not effective in analyzing a reading.

- Identify the arguments and evidence that support the thesis or the methods used to elucidate the purpose. Again, jot down brief notes.

- Evaluate this material. Do you think the thesis is valid? The purpose worthy? Do the arguments or activities support the thesis or purpose? Make brief notes of your evaluation.

- Finally, is the material relevant to library materials and services? Note briefly your assessment of relevance.

- Bring these brief notes to the cooperative learning activity. By brief, I mean words, phrases, sentence fragments, occasionally a complete sentence.

Figure 1   Cooperative Learning Guidelines

method, I have prepared a handout that addresses the students directly and spells out the objectives of cooperative learning for the course, responsibilities of the teacher, responsibilities of the students, and suggestions to the students on preparing for a cooperative learning activity. The content of this handout changes as my perception of cooperative learning evolves. Essentially, however, I emphasize the same basic ideas every semester. A recent handout is reproduced in Figure 1.

Evaluating Cooperative Learning

Cooperative learning activities such as discussions, learning exercises, and writing groups do not require evaluation, at least not formal, graded evaluation, but group projects do. Evaluating these can be difficult. I will discuss difficulties involved with evaluating group projects in the next section.

Fortunately, cooperative learning activities need not replace individual work for the course. Formal evaluation of individual contributions to group projects, individual assignments, quizzes, and examinations will yield adequate information for a fair assessment of each student's academic performance.

PROBLEMS WITH COOPERATIVE LEARNING

Cooperative learning has problems that are inherent to the method. The teacher cannot cover the same amount of content as with the lecture method. Both the students and the teacher spend more time in preparation. A certain amount of student resistance, varying from class to class, invariably presents itself. Even students who support the idea of cooperative learning may not fulfill their responsibilities to themselves and their fellow learners. The learning environment may affect cooperative learning activities adversely. Teachers may fail to evaluate cooperative class projects fairly.

Covering the Course Content

No instructional method surpasses the lecture in providing a logical, coherent, fast-paced presentation of subject content. The teacher controls the selection, organization, and presentation of information. The process remains on task and on track.

In contrast, cooperative learning is not an efficient method to cover the material. Group discussions take time, more time than presenting the topic in a lecture. The teacher accepts this limitation, if it is a limitation, and aims for depth rather than breadth of a coverage, for less information but more knowledge. The active, albeit time-consuming, participation of the students in discussion enables them to both assimilate and conceptualize the subject. Because the student is actively involved, retention may be greater than in the more passive mode of the traditional lecture.

Preparation Time

The cooperative method requires more preparation, much of it extremely time-consuming, from both the teacher and the students. Moreover, this in-depth preparation is necessary for every class meeting. No one, teacher or student, can "slip through" a single class.

The teacher must prepare discussion questions or cooperative activities that meet the learning objectives for the topic, achieve these objectives in the time available, stimulate critical thinking, and enhance problem-solving skills. Such thorough preparation consumes considerably more time than is necessary to prepare lecture notes. Despite the most careful preparation, however, university teachers who use cooperative learning sometimes feels that the legendary Murphy's Law singles them out. If anything can go wrong, it will go wrong. Students misinterpret questions that had seemed impervious to misinterpretation. A key student to the planned class activity is absent. Essential equipment, learning materials, or physical facilities are suddenly unavailable.

Matters of little consequence to teachers using the lecture method can seriously affect planned cooperative learning activities. Lecturers are not greatly inconvenienced when overhead projectors mysteriously disappear, the xerox machine breaks down, the scheduled video vanishes, or the regular classroom is pre-empted. But such small matters can torpedo the most carefully prepared cooperative learning activities. Fortunately, a sense of humor and an alternative set of plans for the class will keep Murphy's Law at bay. But the alternative set of plans, obviously, adds to the already burdensome preparation time.

Students also must spend more time in preparation. They cannot slide through a class meeting without having done the readings as they can with a lecture. And they, too, must be thorough in their preparation. Our students at SLIS are conscientious. They feel they will let down their classmates if they do not prepare adequately. Although keeping up with class activities enhances learning, the pressure to do so regularly and without fail can become stressful. Students apologize profusely to the other members of their discussion group when illness, other pressing responsibilities, or unforeseen events prevent them from preparing adequately.

Student Resistance

Students who have had no experience with cooperative learning often resist an unfamiliar approach to education. They have become familiar with the lecture method in university classes and are comfortable with taking notes of the professor's lecture and having minimal class interaction. To them, this is *the* appropriate method for university education. Cooperative learning is an "elementary school" methodology. They can become very hostile to a professor they feel is not doing his or her job. They define the job in this instance as lecturing. A very few are totally imbued with the idea of the superior knowledge of the teacher and have little or no faith in the contribution their classmates can make to their learning. A few students are uncomfortable working with others. For them, learning is a solitary activity. They confuse class discussion with "shared ignorance."

Students' Failure to Meet Responsibilities for Cooperative Learning

Students at the School of Library and Information Studies seldom fail to meet their responsibilities for cooperative learning activities. Those who do so may lack the ability to work at the same level of others in their group, may not understand the requirements of the activity, or, infrequently, may simply freeload. Other students try to help a group member who lacks the ability to achieve at the group's level. They may be less tolerant of the student who doesn't understand the requirements of the activity, especially if they feel that person hasn't made a genuine effort to understand. As one would expect, most students become angry with the freeloader in their midst. Others accept a freeloader as a reality they will have to deal with at times in their professional careers. No matter how philosophically some members of the group react, the student who deliberately refuses to accept a reasonable share of responsibility for the cooperative activity presents a problem to the group, to the other students in the class, and to the teacher. The responsible members of the group must carry an additional work load. The quality of the learning activity may suffer, thereby depriving the class as a whole from learning as much as they might reasonably have expected from the group's project. The teacher's objectives may not have been met at the anticipated level. As a result, fair and impartial evaluation of a group that has not functioned as a working unit is difficult.

COOPERATIVE LEARNING AND THE LEARNING ENVIRONMENT

The learning environment includes all the conditions that affect learning, such as the physical facility, the personality of the class, interaction among students, interaction between the students and the teacher, and class size. Although the environment affects all instructional methods, cooperative activities may depend more than other types of instruction on a positive learning environment.

Physical Facility

The physical facility impacts upon cooperative learning activities. Most of us remember the university classroom with student desks bolted to the floor. The larger ones had a raised dais where the professor stood behind a rostrum on which he set his notes. These classrooms, more accurately called lecture halls, were planned for the traditional university lecturer. They do not lend themselves easily to cooperative learning although an imaginative teacher can adapt them to group activities. On the other hand, a spacious classroom with movable student chairs, desks, or study tables facilitates cooperative learning.

Class Personality

As every teacher knows, every class has a unique personality. Two sections of the same course can be so different that a teacher has to adjust instructional methods and course requirements. Attitudes, either positive or negative, of individual students, especially students who are natural leaders, affect the learning environment. Students' attitudes, academic ability, background knowledge, and life experiences combine to create a distinctive class character. Teachers, no matter what type of instructional methods they use, react to negative messages students send them. This holds true whether the students communicate verbally, through body language, poor academic performance, frequent absences, or in other ways. The university professor who relies primarily on the traditional lecture method, however, controls learning activities to a greater degree than the teacher who emphasizes cooperative learning. Student negativism, always difficult to deal with, can torpedo the best-laid plans for an instructional method predicated upon student cooperation.

Interaction Among Students

We have such interesting people in this class. They've done so many different things and have such a variety of backgrounds.

We all work together and learn from one another. We don't compete for grades.
—Graduate students, School of Library and Information Studies

Positive interactions between students promote cooperative learning. Such attitudes include the willingness to share, mutual trust, making the effort to get to know one's classmates as individuals, enthusiasm for a free and open exchange of ideas, and ability to form good working relationships. These attitudes characterize students who will interact positively and create a class environment conducive to cooperative learning. In contrast, students who prize their individual prerogatives, focus narrowly on their own objectives, fear competition from other students, find exchange of ideas threatening, and resist forming working relationships do not interact successfully with other students. They perceive cooperative learning as limiting their intellectual horizons. Several of these students in a class, especially if they have leadership ability, may inhibit classmates who might otherwise have found cooperative learning consonant with their personalities and learning styles.

Interaction Between Students and Teacher

Successful cooperative learning activities depend upon free and frequent interaction between the students and the teacher. Students who feel comfortable seeking out the teacher for help and advice will achieve at a higher level than students who are hesitant to ask a teacher for suggestions on how to approach a course requirement, for clarification of guidelines, or for assistance in solving problems related to a learning activity. Likewise, teachers who are not accessible to students will not

realize the full potential of cooperative learning. As with class preparation, this interaction between students and teacher absorbs considerably more time than traditional instructional methods. Both the students and the teacher may find it difficult to fit this additional time into already crowded schedules. These barriers to student and teacher interaction may create problems that adversely affect cooperative learning activities.

Class Size

Class size affects planning, implementation, and evaluation of cooperative learning. Classes of fifteen or fewer students fall naturally into the cooperative learning mode. Small classes can accommodate a variety of cooperative learning activities effectively and efficiently. Conversely, classes of thirty or more graduate students are more challenging to handle in a cooperative mode. Large classes require more detailed planning, may not be able to accommodate as many cooperative learning activities, and present obstacles to precise and impartial evaluation. Despite these problems, cooperative learning will also work with large graduate classes. Teachers and students are able to meet course objectives using this method, but they must be willing to expend more effort and to realize that some negotiation and adjustment of evaluation procedures may be necessary. In short, cooperative learning works well in large classes if both teachers and students remain patient and understanding throughout the academic term.

EVALUATING COOPERATIVE CLASS PROJECTS

How does a teacher evaluate a cooperative class project fairly and accurately? What problems does one need to solve in doing so? Do some of these problems elude solution? If so, how can a teacher avoid the pitfalls inherent in evaluating cooperative class projects and yet provide students with these valuable learning experiences?

First of all, we need to realize that evaluating the project is not really the problem. What concerns the teacher and the students is evaluating each student's contribution to the project. If the project is truly cooperative, that is, if it is not possible to identify each student's contribution, evaluation may be difficult. If, on the other hand, the individual student's contributions to the project can be rather easily identified, evaluation becomes only a minor problem. So we will deal only with those projects that are truly cooperative.

Let's say the teacher evaluates the project as excellent and gives it an A. But something seems amiss. The students are not at ease about the grade. The teacher might conclude that not all members of the group deserve the A, not a difficult conclusion to reach. Much more difficult is to find out which student or students did not contribute adequately to the project.

One can ask the students to evaluate one another, perhaps not to give a letter grade but to write comments on each student's contribution. This may or may not work. Most likely it will not. Students' reluctance to evaluate one another is legendary.

Another approach is to discuss the project with each student individually. In doing so, one can emphasize the process the students followed in reaching their final product, namely the completed project. This may elicit helpful information. Or it may not. The legendary code that says you do not squeal on your buddy is still in effect. Yet the teacher can discern enough information from what is not said or is implied to be able to make a fairly accurate assessment of individual contributions to the project.

Let's assume the teacher obtains a reasonably accurate assessment of each student's contribution and decides upon individual grades based on this assessment. What then? In the best possible scenario, all of the students who worked on the cooperative project will accept their individual grades as a just and fair evaluation. But the process is difficult and time-consuming.

In the worst possible scenario, however, one or more students may not accept their grades and may take their complaint to the department chair or the dean of the school. Then the teacher must prove the accuracy and fairness of the individual grades. What proof was obtained? What documentation, if any, resulted from the interviews? What other evidence can the teacher present? Now the evaluation process tee-

ters on the threshold of the university's procedures for dealing with student complaints. The weary teacher can be excused for asking, "Is it worth it?"

In most instances, however, a cooperative project reflects similar commitment and involvement from all of the students. Problems in evaluation usually do not arise. Teachers should not avoid assigning cooperative group projects because they fear evaluation may lead to student complaints. They may wish, however, to design the project in a way that allows them to identify individual contributions to the final product.

I have had no problems with evaluating group projects, but I have attempted to design these activities so that I could identify individual contributions. I feel that I have been fair and accurate within an acceptable margin of human error. No student has ever questioned my grades to individual members of the group for a cooperative project.

CONCLUSIONS AND RECOMMENDATIONS

Cooperative learning in my class at SLIS has been increasingly successful through the years. This is indicated by student performance, student response, and student evaluation of my courses. Students' critical thinking and problem-solving skills have improved. Students have consistently performed at the higher levels of Bloom's *Taxonomy* analysis, synthesis, and evaluation (Bloom, 1956). With very few exceptions, they have responded positively to cooperative learning activities. As my skill in using cooperative learning as an instructional method has improved, so have the students' evaluations of my use of it in my courses.

I recommend cooperative learning to teachers in professional graduate schools. It works. I suggest, however, that no one follow my trial-and-error method. Reading the professional literature and attending workshops would result in more immediate success than I experienced. But I have no regrets. I found the rewards to be well worth the occasional disappointments that accompanied my failure to foresee and forestall problems and pitfalls inherent in my learn-as-you-go approach.

NOTES

1. I prefer to use "teacher" rather than "professor" when referring to my role as an educator. "To teach" more precisely describes my responsibilities at SLIS than "to profess" does.

— —

REFERENCES

Adams, D. M., & Hamm, M. E. (1990). *Cooperative learning: Critical thinking and collaboration across the curriculum.* Springfield, IL: C. C. Thomas.

Bloom, B., (Ed.). (1956). *Taxonomy of educational objectives, the classification of educational goals, handbook I: Cognitive domain.* New York: David McKay.

Costa, A. (1985). *Developing minds: A resource book for teaching thinking.* Alexandria, VA: Association for Supervision and Curriculum Development.

Dishon, D., & Wilson-O'Leary, P. (1989). Tips for teachers. *Cooperative Learning, 10*(3), 30-40.

Graves, T. (1990a). Cooperative learning and academic achievement: A tribute to David and Roger Johnson, Robert Slavin, and Shlomo Sharan. *Cooperative Learning, 10*(4), 13-16.

Graves, T. (1990b). Non-academic benefits of cooperative learning. *Cooperative Learning, 10*(3), 16-17.

Griffith, S. C. (1990). Cooperative learning techniques in the classroom. *Journal of Experiential Education, 13*(2), 41-44.

King, A. (1990). Enhancing peer interaction and learning in the classroom through reciprocal questioning. *American Educational Research Journal, 27*(4), 664-87.

Kluge, L. (1990). *What we know about cooperative learning.* Arlington, VA: Educational Research Service.

Kohn, A. (1991). Don't spoil the promise of cooperative learning: Response to Slavin. *Educational Leadership, 48*(5), 93-94.

Krathwohl, D., Bloom, S., & Masia, B. (1964). *Taxonomy of educational objectives, the classification of educational goals, handbook II: Affective domain.* New York: David McKay.

Prescott, S., & Wolff, D. E. (1990). Cooperative learning as a teaching strategy in elementary and secondary teacher education courses. *Teacher Education Quarterly, 17*(2), 41-58.

Rockman, E. F., (Ed.). (1991). Reference librarian of the future: A symposium. *Reference Services Review, 19*(1), 71-80.

Slavin, R. E. (1991). Synthesis of research of cooperative learning. *Educational Leadership, 48*(1), 71-82.

CHAPTER
22

AN AGENDA FOR ALL SEASONS

—

James Bellanca

Upper Jay, New York may well be the birthplace of the modern cooperative learning movement. In the early seventies, Roger and David Johnson migrated from the Midwest to a small conference center buried in the Adirondack Park. There they conducted—usually for three or four people and millions of black flies—their early rendition of basic cooperative learning.

What started as a move to make the teaching of constructive social skills and the resolution of conflict easy for the classroom teacher has grown into a movement with many purposes. These include: teaching social skills and increasing self-esteem (Kohn, 1986), improving student achievement (Slavin, 1983b), resolving conflict (Johnson & Johnson, 1979), developing cooperative social skills (Cohen, 1986), embedding graphic organizers (McTighe & Lyman, 1988), and building higher-order thinking (Bellanca & Fogarty, 1991). Unlike many other educational movements, cooperative learning carries with it a substantive body of research. This research supports the claims of cooperative learning. For those educators who work cooperation into the future of their schools, cooperative learn-

ing has established itself as an agenda for all seasons.

Cooperative learning is a philosophy, an instructional strategy, and the bedrock of cognitive instruction. When a school combines all three into a single approach, a strong foundation for teaching, learning, and living is set in place.

Cooperative learning is based on the belief that school life, family life, and work life are enhanced when individuals care about each other and work together for mutual goals. "We sink or swim together," "All for one and one for all," and "Three heads are better than one" are common expressions of the cooperative spirit. In the schoolhouse, cooperative learning takes many forms. When the belief system of cooperation and caring saturates all corners of all classrooms, it is possible to see the most powerful effects.

Espousing the principles of cooperation is not enough. The philosophy entails a host of carefully scrutinized strategies. The strategies are the practical tools which enable teachers to enable learning in new ways. As teachers expand a repertoire of cooperative strategies, they build a strong foundation for students not only to work together, but also to take greater responsibility for individual learning (Johnson & Johnson, 1987).

It is very easy for the uninitiated to confuse cooperative learning with general grouping practices. The definition of cooperative learning, two or more students of different ability working together for a common goal, gives the first clue that cooperative learning is more than assigning students to work together. In general grouping practices, students may work together, but each retains individual goals. These students learn individually ("I have my science lab book") or competitively ("My answer is better than yours"). In cooperative learning, however, the students work to achieve a single goal ("*We* did it").

The skilled teacher who uses cooperative learning calls upon several key elements—the critical attributes of cooperative learning—which make this strategy unique. When all these attributes are present in lessons, purposefully created by the teacher, there is true cooperative learning. When one or more of the attributes is absent, there is little more than a group doing individual work in the same location.

The cognitive model of cooperative learning has five critical attributes summed up in the **BUILD** acronym:

Build on higher-order thought.

Unify the teams.

Invite individual accountability.

Look back and evaluate the quality of thinking and cooperating.

Develop social skills.

The best of cooperative lessons integrate all five attributes. The best of cooperative classrooms do so day in and day out as the heart of instruction. When a skilled teacher builds such a classroom it is a common sight to see students working together cooperatively 60 to 75 percent of the day.

The list of cooperative strategies a teacher can use to facilitate these attributes is about as endless as the stars. Teams, Games, and Tournaments (Slavin, 1983a); thought teams (Bellanca & Fogarty, 1991); four heads together (Kagan, 1990); jigsaw (Kagan, 1990); three-to-one questions (Bellanca &

Fogarty, 1991); team organizers (Bellanca & Fogarty, 1991); tribes (Gibbs, 1987); roles (Johnson & Johnson, 1979); BUILD charts (Bellanca & Fogarty, 1991)—the volume of strategies is both a blessing and a curse.

First, consider the curse. It is easy for a teacher to dabble in cooperative groups: Teacher A learns jigsaw. Teacher B does Teams, Games, and Tournaments. Teacher C posts guidelines for cooperative work. Teacher D loves four heads together. By picking a strategy or tool to throw into the classroom milieu now and then, each can assume he or she is doing cooperative learning.

Now, consider the blessing. When a teacher elects to teach students *how* to work as a team, he or she is laying the foundation for a cooperative classroom. Whether the teacher uses cooperative strategies synthesized into a personal approach or a pre-packaged model matters little. What matters more is making a serious, regular, and consistent effort to use cooperative learning as the foundation of learning in the classroom and the core for improving basic skills, social skills, and thinking skills.

The full potential of cooperative learning, however, is not reached by limiting it to helping students score better on memory work, vocabulary, spelling, or math worksheets. Such improvement of basic skills is necessary, but it is just a start. Cooperative learning's full potential is used when it is the bedrock for caring and thoughtful classrooms. When the teacher—better yet, the entire teaching family in a school—uses the cooperative social skill model to build the cooperative spirit throughout every classroom (Glasser, 1986; Kohn, 1986) and takes advantage of cognitive strategies to make every classroom a "home for the mind" (Costa, 1991), the outcome is much more likely to stretch children and teachers far beyond normal performance expectations.

In this context, effective teaching and learning occur when the teacher is skilled enough to manage cooperative learning as the foundation for a triple agenda classroom. This triple agenda encompasses content, cooperation, and complex thinking. When all three elements are entwined, the effectiveness of each approach is exponentially powerful.

Consider how a triple agenda lesson differs from the ordinary content-only lesson, or even the cooperative lesson that is limited to recall outcomes.

A HIGH SCHOOL EXAMPLE

A Single Agenda: Content Only

In this lesson, a U.S. history teacher assigns all students in the class to "read the next chapter." On the following day, the teacher gives a quiz (the grades include five As, twelve Bs, thirteen Cs, seven Ds, and three Fs) and puts the grades in the grade book. He or she next lectures on the materials. In the lecture he or she shows several studies, asks three theoretical questions, and uses a colored overhead as an outline. For the next two days, the teacher spends ten minutes in a guided discussion asking students' opinions on the causes of the Civil War. The discussion is closed with a summary review and an admonishment that everyone study for the unit final.

The Double Agenda: Cooperation and Content

In this lesson, the teacher assigns previously established base groups to jigsaw the next chapter. Each one of the three students in a group reads one-third of the material. The students then teach each other about their respective portions. On the next day, the teacher uses expert groups to check for understanding of their reading about the war's causes. After the expert groups are finished, each base group works on a three-to-one worksheet (Bellanca & Fogarty, 1991) to help them pull together the key information. On the next day, each group recorder reports on what the group has learned about the causes and explains why it has made its selections. On the overhead, the teacher records the key concepts reported by each group. Next, the teacher guides a discussion to clarify the main points. On the third day, he or she instructs the base groups to review the material from their notes; check that every group member can explain all of the material; and make a list of the ways they have helped each other learn. On the fourth day, the teacher tests individual students' knowledge of the Civil War's causes.

The Triple Agenda: Content, Cooperation, and Complex Thinking

In this lesson, the teacher uses a KWL goal-setting chart in the pre-set base groups (Bellanca & Fogarty, 1991). Each group lists what it already knows about how the Civil War began and what they want to learn about the war. By now, they are used to the learning expectations.

After the groups finish their lists, the teacher elicits a comprehensive list for the whole class for both categories. The base groups then do a jigsaw reading in the text with instructions that each individual make a causal web (Bellanca & Fogarty, 1991) of an assigned section. (At this point in the course, they have already learned how to do this.) The teacher writes on the board the triple agenda objectives:

At the end of this unit, you will:

- identify the causes of the Civil War,
- evaluate the causes of the Civil War, and
- apply the conflict resolution skill of persuasion.

On the next day, the teacher assigns expert groups to compare webs on each section. After the expert groups do their work, students go back to the base groups with instructions on how to use a fishbone organizer (Bellanca & Fogarty, 1991). In the base groups, the recorder notes the instances of positive persuasion used by members to resolve disagreements.

On the third day, each team is instructed to place in rank order the principle causes of the war. After agreeing on the number one cause, each team develops its rationale. In the second half of the class period, each team has the chance to make its case. For homework, students are assigned to review their team's case for the number one cause and to prepare an evaluation of the case using the teacher's standard check form.

On the fourth day, the teacher gives a quiz asking each student to identify the causes discussed in the class; explain the importance of two persuasion methods used; and write a short paragraph evaluating defense of the group's number one choice. The quiz is followed by a discussion of persuasion techniques. In this discussion, each group lists its

HIGH SCHOOL INSTRUCTIONAL STRATEGY

SINGLE AGENDA

(Content Only):

- homework
- reading quiz
- lecture
- theoretical questions
- opinion discussion
- summary
- recall test

DOUBLE AGENDA

(Content and Cooperation):

- base group/homework
- expert groups/check for understanding
- base group/three-to-one questions
- recorder reports and defends
- clarification discussion
- base-group review
- base-group evaluation
- test-recall and explanation

TRIPLE AGENDA

(Content, Cooperation, and Complex Thinking):

- KWL goal-setting chart
- class list—advanced organizer
- base groups
- jigsaw homework
- triple objectives
- base groups/attribute webs
- fishbone organizer
- recorder observes
- persuasion
- rank order
- case study
- evaluation
- test—identify, persuade, and evaluate teamwork

Figure 1   High School Instructional Strategy

favorite techniques and then the teams debate each other (see Figure 1).

AN ELEMENTARY SCHOOL EXAMPLE

A similar outline contrasting the three agendas is possible with a third grade science lesson:

A Single Agenda: Content Only

In this lesson the teacher distributes a science text to each student. The unit is trees. The teacher calls upon individuals to read aloud each paragraph. When the reading is done, the teacher instructs the students to answer the questions at the chapter's end. After ten minutes, the teacher tells them to put away their materials. Those not finished with the questions must complete the work at home.

On the next day at science time, the text questions are reviewed and different students are called on to answer each question. If the answer is correct, the teacher says "good answer" and proceeds to the next. If the response is incorrect or incomplete, he or she says, "No, that's wrong," and asks another child to answer. After the last answer, all the answer sheets are collected and graded.

The Double Agenda: Content and Cooperation

To begin the trees unit, each student is assigned to a three-person task group. Each group has a strong reader, an average reader, and a weak reader. Each student is assigned a specific role (reader, recorder, and checker). With the entire class, the teacher reviews each role's job, the team guidelines (one person talks at a time, use six-inch voices [voices that can only be heard by someone who is no more than six inches away from the speaker], use first names, no put-downs, stay with the group), and the lesson objectives (to identify the differences between hardwood and softwood trees and to practice teamwork).

TREES

1. The answers to these questions are in the science book. After your team has found the information to answer the question, each team member is to answer the question. After the recorder writes each answer, the team will agree on the best group answer.

2. Check that each team member can explain the group answer.

3. When finished, each person who helped should sign the worksheet.

Team Name _____

Members _____

_____

_____

Date _____

1. Each person name one hardwood tree and one softwood tree.

Hardwood	Softwood
A.	A.
B.	B.
C.	C.

Each team agree on at least three important characteristics of hardwood trees and three of softwood trees.

Hardwood	Softwood
A.	A.
B.	B.
C.	C.

2. Each person list at least one use of each tree type.

Hardwood	Softwood
A.	A.
B.	B.
C.	C.

Team: agree on which use of the trees is most valuable to your family.

_____

_____

Figure 2   Trees Worksheet (Elementary School)

The teacher distributes one text and one worksheet to each group. He or she reviews the three-to-one questions on the worksheet and instructs the teams to read the text and agree on the answers.

After the teams finish the worksheets, the teacher asks a student from each group to share the group's answers. After several answers, each group's answer sheet is collected, signed by each member.

On the next day, the teacher gives each group a worksheet with the outlines of hardwood and softwood leaves. The teams stay together while the class walks through the nearby park. In the leaf hunt, each group is to find a sample leaf for each outline on the worksheet.

When the class returns from this trip, the groups paste the leaves to the matching sketch and each member signs the sheet. On the back of the sheet, each group uses a scale of one to five to rate how well members worked together, how well each member did his or her assigned job, and how well they encouraged each other (see Figure 2).

The Triple Agenda: Content, Cooperation, and Complex Thinking

In this lesson, the teacher begins the study of trees by reading Joyce Kilmer's poem, "Trees." After the poem, students turn to a neighbor, "put two heads together," and decide how Kilmer felt about trees. While they are sharing, the teacher projects a large leaf on the overhead screen. After two minutes, he or she signals for their attention and asks for their decisions. He or she then announces that the class is going to make a leaf poem with their ideas, and asks that each group provide just one word to describe Kilmer's feelings. As each group in turn

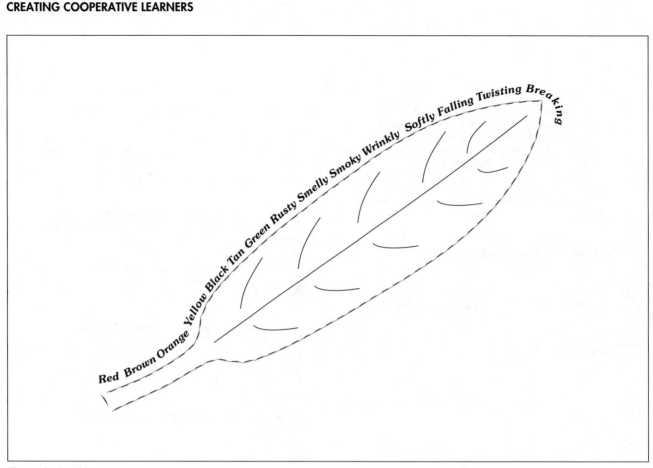

Red Brown Orange Yellow Black Tan Green Rusty Smelly Smoky Wrinkly Softly Falling Twisting Breaking

Figure 3   Leaf Poem

responds, the answers are written on the leaf out-line (see Figure 3).

After the last contribution is made, the teacher uses a second overhead to outline the multiple lesson objectives.

- To know what makes a tree special.
- To show how trees are alike and different.
- To create a poem about a tree.
- To practice encouragement.

After checking for understanding about the objectives, the teacher divides the class into heterogeneous groups of three, assigns roles, reviews group guidelines, and reviews the encouragement T-chart (Bellanca & Fogarty, 1991). Each group's lab technician is invited to get a package of materials from a side table and share its contents with the group. (Each packet contains a piece of bark, a leaf, a seedling, a small limb, the tree name on a card, and a worksheet with the part names). The groups match the tree parts with

the worksheet. The teacher also reminds them to encourage each other.

Wandering among the groups, the teacher is able to help the groups, answer their questions, and observe how they encourage each other. When most of the students are finished, he or she signals for their attention and asks that the data collector in each group show its completed arrangement.

In the center of the room, there is a large sheet of newsprint showing a web labeled with the tree parts on the floor. The researchers from each group bring the labeled parts and glue them to the newsprint.

After the last piece is in place, the teacher asks students to explain what is similar about the objects on each ray and what is different. He or she probes and cues for small distinctions.

On the next day, the teacher directs a summary of the similarities and differences between the various trees to bridge into a discussion of the distinction between hardwoods and softwoods. The class

OBSERVATION WORKSHEET

Sample	1	2	3	4	5	6
Shaving	easy	hard	hard	easy	hard	easy

Figure 4   Trees Unit Observation Worksheet

observes as the teacher uses a penknife to shave each limb sample. After the samples are shaved, the groups are asked to agree whether the job of shaving was hard or easy (see Figure 4).

The technicians share the results. Where there is disagreement among groups' answers, simple voting is used to resolve the conflict. After the last agreement is reached, the teacher facilitates a summary of what the students have learned by a series of open-ended questions based on the web. These questions then lead to the labeling of the hard-to-shave samples as hardwood and the easy-shaving limbs as softwood. To conclude, the stu- dents in each group are asked to complete a prediction chart (see Figure 5).

After ten minutes, the groups are called back to work as a whole class. In turn, each group gives its response to an item on the chart. Other groups then agree or disagree. Where there is disagreement, students are encouraged to give reasons and persuade. When the entire group agrees on a response, the class moves on to the end. The teacher concludes this activity by correcting mistaken predictions, affirming correct predictions, and soliciting generalizations about hardwood and softwood.

PREDICTION CHART

Hardwood	Softwood
Will burn longer	Will saw faster
Will give more ashes after burning	Will take a nail more easily
Will last longer on a house	Will split more easily with an axe

Figure 5   Trees Unit Prediction Chart

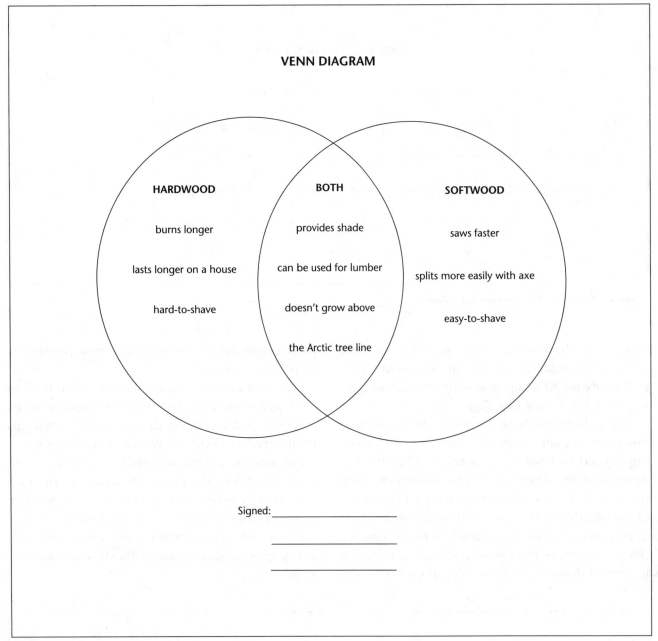

VENN DIAGRAM

HARDWOOD

burns longer

lasts longer on a house

hard-to-shave

BOTH

provides shade

can be used for lumber

doesn't grow above

the Arctic tree line

SOFTWOOD

saws faster

splits more easily with axe

easy-to-shave

Signed: _____

_____

_____

Figure 6   Trees Unit Venn Diagram

On the next day, the teacher models how the students can create a Venn diagram to compare and contrast hardwood and softwood trees. Then each group works on its diagram and signs its completed work (see Figure 6).

After checking the groups' work, the teacher re-reads the Kilmer Poem and the class's leaf poem created at the start of the lesson. Each group reviews what it has learned about the unique qualities of all trees and the differences between hardwood and softwood trees. Students then create a tree poem with that information.

Each group uses a sheet of newsprint and crayons for the paper poem. The teacher informs students that he or she is going to observe how well they work together, encourage each other, and how accurate the information that the group uses is. He or she also lets students know that each individual in each group should be ready to explain why the group has used the selected information.

ELEMENTARY INSTRUCTIONAL STRATEGY

SINGLE AGENDA LESSON
(Content Only):

- selected students read text aloud
- individuals answer chapter questions
- selected students read aloud
- positive reinforcement

DOUBLE AGENDA LESSON
(Content and Cooperation):

- assigns heterogeneous groups
- assigns roles in group
- reviews roles and guidelines for cooperation
- identifies cooperation and content objectives
- three-to-one worksheets reviewed
- group signatures
- reviews group answers
- team worksheet for leaf search
- group rating
- group agreement activity

TRIPLE AGENDA LESSON
(Content, Cooperation, and Complex Thinking):

- Think, Pair, Share set (Bellanca & Fogarty, 1991)
- model leaf poem
- group wrap around (Bellanca & Fogarty, 1991)
- overhead to review content, cooperation
- cognitive objectives
- check for understanding
- assigned heterogeneous groups with roles
- reviews roles, group guidelines, and encouragement T–chart (Bellanca & Fogarty, 1991)
- distributes prepared packet to each group
- monitors
- web for entire class

- questions similarities
- differences
- probing questions
- teacher-directed summary by groups
- conflict resolution—voting
- prediction chart
- agree/disagree discussion
- Venn diagram for compare and contrast group task
- groups make own leaf poem
- observation for encouragement during group task
- random quizzing of knowledge; tests individual ability to explain material.

Figure 7   Elementary School Instructional Strategy

The three ingredients—knowledge of trees, observed encouragement, and the ability to explain serve as the "test" (see Figure 7).

What becomes readily apparent in the triple agenda classrooms is that the most skilled teachers are able to cover the same amount of material and to engage each child's active thinking about the topic with interest and variety. By purposefully preparing their students to incorporate the triple agenda, teachers create learning conditions conducive to complex thinking about the content without losing time to off-task misbehavior. In the single agenda lesson, the teachers lose time when disinterested students lose concentration and distract each other.

The challenge of the triple agenda classroom is the careful preparation of the students with the "shareware" (the tools and skills to work cooperatively) and the "mindware" (the tools and skills for thinking) needed to achieve the cooperative and cognitive objectives with the content objectives. This means that the triple agenda teacher must take time at the year's start to frame the conditions for cooperation and complex thinking and to provide instruction in the skillful use of shareware and mindware. Although time devoted to mindware and shareware instructions eats away at allotted time early in the school year, that time enables the teacher to move at least as quickly—and more completely—into the content as the year progresses. Time ordinarily lost in the single agenda classroom to the discipline problems of unengaged and often bored students is recaptured by the skillful cooperation and the active, self-directed mental engagement of students well prepared to work together and to engage each other in thoughtful tasks. In the thoughtful classroom, the students know that they are individuals accountable not only for content mastery, but also for how well they use their cooperative and cognitive skills. Moving beyond superficial coverage of facts the teacher has the opportunity to delve into critical concepts as well.

In this context, cooperative learning opens windows of opportunity not found in a content-only classroom. If needed, the teacher can intensify instruction in the cooperative social skills as the means to help students become more caring and more cooperative with each other. Without changing the direction of the curriculum, he or she can focus on the cooperative development of one or more students by expanding or contracting the time spent in learning the cooperative skills.

As the teacher guides students toward conceptual objectives in the content, the teacher will have the chance to bond students into high-trust teams that support each member. No longer is the teacher the sole motivator; students begin to help each other.

To picture the effect of the triple agenda, imagine a crew preparing for a rowing race. The coach takes great care to teach each member the technique of synchronized rowing. Each member has a job. In the beginning of the session, the members struggle to flow with the team. With practice, coaching, and more practice, the team members learn to pull together, to row as a unit.

The cooperative classroom with the learning groups is very much like the rowing team. The teacher not only shows the students how to row (the content); he or she also teaches them how to work as a team (cooperative skill). Practice and coaching of the rowing and teamwork go hand in hand. Success is measured by how well the students row together; the most powerful teams are those that master the double agenda.

Explanations of cooperative learning often miss this salient point. Traditionally, the arguments outlining the benefits of cooperative learning point out the achievement successes and the future work benefits of the teamwork to the creative classroom climate. This improved climate fosters internal motivation, accelerates learning, and makes traditional discipline problems less problematic. It may well be argued that teachers who take the time to teach students how to work, solve conflicts, and make decisions in small cooperative groups, make their own jobs easier and provide themselves with the time to accomplish their primary career agenda—teaching every child.

The effects of serious cooperative learning—concentrated instructional time devoted to the double agenda—extend beyond the classroom. Cooperative learning offers another, often missed, benefit—a cooperative school climate. To feel this effect, one need only visit a school dedicated to the cooperative model such as ones found in Chicago Heights, Illinois; Parkersburg, West Virginia; Lawton, Oklahoma; or Rockford, Illinois.

A visitor walking into any of these schools—all serving more than 85 percent Chapter I students—will *feel* the difference. The tone goes beyond posted mission statements on the entrance doors, bright bulletin boards celebrating student and teacher achievements, and drug-free school posters. The visitor will observe the easy way "big sisters" and "big brothers" mentor their primary grade partners with smiles and laughter; the cooperative games that include every student on mixed-age teams during recess; the cafeteria-table teams earning points together for cooperative lunch-time behaviors; the schoolwide goal of 1000 recorded encouraging words or actions a month; weekly goal-setting activities by base teams in every class-room; and sample after sample of students encouraging and helping each other throughout the building. In spite of the fact that most students in these schools live in poverty, surrounded by drugs, crime, and family dysfunction, the focus in every classroom is on cooperative work as the base of learning. In the earliest grades, the children learn how to move in and out of groups; how to care for each other; and how to work as a team in the classroom, hallways, cafeteria, playground, gym, and bus lines. Students in these schools avoid negative put-downs ("nerd," "jerk," or "stupid"), competitive criticisms ("you idiot, why can't you..." or "she can't do anything right"), foul language (no examples needed!), and rejections ("Do we have to work with him?" or "Why does she have to be in our group?"). Instead, students seldom forget to give each other and their teachers positive recognition ("Good job"), encouragement ("This is hard but we can do it if we work together"), and support ("We'll do it together"). As a result, students in the schools are bound with the feeling of "one for all, all for one" not only in classroom groups, but across grade levels.

The schoolwide cooperative goals impact the faculty as well. When cooperative learning methods are used to develop the students' social skills and the classroom's social climate on a consistent basis, a teacher can expect significant gains in students' basic skills. These gains are most dramatic when the social skills are taught first independently and then embedded into basic skill instruction. In a sense, the students learn the cooperative social skills in "spring training" and apply them in the "regular season." In the regular season, the teacher as coach continues to help students refine social skills. As students work together "in the game," the teacher gives feedback on their cooperation and elicits their assessment of team progress.

While the evidence is clear about the potential for cooperative learning—especially when it inculcates serious integration of the social skills into the curriculum as advocated by Johnson and Johnson, or schoolwide as advocated by Cohen, Kohn,

Bellanca, Fogarty, and Burke—it falls short of this potential if it is not combined with strategies to help all students become complex thinkers and problem solvers in triple agenda classrooms.

The triple agenda classroom works best in a schoolwide context. In this context, every teacher purposefully endeavors to help each student become a mindful learner. This suggests that thinking, along with cooperating and content mastery, is a critical component of each instructional day. Thinking in this sense, however, is not something that just happens or occurs in isolation from the cooperation and content. All three are treated as a single approach to instruction. (Returning to the sports analogy, the triple agenda teacher/coach does not isolate thinking instruction to a special period each day. As with the cooperative social skills and group learning procedures, she or he introduces students to the thinking skills and problem-solving processes appropriate to their level. This begins in "spring practice." After the students learn the new plays, they go into "the regular season" where the games count. The teacher helps each student perfect the skills. In the triple agenda classroom, the teacher also may make use of the team spirit. Students are encouraged to help each other with feedback and support. The more each individual masters the game, the greater the chance for team success.

From a practical point of view, the students' cooperative skills are the chief enablers of complex thinking in the classroom. If a teacher has to take the time to hear how each student in a classroom is progressing and to read and analyze each assignment, paper, or project, one-by-one; current time limits require either superficial evaluation, long time lapses between assignment collection and assignment return, or huge time investments. When students are able to function skillfully in thoughtful and challenging tasks, having mastered cooperative learning and complex thinking, the teacher spends considerably less time on off-task diversions and considerably more in-class time on coaching both individuals and groups. Does a slower student need a new explanation? A review of the problem-solving process in use? A word of encouragement? Do the three fastest learners need more difficult problems to solve? More in-depth feedback? A special team project applying complex principles? A cooperative learning teacher has the time to provide for these needs.

Just as the double agenda impact is increased when it becomes a schoolwide goal, the triple agenda increases its impact when the entire school integrates complex cognition into the curricular fabric. Indeed, there is some indication that when cognitive instruction is added to cooperative and content learning, the results are exponential rather than additive. This means that all students not only cover more content, but also understand it more deeply and apply it more accurately.

Looking back at the common definition of cooperative learning as a group of students of mixed ability working to achieve a common goal, it is apparent that the definition is both simple and profound. In its simple sense, cooperative learning is an instructional tool, one among many, that can help most students obtain better test scores on the basic skills of reading or math. In the more profound sense, it is an instructional model, which, when integrated with cognitive instruction and curricular content, provides a school with multiple opportunities to better prepare all students for learning and living in the twenty-first century.

REFERENCES

Bellanca, J., & Fogarty, R. (1991). *Blueprints for thinking in the cooperative classroom*, (2nd ed.). Palatine, IL: Skylight Publishing.

Cohen, E. (1986). *Designing groupwork: Strategies for the heterogeneous classroom*. New York: Teachers College Press.

Costa, A. (1991). The school as a home for the mind. Palatine, IL: Skylight Publishing.

Gibbs, J. (1987). *Tribes: A process for social development and cooperative learning*. Santa Rosa, CA: Center Source Publications.

Glasser, W. (1986). *Control theory in the classroom*. New York: Harper and Row.

Johnson, D., & Johnson, R. (1987). *Learning together and alone: Cooperative, competitive, and individualistic learning*. Englewood Cliffs, NJ: Prentice–Hall.

Johnson, D., & Johnson, R. (1979). Conflict in the classroom: Controversy and learning. *Review of Educational Research*, 49, 51-70.

Kagan, S. (1990). *Cooperative learning resources for teachers*. San Juan Capistrano, CA: Resources for Teachers.

Kohn, A. (1986). *No contest: The case against competition*. Boston: Houghton Mifflin.

McTighe, J., & Lyman, F. (1988). Cueing thinking in the classroom: The promise of theory-embedded tools. *Educational Leadership*, 45(7), 18-24.

Slavin, R. (1983a). *Cooperative learning*. New York: Longman.

Slavin, R. (1983b). When does cooperative learning increase student achievement? *Psychology Bulletin*, 94, 429-445.

ASSESSING SIGNIFICANT OUTCOMES

A friend of ours who is a fifth-grade teacher in California declared that she was not going to teach her music this year. Knowing that the fifth grade United States history curriculum included a unit on the westward expansion, and that our friend was very fond of playing her guitar and singing songs of the new frontier with her students, we were puzzled. We wondered why she had made the decision to exclude the music component.

"Because," she countered, "my students are not being evaluated on how well they enjoy or know music. They are being evaluated on how well they are mastering reading, writing, and mathematics!"

This last section addresses the complex task of assessment. Whether aesthetic, scientific, technological, educational, or physical, there is a strong desire for feedback in any human endeavor. We want to know how well we did, if it worked, and we want to know the results. With new and more complex goals on the agenda for educating the citizens of the 21st century, the question is: How will we know that these new goals are being achieved?

This final section begins with a reassessment of assessment itself. Two premises are set forth. First, we cannot measure these new process-oriented goals with product-oriented assessment techniques. Second, changing the forms of assessment can be used as an influential tool and significant impetus for restructuring schools—what is inspected is what is expected; what is tested is what is taught.

Following this reassessment, a renaissance in practices is envisioned. One chapter examines the issue of "finding out what we need to know," while another chapter takes a pragmatic look at grading as one compelling component of assessment that continues to haunt the student, the parent, and the teacher. Still another chapter espouses a more liberal approach of evaluation as an ongoing collaborative process for the student, parent, and teacher. Further chapters elaborate on methods and models for assessing and provide a strategic planning process for systematic assessment as well as one way to actually track student transfer of learning.

REASSESSING ASSESSMENT

—

Arthur L. Costa and Bena Kallick

The task of curriculum designers usually involves three major decisions: (1) establishing the outcomes or goals of the educational enterprise, be it at the classroom, school, district, state, or national level; (2) designing the delivery system by which these goals will be achieved, including instructional design, materials selection, allocation of time, and placement of learnings; and (3) developing procedures to monitor and evaluate the achievement of our goals as a result of employing that delivery system. Curriculum alignment means that these three groups of decisions are consistent with each other; it means that our delivery system is designed to meet desired outcomes and that our assessments evaluate the established goals (see Figure 1).

In the curriculum alignment process, sound educational practice dictates that the first group of decisions—the goals—drives the system. Like it or not, what is inspected is what is expected; what you test is what you get. The traditional use of norm-referenced, standardized tests has dictated what should be learned (the goals) and has influenced how it is taught (the delivery).

As evidenced in the preceding chapters, educators realize that new goals for the next century are becoming increasingly necessary for our children's future, for the continuity of our democratic institutions, and even for our planetary existence. Such goals include:

- Capacity for continued learning,
- Knowing how to behave when answers to problems are not immediately apparent,
- Cooperativeness and team building,
- Precise communication in a variety of modes,
- Appreciation of disparate value systems,
- Problem solving that requires creativity and ingenuity,
- Enjoyment of resolving ambiguous, discrepant, or paradoxical situations,
- Organization of an overabundance of technologically produced information,
- Pride in a well-crafted product,
- High self-esteem, and
- Personal commitment to larger organizational and global values.

These new goals need to drive the curriculum alignment process in thoughtful schools of the future. The delivery system—curriculum materials,

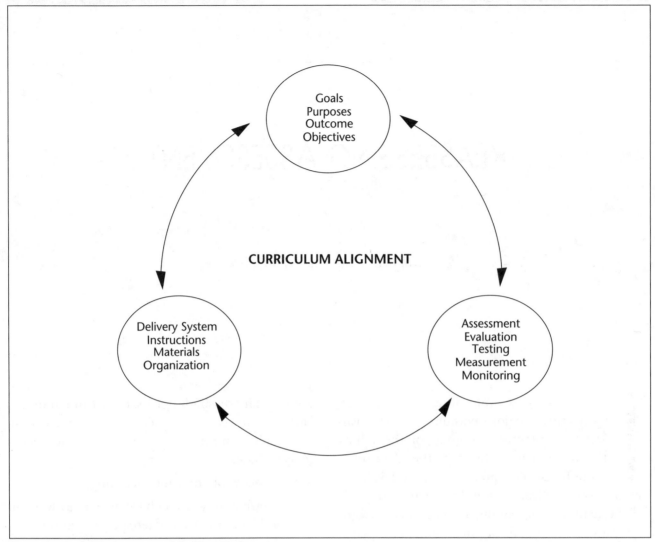

Figure 1 **Research Outcomes of Cooperative Learning**

instructional strategies, school organization—and the decision-making processes employed need to embody these goals. Furthermore, these goals are valid not only for students but for all of the school's inhabitants.

Likewise, our methods of assessment must be transformed to become more consistent with our new goals. We cannot employ product-oriented assessment techniques to assess the achievement of these new, process-oriented educational outcomes. Standardized test scores give us a static number that reflects the achievement and performance of isolated skills at a particular moment in time. Thinking, however, is dynamic; we learn from experience, react emotionally to situations, exper-

ience power in problem solving, and are energized by the act of discovery. Thus, testing thinking may indeed be an oxymoron.

We are witnessing a nationwide surge to "go beyond the bubble" of standardized, norm-referenced, computerized testing (California State Department of Education Curriculum Assessment Alignment Conference, 1989). State departments of education (including New Jersey, Vermont, Colorado, Maryland, Michigan, and Illinois) are providing leadership by experimenting with and advocating innovative assessment methods such as writing samples, materials manipulation, open-ended multiple answer questions, portfolios, performances, and exhibitions.

Such innovative methods are more useful than traditional testing procedures for several reasons. First, they resemble the situations in which real problem solving and creativity are demanded; they are not contrived. Second, they allow teachers to more accurately diagnose students' abilities. Third, they take place during instruction rather than after instruction is completed. Furthermore, they provide more immediate results that assist teaching teams in evaluating the effectiveness of their own curriculum decisions and instructional efforts. Finally, they provide "real-time" feedback to students themselves who must become the ultimate evaluators of their own performance.

To ensure the success of new assessment efforts in the restructured school, educators need to address at least the following six tasks:

1. Re-establish the school-site team as the locus for accountability.

2. Expand the range, variety, and multiplicity of assessment techniques.

3. Systematize assessment procedures.

4. Re-educate legislators, parents, board members, and the community.

5. Any assessment of student performance must also include an assessment of school and classroom conditions.

6. The process of evaluation will become internal for students.

RE–ESTABLISH THE SCHOOL-SITE TEAM AS THE LOCUS FOR ACCOUNTABILITY

For too long the process of assessment has been external to teachers' goal setting, curriculum, and instructional decision making. School effectiveness, student achievement, and teacher competence have often been determined by a narrow range of standardized student achievement test scores in a limited number of content areas: reading, math, and language acquisition. Awards of excellence have been granted to schools that show the highest gains in scores. Teachers have been given merit pay based on their students' performance on standardized tests. Test results have been

published in rank order in newspapers. (The real-estate industry loves this: "This is a ninety-eighth percentile community," say the agents. Houses are priced accordingly.)

Lord Kelvin said, "When you cannot measure it; when you cannot express it in numbers, your knowledge is of a very meager and unsatisfactory kind." Based on this archaic, reductionist theorem, we have tried to translate our educational goals into observable, measurable outcomes. We have become fascinated and enamored with:

- The amount of time spent on a task,
- The number of questions asked at each level of Bloom's Taxonomy,
- Score gains on achievement tests,
- Class size: numbers of students or the ratio of students to adults,
- Length of time in school,
- I.Q. scores as a basis for grouping,
- Numbers of days in attendance,
- Minutes of instruction,
- Percentages of objectives attained,
- Numbers of competencies needed for promotion, and
- School effectiveness judged by published test scores.

In the process, teachers have become disenfranchised. Educators in the classroom have had little say about what tests measure. In fact, what tests do measure is usually irrelevant to the curriculum, and the results of testing disclose little about the adequacy of teachers' decisions. In many ways the desire for measurable outcomes has signaled teachers that they are not competent to assess students themselves. The message is that they can not be trusted to collect evidence of student's growth, that the observations they make daily in the classroom are suspect and of little worth.

The accountability movement has caused educators to search for "hard data" by which to assess their efforts. What teachers observed, therefore, was "soft data." We propose that the "hardest," most objective data available is collected by an enlightened teaching team which systematically and collectively gathers data over time in the real-life, day-to-day interactions of the classroom. Conversely, the most suspect data is that designed and collected by testing "experts" external to the school setting and ignorant of the school's mission, values, and goals; the community's culture and socioeconomics; and the classroom mix of learning styles, teaching strategies, and group dynamics in which their tests are administered.

Someday we will reflect on this era and think: "What was educationally significant but difficult to measure was replaced by what was insignificant but easy to measure." Someday we will realize to what extent we've measured our effectiveness at teaching what is no longer worth learning! To paraphrase Jacob Viner, "When you can measure it, when you can express it in numbers, your knowledge is still of a meager and unsatisfactory kind!"

In the restructured school, accountability will be relevant to the staff because it will be used as feedback and as a guide to informed and reflective practice. Staff members will need training to learn how to design ways of gathering such data, establishing criteria for judgment, and working together to develop their common understanding, reliability of observations, and reporting of results.

EXPAND THE RANGE, VARIETY, AND MULTIPLICITY OF ASSESSMENT TECHNIQUES

For too long we have relied on a limited range of acceptable measures, primarily paper-and-pencil tests. Enlightened, skillful teachers—being the best collectors of data about student's growth toward the process goals of the restructured school—are able to observe students daily in problem-solving situations that demand performance of the goals of the restructured school: cooperation, problem solving, and creativity. This requires an expansion of our repertoire of assessment techniques including:

- Direct observation of student performance in problem-solving situations,

- Collecting portfolios of selected student work over time,
- Observing performance in extended projects,
- Inviting students to keep logs or journals,
- Interviewing students about their own self-concept and perceptions of themselves as learners,
- Making videotapes of student interactions,
- Collecting writing samples over time,
- Keeping checklists recording indicators of dispositions and habits of mind exhibited during group projects and discussions,
- Assessing student displays, exhibitions, and performances according to a set of agreed-upon criteria,
- Inviting students to display thinking skills using graphic organizers,
- Engaging in child study by keeping anecdotal records,
- Recording critical incidents: vignettes, sayings, and uses of terminology which indicate transfer, application, and internalization of concepts and strategies,
- Keeping checklists, logs, diaries, and journals about students,
- Employing technology to assist in collecting and recording information about students over time.

SYSTEMATIZE ASSESSMENT PROCEDURES

Skillful teachers already assess their students in many of the above ways. Teachers can describe students' progress: the lights that go on in students' eyes; the voice inflections of students when they've "got it," or the "a-ha" of discovery in students' exuberance. These reflect the collaborative sharing and interdependence of group work; the serendipitous application of skills and concepts beyond the context in which they were learned; and the reports from parents and other teachers of learnings applied.

What is lacking is a systematic way of collecting and reporting such evidence. Staff members need to refine their skills of observation and work for assessment that is reliable independent of the specific assessor. They need to identify and define terms and adopt common goals. They need to continually scrutinize the curriculum to ensure that goals, instruction, and assessment are aligned. Teachers, parents, administrators, and students all will need to see clearly the school's objectives and purposes, and all will become more involved in collecting data, revising perceptions, and realigning practices.

Limitations of time and communication in school settings often prevent teachers who work in different departments, grade levels, and disciplines from meeting together. The mutual support, continuity, reinforcement, and assessment of these new goals of the restructured school throughout the grade levels and across the subject areas has yet to be accomplished. Critical reading, the scientific method, problem solving, modes of inquiry, and study skills can be applied to mathematics, literacy, or numeracy. The distinctions and connections are still vague, however, when deciding which skills should be taught in a particular discipline and how they all fit together.

Until we consider thinking as the core of the curriculum and that content should be selected or rejected based on its contributions to the thinking and learning process, we shall continue to endure this dilemma. The sooner we admit that these new processes have become the content, the sooner we will find ways of infusing and assessing these goals throughout the curriculum. Our obsession with content is what holds us back.

RE-EDUCATE LEGISLATORS, PARENTS, BOARD MEMBERS, AND THE COMMUNITY

As a goal of education, the development of the intellect is not yet valued or understood by the majority of the public. Business and industry leaders are increasingly supportive of schools' endeavors to educate the future generation to become better individual and group problem solvers, to develop creative capacities, to be open to new and continued learning, and to work cooperatively in teams. However, there are still legislators, governors, school boards, and even an "education president" who fail to include thinking, creativity, and cooperation in our national goals for the twenty-first century.

Educators have allowed the public—parents, school boards, legislators—to use these scores to evaluate their schools, students, and teachers without helping them see that other, more significant nonmeasurable objectives can also be documented using a variety of reliable sources and techniques. Political decisions about testing, schooling, curriculum, and teacher competencies need to give way to sounder educational principles.

Educators, in conjunction with test makers, textbook publishers, professional organizations, business and industry leaders, parents, and the media, need to mount a massive information and educational program to shift public policy and national values toward support of more rational, cooperative, and compassionate public education.

Any assessment of student performance must also include assessment of school and classroom conditions. The conditions in which people work send powerful signals as to the values, mission, and purposes of the institution. Jack Frymier (1987) writes:

> *In the main, the bureaucratic structure of the workplace is more influential in determining what professionals do than are personal abilities, professional training, or previous experience. Therefore, change efforts should focus on the structure of the workplace, not on the teachers. It can be assumed that teachers will more likely teach for thinking, creativity, and cooperation if they are in an intellectually stimulating, creative, and cooperative environment themselves.*

We must therefore also assess the quality of the environment in which teachers, students, and administrators operate. We must constantly monitor the intellectual ecology of the workplace to insure that intellectual growth for all the participants does not become endangered, or worse, extinct.

Some questions by which to assess the intellectual ecology of the school environment include:

- Have curriculum materials been developed and materials adopted to support thinking, cooperation, creativity, and the other new goals of the restructured school?

- Are the reward systems for students and the teacher evaluation system aligned with the new values and mission of the restructured school?

- Do the communications—such as report cards, newsletters to parents, school mottoes and logos—reflect the values of the restructured school?

The process of evaluation will become internal for students. We must constantly remind ourselves that the ultimate purpose of evaluation is to have students become self-evaluating. If students graduate from our schools still dependent upon others to tell them when they are adequate, good, or excellent, then we've missed the whole point of what education is about. The highest level of Bloom's Taxonomy (1956) is generating, holding, and applying a set of internal and external criteria. For too long, adults alone have been practicing that skill. We need to gradually shift that responsibility to students. Our goals for the restructured school must be to help students develop the capacity to modify themselves.

REFERENCES

Archibald, D. A., & Newmann, F. (1988). *Beyond standardized testing: Assessing authentic academic achievement in the secondary school.* Reston, VA: National Association of Secondary School Principals.

Arter, J., & Salmon, J. (1987). *A consumer's guide: Assessing higher order thinking skills.* Portland, OR: Northwest Regional Laboratory.

California State Department of Education Curriculum Assessment Alignment Conference. (1989, October 16). Sacramento, CA.

Costa, A. (1991). Assessing growth in thinking skills: Part VIII. In A. Costa (Ed.), *Developing minds: A resource book for teaching thinking.* Alexandria, VA: Association for Supervision and Curriculum Development.

Bloom, B. S. (Ed.). (1956). *Taxonomy of educational objectives, Handbook I: Cognitive domain.* New York: David McKay.

Frymier, J. (1987, September). Bureaucracy and the neutering of teachers. *Phi Delta Kappan*, p. 10.

Norris, S., & Ennis, R. (1989). *Evaluating critical thinking.* Pacific Grove, CA: Midwest Publications.

Perrone, V. (1991). *Expanding student assessment.* Alexandria, VA: Association for Supervision and Curriculum Development.

Stiggens, R., Rubel, E., & Quellmalz, E. (1986). *Measuring thinking skills in the classroom: A teacher's guide.* Portland, OR: Northwest Regional Laboratory.

Worthen, B. R., & Sanders, J. (1987). *Educational evaluation: Alternative approaches and practical guidelines.* White Plains, NY: Longman.

FINDING OUT WHAT
WE NEED TO KNOW

—

Sharon Jeroski

Evaluation is much more than a way of monitoring change—it is the single most powerful way in which teachers communicate their values and beliefs to students, parents, and colleagues. The way we look at evaluation is connected to the way we look at and interact with the world around us. The issues we encounter as we assess and monitor changes in our students reflect fundamental issues in education; these issues, in turn, are shaped by the concerns of larger communities.

Until relatively recently—two to three hundred years ago—education in most of the Western world was largely a private undertaking. Children of prominent families developed the skills and knowledge they needed to take their expected places as leaders in the church, state, or the military. Their evaluation was almost entirely based on their performance in dynamic and interactive situations—on their abilities to speak informatively and persuasively and to draw on the knowledge they had acquired to illuminate moral or strategic issues. As participation in schooling increased, the goals of education expanded and reflected the prevailing view that children were not inherently "good"—that they had to be instructed and shaped

in order to assume a proper moral character. Evaluation, quite logically, focused on the state and condition of children's minds, and was often undertaken by clergy or other members of the community known to be of high moral character. They visited the schools to listen to recitations, to interview and inspect the children. This view prevailed until the close of the nineteenth century, when Western societies embraced the scientific paradigm. The zeal for empiricism, combined with the increasing universality of education, focused attention on a new role for schools: sorting students to determine their appropriate role in society. Evaluation focused around such quantitative measures as the intelligence test and "objective" written measures of achievement that held the promise of identifying the appropriate role for each student. In this century, schools in North America have reflected both the intuitive appeal of egalitarianism and the success of assembly-line industry. Schools have been expected to "produce" students who acquire set content and master specific skills. In this reductionist approach, evaluation is largely a matter of quality control—of monitoring the "products" to ensure that they met standard specifications.

Today, as we approach the twenty-first century, the information age is shifting the influences that shape our views of education. New interest in the integrated nature of knowledge, in the connectedness of our world, in systems and patterns, and in networks and teams pervade science, economics, ecology, business management, and, of course, education. And, quite logically, the emphasis on evaluation is shifting from monitoring, which is largely a managerial function, to supporting learning and enhancing development, a learner-focused orientation.

Of course, the two functions—monitoring and enhancing—are not mutually exclusive. By monitoring development, teachers and students are able to make informed decisions about teaching and learning. But effective evaluation can also shape learning when teachers and students work together to focus on what they really value about themselves as powerful learners and thinkers.

EVALUATING WHAT WE VALUE

"It's almost like we've been on a journey in connections," Robert explains.

"Yes," Ronsor chimes in; "Just in a period of time—not even half a year—we've been on a learning journey from not even thinking about connections to now, where we can connect anything!"

"Can you remember how you got started on connecting?" their visitor asks.

"It was Mrs. O.—it was when we came to Mrs. O.'s room that the connecting started," Daniel suggests.

"I remember!" offers Jason. "First we brainstormed connections—all the connections we could think of—and then we represented them!"

"I did a dinosaur skeleton with the bones connected!"

"I showed how Lego connects to make things!"

"My first one was a truck pulling a trailer."

"I showed a pen with a top that connected to it."

"Then we had the connecting chain," Alli remembers. "Whenever anyone made a connection they put their initials on a piece of paper and made a new link in our connecting chain."

"And we wrote our connections, too," Tara adds, "and put them in our special connections jar—do we still have that?"

"And we did connecting journals, too. But pretty soon we didn't need to do that—we just made connections all day long," Ronsor explains, "and now we mostly connect ideas."

*Jason nods, "We've sure changed—last October we could only connect **things**."*

"You know," Aerhyn says, "connections are hard to think and connections are easy to think. And when you fill up with new information, your brain takes each piece and sorts into hard connections and easy connections."

*"Do connections help you learn new things?" asks Mrs. O. "When there's something that you **almost** know does it help to connect it to something you already know?"*

"I think so," Alli agrees, "and when you're learning and it's hard, you've just got to keep thinking for the connections—like I did with regrouping."

"I notice that you all seem to have a signal for connections—you lace your fingers together. How did that start?" asks the visitor.

"Well, I think we saw Mrs. O. do it first," Ronsor explains, "and she was our role model. It's good because sometimes if we're watching a videotape or something and it's not appropriate to talk, we can still show our connections silently."

Aaron nods and shows the connection symbol: fingers on the right hand interlaced with fingers on the left.

"And in writing, Mrs. O.'s given us a new connections symbol for our reflections. Sometimes we circle the one that tells about our work that time, but sometimes we just draw the circles ourselves." Robert displays the "connecting scale"(see Figure 1).

These seven-year-olds value connections. Their teacher, Kim Ondrik, believes that helping them make connections will help them to become more independent and powerful thinkers. As the chil-

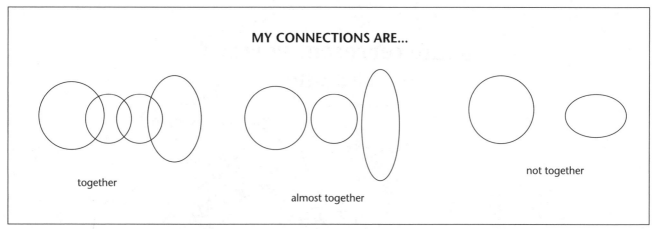

Figure 1 Kim's Connecting Scale

dren explained, they began with concrete representations, extensive modeling, and discussion. Now, six months later, they say, "We can connect anything!" They continually monitor their connections. As they discuss classroom behavior, books, arithmetic, their writing, and themes such as families, they frequently announce, "I have a connection," or silently lace their fingers together. When one group of children was called for music, Tara announced, "I have a connection. Wendy, Wednesday, and Wu start the same—that's alliteration." They also evaluate their own development in terms of their connections. They don't talk about what they don't know or what they can't do; instead they explain that not all of their connections are together. For example, Eric, who is six, describes his learning:

My connections are together for dinosaurs and space. They're almost together for diplodocus, for writing, and for reading. But my connections for math are not together yet.

As Kim observes and conferences with the children, she notices that they are developing increasingly complex and sophisticated connections and often notes evidence that they:

• notice patterns,

• make connections between classroom activities,

• make connections to out-of-school experiences,

• enjoy exploring and finding new connections,

• refer to previous activities, and

• connect their experiences with the literature they read.

Learning, instruction, and evaluation are integrated and purposeful in Kim's classroom. Everyone knows what is valued, and this knowledge helps them to focus on key aspects of their own thinking and learning. See, for example, these values reflected in Kelsey's self-representative cluster (Figure 2).

Teachers sometimes feel that the amount of information they need to note and record is overwhelming—particularly as they move toward the kinds of qualitative information that develop through conferencing and observation. Setting priorities is difficult, but clearly establishing and sharing your priorities makes evaluation manageable. Many teachers, like Kim, choose three or four key aspects of children's development to focus on. They explicitly identify the behaviors they want to see "more of, more often"—not so much as outcomes but as "outcomings" of their programs. For example, one group of kindergarten through high school teachers chose to focus learning, instruction, and evaluation around four aspects: questioning, making connections, representing in a variety of ways, and reflecting. These threads wove through all of their classroom activities and provided a focus for their observations and record-keeping, and for the student's self-evaluation.

In Louise Zappitello's class of seven- to nine-year-olds, the children know that questions are important: they have a "burning question" board in their room;

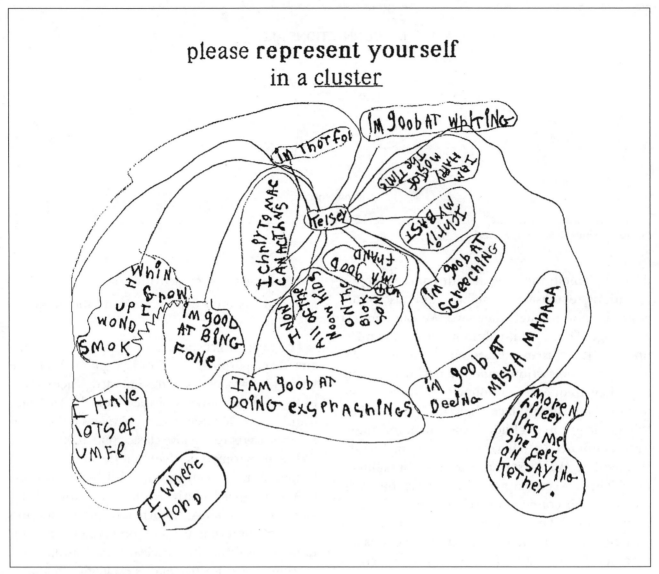

Figure 2 Kelsey's Cluster

each new area of study starts with questions which they continually revise and add to; the "audience" is expected to offer thoughtful questions to the presenters. Louise focuses her observations and comments around such questions as:

- How often does the student spontaneously ask questions?

- To what extent are the questions: appropriate for the situation? unusual or innovative? challenging or thought provoking?

- What does the student do with his or her questions?

- How does the student deal with his or her questions when they are not easily (or completely) answered?

- To what extent is the student able to extend a question or questions to sustain a project or learning activity?

- To what degree does the student evaluate his or her own questions?

Katie has been developing a list of questions during the first three days of her study of ocean life. Her questions are appropriate; many of them are innovative and challenging. She is not just idly generating questions: and one question is especially important to her. She wants to know how long it takes for an egg to hatch, and leaves space for the teacher to provide an answer (see Figure 3).

Bill Polkinghorne's tenth grade history class also focused on questioning. After overviewing a chapter in their text, each student chose one section and generated five questions they'd like to investigate. After their questions were evaluated (and where appropriate, revised) they developed an answer to one question. Bill and the students worked together to develop the following criteria for thoughtful questions:

Powerful

- asks for an interpretation by reader
- makes connections to other events, people, causes, or purposes
- answers "why" and "how"
- gives purpose
- is open-ended

Satisfactory

- links cause and effect
- asks for chronology (events in order of time)
- is closed (finite or complete within itself)
- answers "how"

Developing

- answers "who," "what," or "where"
- asks for a brief, specific, text-explicit answer
- makes no connections

STUDENTS AND TEACHERS WORKING TOGETHER

Students and teachers at Dunsmuir, Spencer, and Claremont Junior Secondary schools on Vancouver Island are exploring strategies for creating meaningful conversations about their learning. Teachers model and support oral reflections around such questions as:

- What do you like other people to notice about your work?
- What parts of your work are especially satisfying to you?

- What did you struggle with today? How did that turn out?
- Who helped you with your thinking and learning today? How? Is there anything else someone could have done to help you? What? Who did you help? How?
- How can I be fair when I mark your work? What should I keep in mind?

Students also develop written reflections in learning logs, dialogue journals, end-of-term summaries, and notes that accompany their assignments. Students in Kathy Coleman's eighth grade French and English classes initiate evaluation conversations by letting her know what they value and would like her to notice about their work:

> *Three things I want you to notice about this work: I had a fairly positive attitude; I asked lots of questions; it was punctually correct.*
> *(Jenni)*

> *By doing this piece of work I learned some "er" verbs and sentence parts. I want you to notice that I put a lot of effort into this.*
> *(Julie)*

> *I want you to notice that this is the first time I have ever sat down and written a paragraph in French and that I tried my best. I'm proud that the only mistakes I made were that I didn't write the date in French and I left the "e" off of "une."*
> *(Tracy)*

> *Something that I want you notice about my paragraph about the sixties is that this may not look like much but I worked hard to get the information. My printing is quite small and I can fit a lot of words on one line so it looks like I haven't done much. If I had to do this again I would like to try to do it a little bit neater.*
> *(Tracey)*

It is clearly a major source of worry to many students that their effort will go unrecognized—that their teachers will think they "didn't try" or that their work "might not look like much." Those worries evaporate when evaluation is collaborative and purposeful. There is no longer any mystery about

I WONDER

wiy do fish live in
the sea and dont
liv on the earth?
haw do fish cumunacat?
haw can fish breth in th
wotr and we ned tancs?
I wondeR way we cant live
in the wotr? can crabs
eat fish? can shrimp
cat litul rocks? can big
fish eat 20 litul fish,
haw long can wotr cre
live??? Haw long is

Can fish sta in the
wotr and cum up??
wiy do we have no fins
and fish do?? Mrs. Z
haw long dus it

tac for a aggth ach

yoranso ples

haw meny fish livin t
wotr? wiy or ther so
meny crabs? wen will
the hol unufrs of o
Seascreehrs
stop living!

Figure 3 Katie's Questions

how the process works and rather than inhibiting students' learning (by causing unnecessary anxiety), evaluation enhances learning.

Julie Davis' ninth grade English students offered her some thoughtful advice about evaluation in responding to her question, "How can I be fair when I evaluate your work?" Her question let them know that she expected them to be partners in the evaluation process; their answers showed their willingness to collaborate with her.

> *You can be fair by putting yourself into our places. Such as if one has a talent for writing and for drawing then you mark the drawing from how much effort was put into it. If it's the other way around you mark the same way. I would mark the projects by the following: completion, effort, and imagination.*
>
> *(John)*
>
> *I think it's hard to be fair for opinion answers since it is your own opinion. Maybe when marking opinion questions you could be marked on the depth of your ideas rather than the ideas themselves. In normal questions I think that it is simple to be fair because most questions are either right or wrong.*
>
> *(Michelle)*

Doug Smith's music students assess their own performance in terms of concerts, practice, contributions to class, goals, and areas they need help with. They also indicate the letter grades they feel they deserve. Joslin wrote:

> *I think that I have improved a lot since last term and I think the whole choir has as well. The concerts were excellent and fun, although I think we should all work a little harder to learn our words for "Phantom of the Opera...." I give my voice and musical experience to the class. I enjoy singing and music very much. I would like to improve my breath control and improve the break between the middle register and my head-voice.*

The students' clear understanding of the expectations for their class is striking. So is their honesty and trust. As Selina shows below, they are engaged in a meaningful and real conversation with their teacher:

> *I think the class really improved this term even though we were really sick of "Song of the Sea" and "All I Ask of You." I have improved my sight reading a little. I could have learned more words of "All I Ask of You." My behavior was fine at the concert (and in class) although others were talking. I think that the songs you pick are getting better (more upbeat)...*

These students know that they are engaged in a collaborative effort; and they know that their teacher is interested.

In Fred Birkenhead's eighth grade woodworking class, evaluation is shared; students are expected to keep track of their accomplishments and summarize their learning processes. For example, Colin wrote:

> *In woodwork 8 second term, at the beginning I made a cube with sanded edges that I painted so it only went together one way and nobody could figure it out.*
>
> *Next I learned to use the plane, did notes on the plane and did all my homework on the plane. I also took a rough piece of wood, planed it, and made a perfect 90-degree angle. I learned every part of the plane and how to put it together. I also helped a lot of people with the plane.*
>
> *I learned how to sand things with sandpaper and block, I learned all about the edge grain, the face grain, the grain direction, which way to sand, different types of sandpaper, etc.*
>
> *I learned how to use the band saw and did both sheets on the band saw. I even worked on the band saw.*
>
> *In extra time I made salt and pepper shakers and a mail opener. I also learned how to use the power drill.*

Colin's summary is probably more comprehensive than any his teacher could have written; it is also personal. It highlights the accomplishments that are most meaningful to him—his inventiveness and skill in creating a puzzle; his skill with the plane saw; and the fact that he "even" worked on the band saw. His teacher read and concurred with Colin's assessment. For most students, the written summaries stimulated brief oral or written exchanges with the teacher. In a few cases, they prompted extensive individual conferences.

Students in Bill Cook's seventh grade class frequently make decisions about the books they read and the ways they will represent their understanding. After reading his novel, Darren engages in written conversations with his teacher about his plans and the reasons for his choices. He also alerts him about what he wants noticed. Bill replies, in turn, sometimes simply with a check mark, other times with a question or comment (see Figure 4). Student and teacher share responsibility not only for the learning that is developing, but also for the demonstration of that learning that makes evaluation possible.

Elementary teachers are exploring a variety of ways of stimulating evaluation conversations with the children they teach. Often, these conversations are shaped around a few key questions. For example, in Mrs. Juliano's fourth grade classroom, students are accustomed to responding to three questions after each assignment. After completing a sequencing activity, where he was asked to arrange sentences in a logical order, Kamal offered the following responses:

What were you trying to do?

I tried to put sentences in order.

How do you feel about it?

I think I hate this activity because I hate gluing and cutting. But if I have to do a pattern with coloring I will like it!

How can I help you?

Mrs. Juliano, please try to make the stories that you pick shorter.

In primary classrooms, most of the evaluation or self-assessment conversations are oral. Many of these conversations are informal and spontaneous—a child shares or comments on an activity, and the teacher responds with a question that prompts further reflection. Other conversations are planned. In Mary-Eileen Johnson's class of five-

to eight-year-olds, the children not only enjoy talking about their work, they expect to offer their reflections and suggestions in response to familiar and repeated questions. For example, after offering their representations of a book they had read, the children's reflections were videotaped. One group dressed up like the characters in the book and role-played a television news interview. After their performance, they responded to Mary-Eileen's questions:

What would you try to remember for next time if you were going to do this project again?

To remember what to do. We forgot a bunch of things that we planned.

What do you think you learned from this activity?

Audiences really like interviews. And costumes made it more fun for us and more interesting for the audience—they made it more like the real characters in the book.

What suggestions would you give other people who wanted to do an interview presentation?

Speak up. Wear costumes. Remind each other about the parts they forget.

Four-year-old Brody has no difficulty reflecting on his work and sharing his concerns. After illustrating a train, he explains, "The train should be on the tracks. I couldn't figure out how to do it. So I kind of put it beside the tracks. But that's not how it really is. Trains are supposed to go right on the tracks. Could you show me how?"(see Figure 5).

KEEPING TRACK OF CHANGES

The teachers at David Cameron School, like many others in British Columbia, are choosing to document student growth by collecting and organizing samples of accomplishments. These portfolios or collections offer a rich resource for teacher evaluation, self-evaluation, and for prompting informed communication about a student's development. Because they provide something concrete to reflect on and talk about, the collections facilitate communication among students, parents, and teachers (see Figure 6).

I have chosen to represent my understanding of the aforementioned novel by producing the following products.

1. <u>Pictorial Journy</u> _____ because it shows ......

   | all the real big events as the story goes along. ——→ | Comments:
→ why? |

2. <u>Charachter Sketch</u> because it shows ......

   | all about the main character in the book like his age, where he lives... | Comments:
How will this help me understand his quest? |

3. <u>Newspaper</u> _____ because it shows ......

   | The main events in the story. | Comments: |

| What I want you to notice.

How hard I am going to try on the projects. ——→ | Comments:
I will notice I'm sure. |

"The Hostage"

Figure 4 Darren's Novel Evaluation

Figure 5 Brody's Train

Portfolios also help to emphasize that subjective or qualitative evaluation can and should be just as systematic as any objective measurement. For example, many teachers document students' literacy development by collecting a response to an open-ended response task (e.g., "Read the poem. Use your ideas, feelings, and images to show your understanding") at regular intervals through the year.

WE ARE PROUD OF OUR LEARNING

As we know, our schools are changing. The focus of the new Intermediate Program is on helping students become active participants in all aspects of their learning experiences and building a sensitivity toward lifelong learning. The aims of reporting to students and parents are to:

(1) recognize successes and give guidance for continued success.

(2) build self-confidence.

(3) continue the process of making learning worthwhile and enjoyable.

This folder contains materials selected by both your child and his or her teacher which will give you a sense of projects and assignments completed and progress made. One of the major purposes of this endeavor is to allow students to choose and evaluate those things they consider to be important representations of what they have learned and what they value from their learning.

Students have been encouraged to consider the following criteria when choosing material for their folder: care and effort, presentation, clarity, originality/creativity/artistic skill, improvement, and scores which indicate success.

We hope that you will take the time to respond to this small collection by commenting on those aspects you feel are well done. A response sheet has been provided for this purpose. We urge you to focus on the positive.

Guiding your child on to continued growth and success at school by helping to set reasonable goals is a valuable process. Your child's teacher would welcome a note or call at the school if he or she can help in making this report more worthwhile for you and your child.

As this collection constitutes an interim report, please sign the parent response sheet and return the entire collection to the school. Thank you.

The Intermediate Teachers

Figure 6   Letter to Parents About Student Portfolios

Others videotape "think-aloud" problem-solving sessions each term and make the tapes available for student and parent (as well as teacher) review. In some schools, children are developing scrapbook collections that continue over several years of school: each month, the children pick one or two pieces of work to put in their scrapbooks. At the end of the year, the scrapbook goes on to the next teacher as part of the students' permanent record.

Students' self-evaluation plays an important role in developing effective collections. In David Layzell's class, students focus on pride and improvement as criteria for selecting work for their collection. Kelly included a math worksheet:

> *I selected this piece of work because I am really proud of the multiplication that I learned so quickly so it improved my marks.*

> *I would like you to notice that I'm not that good at problem solving but I got 6 out of 8.*

> *This piece of work was chosen because I wanted to show you how much I have improved at all of my multiplication tables very quickly.*

She comments on her improvement in other areas:

> *Novel study: This piece of work was chosen because I wanted to show you how much I have improved at my handwriting and how all my work is in order and underlined.*

> *Social studies: I wanted to show you how much I have improved at being exact with the way I drew this map.*

In the same classroom, Catherine comments:

> *Math: This piece of work was chosen because I wanted to show you how much I have improved at working with decimals and my times table.*

> *Geography: . . . how much I have improved at what I know of Japan. I feel great that I know so much.*

Catherine, like all students in David Layzell's classroom, completes a goal-setting activity at the end of each term (see Figure 7).

Children in Louise Zappitello's primary classroom also keep collections that they share with their parents. Each piece of work is accompanied by comments from Louise and the student. In the sample in Figure 8, Ryan notices a big difference ("bivrets") in his clusters. Saulo, Greg, and Sonia commented on other assignments (see Figure 9).

Each term the children take their portfolios home as part of their reporting. Louise includes a letter to their parents that offers some insights about change. Her letter reads in part:

> *A unique feature of this portfolio is that it contains your child's reflections on his/her own learning and work as well as my comments. When students respond, their initial comments may be simple and lacking in detail. For example, "I chose this piece of work because it is nice." You will see a progression from this type of comment to more detailed ones as time progresses.*

> *Another unique feature of this portfolio is our "Portfolio Review" wherein we want to involve you in responding to your child's growth and progress. Several times this year your child's portfolio will be sent home. You will notice a blank pink form on the inside front cover. We would appreciate it if you would please review this folder with your child and respond to the Portfolio Review Sheet. As you look through the portfolio pages please look for "two stars and a wish." A star is a compliment. You might compliment your child on the detail contained in a piece of writing, the imaginative drawings, some unique thinking or humor, an effective way of presenting something, etc.... After listening to your compliments, your child will be ready to listen to your wish. Wishes indicate an area for improvement. Only one wish is required as too many wishes may do more harm than good.*

Parents were delighted with this form of reporting and participated enthusiastically (see Figure 10). As Louise describes:

> *Three things happened that I didn't expect. First, I got the reviews back before parents came for their interviews—that really helped me to prepare because I knew about their concerns in advance. The reviews helped the children to see what was valued at home as well as at school and that helped to motivate them. Finally—and almost best of all—the parents*

<u>STUDENT GOAL SETTING - GENERAL</u>

The most important thing I am trying to accomplish right now is *to get better in Math for Area!* ✓

To do this I will need to *study harder & get more help & do my homework as soon as I get home!* ✓

This is important to me because *I want to be really good at it so to me its a piece of Cake!*

Sure! You can do that, Cath. Keep your chin up when you start getting confused. Ask questions & get help

<u>PARENT RESPONSE SHEET</u>

The things I noticed about your collection were:

That Catherine has worked very hard and takes great pride in her achievements she finds some things a little difficult but she seems to have the determination to succeed with it!

The most important thing I would like to say to you now is: *Keep working hard and your achievements will continue to grow and give you great satisfaction.*

Parent's Signature : *B.A.*

Figure 7   Student Goal Setting and Parent Response

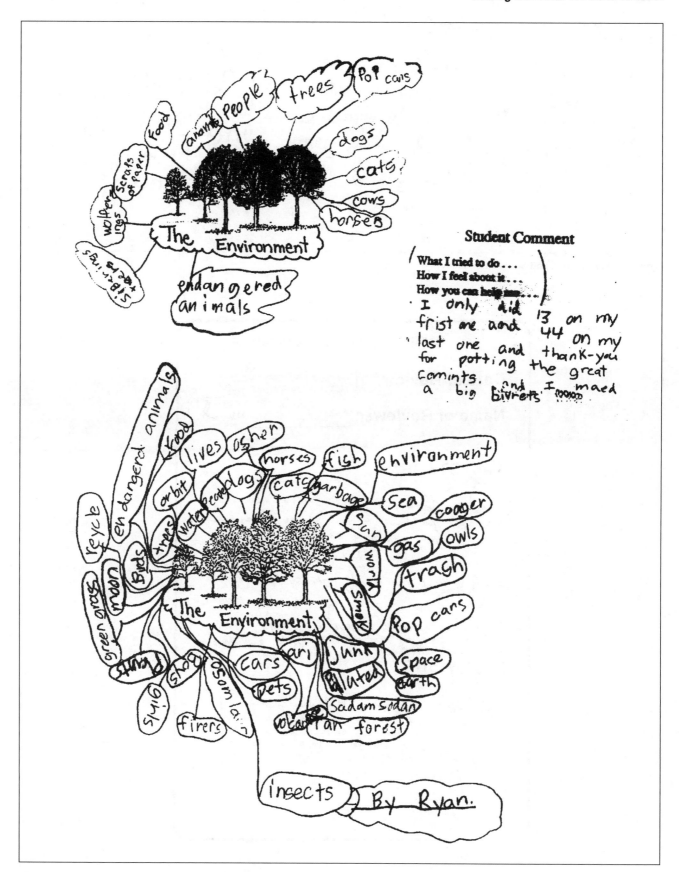

Figure 8 Ryan's Clusters and Evaluation

it is exelent
and hard warkn
and it had
vantastich colaring

What I tried to do was
to finish this but I
couldn't. And when I work
on these works again
please give us more
time !!

I feel about it
is that it wus
like I wus
goona be u
Othr.

Figure 9   Saulo, Greg, and Sonia's Comments

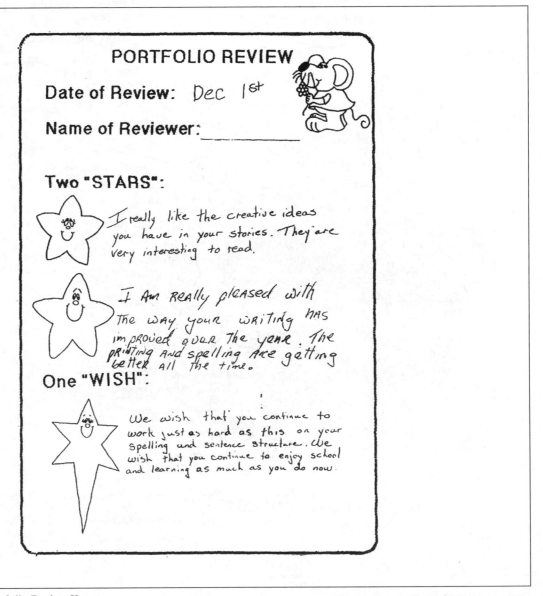

PORTFOLIO REVIEW

Date of Review: Dec 1st

Name of Reviewer: _____

Two "STARS":

I really like the creative ideas you have in your stories. They are very interesting to read.

I Am Really pleased with the way your writing has improved over the year. The printing And spelling Are getting better all the time.

One "WISH":

We wish that you continue to work just as hard as this on your spelling and sentence structure. We wish that you continue to enjoy school and learning as much as you do now.

Figure 10   Parent Portfolio Review Sheet

learned so much about the evaluation processes we are using, how and why they can be effective in helping children learn and grow, and also how much work it really takes. Several commented, "Sure appreciate the efforts you go to for our kids, Mrs. Z." Both the children and I felt great after this reporting period.

These are real achievements and real conversations, centered around shared values. The students, teachers, and parents I have described are finding out what they need to know.

———

REFERENCES

Brown, R. (1987). Who is accountable for 'thoughtfulness?' *Phi Delta Kappan, 69*(1), 49-52.

Brown, R. (1991). *Schools of thought.* San Francisco: Jossey-Bass.

Brownlie, F., Close, S., & Wingren, L. (1990). *Tomorrow's classroom today: Strategies for creating active readers, writers, and thinkers.* Portsmouth, NH: Heinemann and Markham, Ontario: Pembroke.

Brownlie, F., Close, S., & Wingren, L. (1988). *Reaching for higher thought: Reading, writing, thinking strategies.* Edmonton, AL: Arnold Publishing Ltd.

Cameron, C., & Gregory, K. (Eds.). (1991). *The having of wonderful ideas.* Sooke, BC: Sooke School District #62.

Chittenden, E., & Courtney, R. (1989). Assessment of young children's reading: Documentation as an alternative to testing. In D. Strickland & L. M. Morrow (Eds.), *Emerging literacy.* Newark, DE: International Reading Association.

Jeroski, S., Brownlie, F., & Kaser, L. (1990a). *Reading and responding: Evaluation resources for your classroom.* (Primary; Vols. 1-2). Toronto, ON: Nelson Canada. (Available in the U.S. from The Wright Group, Bothel, WA).

Jeroski, S., Brownlie, F., & Kaser, L. (1990b). *Reading and responding: Evaluation resources for your classroom.* (Vols. 1-3). Toronto, ON: Nelson Canada. (Available in the U.S. from The Wright Group, Bothel, WA.)

Ministry of Education. (1991). *Thinking in the classroom: Resources for teachers.* Victoria, BC: Author.

Perrone, V. (1991). *Expanding student assessment.* Alexandria, VA: Association for Supervision and Curriculum Development.

HOW TO GRADE
(IF YOU MUST)

—

James Bellanca

The flush rose on Alan's face. His hands quivered. "It's not fair," he shouted. "I worked hard. I didn't deserve a B+. This will wreck all my chances for Harvard."

Mr. Beaster stood silent. As Alan took a breath, Beaster interjected; "Alan," he began, "your grade...."

Alan glared. "It's not my grade. I worked for an A. I deserve an A. I need it. This is the last semester. The good colleges will look at my grades. If you don't give me an A, my class rank drops."

Again Beaster tried to interrupt, but Alan kept on, nostrils flaring, his face now beet-red. "You're cheating me," he screeched. "You're ruining my life. My father will kill me. There's no way this grade is O.K. If you liked me, you would give me an A. You're not fair."

"Alan," countered Beaster, "I'm not going to debate this grade with you. If you want to discuss it when you are calm, I'll be glad to."

"Bull _____. You'll never change it," Alan pouted as he turned to leave. "You teachers are all alike. You _____."

What teacher has not faced an angry Alan or his parents, unhappy with a grade? From first grade on—now even in preschool—grades become a consuming passion for high-achieving, earnest students. If Alan doesn't get the best grades, he does not see himself as the best. Without being the best, how will he get in the top track or the best college?

Alan learned from his first years in school that grades count. Teachers praise students with the best grades; they scold or ignore those with low grades. Teachers assign front-row seats to students with high grades; those with low grades are banished to the back. Parents give rewards for high grades and frown and lecture about low grades and being a failure.

By the seventh grade, Alan knew the game well. Study hard. Do all the homework. Memorize all the vocabulary. Raise your hand first. A is the target. Get the most A's. They count for high school. They guarantee the fast track. The fast track is a ticket to fame, fortune, and happiness.

Alan was prepared for high school. He charted his grade point average each semester. While taking the college prep curriculum, he learned how to bail out of classes with "tough" teachers. He discovered which electives would pad his GPA. By the end of his junior year, Alan could memorize a page of course notes in a half-hour, disguise Cliffs Notes in well-formatted and grammatically perfect essays, and copy lab notes with total precision.

* * *

*C*armela stared at the floor. Mrs. Martinez sat beside her. Carmela did not move. "Carmela, what am I going to do with you?" Mrs. Martinez asked. "Your grades are getting worse. You are a bright girl. You should be doing better. You are not a D student."*

Carmela still did not move. "I do care," she thought, "but it's not so easy. It never has been easy. I've got more to think about than school. School doesn't help me make the dinner or watch my brothers and sisters at night—especially when there is no dinner. And even if I do study, I'm always getting a C or a D. So why bother? I can do C or D without studying."

"Carmela," pleaded Mrs. Martinez, "Don't you know you are wasting your life? Look at me, Carmela. What do you have to say?"

Carmela shook her head. "It doesn't matter."

What teacher has not counseled a Carmela? Her mother works long hours. Carmela, the oldest of six children, is responsible for their care before and after school. She dresses them and hurries them out the door in time for school. After school, she walks them home. Even in winter, they walk together. "You will be safe from the gangs, if you do," her mother admonishes. "You keep them together." Once home, she locks the door and starts dinner. By the time her mother arrives, the young ones are ready for bed. Only then, dog-tired, does she open her history text.

Carmela learned in first grade how grades counted. After school, Carmela's mother helped her do homework. Together, they practiced her English, read the story sheets, and marked the answers. When the teacher gave Carmela a smile sticker or a star, Carmela was pleased. Her parents praised her good grades. But in the fifth grade, when her father died, things changed. Carmela's mother went to work. She left each morning at 7:00 and arrived home after 9:00 at night. With her two jobs and Carmela's help with the children, Mrs. Ruiz managed. But there was little time or energy for Carmela's schoolwork or the other children. "Just graduate," she would admonish Carmela.

Carmela wanted to tell her teacher what was wrong. But what could Carmela say? It was best to stay quiet. She knew grades were important, especially if she wanted to please her teacher. But her family was more important. No matter how Carmela tried to study, someone interrupted: Miguel was hungry or Tomas wanted help with his schoolwork.

What could she do?

Grades, especially those based on the competitive curve, create fearsome anxieties for students like Alan and Carmela as well as for their teachers. In our highly individualistic society, the grading curve exacerbates the most negative anti-learning attributes of competition. Because the grading curve brands winners and losers, it works against the goal of successful learning for all students. First there are the Alans who have been programmed from birth to earn the right grades in order to enter the right schools. Next, there are the Carmelas torn between an array of real-life priorities and pressed by forces over which they feel they have little control. These are joined by those who learn slowly, but well; those who are bright but not yet language proficient; those with small motor deficiencies that prevent fast writing; those who fear beatings for low marks; and those whose whole lives are measured by good grades.

For every student who "wins" with an A, there is one who "loses" with a B, C, or F. For the ten percent with the top GPAs year in and year out, there is at least an equal number who sit at the bottom. As the top scorers become more enamored of their successes in school, one by one, the bottom dwellers give up and go elsewhere. Top scorers are motivated by their great grades to do better; poor grades in a competitive system only encourage the bottom scorers to languish or leave.

THE AIKIDO PRINCIPLE

For many teachers who confront the practical and moral issues of school grading practices, the pressures to use a mere letter or number to sum up a student's performance over a day, week, or semester never subside. Some handle the stress by ignoring all assessment. Others burden themselves with elaborate accounting procedures, searching in a plethora of numbers for some way to quantify what a student learns. All too many succumb to the pressure to teach only what is measurable, in spite of the knowledge that very little that truly challenges students in their learning is, as yet, measurable by conventional grading practices.

The cooperative and thoughtful classroom requires a teacher with the skill and the will to teach with a **triple agenda classroom**: the curricular content; the cooperative attitudes and skills; and the thoughtful dispositions, processes, and skills which mark mindful students. In this classroom, the teacher must structure lessons so that students not only learn facts, concepts, and subject skills, but also incorporate cooperative learning as a base to develop each student's capabilities as a critical and creative thinker in search of thoughtful results. As classroom teachers who are skilled in the delivery of triple agenda lessons can testify, this is no easy path. They can also argue that the biggest thorns in their side are the lingering demands from administrators, parents, and students that they use the archaic grading system and that they limit instruction to what is gradable. It seems no matter how creative the teaching and learning, traditional perceptions of good schooling are still reflected in the same old "wad-ja-get?" mentality (Kirschenbaum et al.,1971).

Given the pressure to maintain the traditional report card with its standard way of answering the wad-ja-get question, the question most often asked by teachers attempting to implement the triple agenda classroom is: "What do I do? I may be challenging students to think, to cooperate, and to work on authentic tasks, but my district says that I must summarize it all with a grade on the report card."

To answer this question, I have found it most useful to start with the Aikido principle. In the martial art of Aikido the essential rule is to use the defense as the offense. Rather than attack the opponent, skilled Aikido practitioners learn to step aside from their opponent's thrusts. As the assault passes, the Aikido practitioner seizes the passing energy and uses that force to "assist" the attacker to defeat him- or herself. When using this principle, the triple agenda teacher avoids taking attacks that attempt to force simplistic grading practices on complex learning tasks. Instead, the teacher lets the opponent expend the force of the attack and turns the energy of the attack back into itself. Because triple agenda teachers know that instruction and assessment are twin inhibitors of substantive learning, they side-step the arguments that seek to preserve the grade at all costs. They know it is a fu-

tile task to convince parents and students—especially those overachievers who have learned well the value of grades for upward mobility—that grades are contrary to cooperation, destructive to learning, and counterproductive to skillful thinking by all students. The wad-ja-get mentality is ingrained too deeply. Rather than do combat with the argument, the teacher knows it is more helpful to step to one side and concede to the demand for grades and develop an assessment format that connects feedback to performance without a curve. He or she can, if necessary, reduce the more valid and authentic assessment information to a simple letter grade. Although this is not the ideal solution, it is an important trade-off. By giving in on the grading curve issue, triple agenda teachers are free to focus students' full energy on complex learning and cognition. In this context, grades satisfy the short visions of those who value letters and numbers at the end of a school year more than the learning that takes place day in and day out. Grades are not allowed to jeopardize the essence of the thoughtful classroom.

THE TRIPLE AGENDA CLASSROOM: PART ONE

In the triple agenda classroom, the teacher has multiple means to motivate students' thinking, cooperation, and mastery of content without relying on grades.

Expectations will determine how high a level of thinking and cooperation will come from every student in every lesson. The lowest expectations come from those who signal students that the only important learning is that which is rooted in recall or regurgitation of textbook facts. If a teacher limits standards and teaching expectations to low-level outcomes—the single agenda—that is what students will provide. Such performances are easy to grade. If, however, the demands of serious cooperation and high-level thinking outcomes are added to each lesson, the expectations will result in students who use their cooperative skills and their thinking strategies to produce triple agenda results. Any visitor to such a classroom will see heads together, engaged in high-level thinking tasks. In this context, triple agenda assessment is less a worry and more a window of opportunity that challenges students to behave intellectually in ways they would not believe possible in a recall-oriented classroom.

For example, while students are doing their learning tasks (e.g., vocabulary study, math problem applications, or biology lab experiments), the teacher moves among the small groups. In addition to answering content questions, he or she observes instances of students using cooperative social skills and keeps a check sheet on a focus skill such as encouragement. When the task is finished and students have reviewed their own cooperation, the teacher uses the check sheet to give feedback on their progress with the key social skills.

After the first few practices, the teacher adds an observer as a role in each group. He or she gives the observers check sheets. Each observer has the task of recording observed cooperative skills used in his or her group and of giving feedback during the group processing time.

As the week progresses, the teacher can initiate a group or class chart that graphs the improvements. Once the graphing begins, he or she can establish performance standards with clear benchmarks. Each group takes charge of its own practice and the assessment of its progress.

If grades are required, the teacher can assign a letter grade for each numerical benchmark (observed instances of the expected social skill). At the end of one marking period, each member of a group will receive the grade of the benchmark attained by that group. That grade is averaged into the individual's group grade.

Benchmarks	Grades
30	A
25	B
20	C
15	D

Individual Assessment

In addition to assessing students in groups, the teacher may elect an individual assessment of each student's use of the focus social skill in various

groups. Issues for the teacher to assess include: How regular and natural is the student's use of the skill in task groups, informal groups, or large class activities? What improvements are observable? A page of Likert scales will make the task easy.

What I did well:

- listened
- did my job as checker
- did not interrupt
- looked at the speaker
- spoke quietly

| Not Yet | Sometimes | Daily |

The reverse side of the assessment sheet identifies the words and behaviors associated with the cooperative social skill and matches a chart hung in the classroom. Each student fills out a scale with appropriate comments before the teacher adds to it. The students may take the weekly charts or a quarterly summary home to parents or they may insert the charts in their portfolios. Another option is to have students write a commentary in their journals about improvements they are making on applying the social skills. Younger children may use a check sheet.

If the teacher must provide a grade for the social skill, there are several options.

- Use the all-class norm as the C grade. For instance, the all-class norm for use of the designated behavior is five per week. A grade scale would look like this:

  A = 9+   B = 7
  C = 5   D = 3

- Base the grade on individual improvement:

  D = increased average daily use by 1
  C = increased average daily use by 3
  B = increased average daily use by 5
  A = increased average daily use by 7

- After the class has had sufficient practice, set standards for observations. After posting the standards, inform the students how each may earn a grade for social skill use during this test week.

C = 6 instances observed

B = 9 instances observed

A = 12 instances observed

- Use an individual observation sheet. Each day during the week focus on one-fifth of the class and record the instances noted.

During the term, repeat the test week at least three times. After the first test week, it will be necessary to put the students on notice. The teacher announces that there will be at least two unannounced test observations in the month.

If the social skill is not a separately listed grade, but only a part of a total grade, the teacher can decide on the percentage the social skill grades will count. He or she may adapt the chart and send it to parents, explaining how he or she arrived at the social skill grade and describing its weight in the grading scheme.

THE TRIPLE AGENDA CLASSROOM: PART TWO

Can a teacher assess thinking? Many say no. They argue that thinking is individual, internal, an ability fixed by birth, and something a student either has or doesn't. Others argue that grades inhibit creative thinking by imposing too much prior judgment. Because of these factors, the naysayers argue that it is neither fair nor possible to assess thinking. Given certain conditions, however, a teacher can and must assess improvement in a student's thinking patterns. Although not recommended, a teacher can even assign a grade to such improvement.

It is true that what happens in the mind is not something a teacher can easily assess. What happens outside the mind is something a teacher can assess: words, spoken and written, artifacts in many forms, and thoughtful behaviors reflect much about each student's thoughts, dispositions, and conceptual processes. The skillful teacher, under-standing that thinking is an alterable process, knows that it is possible to teach and improve both the quantity and quality of a student's thinking skills, thinking processes, and thinking dispositions. To help the student understand the degree of this improvement, the teacher will use all available tools to assess observed behaviors. When required, he or she can reduce what is most important in a student's thoughtful progress to a grade.

The most basic assessment of thinking begins with the teaching of thinking skills. In an instructional framework, the teacher will select two to four specific thinking skills already implicit in the chosen curriculum. For instance, in the primary grades, attributing, sorting, and sequencing are often-used skills. In the late primary grades, inferring, predicting, and classifying are buried in the reading and math curricula. In high school geometry, estimating is a core thinking skill.

There is little need for introducing a plethora of thinking skills. It is more beneficial to students' conceptual development for the teacher to identify a few skills implicit in the curriculum and to make them explicit. There are several advantages to this model:

- It avoids overloading the curricula.

- The skillful teacher can use thinking skills as an integrating thread. The thinking skills can link various topics, units, and courses that otherwise might appear fragmented and separate to students.

- It allows the skillful teacher to design a thinking focus that will encourage student transfer across the curriculum.

- The teacher can introduce each thinking skill at the level of concreteness and simplicity appropriate to the students' cognitive development. For example, in kindergarten, students learn to sort objects by color, size, and shape; in the middle grades, the students build on this expertise by learning to classify animals, cultures, or historic periods; in high school, they extend their classifying skills in biology, literature, social studies, or practical arts with more abstract or more complex data.

- It encourages students to learn thinking strategies that apply to many types of material.

- The teacher has opportunities to assess thinking skill use and development with easy-to-use tools.

- It encourages students to become more reflective about their own thinking and more responsible for self-assessment.

- It builds a foundation for more sophisticated assessment of student dispositions toward thoughtful learning.

- It makes it possible, if required, to grade students' understanding of thoughtful behavior and their use of these behaviors in different situations.

What follows are suggestions for authentic assessment—and grading if required—of significant and thoughtful classroom tasks.

Primary School Assessment: Sorting

Evaluation Tools   Make a sorting mastery matrix for each child. Keep all the sheets in a loose-leaf binder until you are ready to place them in each student's "For Home" portfolio. When the child demonstrates the item, enter the date (see Figure A1) or a check (see Figure A2).

Share the assessment matrix at the parent conference. In this case, you can personalize discussion of the student's progress and where the student stands in relation to your expectations.

Grading   If your school expects a report card grade, the criterion checklist (below) is an easy option.

1. Equivalent Points. If you want a specific grade, each time the student demonstrates an item on the matrix or check sheet, award a point. Set criteria for letter grades by quarters of the year.

Quarter	C	B	A
1	3	4	5
2	6	8	10
3	9	12	15
4	12	16	20

2. If sorting is only part of your class grade, establish the percentage of the total grade for which the sorting grade will count. For example, if sorting is ten percent of the total final grade, calculate the number of points earned by the student in the sorting work and add that number into the student's total (see Figure A3).

Middle/High School Assessment: Classification

Evaluation Tools   There are multiple ways to assess individual work at this level.

1. Check for understanding using a knowledge quiz or test of the thinking skill (see Figure A4).

2. Check for performance using a new application (see Figure A5).

Decide what percentage of correct answers from above equate with what letter grade. If you used all items from the above knowledge questions, your scale might look like this:

Letter Grade	Point Scale
A	93
B	85
C	78
D	70

Using the fluency criterion (the number of correct answers generated on an open-ended question), set a grade standard.

Correct Answers	Grade
13	A
10	B
7	C
5	D

3. Provide ongoing feedback to group products.

- On each of the group Venns, praise those that either increase fluency from the previous Venn or that surpass the top standard. Encourage those that remain at the same fluency level from task to task. ("Good start. Let's see one or two more items on the next Venn.")

- Chart individual improvements on the fluency criterion.

4. Invite students to assess their thinking improvements:

Card Talk   Give each student a 3 x 5 index card once a week. After each has named and dated the card, provide a self-assessment stem. ("I know I am getting better at classifying because…"; "I'd rate my improvement at classifying as _____ because . . . .") Collect the cards, select a few to read aloud (keeping names anonymous) and a few to review each week to write a return message to the students. The message should provide a positive comment about the student's completed stem. Explain this to the class. File the others in the students' portfolios.

Journal Entry   Several times a week, conclude the thinking work by inviting students to comment about their thinking in a journal. Let students know you will select five or six journals to review each week. Provide cues to help them focus their thinking for this skill:

Rate your knowledge and use of **classifying**. Give your reasons for this rating.

1	5	10
dead in water		soaring high

Rate how much you think you are improving with your use of the Venn. Give your reasons for this rate.

Think about how you could improve on your use of the Venn. Explain.

_____

_____

_____

5. Use charts and graphs to show progress by groups and/or individuals.

Class Thermometer   On a bulletin board or blank wall, post a thermometer on newsprint. Mark the graduations. After each practice, tally total points earned in each classifying practice. Give bonus points for each group that improved its score from the previous practice round.

Group Bar Graph   Post a bar graph on the bulletin board. After each practice, have the recorder add to the graph with accumulated points and improvement bonus points.

Individual Improvement Chart   Insert a chart in the back of each student's journal. After each round of group practice, give students an individual task for making a Venn. Have the groups check each other's finished project and chart the score including an improvement bonus on the chart.

Grading   If you must reduce the student assessments to a grade, here are two options:

a. To grade the knowledge base, scale your quizzes and tests (see Figure A6).

b. To grade guided practice, indicate the student's performance on each scale. Provide five points for Regular, three for Sometimes, and zero for Not Yet. Scale the totals as above (see Figure A7).

c. To grade independent practice and transfer, assign points to each mark on the Likert scale, total the points and then make the final grade scale or ask the student to select his or her best work, indicate to you the reason, and give a Likert scale rank. Review and use as the basis for a final grade.

Transfer   Once students demonstrate proficiency in using the Venn with assigned reading materials that you selected for classifying, you have the opportunity to promote independent practice and transfer. If necessary, you can grade the results.

If you are teaching a self-contained classroom, structure transfer or independent practice:

• Provide materials or readings to classify. For instance, in science, assign two animals to each observer; in social studies, two cultures to compare; in language arts, two characters or two settings in a story or two poems by the same author; in fine arts, two compositions by the same artist. Instruct the students, either singly or in a cooperative group, to review the procedures for classifying by using a Venn.

• Send pairs of students on a search for materials or readings to classify with a Venn. When they find the materials, each pair will write instructions for the clarification task. Check the instructions and trade assignments among the pairs. After pairs have completed the assignments, they will give the completed Venns back to the originating pairs. These pairs will review the work and respond with what they thought was done well.

- Instruct individual students to find materials or readings to classify in their other classes or at home. (This is where middle school interdisciplinary teams are especially helpful. All teachers on the team can reinforce the classifying thread across all areas of the curriculum.)

- Provide a list of new vocabulary words. Instruct individuals or teams to find the meanings in a dictionary, sort the words into at least two (three or four is more challenging) groups using a Venn on an overhead transparency and label each group by its common elements. If there are items in common, students should insert these in the overlaps. Complete the task by asking the students to explain to the class why they made each group. (Have them write and cut the words from a blank overhead. They can place these words on the overhead Venn transparency for all to see.) To assess this task, here are several options.

Self-assessment Instruct the students to attach a PMI (Plus/Minus/Interesting) summary to their completed work. (Edward de Bono invented this evaluation tool. It is an excellent vehicle for helping students develop their disposition to evaluate their own work.) Students should ask themselves: What were the pluses of their project? What were the minuses? What interesting questions do they have about this project? (Or what interesting questions might others ask?) Encourage three or more responses in each element.

PLUS

- lots of words
- five groups
- groups all agreed
- mostly good
- followed instructions
- all can explain

MINUS

- #2 no why
- argued about #4
- two leftovers

INTERESTING QUESTIONS

- what would happen if we grouped in a different way?
- why were the "whys" so hard?
- where can we use these words?

Group Assessment Invite the groups to use evaluative questions about the thinking they did:

- What did you do well in your classifications?
- How might you have classified the information in a different way?
- Where might you use the ability to classify?

Individual Assessment Invite individual students to rate the thinking they applied:

In a scale, tell how you did a classifier.

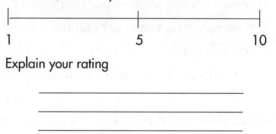

1   5   10

Explain your rating

_____
_____
_____

Transfer Scale Provide students with a transfer scale. Show examples of what that transfer looks like or sounds like at each point on the scale.

NOT YET:

"I don't see how to use this."

"This is dumb stuff."

"What's the connection?"

A SMALL LEAP:

"I can compare short story characters using a Venn."

"It will help with math sets."

A WORLD-CLASS BRIDGE:

"We can compare job benefits after an interview."

"I can contrast political beliefs before voting."

The students might share what they have written with each other or the whole class, enter it in a journal, write a parent letter, or deposit the assessment responses in their portfolios with the "thinking products" they created. To emphasize the transfer element, it is important that the teacher close the transfer activity by reviewing both the basic thinking skill and ways to use the skill in school and in life.

The grading of transfer may be the ultimate absurdity. A grading requirement, however, is not sufficient reason for leaving this crucial learning opportunity out of the curriculum. The following option, built on the above assessment, is suggested.

Grade the PMI with a fluency criterion (how many acceptable examples) or uniqueness criterion (how many "a-ha!" insights). For fluency, you might use the chart.

- less than three acceptable answers per column "not yet; add some more and I will give a grade."
- three acceptable answers per column = C
- five acceptable answers per column = B
- seven acceptable answers per column = A
- one bonus point for each additional acceptable answer per column

You can also award bonus points for each response given that shows insight and was not given by anyone else in the class.

For each evaluative question, you might use the fluency or insight criteria. Or you might use logical extension with more mature students. In this criterion, the students are asked to give reasons why they answered as they did. For each rationale or piece of evidence supplied, the student earns points. For instance, here is a grading scale for responding to the first question with logical extensions.

- one justified example or one justified reason = C
- two examples or reasons = B
- three examples or reasons = A
- additional examples or reasons = bonus points

For the transfer scale, grading becomes simple.

NOT YET: No grade earned. Keep at it.

SMALL LEAP: C

WORLD-CLASS BRIDGE: A

THE TRIPLE AGENDA CLASSROOM: PART III

When a teacher ties cooperation and thinking into learning tasks with significant content outcomes, he or she completes the triple agenda. In the "integrating the curriculum" literature, this is known as the nested model. Not only does this model make thinking and cooperating an integral part of every lesson, it also allows for the most logical and simple way to assess and grade student attainment of complex and significant outcomes.

When integrating the three elements of thinking skills, cooperation, and content into a single lesson, it is helpful to follow these guidelines:

1. KISS: Keep it simple and structured. The "it" is the process of assessment and evaluation.

2. START with a significant outcome. As Sizer (1992) suggests, these are best framed in an "exhibit" framework.

An Elementary Language Arts Sample

Your team will write a safety book for second grade children. It will include:

- pictures and words
- a cover with title
- the dangers
- the ways to avoid the dangers
- quotes from parents, safety officers, teachers, and other members of the community.

Be prepared to read and to tell the first grade class why you picked each danger.

A Middle School Science Sample

Act as your village's waste disposal research team. You have a budget of $12 per household to dispose of the glass waste in the village. Make three plans (good, better, best) to recommend to the village council. Provide a budget that is maximally efficient and will leave the village free of glass litter. You will need to consult with village officials and research village data in the library. Be prepared to defend your recommendations and your reasoning. You will submit your plans to the entire class the class will select the best plan for the village.

A Secondary Geometry Sample

By using knowledge of radius and circumference, compute the time it will require a plane pilot, a truck driver, and a bicyclist to complete each of the following circular routes. Be prepared to explain all procedures you selected and the variables attendant on your solution to the class.

- New York to New York on the class globe

- Dupont Plaza to Columbus Hotel to Library Park to Dupont Plaza

- Michigan City to Johnsonville to Bloomington to Saleto to Michigan City

Identify and share the indicators of success with the students before the lesson or unit starts. In a triple agenda lesson, the teacher and students will use the indicators for the assessments. As the class works through the lesson, some assessments will focus on progress. Others will assess terminal results or transfer. The indicators make clear and easy benchmarks or signposts that the students can follow. They also prevent students from confusing benchmarks with outcomes.

Let student self-assessment precede your feedback. This helps students learn the skills and value of self-evaluation. In this scenario, your feedback fills out or extends the students' self-evaluation. The double-entry journal (student writes on one-half the page; teacher responds on the other) is a helpful tool for this, especially when the students are focusing on progress.

Have students use a consistent tool. The Likert scale with reasons or the PMI are easy frameworks for students to adapt. Skillful and careful practice in using one tool will yield more realistic assessments.

Delay any grade until the very last. Grades are for report cards. Whether using letters, numbers, or symbols, a teacher saves grief by not entering a grade for every paper that crosses the desk. While students who are grade hungry may pester for grades on every task, just say no! If a teacher indicates how students will receive the final grade and sticks with the plan, the students will focus on assessment quality more readily.

Use the funnel model of assessment. It begins with the three-level outcomes for the lesson or unit. Next come the indicators of success and the assessment tools, beginning with self-assessment of products, and knowledge tests that the students will use. As students progress through the unit, they will organize in a portfolio the completed work and assessments. At the end of each unit, each student may select his or her best work or three works and write a rationale for the selection.

With this final assessment submitted by the student, samples of the best work for the unit, and knowledge test results, the teacher has more than enough data to judge to what degree the student has met the three-level outcomes: Not yet, O.K., or WOW! With all work funneled through this process, attaching a meaningful grade is an easier task.

When you use *Not Yet*, you will need to reteach and encourage more effort. This approach has the advantage of signaling to students that *all* outcomes are possible and necessary to attain. Not "getting it" is *not* a terminal illness. All learning is possible. Some need more help and more time, especially with transfer.

IN SUMMARY

Triple agenda instruction provides the opportunity for triple agenda assessment. It enables the classroom teacher to make assessment authentic. Although the triple agenda model requires more up-front work to prepare what the students will learn, it enables the teacher to focus on the quality of students' collaboration and cognition. In its simplest form, the model focuses on skill acquisition and application. It makes teachers the center of classroom intellectual activity; their modeling, planning, facilitation, and assessment help the student become both a cooperative team player and able to thoughtfully apply thinking skills and processes.

In the triple agenda model, the teacher's expertise as a facilitator is crucial. She or he doesn't dump information into empty minds. The teacher provides students with the skills and the dispositions to learn: how to acquire, understand, and assess their own learning. This is seldom compatible with or even allowed by conventional school practice, especially when it comes to the demand for grades in a grade book.

The excellent teacher facilitates, making learning happen for every child, no matter what the child's handicaps or limits. The teacher's job is not to be an accountant. Current classroom practice—which pressures the teacher to pour information into empty vessels, and to test for the purpose of grades and grade point averages—hampers effective teaching. However, because grading traditions are so deeply ingrained in the American school psyche, it is probably not worth the teacher's time to fight the wad-ja-get mindset. Instead, it is probably best for the teacher who values thinking to concentrate on improving triple agenda instruction and to compromise in the grading game with standard-based grades that do not interfere with the ability to help all students to think and cooperate.

FIGURES

MASTERY MATRIX

NAME _____   START DATE _____

THINKING SKILL _____   END DATE _____

Names	Carmela	Alan	Roberta	Robin
1. Can sort by shape	9/15	9/17	9/24	9/20
2. Can sort by color	9/20	9/20	9/25	9/21
3. Can sort by size	10/1	10/1	10/8	10/5
4. Can sort by thickness	10/9	10/12	10/12	10/12
5. Can sort by symbols	10/14			
6. Can sort by _____				

Figure A1   Mastery Matrix

CHECK SHEET

Name: Class:

	Not Yet	Adequately	Very Well
SKILL			
Sorts by shape	X		
Sorts by color			X
Sorts by size		X	
Explains sorts		X	
Mixes sorts		X	
Helps others sort	X		

Figure A2   Check Sheet

ESTABLISHING PERCENTAGE OF TOTAL GRADE

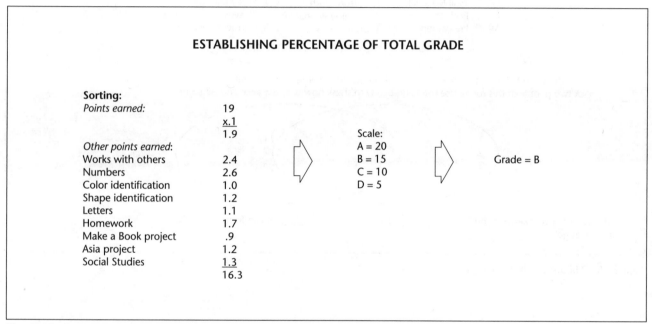

Sorting:
Points earned: 19
                         x.1
                         1.9

Other points earned:
Works with others   2.4
Numbers   2.6
Color identification   1.0
Shape identification   1.2
Letters   1.1
Homework   1.7
Make a Book project   .9
Asia project   1.2
Social Studies   1.3
                        16.3

Scale:
A = 20
B = 15
C = 10
D = 5

Grade = B

Figure A3   Percentage of Total Grade

SAMPLE KNOWLEDGE QUIZ

NAME: DATE: CLASS:

- Answer True or False.   (ANSWERS)
  1. To sort is to put items into a step-by-step order.   T   F   (F)
  2. To sort means to group objects that are alike.   T   F   (T)
  3. Likenesses and differences help us classify.   T   F   (T)
  4. A Venn diagram is a classifying tool.   T   F   (T)

- Eliminate what doesn't belong in each group.
  5. a. elephant   b. tiger c. lion   d. dog   _____   (d)
  6. a. house b. tree   c. flower d. grass _____   (a)

- Put the steps in order for classifying with a Venn.
  7. label the Venn parts   _____   (2)
  8. put items in each part of Venn   _____   (3)
  9. draw your Venn   _____   (1)

Figure A4   Knowledge Quiz

SAMPLE APPLICATION CHECKUPS

I.   Read the following two paragraphs from a clothes catalog. In the Venn below, label the three parts. Enter the likenesses and differences that fit each part. (1 point per correct answer)

Twill Jeans

Jeans that follow in the same tradition as our blue jeans, except these are made from sturdy 10 oz. cotton twill. The color is also notable: our special piece dyeing process lends every color a wonderfully saturated quality. We then garment wash these jeans for immediate softness and comfort. Traditional fit. Riveted front pockets. USA. Machine wash. Unisex 26-34, 36, 38, 40. Order hemmed up to 36", or unhemmed.

Plain-front Jersey Tee

A substantial shirt of midweight cotton jersey. Densely knit for opacity and smooth texture. Garment dyed for depth of color. Generous fit. Domestic and imported. Machine wash. Unisex (same as men's) sizes S, M, L, XL. Short sleeve or long sleeve.

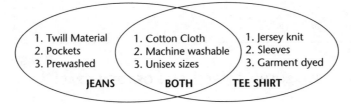

Make the Venn below. Show how sorting and classifying are alike and different.
Pick two people in this room. Use the Venn below to show how they are alike and different.

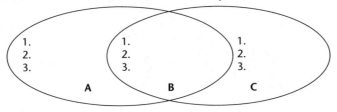

In the Venn above, likenesses go in _____ and _____. (Select from A, B, C.)
Differences go in _____.

Figure A5   Thinking Skill Checkups

GRADING SCALE

Correct	Number	Letter	Comment	Symbol
28	90%+	A	Exceeds expectations	++
22	80%	B	Meets expectations	+
15	70%	C	Meets minimum	0

Figure A6   Grading Scale

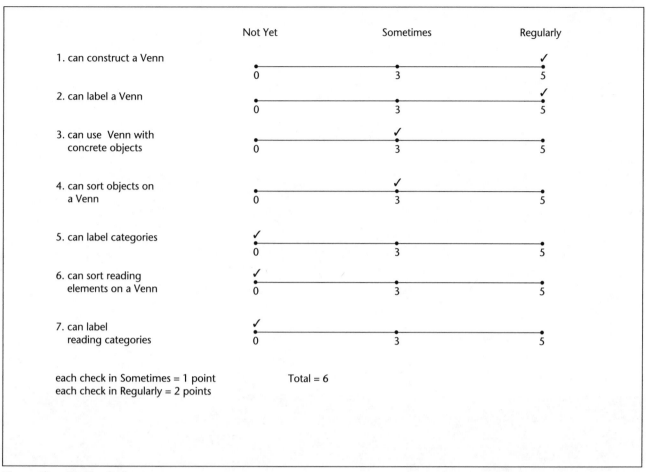

Figure A7   Grading Scale

REFERENCES

Belmont, P., & Dickison, M. (Eds.) (1991). *Portfolios: Process and product.* Portsmouth, NH: Boynton/Cook Publishers Heinemann.

Bellanca, J. (1991). *Building a caring, cooperative classroom.* Palatine, IL: Skylight Publishing

Board of Education for the City of Etobicoke. (1991). *Making the grade: Evaluating student progress.* Scarborough, Ontario: Prentice-Hall Canada.

Gerhard, C. (1991). *Assessment of conceptual organization (ACO): Improving writing, thinking, and reading skills.* Philadelphia: Research For Better Schools.

Kirschenbaum, H., Simon, S. B., & Napier, R. W. (1971). *Wad-ja-get? The grading in American education.* New York: Hart Publishing.

Mitchell, R. (1992). *Testing for learning: How new approaches to evaluation can improve American schools.* New York: The Free Press.

Perrone, V. (Ed.) (1991). *Expanding student assessment.* Alexandria, VA: Association for Supervision and Curriculum Development.

Simon, S. B., & Bellanca, J. A. (1976). *Degrading the grading myths: A primer of alternatives to grades and marks.* Washington, D.C.: Association for Supervision and Curriculum Development.

Sizer, T. (1992). *Horace's school.* New York: Houghton Mifflin.

EVALUATION: A COLLABORATIVE PROCESS

—

Bena Kallick

"D id I get this right?" "Is this what you had in mind?" "Is this work good enough?" So much of a student's sense of "good" work depends on someone else telling us if we have it right. I am not talking about the kind of work for which there is a single right answer. I am talking about work that requires complex thinking, problem solving, divergent ideas, a new synthesis of one's knowledge base, or applying knowledge through performance—the kind of answer that requires the student to be the producer of knowledge rather than the reproducer of knowledge. When we move into that zone of uncertainty in which right and wrong are a matter of a shared understanding of expectations and criteria, we need response. We need a mirror placed before our work that provides an opportunity for reflection and constructive criticism for improvement. We need to be provided with an opportunity to talk about our work with others as we develop our capacity to be sharper in our self-evaluation. The learner's task in the evaluation process is to:

- internalize external standards and expectations for good work,

- understand explicit ways to improve performance to meet those standards,

- develop a self-determined set of standards for high-quality work, and

- learn how to engage in a dialogue about appropriate standards for good work and to negotiate standards based on justifiable evaluative reasoning.

In order for the learner to be successful in this task, classrooms must provide opportunities for collaborative evaluation processes.

OWNING THE EVALUATION DATA

A first and most important assumption is that if learners are to change their behavior as a result of newly learned knowledge or skills, they must own the evaluation data. Unless the learner sees the reason to change; believes that the change is worthwhile; and sees a way to integrate that change into already existing behaviors, attitudes, and knowledge, the change will not take place. If these criteria are not met, learners may be able to reproduce knowledge in a limited way for a limited time, but integration of the new knowledge or skill by the learner as an actor in the world will not happen. Performing as a learner is analogous to performing as a teacher—to get better you need to practice; receive accurate, descriptive responses to your work; receive sound advice from a coach or mentor; and develop the capacity to reflect on your practice and judge your performance in relationship to targets determined by self and others.

Improvement, in the sense of being able to perform better, is judged both by coach or mentor and by self. If either source is considered unreliable, the use of the evaluative data is placed in question and improvement hindered. When the gap is too great between the external sources of evaluation and the internal sources of evaluation, the learner may fall prey to one of many scenarios—"I will do this learning for you but not because there is an intrinsic value for me" or "I do not believe what you say about my work and will resist learning from you" or "I don't know how to think about my work and feel badly about myself as a learner" or "If I can't do what you want me to do, then I just won't work at all for you." Any of these scenarios leaves the learner in conflict about his or her work and creates a tension that pulls the learner away from independent learning and toward learning for approval. I am impressed with how frequently I hear people use the phrase "Won't you just do this for me?" not realizing that people might be able to do work for its value for themselves.

At the center of self-esteem is the question of worthiness—**worth**. As Freud illuminated in his discoveries, one's sense of worth comes from two life-sustaining drives—the capacity to love and to work. When we ask, "What motivates the student to perform in school?" we often forget that the most significant motivating force is the student's discovery of his or her capacity to do successful and good work. How one determines whether a student is doing successful and good work should be a collaborative process of standard setting. In most educational settings this is not the case. Rather, standards for successful and good work are set outside of the student's own sense of performance. The standards are presented to the student as an immutable fact, non-negotiable regardless of the student's justifiable reasoning about his or her own performance. When students are brought into a dialogue about standards, ownership of the evalua-

tive data is more successful. The learning targets are agreed on based on a dialogue about the quality of effort and worthiness of one's work in relation to the developing expectations of self and coach or mentor.

Our objective is to bring the learner into the evaluation process in such a way that he or she will become a partner in the learning process; a person who will be able to participate fully in the learning experience with a sense of control over its results.

COLLABORATION BETWEEN STUDENT AND TEACHER

There are many opportunities to develop evaluation as a collaborative process in the classroom. I will mention a few of the most frequently tried practices.

Conferences or Student Interviews
A conference can be a wonderful opportunity to hear how students are thinking about their own work. The quality of the conference is far more significant than the quantity of conferences. Some schools state that a student will be interviewed at least once a month. Given a class size of between twenty-five and thirty students, a teacher in an elementary school will be required to have one conference a day; in a secondary school it may require four or five conferences in a day. Each student is assured an opportunity to discuss his or her work with a teacher on a monthly basis. In addition, some schools have required that teachers also talk with one parent every day. Regardless of whether a student is in particular trouble, has special needs, or has done something exemplary, regular conversations about student work are built into the daily life of school. Other teacher conference time is provided by allowing students to do independent work during conference time. Or perhaps students may be engaged in group work. Some teachers provide time for student peer conferences as a regular part of their work with students. At this time, students conference with one another about their work and the teacher pulls aside individual students for conferences. Group interviews provide another option. At this time, the

teacher pulls together a group of students and confers about their work.

Questions For An Interview   Imagine that you were to have the opportunity to interview Jean Piaget, John Dewey, or Sylvia Ashton Warner. If you were able to resurrect them for only fifteen minutes, what would be your questions for them? Most of your questions would probably start in the following way:

- How do you feel about…?

- In your opinion, do you think…?

- Why do you suppose…?

- What was on your mind when…?

- Now that you have accomplished your work, what do you think about…?

- How does what you say compare to ＿＿ in your opinion?

In other words, you would be asking questions that would elicit responses that only they could provide. You would not ask them questions that you could find the answer to through other means. You would consider the time with them so valuable that you would think of the opportunity as one in which you had access to primary source information. Any information that could be gleaned from secondary sources should not use up your precious time.

Consider the interview or conference with a student in the same light. If there is information that can be gleaned from other places, then why use your precious interview time for that? Why not consider the student, during the interview, as a primary source for you? It is only at this time that you can gain access to his or her original thinking; his or her thinking about self and work in original ways. Try constructing an interview for your student using the above starters. For example: How do you feel about reading? How does the book you just read compare to the one you read last week? In your opinion, what is the significance of learning fractions? Why do you suppose that I chose to teach the class about the Civil War?

Questions For Reflection on Portfolio   One of the most significant aspects of portfolio assessment is the opportunity to reflect on your portfolio with another thoughtful person. The portfolio represents selections from a collection of a student's work. Over the course of a few months, a student collects work. The student is then asked to choose from the work examples for the portfolio. The examples in a writing portfolio might include: best final product with drafts stapled together; best example of change within drafts; and best example of risk taken by learner in trying to acquire a new skill or style. When the student chooses, he or she justifies the choice. A conference can reflect how the student has evaluated his or her work and where there are targets for growth. Sometimes the teacher will also choose best examples from the student's work. In that case, the conference provides an opportunity for the teacher to share his or her choices with the student's choices. Suppose the teacher's choices do not match the student's choices. This provides a marvelous opportunity to talk about expectations, standards, and quality of work. And what a marvelous opportunity for the teacher to understand the student's developing criteria!

Building Criteria

The whole class can participate in the development of criteria. For example, in a given project, students can collaborate, as a classroom community, in setting the standards and criteria by which they will judge the project results. These expectations should be established before the students begin their project work. In this way students are building their capacity to critique work as well as do work.

An elementary school project with a group of bilingual students focuses on building criteria for what makes a good story. The teacher and children begin to build a set of criteria for what, in their opinion, makes a good story. After they read a story together, the class discusses whether the story met their criteria. In some instances they find that they have to expand their criteria based on their reading. In some instances they find that certain criteria are specific to a story genre. After they become more skilled in their capacity to evaluate stories on the basis of established criteria, they decide to look at their own story writing in the same way. The students use peer conferences about their story writing as a basis for examining the story in light of the criteria. The levels of collaboration and evaluation become a powerful learning opportunity. Students are eventually able to examine their criteria for what makes a good story with some of the criteria literary critics have used. Students may converse with literary critics and inform their evaluation process through those conversations. In this way, students are working as critical thinkers—making their evaluative judgments through informed reasoning.

Group Evaluation

When students are working in groups, they have another opportunity to develop a collaborative evaluation process. Group work requires evaluating the content of the group effort as well as the group process. Although the criteria for good group project work may be set with the class, each group may set its own criteria for good group process. The "How are we doing?" chart is an example of a group process evaluation form (See Figure 1).

Students are asked to rate themselves in one of three categories: Often, Sometimes, and Not Yet (a positive developmental way of looking at behavior). After the student has evaluated himself or herself, the activity can expand so that all of the students in the group evaluate one another and give each other feedback about their behavior. Finally, the teacher can monitor the groups with a clipboard with the same charts for each group. In that way, students can have three perspectives on the same event—self, peer, and teacher. Goals can be set for new behaviors based on interpreting the evaluative responses.

When a classroom is focusing on thinking, the process behaviors should foster better thinking. An excellent list of such behaviors is provided in Art Costa's work on intelligent behaviors (Costa, 1991). Teachers and students might generate a set of criteria for what intelligent behavior looks like. That list can be transposed onto the "How are we doing?" form (See Figure 1).

ESTABLISHING SCHOOLWIDE STANDARDS

If teachers and students are collaborating in the evaluation process, how does this begin to translate to schoolwide criteria and standards? This is an excellent initiating conversation for a schoolwide discussion. Usually the discussion starts from another perspective—what standards we establish (or the state or district establishes) that we require of our students. I am suggesting that we reverse the process and that we start in collaboration with students and work our way out from the classroom to the school to the district and to the state. If we reframe the question from this perspective, we may learn something new about accountability. We may learn something more about how to encourage student accountability and self-evaluation in relationship to the larger set of expectations that surround students and their work. We may also provide a more constructive framework for instruction in relationship to student learning because teachers will stay closer to the authentic, daily performance of the work of students as they develop their criteria for evaluation. When teachers bring the data from their classrooms to the whole-school discussion on standards and criteria setting for evaluation, the discussion remains closer to the realities of the classroom. The whole school can engage in conversations based on the work of students rather than impressions of what ought to be. To emphasize this point, the following situation occurred in an elementary school. A group of teachers brought writing from kindergarten through sixth grade classes. They had agreed that one of the ways that they would produce a common experience for discussion would be to provide the students with a writing prompt. In that way, all students would submit their writing sample for examination. The prompt they used was offered in early November: "Suppose you were the last turkey in the barn—describe your feelings and experience." Children were encouraged to draw as well as write and adults were available to capture stories from nonwriters. The teachers, one from each grade, came to the meeting with their class's writing samples. They were asked to switch papers so that no one scored their own set of papers. The task was to choose the best three examples of writing from their twenty-five or thirty samples. One of the first questions a teacher asked was, "Suppose you cannot find three best pieces?" The teacher's ques-

HOW ARE WE DOING?
ATTRIBUTE: FLEXIBILITY IN THINKING

OBSERVABLE INDICATORS	OFTEN	SOMETIMES	NOT YET
Is willing to change her or his mind			
Accepts another point of view ("I agree..." "I understand..." "I see...")			
Accepts or offers multiple solutions to the problem			
Is able to change focus without panic or fretting			
Is able to compromise (gives up "ownership" or role)			
Is willing to consider more than one thing or source at a time			
Is willing to accept that there may not be an answer			

Source: Bena Kallick, Westport, CT.

HOW ARE WE DOING?
ATTRIBUTE: OVERCOMING IMPULSIVITY— DELIBERATIVENESS

OBSERVABLE INDICATORS	OFTEN	SOMETIMES	NOT YET
Listens to directions before starting			
Listens to response of others and does not repeat what has been said or asked			
Asks questions to clarify the task or direction			
Decreases number of erasures			
Reduces the number of unnecessary, repetitious questions			
Analyzes the problems and develops a plan (uses visual strategies—e.g. mind map)			
Thinks before answering			
Takes time to use thoughtful, precise language			
Can paraphrase when called upon			

Source: Bena Kallick, Westport, CT.

HOW ARE WE DOING?
ATTRIBUTE: PERSISTENCE—Persevering when the solution to a problem is not immediately apparent

OBSERVABLE INDICATORS	OFTEN	SOMETIMES	NOT YET
Stays on task			
Seeks alternative sources of data			
May take a break, but returns to task			
May say "Don't tell me, let me figure it out"			
Shows intenseness of thought			
Says, "Wait a minute, I want to finish"			
Completes task or project			

Source: Bena Kallick, Westport, CT.

HOW ARE WE DOING?
ATTRIBUTE: LISTENING TO OTHERS— With understanding and empathy

OBSERVABLE INDICATORS	OFTEN	SOMETIMES	NOT YET
Maximizes eye contact			
Pays attention			
Paraphrases others' responses			
Demonstrates body language (e.g., nods approval, sits up, etc.,)			
Asks questions related to the topic			
Responds by actions or words			
Gives accepting response (the way in which the responses are given)			

Source: Bena Kallick, Westport, CT.

Figure 1   "How are we doing?" chart

tion reflected external standards for a good piece of writing, standards not based on the work of the children in the classroom. Suppose none of the children meet that expectation? In fact, the task was to choose a relative measure from within the population they were given. It is not difficult to see how that attitude begins to translate to (1) expectations for students that do not match the capabilities of students, (2) disappointment that the students' work is not "good enough," (3) when accepting the student's work, feeling as if one has lowered one's standards, and (4) having difficulty providing realistic learning stretches from within the students' work.

The teachers finally got to the task and chose the three best pieces. We then, starting from the kindergarten class and moving through to the sixth grade class, described the characteristics that made those pieces "best." At the end of the exercise, we had an interesting story of the development of writing for these students. We could then compare that to what theorists in the writing process were suggesting. We had established a knowledge base about our students that provided a lens through which we could examine the work of other practitioners and theorists.

Two additional powerful insights came from this experience:

> The teachers were viewing the work of the children in early November against last year's class in June. In other words, what they remembered as the performance of their last year's class at the end of the year, they were carrying into their expectations for this year's class at the beginning of the year. One of the most difficult aspects of losing a class in June is that you just about have them where you want to see them and you have to let them go and start all over again!
>
> The first grade teacher exclaimed when she got her class's papers back—"I am amazed that these are the best three examples— they are my worst readers!" This teacher revealed the bias we bring to viewing our students' work—a bias that often remains

hidden in our grading system. The teachers all agreed that it was important, especially if they were looking for a collaborative understanding of evaluation in the school, to read and evaluate each other's student work at least once a month.

Instituting practices that facilitate teachers' talking about criteria, standards, and evaluation practices is one powerful way to change the accountability system. Such practices as evaluation study groups, teacher-as-researcher groups, or teachers working in partnerships with one another to exchange papers all can be organized as a part of staff development.

DISTRICT STANDARDS

As these conversations grow out of individual schools, they can be a part of the development of a school-based management system that reports to the superintendent. At the central level, the district can orchestrate school-based understandings and, through collaborative processes, can arrive at realistic expectations for students at elementary and secondary levels. The orchestration of curriculum, instruction, and assessment practices is a necessary part of school accountability. But a little voice is saying to you right now, "What about the state?" The state might also reverse its perspective. Rather than developing the accountability measures, it might see its role as facilitating district processes for greater accountability. The state might serve as a legitimizing agency for district practices. In that way, the state might establish policy for criteria for a solid evaluation system or process rather than trying to establish procedures for measuring what might be differing strategies of instruction and—in some states where there is not a statewide curriculum—differing curricular requirements.

CONCLUSION

The process of collaboration should be thoughtful enough to improve learning and teaching. We know that the process of evaluation presently in place is seen as detracting from teaching and learning. The measures that are mandated are often perceived as punitive, not authentic, and do not adequately describe what teachers and students value. By developing collaborative processes for setting evaluation standards, we can enlarge our understanding of what it means to examine a human process as dynamic and complex as learning. We can learn to value more than one perspective regarding the question of standards. And finally, we may make our way out of an accountability process that represses rather than enhances thinking at all levels of the educational enterprise.

——

REFERENCES

Chittenden, E. (1990). Young children's discussions of science topics. In G. E. Hein (Ed.), *The assessment of hands-on elementary science programs* (p. 220-247). Grand Forks, ND: North Dakota Study Group on Evaluation.

Costa, A. (1991). *The school as a home for the mind.* Palatine, IL: Skylight Publishing.

Duckworth, E. (1978). *The African primary science program: An evaluation.* Grand Forks, ND: North Dakota Study Group on Evaluation.

Goodman, K., Goodman, Y., & Hood, W. (1989). *The whole language evaluation book.* Portsmouth, NH: Heineman.

Hein, G. E. (Ed.). (1990). *The assessment of hands-on elementary science programs.* Grand Forks, ND: North Dakota Study Group on Evaluation.

Kallick, B. (1989). *Changing schools into communities for thinking.* Grand Forks, ND: University of North Dakota Press.

Wiggins, G. (1989). A true test: Towards more authentic and equitable assessment. *Phi Delta Kappan, 70,* 703-713.

HOW DO WE KNOW
WE'RE GETTING BETTER?

—

Sharon Jeroski and Faye Brownlie

The minute we begin to articulate our feelings, ideas, and judgments about a piece of literature, it begins to take another shape. We see things we had not seen before, and we begin to forget those things that do not relate to the account we are giving of the story. This is true whether we are simply retelling the story to friend, asking a question of a trusted colleague, expressing our opinions to a stranger on the street, or pausing a moment to talk silently to ourselves about what we have just read.

—(Nelms, 1988, p. 7)

Teachers today are struggling to reconcile their beliefs about how students develop as thoughtful, responsive readers with their need to offer clear evidence that students are becoming "better" readers. It seems clear that traditional indicators such as standardized test scores, percent correct, or rank-in-class do not offer the kinds of information teachers find helpful in supporting students who are actively constructing meaning as they read. What features might characterize assessment of authentic achievement in reading real accomplishments of active, responsive readers?

- The student makes critical choices about such features as materials, use of time, and representation of response.

- The student makes connections with previous knowledge and experience in shaping a response.

- The student personalizes the reading experience and shows some depth of understanding.

- The student's response reflects or stimulates thoughtful interactions about the reading experience.

- The text and the response task are meaningful to the student.

MAKING CRITICAL CHOICES

Active readers are continually making choices—choices about what they will read, when they will read, and how they will read. They also make choices about what they will do with their reading—how they will respond and represent their ideas, and whether or not they will seek an audience.

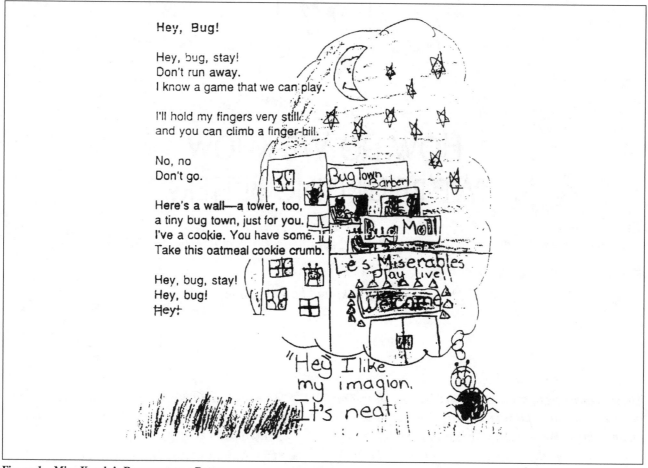

Figure 1   Miya Kondo's Response to a Poem

From *Reading and Responding: Primary* by Jeroski, S., Brownlie, F., & Kaser, L. Copyright 1991. Used by permission of Nelson, Canada, a division of Thomson Canada Limited.

In working with young readers, we very quickly discovered that assessing and evaluating their development was much easier when we encouraged them to make their own choices. Rather than offering carefully structured reading assignments, we began inviting the students to use their feelings, ideas, and images to demonstrate their understanding of a reading. Freed from our expectations, the children responded in wonderful and diverse ways. In Louise Zappitello's primary classroom, children aged six to nine have frequent opportunities to make choices about their reading and their representations.

Miya

Miya is an eight-year-old author and illustrator who is strongly drawn to the imagery of poetry (See Figure 1). Miya explained, "I thought it would be fun to show you what the bug was thinking. I put myself into the bug's mind and I got a really strong picture of the kind of town it might like." Miya's illustration offers a delightful personal perspective with "Les Miserables" playing at the local Bug Mall. Miya's "bug"—like Miya herself—is enjoying the images it has created.

Miya is also the principal illustrator of the collaborative novel she is working on. "I write the words and draw the pictures; they [her partners] color them," she explains. The novel features three beautiful, rich, and independent young women who move from one fortunate adventure to another. It is carefully written and exquisitely illustrated.

Stina

In the same classroom, Stina (who is collaborating on a mystery novel) chose to read and respond to a poem about a dog "thin as a rail" whose fleas hop

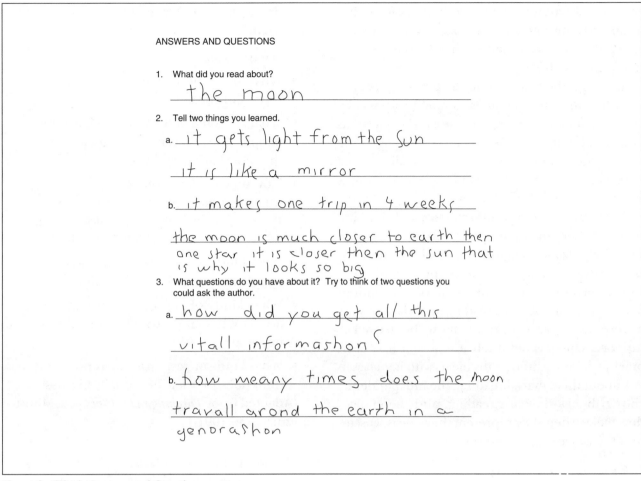

ANSWERS AND QUESTIONS

1. What did you read about?

     the moon

2. Tell two things you learned.

   a. it gets light from the Sun

      it is like a mirror

   b. it makes one trip in 4 weeks

      the moon is much closer to earth then
      one star it is closer then the sun that
      is why it looks so big

3. What questions do you have about it? Try to think of two questions you
   could ask the author.

   a. how did you get all this
      vitall informashon

   b. how meany times does the moon
      travall arond the earth in a
      genorashon

Figure 2   Stina's Answers and Questions

from the bottom to the top whenever he waves his tail. Stina wrote:

> *I wonder why he only hase flees on his tail but if he hase fles on his tail why whene he waves his tail they don't go all over his body. If he is as thin as a rail he must not be a healthy dog. where do the fleas that are on the top go whene he waves his tail.*

Stina has a dog and she is intrigued by some of the detail in the poem. In conversation she explained that her dog sometimes had fleas, but he was much healthier than the dog in the poem. Stina is characteristically curious—she poses a number of questions that demonstrate her connections to what she already knows about dogs: Why does he only have fleas on his tail? Why when he waves his tail don't they go all over his body? As an author, Stina is currently much more interested in exploring and playing with language and ideas

than with illustrations and images. We see these choices extending to her novel, which she and her partner, Tim, have been working on intermittently for several weeks.

Stina and Tim are obviously enjoying their collaboration, although they explain that they sometimes get tired of their book and stop writing it for a week or two. It features a complex Halloween/mystery plot and they explain that they usually get their ideas by talking together, "but sometimes when we're writing we really don't know what's going to happen." Although they are keen to find a new audience for their novel, they have obviously had so much fun writing it that sharing it is almost anticlimactic.

Stina's enthusiasm for language and learning is also apparent when she selects **answers and questions** as a way of demonstrating her understanding of a selection about the moon (See Figure 2 above). (Children were offered four choices: illustrating; writing a note to someone at home; writing about the new information they learned; or answers and questions).

Although the assignment asks for two pieces of information, Stina includes as much as possible. Her questions are delightful—clearly the questions of a developing author who loves language. She wants to find out where the author got all this vital information and how many times the moon travels around the earth in a generation.

The wide range of representations of thinking reflects the opportunities present in the classroom. These children recognize their ability to both choose from among a repertoire and to apply their choices in a variety of contexts. All of the children were able to choose both reading material and ways of responding and representing without teacher support. This was definitely a skill that had been practiced. Louise frequently meets with her class to talk about their shared reading, the independently chosen books they are reading, and the choices they make when they represent their ideas. Discussion focuses around questions such as:

Choosing Books:

- How did you pick that book? Was it a good choice for you?

- Who do you know that might like this book? Why do you think they would like it?

- Do you ever give other people advice about books and stories they might like? Who do you give advice to? Do you think your advice helps them?

- Who tells you about good books to read? How do their ideas help you?

- What books have surprised you—books that you thought you might not like that turned out to be interesting? Books that you thought you would like but found out you didn't?

- What do you do when you find you have made a mistake in choosing a book?

- What do you usually do when you finish reading a book? (Do you tell other students about it? Write about it? Read it again?)

Choosing Responses:

- What are some of the ways you like to represent your ideas?

- What are some of the ways you like other people to represent their ideas when they are sharing with you?

- How do you like to represent your ideas when you are working with a partner? With a group? With an older or a younger buddy? Outside of school?

- What kinds of representations do other people ask you to help them with?

- What kinds of representations do you avoid? What kinds would you like to be better at?

- What kinds of responses or representations does your teacher usually like best?

(Adapted from *Thinking in the Classroom*, Ministry of Education, 1991.)

The teachers and students we work with value and monitor the choices they make through their oral and written reflections in conferences, learning and thinking logs, portfolios, and classroom sign-up sheets where they indicate the genres, books, stories, and forms they are currently exploring (See Figure 3).

MAKING CONNECTIONS

Connecting—between the known and the unknown, with others, with personal experience, and with the world—is fundamental to assessing growth in learning. Children can be encouraged to connect their prior experiences with reading by activities such as in Figure 4.

The importance of the connections is made explicit by the teacher's question: "Does the information agree with your ideas?" Jenna, a seven-year-old in Lynn Hoeteker's class, clearly indicates that while reading, she has held her prior knowledge in mind and looked for substantiating evidence (See Figure 5).

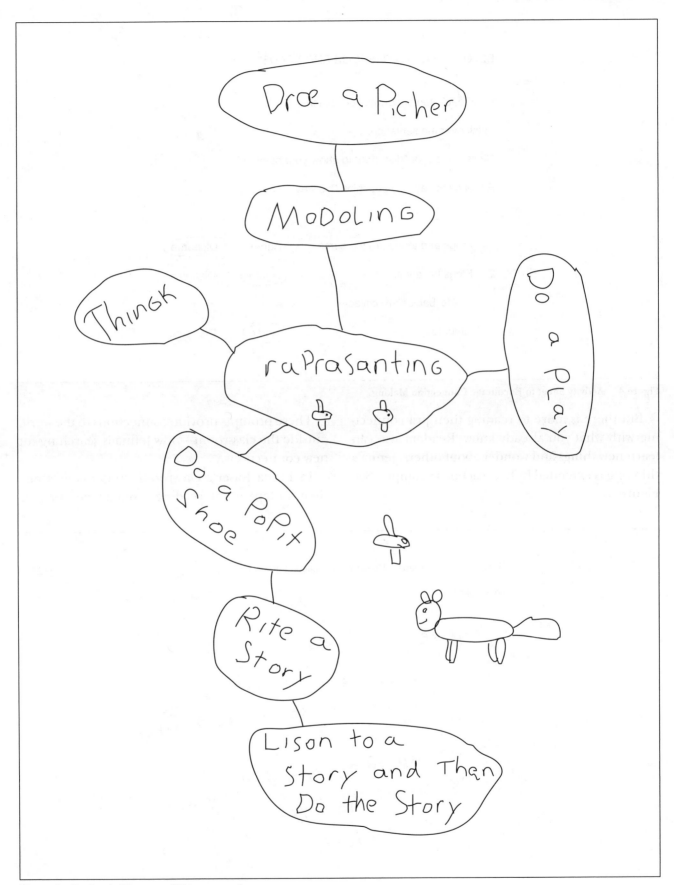

Figure 3   Student's Diagram of Representations

BEFORE YOU READ "FROGS AND TOADS"

Read each sentence with your teacher.

Think over the sentence.

Circle "agree" or "disagree" to show your opinion.

Be ready to say why you think this way.

1. Frogs and toads are the same.   Agree   (Disagree)

2. Frogs lay eggs.   (Agree)   Disagree

3. Toads' babies are called

   tadpoles   (Agree)   Disagree

Figure 4   Activity Sheet to Encourage Connection Making

But there is more to reading then just connecting with what you already know. Readers also can learn new things and wonder about others. Jenna's thinking is extended by her teacher's prompts (See Figure 6).

These prompts provide connections to the world outside the classroom—now Jenna is searching for new connections.

In Linda Kaser's classroom, students examine their independent reading from three perspec-

Read "Frogs and Toads." Does the information agree with

your ideas?

1 agree

2 Yes because it showed an egg and there was some informashon on the egg

3 the auther agreed because he said that the egg turns in to a tadpole

Figure 5   Jenna's Response to Reading "Frogs and Toads"

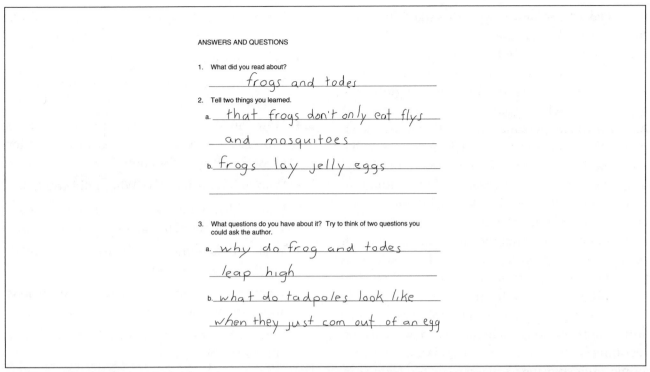

Figure 6   Jenna's Answers and Questions

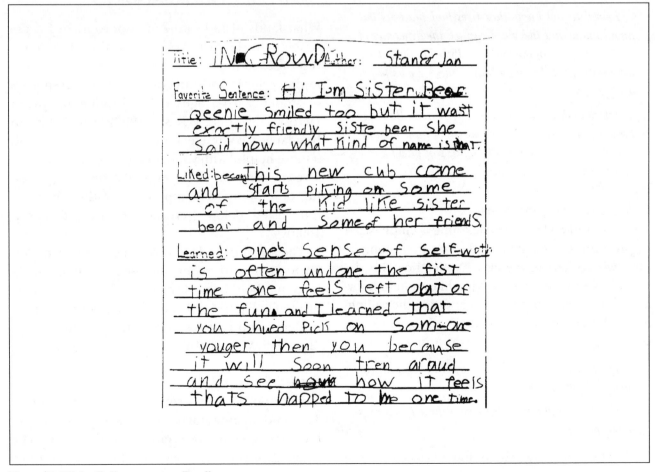

Figure 7   Michael's Response to a Reading

tives: a favorite sentence, what they liked, and what they learned. Michael was able to respond from all three perspectives (See Figure 7).

Michael's "learned" reflection connects the experience of the character not only to a global lesson (not to pick on someone younger than you) but also to his personal world (that's what happened to me one time). Michael chose a book that was meaningful to him: Linda offered a task that supported him in making sense of his reading. In turn, he provided her with clear, valid information about his development as a reader.

Another way to examine the connections with content or expanding bodies of knowledge is through learning log prompts such as "I used to think…but now…" Reflections such as this help students recognize their need to make connections and adapt existing schema as new learning reconnects and reshapes information. For example, after studying a unit on trees, two eight-year-olds in Laura Smith's library reflected:

> *I used to not know that trees had patterns but now I know that they do. I can tell the difference of the trees because of the patterns. I used to think trees were not useful, but now I know they give us paper and oxygen.*

> *I used to think all the trees had…leaves. But now I know not all trees have leaves—they have needles. I used to think trees weren't useful. But now I know they breathe carbon dioxide.*

Collaborative Connections

The power of collaborative learning is emphasized by prompting students to reflect on their connections with others in the class. Notice how this six-year-old's entry informs us as to what students know about learning—the value of expertise, the willingness of people to share their ideas, and the strengths of individuals within groups.

> *Jay has tote me. I think more than 1 hanjrid things abuot ANTS.*

> *(Jay has taught me. I think more than 100 things about ants.)*

Teachers' questions help students to make connections in their reading and thinking.

- What did we do today that helped us to become better learners? How did it help?
- How can we use what we learned?
- What did you notice about your thinking in this class today?
- How can you use the reading and thinking strategies we worked on today in your other classes? Outside of school? At work?
- Who helped you today? Whom did you help?
- What did you like about your reading today? What was challenging in your reading today?
- What was something you learned from reading that surprised you?
- What are questions which you are still curious about and would like to find some answers to?
- What are new questions you thought of after talking to your group?

DEPTH OF UNDERSTANDING

What kinds of indicators are appropriate for describing the depth and personalization of students' responses to their reading? We developed the following criteria and categories from the responses of students from ages eight through seventeen (Jeroski, Brownlie, & Kaser, 1990). The scales can be adapted to any age: for example, we have found it more helpful with younger children (ages four to seven) to describe three levels of responses (powerful, developing, and supported) rather than the four listed below (Jeroski, Brownlie, & Kaser, 1990).

The scoring guide and comments offer models for teachers and students to use in developing criteria in their own classrooms. The samples reprinted in Figures 8, 9, and 10 are from sixth grade students who had responded to a poem entitled "The Wild Wolves of Winter."

Powerful

The response is personalized and thoughtful. The student integrates previous experience and includes specific references to the text. The ideas expressed go beyond the text, describe the comparisons or metaphors, and indicate a

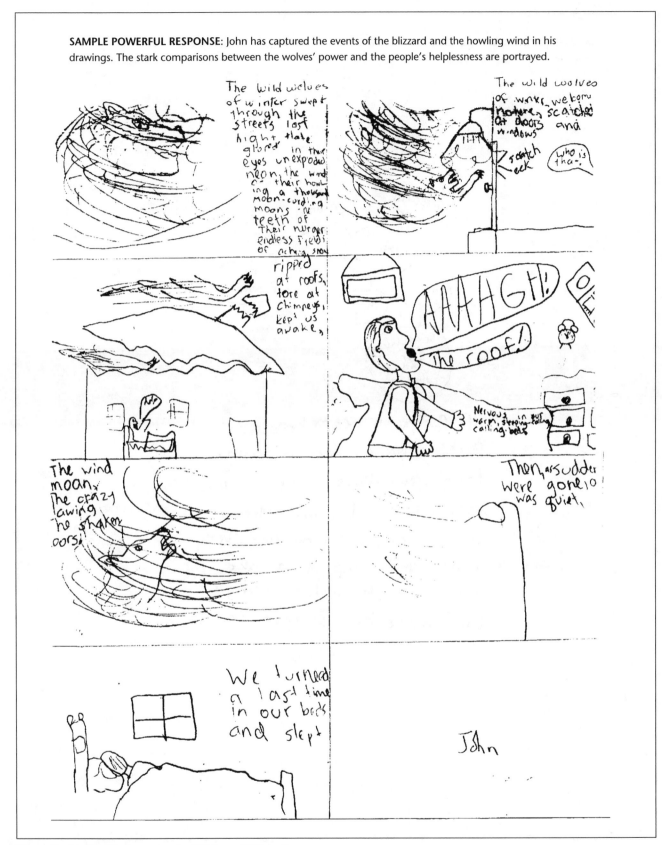

Figure 8   Student Response to the "Wolves of Winter"

From *Reading and Responding Grade 6* by Jeroski, S., Brownlie, F., & Kaser, L. Copyright 1990. Used by permission of Nelson Canada, a division of Thomson Canada Limited.

SAMPLE PARTIAL RESPONSE: Lauren identified with the poet, the sleeplessness, and the fear, but she attributes this all to a pack of wolves. She has not recognized the wolves as representatives of a winter wind.

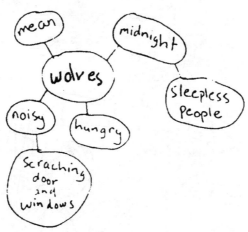

life for me is scary because
packs of wolves keep on coming
though my village. My life is also
very sleepless because the
wolves scrach at my door every
night and keep me awake. I
wish that the wolves will go
back were they came from.

Lauren

Figure 9 Student Response to the "Wolves of Winter"

SAMPLE COMPETENT RESPONSE: Jim understands the metaphor of the blizzard, but does not provide much detail in his description of it. He uses text information and personally responds to the fierce wind.

I think in the poem "The Wild Wolves of Winter" the wolves wher like a bliezard. The scratches at the door are like when the wind blows and you're all allone you Could almost think there was Someone at the door. The poem is good

Jim

SAMPLE UNDEVELOPED RESPONSE: Lindsay attempts to interpret the wolf in the poem, but misses the intent and seriousness of the poet.

The Wild Wolves of winter   Lindsay

I think this poem is about a person wearing a wolf skin jacket trying to stay intsead of outside in the cold.

Figure 10   Student Responses to the "Wolves of Winter"

From *Reading and Responding Grade 6* by Jeroski, S., Brownlie, F., & Kaser, L. Copyright 1990. Used by permission of Nelson Canada, a division of Thomson Canada Limited.

relatively deep or sophisticated understanding of the selection.

Competent

The response is consistent and logical and features some integration of previous experience and includes text references. The student may focus on one aspect of the poem, not describe the metaphor, or deal with the idea on a surface level.

Partial

Some inconsistencies are apparent, suggesting a partial or incomplete understanding of the poem. Typically, the student makes less frequent use of images, emotions, and specific text references.

Undeveloped

The response is inconsistent or illogical. The student may offer broad general statements without explanation. If any text references are included, they may be inappropriate or illogical.

THOUGHTFUL INTERACTIONS

Student interviews are one way of finding out what students think about their developing competencies, what their personal evaluation of their growth is, and what support is needed to continue to enhance their language development.

Colin is a seven-year-old reader. He has practiced reading the age-old tale "The Turnip" and has now taped this reading. He is interviewed by his teacher on his reading of the selection. His reading has been very expressive. Each time he came to the repeated line, "But the turnip wouldn't budge," the line became louder and more expressive. He made one miscue—"hungry" for "huge" but corrected himself after realizing that it was unlikely the turnip being pulled from the ground was "hungry."

Teacher: What did you think about your reading on the tape?

Colin: Quite good but for one word when I was practicing it. I felt a little better, then I made a couple of mistakes but I corrected them.

Teacher: Can you tell me about those mistakes?

Colin: Hungry didn't make sense…a man pulling up a "hungry" turnip. So I asked my Mom and she said it was "huge," so I just remembered it. I practiced a couple of times on our way out to dinner and I just kept getting better and better at it. I guess it was quite great except leaving out the "huge" or "hungry."

Teacher: What would you like me to notice about your reading when I am listening to the tape?

Colin: My voice and stuff and how smoothly I was. How it is important in my voice that I put life into it. For example, "But the turnip wouldn't budge!" I make it like it's alive.

Colin's response clearly indicates what he values in his reading development. He prepares to read for an audience, recognizes the entertainment value of real reading, practices for improvement, reads for meaning, and checks with others when he needs support. His ability to talk about his reading with such clarity helps us continue to support his growing independence as a reader and a thinker.

Thoughtful interactions between students and teachers can also occur in print. A critical element in keeping the interaction thoughtful is asking real questions of a real audience with a real purpose.

The following two letters are samples from a second grade class after the Canadian Fitness Test. The teacher had been away for the testing day so the substitute teacher asked the children to write to Miss Kaser, describing their participation in the events.

Dear Miss Kaser,

I slept in this morning and I missed the Canada Fitness Test. I felt a little sad, but I didn't worry and if I was in it I would know that I would do very well on every one of them.

Love, Bonnie

Dear Miss Kaser,

I liked Canada Fitness because I felt I did better than last year. I mostly liked the shuttle run because you got to pick up bean bags and drop them. I mostly liked the 50 meter run because I liked being timed and running through the two cones. When I ran it was like running through two lion statues only with one colour and one eye as round as round can be. The thing I didn't like about Canada Fitness was me and my partner always had to line up last.

from Elsa

Both letters show the students' understanding of the effect of their actions on their performance and their positive performance image. Strong personal voices come through in their letters. They are obviously used to being carefully listened to and are attempting to write to Miss Kaser about what she would want to hear about them.

Julie Davis, a high school English teacher, asked her students to tell her in writing the kinds of questions they most liked to respond to. These are two responses:

I like a question that is slightly cryptic and makes you think. Another question I like is one where there is no correct answer, you just have to let your ideas flow smoothly.

Puzzles have always appealed to me for the simple reason that you know there must be an obvious answer, though it may be hidden.

I hate questions that require a choice of yes or no, for I have learned that there is a compromise, a mutual area, between the absolutes.

Many likes and dislikes of questions originate over the topic.

Deanna

Deanna's response indicates not only that she has carefully thought through her preferences, but that she has also experience with questions which invite reasoning.

My favorite kind of question is one that takes as little time as possible to do. The reason is because I'm always busy and have better things to do than answer big silly useless, school, brainstorming problems. Although I like to tackle practical problems that can be done with ingenuity and skills.

Scott

These are real questions for a real world. Scott's perspective refocuses us on the number of questions which are asked in school by people who already know the answers to their questions.

Another combination is that of the unknown audience, the conversation with someone whom you may know less well. In Linda Hoffman's fourth grade class, the students were writing 'Dear Reader' letters to insert at the beginning of their thinking logs. The purpose of the letter was to guide the reader when he or she looked through the log. Of particular interest in these letters is the students' sense of pride in their accomplishments and their means of describing what they really value in their learning.

Dear Reader,

This is my Thinking Log. I put a lot of work into this so please don't look for spelling, coloring, etc. Some of the things I would especially like you to look at is the ocean garbage one because I think it is wrong to make a dump out of a gorgeous ocean and killing all the ducks and fish. And another thing I would like you to read is the front page of my book it is how I felt about learning at the beginning of the year and I still feel the same way about learning and even better!

Yours truly, Radel

Dear Reader,

I want you to read my book and see if you can find out how my feelings were when I did my Brain, my Collage, my kindergartin and my feelings poem and if you would have the same feelings. The one that I felt best about was thinking inventory. I thought that was my best creative thing. I like it because it showed what I like to do, what my dream was and what I think will happen to me in the future and that's what I think is important. I also think my learning has changed when I have to give a straight answer my learning isn't that different but when I can give all my ideas about it I think it shows you where I've changed in my learning.

Thanks, Dustin

These letters reflect not only the sense of writing for a real audience, but students who have learned from a series of thoughtful experiences and interactions with one another and their teacher throughout the year.

MEANINGFUL TASKS

The ultimate goal of most reading instruction is the development of thoughtful, independent readers—readers who understand and respond to what they read and who are able to integrate and extend each new reading experience in a meaningful way. This understanding and response can only develop when children are engaged in reading texts which they find to be worth reading—because the readings are personally meaningful, entertaining, or enjoyable, useful in accomplishing some purpose, or represent a milestone of some kind to the reader.

The children whose work appears in this chapter were able to make effective choices and develop rich responses because they were engaged in activities that were important to them. They were able to make choices about the form their work would take; it is equally important that they were able to focus on developing meaning. Having initiated a frame of reference, they were able to pursue their ideas until they were satisfied with the result. For example, when Miya and Stina responded to the poems, they completed their representations relatively quickly in order to share them with their visitors; writing their novels, however, extended over several weeks.

Like Miya and Stina, all of the children and teachers we work with assume that reading, responding, representing, and sharing will make sense to them. Although they may struggle with some of the texts they read and the tasks they work on, the struggle is always toward **meaning** (rather than toward "correctness").

Although often students develop their own response tasks, we frequently ask them to work within a structure we provide, especially if they have been practicing or reviewing a particular strategy. We try to ensure that the tasks are open-ended and able to accommodate a range of learners and developmen-tal stages. For example, working with a number of multi-age primary classrooms (our education system in British Columbia features ungraded, continuous progress during the first four years of school) we offered six response options for poems Miya, Stina, and other children were reading:

Listen-Read-Respond

Listen to the poem. Try to make pictures in your head. Tell someone about the pictures you saw. Read the poem yourself. Let new pictures come to your head. Show your ideas. You can write or draw.

Spider Webs

You are going to make a spider web of words, pictures, and ideas! Write the name of the poem in the middle of a blank page. Circle it. Write some words or pictures it makes you think of. Make lines to join them to the name of the poem. Read the poem. Look for words in the poem that give you strong pictures or ideas. Add more words and ideas to your web. Show your web to a friend. Tell about it.

Partners in Poetry

Find a partner. Read the name of the poem together. With your partner, make up two questions about the poem. Read the poem together. Talk about your ideas: What parts did you like? Were your questions answered? Read the poem again. Decide how you will show your ideas. You can use both words and pictures. You might make a web or a cartoon. Work together to show your ideas.

I Noticed, I Wondered, I Liked

Read the poem. Close your eyes and let ideas come into your head. Read the poem again. You can write or draw on the page if you want. Tell one thing you noticed about the poem. Tell one thing you wondered about or wanted to know. Tell one thing you liked.

Take A Poem Home To Meet Your Family!

Find a poem you would like to take home to read with your family. Read the poem to some-

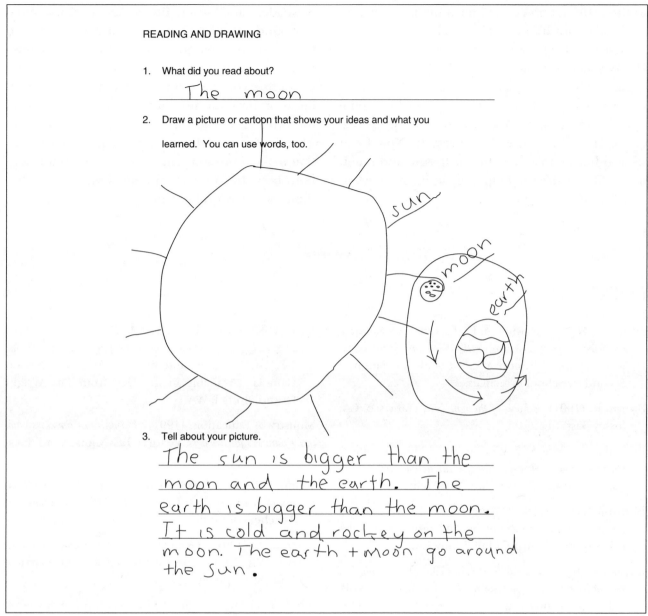

READING AND DRAWING

1. What did you read about?

    The moon

2. Draw a picture or cartoon that shows your ideas and what you

    learned. You can use words, too.

3. Tell about your picture.

    The sun is bigger than the moon and the earth. The earth is bigger than the moon. It is cold and rockey on the moon. The earth + moon go around the sun.

Figure 11   Steven's Reading and Drawing Response

one in your family. Talk about your ideas and the pictures in your head. Remember to encourage other people's ideas. Let them read the poem to you. Work together to show your ideas in pictures or words. Write a notice together telling your teacher how you got along.

Show Your Ideas

Read the poem. Remember you can doodle or draw as you read. Think about the words and ideas. Read the poem over and over again. Show your ideas, feelings, and pictures. You can use words, pictures, cartoons, webs or anything you like.

Responses to all of these options can be connected to a rating scale similar to the one described in "Depth of Understanding" above. That would, of course, be determined by the teacher's purpose in providing assessment feedback.

Steven, who is eight, read the selection about the moon which prompted Stina to ask, "How did you get all this vital information?" Steven, however, brought quite different experiences and interests to the activity, and created meaning in a way that made sense for him (see Figure 11).

Steven is interested in how the universe works. He likes books about space and understands that some kinds of information are most clearly conveyed in a diagram. Steven spent quite a bit of time figuring out exactly how best to develop his diagram. He is pleased with the result: "Now I can show other people how the earth, sun, and moon move. My picture will help them understand when I explain it."

Readers and writers **do** work toward meaning. The kinds of trivial, artificial, and disconnected tasks that once masqueraded as "reading comprehension," were, in fact, unlikely to tell us anything about how young readers created meaning. This is because there was no real meaning to create—all too often, it was just a trick. On the other hand, when we invite children to participate in activities that make sense to them, we develop insights into both **how** they understand and **what** they understand of the world of print.

REFERENCES

Archbald, D. A., & Newmann, F. M. (1988). *Beyond standardized testing: Assessing authentic achievement in the secondary school.* Reston, VA: National Association of Secondary School Principals.

Brown, R. (1991). *Schools of thought.* San Francisco, CA: Jossey-Bass.

Brownlie, F., Close, S., & Wingren, L. (1990). *Tomorrow's classroom today: Strategies for creating active readers, writers, and thinkers.* Portsmouth, NH: Heinemann.

Brownlie, F., Close, S., & Wingren, L. (1988). *Reaching for higher thought: Reading, writing, thinking strategies.* Edmonton, AL: Arnold Publishing Ltd.

Jeroski, S., Brownlie, F., & Kaser, L. (1990a). *Reading and responding: Evaluation resources for your classroom.* (Vols. 1-2: Late primary and primary). Toronto, ON: Nelson Canada. (Available in the U.S. from The Wright Group, Bothel, WA.)

Jeroski, S., Brownlie, F., & Kaser, L. (1990b). *Reading and responding: Evaluation resources for your classroom.* (Vols. 1-3: Grades 4, 5, and 6). Toronto, ON: Nelson Canada. (Available in the U.S. from The Wright Group, Bothel, WA.)

Ministry of Education. (1991). *Thinking in the classroom: Resources for teachers.* Victoria, BC: Ministry of Education.

Nelms, B. F. (Ed.) (1988). *Literature in the classroom: Readers, texts, and contexts.* Urbana, IL: National Council of Teachers of English.

Perrone, V. (1991). *Expanding student assessment.* Alexandria, VA: Association for Supervision and Curriculum Development.

Smith, F. (1991). *To think.* Columbia, NY: Teachers College Press.

ASSESSMENT:
A THOUGHTFUL PROCESS

—

Steven Ferrara and Jay McTighe

The development of student thinking abilities has been recognized as a basic educational goal for the information age (Secretary's Commission on Achieving Necessary Skills, 1991; McTighe & Schollenberger, 1991). With this recognition in mind, many teachers are seeking to involve their students in the meaningful application of knowledge and skills, rather than simply having them memorize facts. These teachers seek to create a thoughtful classroom in which students assume a greater responsibility for constructing meaning for themselves. Such a classroom emphasizes active learning, involving students in working together to examine issues, solve problems, and communicate ideas. The teacher adopts a more facilitative role, guiding students in individual and group work, rather than merely dispensing information.

In addition to changing classroom expectations and the role of teachers and students, such an instructional orientation has implications for the ways in which student learning is assessed. A greater emphasis is placed on the use of assessments that involve students in more "authentic" tasks[1], measure a variety of important learning outcomes, and reflect effective instructional models. Unfortunately, many teachers find that they have received little relevant training in methods of classroom assessment (Stiggins, 1991), either through university coursework or inservice workshops.

In this chapter, we focus on the classroom as we examine principles of sound classroom assessment, introduce a planning process and a framework for selecting appropriate assessment methods, and provide illustrations of the process and framework in use. Rather than examining specific assessment methods in detail, our concentration is on helping teachers develop thoughtful classroom assessments.[2]

PRINCIPLES OF SOUND CLASSROOM ASSESSMENT

The term *assessment* refers to "any systematic basis for making inferences about characteristics of people, usually based on various sources of evidence; the global process of synthesizing information about individuals in order to understand and describe them better" (Brown, 1983, p. 485).[3] Inherent in this definition is an important principle, namely that sound classroom assessment practice requires multiple sources and types of data. Applied to the classroom assessment context, this principle reminds us to rely on more than paper-and-pencil tests to gauge student learning.

To examine the principle of multiple data sources more fully, let's use a photographic analogy. Think of an experience in which someone took a candid photograph of you. You may have been happy if it "captured" you in a pleasing manner. On the other hand, perhaps you were a bit embarrassed because the image was not particularly flattering. In fact, it may have been downright awful, and you may have attempted to get it back so that others would not see it! In either case, would you be willing to say that this single photograph effectively portrays you? At best, it presents a picture of you at a single moment in time within one particular context. In a similar way, the result of a single assessment, be it from a large-scale assessment (district, state, or national test) or an end-of-unit classroom test, provides incomplete information. It would be inappropriate to use such a one-time snapshot of student performance as the sole basis for drawing conclusions about how well a student has achieved desired learning outcomes.

The classroom context offers a distinct advantage over large-scale assessments in that it allows teachers to take frequent samplings of student learning in different contexts. To continue the photographic analogy, classroom assessment enables us to construct a "photo album" containing a variety of pictures taken at different times with different lenses, backgrounds, and compositions. The photo album reveals a richer and more complete picture of each student than any single snapshot provides. Similarly, effective classroom assessment requires multiple sources of data, gathered over time, regarding student learning to enable us to make sound inferences about what our students know and can do.

The use of multiple sources of assessment data is important for summative assessments that form a basis for assigning report card grades. Rather than relying on a single end-of-unit test for assigning grades, effective teachers factor together a variety of sources of information, such as student products, performances, class participation, homework, and conferences. In addition, teachers can use multiple sources of data as the basis for formative assessments. For example, prior to the start of a unit on the Civil War, the teacher might ask students to make a web showing what they already know about this period of history as a means of obtaining information about students' prior knowledge. The teacher might also interview several students at random to check their Civil War awareness. Formative assessment can also be used during instruction to check on student understandings and misconceptions. For instance, teachers often use brief written and oral quizzes and classroom discussions to determine if students have learned course material and can apply instructed skills. Such activities provide teachers with invaluable feedback on their teaching and allows them to adjust instruction to achieve more effective learning.

A second principle of sound classroom assessment practice relates to the relationship between instruction and assessment. It asserts that what teachers assess and how they assess should be congruent with their desired learning outcomes and the instructional methods they use to reach these outcomes. Learning outcomes specify what teachers want their students to know and to be able to do as a result of their educational experiences (Spady and Marshall, 1991). Learning outcomes may consist of knowledge (e.g., the Pythagorean theorem), skills (e.g., a problem-solving procedure), attitudes (e.g., appreciation of literature), or "habits of mind" (e.g., concern for accuracy). Instructional methods may include teacher presentations, cooperative learning, hands-on problem-solving activities, and independent study.

According to this "congruence principle," classroom assessments should be aligned with outcomes and instruction so as to provide valid measures of learning. For example, if teachers want students to demonstrate the capacity to write an effective persuasive essay, then their assessment would include samples of such writing evaluated against specified criteria. The use of a multiple-choice exam, in this case, would be an ill-suited measure of the intended outcome. Likewise, if teachers wish to develop students' ability to work collaboratively on a research project, then they would want to assess group processes and products as well as individual performance. Aligning assessment with curriculum and instruction is crucial because what and how teachers assess sends a clear message to students about what knowledge, skills, processes, and attitudes are most important for them to learn and develop.

Selecting Classroom Assessment Methods

As with instruction, a variety of assessment approaches are available. The selection of methods for gathering information on students' learning should be determined, in part, by the congruence of these methods with desired outcomes and instructional approaches. In addition, teachers should consider at least three other factors when selecting assessment methods. First, assessment methods should be appropriate to the purpose(s) of, and the audience(s) for, a classroom assessment. For example, norm-referenced tests, such as the Iowa Tests of Basic Skills, are used primarily to satisfy demands for educational accountability. Their results are reported to the legislature, the Board of Education, school administrators, parents, and the general public. They are generally designed to determine how well students have learned particular concepts and skills as compared to other students in a norm group. However, at the classroom level, teachers are generally more interested in using assessments for diagnosing student needs, informing students and parents about progress, adjusting instruction, and motivating students. These varying purposes and audiences should determine the methods of assessment and the means by which the results are communicated.

A second consideration concerns the issue of reliability. Reliability refers to the dependability and consistency of assessment results. For instance, a writing assessment would be considered reliable when different raters assign similar scores to the same essays. Likewise, an observation checklist can be used reliably as long as teachers are careful to recognize that their ratings may differ from occasion to occasion (e.g., Monday morning versus Friday afternoon), and that their perceptions of individual students may be influenced by their attitudes toward each student.

Finally, practicality must be considered when selecting assessment methods for the classroom. For example, while a science fair project/exhibition may provide a valid and reliable means of assessing student learning in a science class, the time required to prepare and present the project and the space needed for displaying the exhibit may be difficult to obtain in some schools.

THE FRAMEWORK OF ASSESSMENT APPROACHES

How then do we go about selecting appropriate assessment approaches to use in our classrooms? The Framework of Assessment Approaches[4] (Figure 1) offers a systematic guide to help select and develop assessment methods for the classroom.

Assessment Approaches

Each of the five columns in the framework presents an assessment approach or format. Organizing the five approaches in this way highlights the most important similarities of the methods in the same column, and the most useful distinctions between the methods in different columns. However, the methods could be categorized differently. For example, "essays" could be listed under "constructed response formats," and "oral questioning" might be included under "performance assessments" or "constructed response formats."

The most widely used approaches to classroom assessment appear in the first and second columns. In **selected response formats**, students select the one correct or best answer from several alternatives, for example, multiple-choice items on the Comprehensive Tests of Basic Skills. In **constructed response formats** students generate a response (usually short) to an open-ended question, problem, or task, for example, when students are asked to label a diagram or chart, explain their reasoning, or show their work. However, growing recognition of the limitations of these approaches has led to calls for richer, more "authentic" assessment approaches (National Commission on Testing and Public Policy, 1990), like those listed under the third, fourth, and fifth columns. Teachers may use **product assessments** in which students create tangible products, such as a research paper, science fair project, or art portfolio. They may also use **perfor-**

A FRAMEWORK OF ASSESSMENT APPROACHES

SELECTED RESPONSE Formats	CONSTRUCTED RESPONSE Formats	PRODUCT Assessments	PERFORMANCE Assessments	PROCESS-FOCUSED Assessments
1. multiple choice 2. true/false 3. matching	4. fill in the blank 5. label a diagram 6. short answer 7. "show your work" 8. concept map 9. figural representation	WRITTEN 10. essay, story, or poem 11. research report 12. writing portfolio 13. diary or journal OTHER 14. science fair project 15. art exhibit or portfolio	16. musical, dance, or dramatic performance 17. science lab demonstration 18. typing test 19. athletic competition 20. debate 21. oral presentation	22. oral questioning 23. interview 24. think aloud 25. learning log 26. process folio 27. kid watching

Figure 1   A Framework of Assessment Approaches

mance assessments in which students engage in actual performances that require demonstrations of desired knowledge and skills, for example, oral presentations, demonstrations, or use of an online database to gather information. We draw a distinction between product and performance assessments to highlight the difference between evaluating a performance itself (e.g., students conducting a science lab demonstration) and evaluating the product of a performance (e.g., a science lab report). We further distinguish process-focused assessments, in which teachers elicit students' thinking processes (e.g., process observing, "think alouds"), because they are explicitly intended to provide insight into students' thinking processes rather than the products and performances that result from their thinking.

Assessment Methods

The methods listed in each column of Figure 1 are intended to characterize each assessment approach rather than exhaustively define it. Some of these methods are clearly associated with testing, such as the multiple-choice items. Less formal methods, such as oral questioning and "kid watching," may not necessarily be associated with classroom assessment (Haertel, Ferrara, Korpi, & Prescott, 1984). However, use of these informal methods is essential to providing a complete picture of student learning.

It may be useful to provide examples of these methods. Methods one through five in the framework are generally familiar to teachers because they are among the most widely used classroom assessment methods. They are probably most often used to find out whether or not students can recall and understand factual information.[5]

In contrast, teachers use other assessment methods to get beyond the "correct" answer to more open-ended tasks in which an array of responses is acceptable and expected. Teachers often include short-answer questions in their tests (method six), for example, to pose questions that may not have a single correct or best answer. Math teachers may require students to "show their work" (method seven) to determine what steps students follow in solving multi-step problems. Concept maps, semantic webs (Novak and Gowin, 1984), and other figural representations (methods eight and nine) allow teachers to gain insight into how students organize facts and concepts and to gauge the accuracy and complexity of their understandings.

Teachers assign essays and longer writing assignments such as research reports (methods ten and eleven) to provide feedback about students' abilities to locate and organize information and express ideas clearly in written form. In recent years, we have witnessed increased use of portfolios (method twelve) in language arts and other subject areas to collect representative student work and to chronicle development over time. Product exhibitions, such as science fair projects and art exhibits (methods fourteen and fifteen), allow students to demonstrate their ability to apply knowledge and skills in authentic contexts.

Performance assessments are especially well suited to certain content areas since they allow teachers and others to directly observe the application of desired skills. For example, teachers grade or critique students as they perform a musical piece, demonstrate a laboratory procedure, type for speed and accuracy, or participate in an athletic competition (methods sixteen through nineteen). Teachers may also organize debates and assign oral reports (methods twenty and twenty-one) in order to evaluate students' performances.

Determining what knowledge, thinking skills, and processes students apply in classroom learning situations requires classroom assessment methods that focus directly on thinking processes. Teachers may elicit students' thinking processes using oral questions like "How are these two things alike and different?" (method twenty-two); by interviewing students (method twenty-three) regarding the procedures they follow to generate products or what they think about while performing a task; or by asking students to "think out loud" (method twenty-four) as they solve a problem or make a decision. In addition, teachers may ask students to document their thinking processes by keeping a diary, learning log (method twenty-five), or process folio (method twenty-six). Finally, teachers can learn

about students' thinking processes by watching students individually and in groups as they function in the classroom—that is, by "kid watching" (method twenty-seven). This method is especially well suited to assessing the development of habits of mind, such as persistence and open-mindedness.

We provide these brief examples to highlight the variety of classroom assessment methods available to teachers. How then do we decide which approaches and methods to use? How can we make classroom assessments more thoughtful, sound, and effective? The following process offers a systematic guide to planning and evaluating classroom assessments.

A PROCESS FOR PLANNING AND CONDUCTING CLASSROOM ASSESSMENTS

Assessment is an essential component of the teaching-learning process. Without effective classroom assessment, it is impossible for us to know whether our students are learning what we want them to learn. We have described briefly a framework of assessment approaches and methods available to teachers. In the remainder of this chapter we present a process for planning, administering, and interpreting results from classroom assessments. An Assessment Planning Chart assists in this process. We then illustrate the process in use.

Six Steps for Planning, Administering, and Interpreting Classroom Assessments

1. Identify the learning outcomes to be assessed, the purposes for the assessment, and the audiences for the assessment results.

2. Select methods from the Framework of Assessment Approaches in Figure 1 to assess the outcomes that are appropriate to your assessment purposes and audiences.

3. Record your decisions from steps one and two in an Assessment Planning Chart (see Figure 3). Evaluate the appropriateness of the:

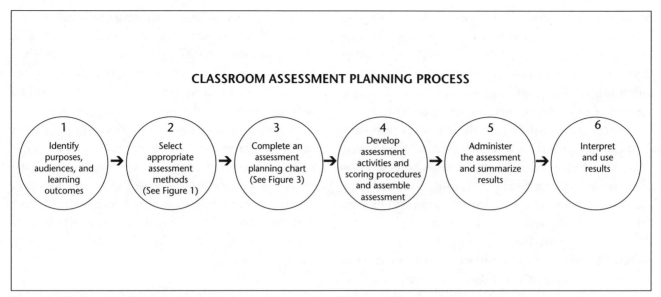

Figure 2   Six Steps for Planning, Administering, and Interpreting Classroom Assessments

a. assessment approaches and methods you have chosen for your assessment outcomes, purposes, and audiences.

b. time allotted to each outcome and assessment activity and the time required to administer, score, and interpret all assessments.

4. Develop and assemble assessment activities and scoring procedures.

5. Administer the assessment and score, rate, or otherwise summarize the results of the assessment for your audiences.

6. Interpret and use the results, keeping in mind the learning outcomes you assessed and your assessment purposes and audiences. Consider potential consequences of your planned uses of the assessment results.[6]

In the next section we present an Assessment Planning Chart, a helpful tool for use in the classroom assessment planning process.

Assessment Planning Chart

Architects create blueprints to communicate their overall vision for a building and to specify details for a builder. The builder then constructs the architect's vision by executing the details in the blueprint. The result is a safe and long-lasting (and,

hopefully, aesthetically pleasing) building. Similarly, classroom teachers can create assessment blueprints to communicate their overall vision for an assessment and to specify details such as outcomes to be assessed and assessment methods to be used. They then can use the blueprint to construct the envisioned assessment, developing activities that assess what has been specified. The result is twofold. First, the assessment that is developed from the blueprint produces valid information about what students know and can do. Second, the assessment clearly communicates to students what they should know and be able to do and what they actually know and can do.

An Assessment Planning Chart[7] is a guide to completing the first two steps in the classroom assessment planning process: identifying learning outcomes to be assessed and selecting appropriate assessment methods from the Framework of Assessment Approaches. The Assessment Planning Chart also helps us reinforce the principles of multiple sources of data and the congruence of assessment and instruction discussed earlier. The generic Assessment Planning Chart (Figure 3) contains three elements necessary for planning thoughtful classroom assessments: content and process outcomes to be assessed, assessment methods to be used, and the amount of assessment time to be allotted to each outcome and method. Teachers can adapt the

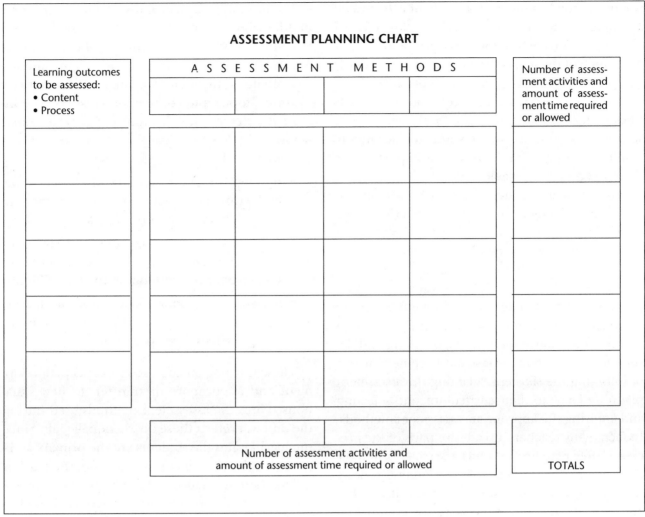

Figure 3   Assessment Planning Chart

generic Assessment Planning Chart to their specific needs and situations, as we illustrate at the end of this chapter.

Using the Assessment Planning Chart

In this section we describe steps to complete an assessment planning chart. First, list each outcome to be assessed, one per row, specifying the desired content, skill or process, and habit of mind. Second, after referring to the Framework of Assessment Approaches, write in one or more assessment methods to assess each outcome, one per column. Next, determine the number of assessment activities appropriate for each content, process, habit, and assessment method. This is a matter of deciding the portion of the total assessment activities and time that should be allocated to

each outcome using each assessment method. It is appropriate to write in numbers or percentages of assessment activities.

Space is provided at the end of each row and column to summarize the coverage of outcomes and use of each assessment method. Teachers can enter in each space the number of activities and amount of assessment time required or allowed to complete the assessment activities in each row and column. The same information can be entered in the space at the lower right-hand corner of the Assessment Planning Chart for a total assessment time. Teachers can refer to and modify each row total to clarify and control how much of any classroom assessment is devoted to each listed outcome, especially if each row total is expressed as a percentage of the total number of assessment activities or assessment time. Likewise, teachers can refer to and modify the column totals to clarify and control how much of the total assessment each method will comprise. Controlling the emphasis placed on each assessed outcome and the reliance on each assessment method is important for thoughtful and sound classroom assessments and for accurately communicating to students what is important for them to know and be able to do.

While teachers generally do not question the usefulness of blueprints like the generic Assessment Planning Chart, they often express concern that such tools are too cumbersome and time consuming to use. We disagree. Experience has shown that, with practice, use of the assessment planning process and tools like the Assessment Planning Chart becomes automatic and efficient. When teachers internalize the process, planning and developing a classroom assessment become a matter of following the six steps, adapting the assessment planning chart to their curriculum, and selecting and applying the appropriate assessment methods. In fact, many teachers already use parts of the process as they plan and conduct assessments in their classrooms. An advantage of the planning process we describe here is its systematic nature; it specifies and clarifies the steps necessary for conducting sound classroom assessments. Similarly, the Assessment Planning Chart explicitly links desired learning outcomes with appropriate assessment methods. Finally, the Framework of Assessment Approaches suggests a wider array of assessment methods than teachers may currently consider and use. The Assessment Planning Chart can be particularly effective when teachers work together to develop "banks" of activities to assess common instructional outcomes. Use of such a systematic planning process by grade-level or department teams results in more coordinated, valid, and reliable classroom assessments.

An Illustration of the Classroom Assessment Planning Process

To demonstrate the classroom assessment planning process, using the Framework of Assessment Approaches and Assessment Planning Chart, we will refer to a hypothetical instructional unit for a middle school social studies class. Imagine a three-week-long instructional unit in which students explore the concepts of citizens' "rights and responsibilities" through an examination of various historical topics and contemporary issues. The intended outcomes for this unit might be as stated below.

Students will:

- develop an understanding of the concepts and principles involved in determining citizens' rights and responsibilities.

- increase their knowledge and appreciation of the rights and responsibilities assured to United States citizens under the Bill of Rights.

- analyze contemporary issues involving citizens' rights and responsibilities by applying concepts and principles developed during the unit.

These learning outcomes stress concept development and application, or transfer, to new situations. Thus, the assessment methods used during the unit will reflect these instructional goals. Since the teacher and the students are the primary audiences for the assessment information, the teacher will use both formative and summative assessments during the unit. Information gained from the formative assessment activities will help the teacher determine if students are developing appropriate understandings of the concepts and principles so that he or she can adjust instruction as necessary and inform students about their progress. Summative assessment activities will be used similarly and as the basis for evaluating student performance in order to assign grades. By identifying purposes, audiences, and learning outcomes, Step 1 in the assessment planning process is complete.

Step 2 is completed by reviewing the methods in the Framework of Assessment Approaches and by selecting several assessment methods appropriate for the identified purposes, audiences, and learning outcomes. The teacher may decide that the summative assessments will include:

- *Written Test.* An in-class test near the end of the unit. Students will write a brief analysis of the rights and responsibilities contained within a specified constitutional amendment, on freedom of speech, for example.

- *Essay.* A persuasive essay that students will develop during the final days of the unit. They will state and defend their views on whether private citizens in the 1990s should be allowed to own firearms. Students will draft and refine these essays based on what they have learned in class, from outside reading and research, and from an in-class debate.

- *Debates.* Students will work on one of several teams to prepare for participation in one of several in-class debates. These debates will address several questions relevant to ownership of firearms: whether the need for U.S. citizens to own firearms for personal protection has increased or decreased since the late 18th century; whether citizens are likely to be more or less safe if the manufacture and sale of firearms were restricted; and whether an increase in safety assumed to result from such restrictions warrants denying citizens the right to bear arms guaranteed in the Bill of Rights.

In order to adjust instructional activities as necessary and to inform students throughout the unit regarding their progress on the learning outcomes for the unit, the teacher has planned several formative assessment activities. Some of these activities will assess students' understandings of the concepts of rights and responsibilities:

- *Written List.* Early in the unit, the teacher will have students work in small groups to discuss the rights guaranteed them as citizens of the United States. Following the discussion, students will individually prepare a written list of their constitutional rights as they understand them. Student responses to this open-ended assessment activity will give the teacher insight into students' understanding of important unit concepts.

- *Oral Questions.* Throughout the unit, the teacher will lead discussions and pose oral questions to the class to determine their understandings of, and ability to apply, the concepts and principles of citizens' rights and responsibilities.

Other formative assessment activities will focus on students' thinking strategies as they prepare for the debates:

- *Kid Watching.* As students work in teams to prepare for the debates, the teacher will listen and observe to determine if they are addressing relevant issues, employing relevant information, developing clear arguments, supporting their arguments, anticipating rebuttals, developing responses, and acknowledging different points of view.

- *Think-Aloud Activities.* Throughout the unit, the teacher will ask students to describe their reasoning processes by thinking out loud. By listening to students as they articulate their thoughts, the teacher can identify misconceptions and fallacious reasoning so as to provide needed clarification or assistance.

Completing Step 3 of the classroom assessment planning process will involve developing an Assessment Planning Chart that summarizes all of the assessment activities planned for the unit. An example is provided in Figure 4.

In this example, we have listed the three intended unit outcomes and the seven assessment activities planned for this unit. We have also indicated numbers of assessment activities and estimated the amount of time required for each activity. With this chart, the teacher has a clear picture of the activities and amounts of time devoted to assessing each outcome and the portion of all assessment activities each method comprises. The completed chart enables the teacher to evaluate the appropriateness and degree of balance between the learning outcomes and methods of assessment. As a result of this step, the teacher may decide to change the emphasis on one or another of the outcomes or to devote more or less time to one or more of the assessment activities. In addition to using the Assessment Planning Chart for planning assessments in an entire unit, the chart can be used to develop a single assessment, such as an end-of-unit test.

Completing Steps 4 through 6 in the process involves developing, administering, scoring, and interpreting the results from the in-class short-answer

ASSESSMENT PLANNING CHART
for unit on "rights and responsibilities"

| | ASSESSMENT METHODS | | | | | | | |
| | FORMATIVE ASSESSMENTS | | | | SUMMATIVE ASSESSMENTS | | | |
OUTCOMES	List	Oral Questions	Kid Watching	"Think-Aloud"	Paper-and-Pencil Test	Essay	Debate	Summary of Assessment Activities
1 Knowledge	open-ended list of rights: 5-10 min. in groups, 5 min. individual work	5-10 questions estimated: 1 minute each	4-5 student groups 30 minutes		1 analysis 15-25 minutes	1 hour		- all seven methods used
2 Understanding				5-10 students 5 minutes each			3 debates 30 minutes each	- oral quest. - kid watching - think-aloud - test - essay - debate
3 Application								- think-aloud - essay - debate
Estimated time for assessment activities	10-15 minutes	5-10 minutes	30 minutes	25-50 minutes	15-25 minutes	1 hour	1 1/2 hours	3 hrs. 55 min. to 4hrs. 40 min.

Figure 4 Sample Assessment Planning Chart

test, oral discussion questions, and all other planned assessment activities. Step 4 is probably the most labor-intensive part of the classroom assessment planning process. In this step the teacher will develop, or select from an existing bank, assessment activities and accompanying scoring procedures and assemble the activities into a form for use with students. For example, the teacher might jot down notes for the listing activity, topics for oral questions, focuses for kid watching and think-aloud activities. But the teacher may want to provide the in-class test, persuasive essay prompt, and debate team assignments and topics to the students more formally and in writing.

Step 5 involves administering each assessment activity, scoring or otherwise evaluating student responses, and summarizing the qualities and charac-teristics of student responses. Using the "rights and responsibilities" unit to illustrate, the teacher may decide to evaluate students' responses in each summative assessment by giving one to two points for each written summary in the in-class test and writing comments in the margins regarding the comprehensiveness and accuracy of each summary; by rating the persuasive essay using a four- or six-point holistic scoring system that focuses on characteristics of persuasive writing and circling any grammatical errors; and by evaluating students' performances in the debates on several dimensions, such as their observance of rules of debating (which the teacher provided as part of the unit), oral discourse style, persuasiveness of arguments, and effectiveness in rebuttals. The teacher may decide to evaluate students' responses to the formative assessment less formally. For example, the teacher may provide one- or two-word comments on student lists of Constitutional rights, only oral comments on students' responses during oral questioning, and a short written note or brief conversation with students after the kid-watching and think-aloud activities. Decisions such as these are determined by the purposes and audiences for each assessment activity.

In the final step of this process, Step 6, the teacher will communicate interpretations, conclusions, decisions, and other actions to take based on the assessment results. As in Steps 1 through 5, the teacher will communicate in ways that are appropriate for students, parents, administrators, teachers, and other audiences. For instance, the teacher may have adjusted instructional activities based on what he or she learned from the four formative assessment activities and told the students about these adjustments. In contrast, the teacher may inform students of their scores on the three summative assessments, perhaps indicating letter grades corresponding to each score, and incorporate these scores into the semester course grade. In order to communicate to students what is expected of them during the unit, the teacher would have informed students ahead of time how each assessment activity was to be evaluated and used. The information from all seven assessment activities could also be used for parent conferences and mid-semester progress reports of student performance and progress.

CLOSING

Effective assessment is part of effective teaching and learning (Schafer, 1991). In this chapter we have discussed principles of sound assessment, described a process for systematically planning classroom assessments, provided a framework for selecting assessment approaches and methods, and illustrated the use of the planning process. While

we could have presented additional principles and practices of classroom assessment, we believe that teachers can go a long way toward developing more thoughtful classroom assessments by applying the ideas and tools in this chapter.

> Authors' note: Our thanks to the Maryland Working Group on Assessing Thinking for their work on the Framework of Assessment Approaches, to Susan Ciotta and Sandi Benson for their fine work on the graphic displays, and to Barbara Reeves for her insightful comments on a draft of this chapter.

NOTES

1. Defined as tasks that are valued in their own right (Linn, Baker, & Dunbar, 1991) because they require students to directly apply valued skills, processes, and knowledge.

2. Thoughtful classroom assessments result from deliberate and systematic planning whereby teachers select methods of assessment that are congruent with their desired learning outcomes and their methods of instruction.

3. Classroom assessments can include paper-pencil tests, oral and written quizzes, homework assignments, class discussions, and other classroom activities in which teachers gather information about student learning. While the terms *assessment*, *test*, *evaluation*, and *measurement* are often used interchangeably, we use the term *assessment*, as defined in this footnote, throughout this chapter.

4. The Framework of Assessment Approaches is based on the work of the Maryland Working Group on Assessing Thinking, whose members during 1987-1990 included state and local school system staff and university faculty in instruction and assessment.

5. However, we stress that these methods are not limited to only this purpose. Many writers and speakers have amply demonstrated the use of multiple-choice items to assess, for example, students' reasoning processes in science and mathematics as well as to determine if students can select a correct answer from among alternatives.

6. There can be negative or positive consequences to our use of assessment results. For example, placing too much faith in a multiple-choice test of science knowledge could mislead a teacher into believing that a student is adequately prepared to perform a laboratory experiment involving chemicals.

7. We have borrowed the term, Assessment Planning Chart, from Stiggins, Rubel, and Quellmalz (1988).

REFERENCES

Brown, F. G. (1983). *Principles of educational and psychological testing* (3rd ed.). New York: Holt, Rhinehart and Winston.

Haertel, E., Ferrara, S., Korpi, M., & Prescott, B. (1984). *Testing in secondary schools: Student perspectives.* Paper presented at the annual meeting of the American Educational Research Association, New Orleans.

Linn, R. L., Baker, E. L., & Dunbar, S. B. (1991). Complex, performance-based assessment: Expectations and validation criteria. *Educational Researcher, 20*(8), 15-21.

McTighe, J., & Schollenberger, J. (1991). Why teach thinking: A statement of rationale. In A. Costa (Ed.), *Developing minds: A resource book for teaching thinking* (rev. ed.) (pp. 2-5). Alexandria, VA: Association for Supervision and Curriculum Development.

National Commission on Testing and Public Policy. (1990). *From gatekeeper to gateway: Testing in America.* Chestnut Hill, MA: Boston College.

Novak, J. D., & Gowin, B. D. (1984). *Learning how to learn.* New York: Cambridge University Press.

Schafer, W. D. (1991). Essential assessment skills in professional education of teachers. *Educational Measurement: Issues and Practice, 10*(1), 3-6, 12.

Secretary's Commission on Achieving Necessary Skills. (1991). *What work requires of schools: A SCANS report for America 2000.* Washington, DC: U.S. Department of Labor.

Spady, W. G., & Marshall, K. J. (1991). Beyond traditional outcome-based education. *Educational Leadership, 49*(2), 67-75.

Stiggins, R. J. (1991). Relevant classroom assessment training for teachers. *Educational Measurement: Issues and Practice, 10*(1), 7-12.

Stiggins, R. J., Rubel, E., & Quellmalz, E. (1988). *Measuring thinking skills in the classroom* (rev. ed.). Washington, DC: National Education Association.

THE MOST SIGNIFICANT OUTCOME

—

Robin Fogarty

Our mission as educators is to help every child become a more active, engaged, committed, and skillful learner, not just for a test, but for a lifetime.—James Bellanca

WHY TEACH FOR TRANSFER?

Transfer of learning simply means the use in a new context of something learned in an earlier context.

All teaching is for transfer. All learning is for transfer. It's that simple. Yet considerable research shows that a startling amount of the knowledge that people acquire in subject matter instruction is "inert." This means that the knowledge is there in memory for the multiple-choice quiz, but the knowledge is passive. It is not retrieved in the context of active problem solving or creativity, such as writing an essay. Inert knowledge does not contribute much to the cognitive ability of the learner except for performance on school quizzes. One of the goals of teaching for transfer is teaching for active rather than inert knowledge.

The mission of the thinking classroom is to extend learning, to bridge the old to the new, and to lead students toward relevant transfer and use of knowledge across academic content and into life situations. Once we accept this mission, we explicitly target skills, concepts, and attitudes for transfer. Once targeted, we mediate or shepherd the transfer of learning within the content we teach, across to other disciplines, and into life situations.

WHAT ARE THE LEVELS OF TRANSFER?

Once transfer of learning becomes the targeted outcome, the search for ways to assess that outcome of course follows. Transfer of learning can be assessed by comparison with a continuum of transfer behavior. This continuum has been developed as a tracking or assessment tool. With it the teacher can begin to track students' transfer, and learners can begin to reflect—using skills of metacognition—on their own levels of transfer.

The continuum in Figure 1 represents levels of transfer that range from simple or near transfer to more complex or far-reaching transfer. Six distinctions are made depicting learner dispositions that overlook, duplicate, replicate, integrate, map, and innovate with transfer. The model is framed, however, by the philosophical stance that these various levels of transfer offer evidence that is extremely situ-

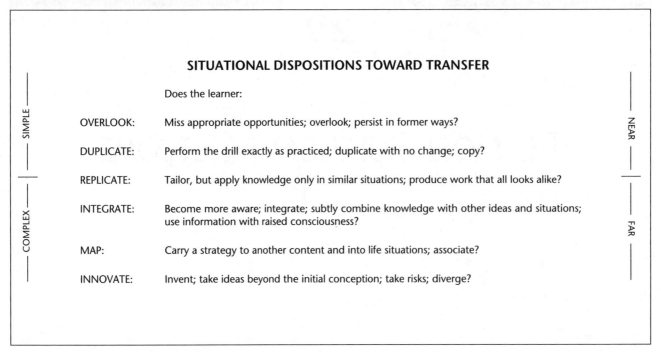

SITUATIONAL DISPOSITIONS TOWARD TRANSFER

Does the learner:

OVERLOOK: Miss appropriate opportunities; overlook; persist in former ways?

DUPLICATE: Perform the drill exactly as practiced; duplicate with no change; copy?

REPLICATE: Tailor, but apply knowledge only in similar situations; produce work that all looks alike?

INTEGRATE: Become more aware; integrate; subtly combine knowledge with other ideas and situations; use information with raised consciousness?

MAP: Carry a strategy to another content and into life situations; associate?

INNOVATE: Invent; take ideas beyond the initial conception; take risks; diverge?

SIMPLE / COMPLEX NEAR / FAR

Figure 1   Situational Dispositions Toward Transfer

ational. That is to say, transfer of learning—using what is learned in one context in an entirely new context—seems to depend on a number of significant variables.

For example, learner dispositions to internalize and apply ideas, concepts, skills, and attitudes may depend on past knowledge and prior experience (How much background does the learner have?); the physical learning environment (Is the climate conducive to learning?); the match between teaching and learning styles (Is the learner enabled by the ways the material is being presented?); the feelings, mood, and emotional state of the learner and teacher (Does the learner [or teacher] have affective variables that are enhancing or blocking learning?) and innumerable other external and internal influences. Thus, the continuum is presented simply as a loose framework of situational dispositions toward transfer. In no way is the model intended for judgmental, summative evaluation. The examples are offered as guides to provide insight into student transfer both for the teacher or observer and the student or learner.

In Figure 2, each of the six situational dispositions for transfer are represented both figuratively and graphically. Each disposition toward transfer is defined and elaborated with classroom examples of what one might see and hear from students at each level. To know what it looks like and what it sounds like provides the concrete clues to the level of transfer occurring.

We *see* in student work, in essence, collected artifacts that provide graphic evidence of transfer. Similarly, what we *hear* students say gives verbal clues to the personal connection making that goes on in their thought processes. Both the graphic representation of students' thinking and the oral articulation of how they are internalizing ideas are helpful (See Figures 2 and 3). One provides evidence of the external product of transfer, while the other provides evidence of the internal process of making the transfer. Both are powerful cues that suggest where students are in the transfer process; what they have learned and how they're using it.

Overlooking Transfer

Ollie the Head-in-the-sand Ostrich overlooks transfer. This learner misses appropriate opportunities, persists in former ways, and may be intentionally or unintentionally overlooking the opportunities for transfer. Sometimes learners choose not to use something new. Whatever the stated reasons—"The com-

LOOKING AND LISTENING FOR TRANSER

Model	Illustration	Transfer Disposition	Looks Like	Sounds Like
BIRDS Ollie the Head-in-the-sand Ostrich		Overlooks	Persists in writing in manuscript form rather than cursive. (New skill overlooked or avoided.)	*"I get it right on the dittos, but I forget to use punctuation when I write an essay."* (Not applying mechanical learning.)
Dan the Drilling Woodpecker		Duplicates	Plagiarism is the most obvious student artifact of duplication. (Unable to synthesize in own words.)	*"Mine is not to question why— just invert and multiply."* [When dividing fractions.] (No understanding of what she or he is doing.)
Laura the Look-alike Penguin		Replicates	"Bed to Bed" or narrative style. "He got up. He did this. He went to bed." or "He was born. He did this. He died." (Student portfolio of work never varies.)	*"Paragraphing means I must have three 'indents' per page."* (Tailors into own story or essay, but paragraphs inappropriately.)
Jonathan Livingston Seagull		Integrates	Student writing essay incorporates newly learned French words. (Applying: weaving old and new.)	*"I always try to guess (predict) what's gonna happen next on T.V. shows."* (Connects to prior knowledge and experience; relates what's learned to personal experience.)
Cathy the Carrier Pigeon		Maps	Graphs information for a social studies report with the help of the math teacher to actually design the graphs. (Connecting to another.)	From a parent: *"Tina suggested we brainstorm our vacation ideas and rank them to help us decide."* (Carries new skills into life situations.)
Samantha the Soaring Eagle		Innovates	After studying flow charts for computer class, student constructs a Rube Goldberg-type invention. (Innovates; diverges; goes beyond and creates novel.)	*"I took the idea of the Mr. Potato Head and created a mix-and-match grid of ideas for our Earth Day project."* (Generalizes ideas from experience and transfers creatively.)

Figure 2   Looking and Listening For Transfer

ASSESSING TRANSFER

WHAT WE SEE (External Product)	WHAT WE HEAR (Internal Process)
• student work	• student conversations
• collected artifacts	• verbal clues
• concrete evidence	• personal connection making
• graphic representation	• oral articulation

Figure 3   Assessing Transfer

puter takes too long"—these learners sometimes unintentionally overlook an opportunity to apply something in a new context, because they just don't "get it"; they miss the connection. If asked, "Why don't you just multiply the number of words in a line by the number of lines—instead of counting every word?" one of these learners might reply, "Oh? I never thought of that."

Transfer that Duplicates

Dan the Drilling Woodpecker duplicates in transfer. This learner performs the drill or reproduces the product exactly as practiced. There is no deviation or personalization. The transfer appears quite rehearsed, mechanical, directed, and procedural. ("Divide, multiply, subtract. Bring down. Divide, multiply, subtract. Bring down.")

Plagiarism is the ultimate example of duplication. "Where can I get a copy of that?"; "I used the definition verbatim"; or "I need a pattern in order to make this," are all verbal clues to duplicated transfer.

Transfer that Replicates

Laura, the Look-alike Penguin replicates. This learner duplicates, but tailors the learning for personal relevance. Using a given model the learner structures the variables to meet personal needs. ("I used the idea of note cards, but I didn't actually use

cards. I just divided the paper into sections so I could do it on my computer.") However, every application (although modified for relevant use) is used in a similar contextual framework. The learner who replicates exemplifies simple transfer and does not break out of the model she or he establishes.

Transfer that Integrates

Jonathan Livingston Seagull integrates with a raised consciousness. This learner, acutely aware of an idea, combines the new learning with prior knowledge and past experiences. The transfer is subtle and may not always be easy to track because the learning is assimilated so smoothly into the learner's existing framework. In fact, sometimes the learner actually says, "I already knew how to outline." or "I've always done my essays from an outline." It's not new—but the prior learning is refined and enhanced. In this integrated level of complex transfer, the learner folds the new learning in with the old, blending the two together.

Transfer that Maps

Cathy the Carrier Pigeon deliberately moves the learning in one context to a different context. The learner makes explicit bridges by strategically planning future applications. The transfer seems crystal clear and application is made with ease. The learner at this level of transfer might comment,

"I'm going to use the science report on pollution in my communications class. We have to develop a public service commercial message."

What distinguishes this transfer from the previous model of integrated use is the explicitness with which the learner applies the ideas. There is obvious intent to move ideas from one context to another in this learner transfer model and the risk taking required is greater than in the previous levels.

Transfer that Innovates

Samantha (or Sam) the Soaring Eagle innovates. This learner creatively transforms learning by grasping the seeds of an idea and researching, reshaping, reforming, and renaming to such an extent that the original learning may be almost indistinguishable or at least vastly modified in unique ways. This learner might say, "Rather than write about my summer vacation from my point of view, I wrote about it from the point of view of my dog, Rags. I bet you wondered why I called it 'Dog Days of Summer.'" This level of transfer is noted for its novel ideas and the risk taking that accompanies

such creative thinking. Sams are wonderful connection makers—anything goes!

CONCLUSION

The six dispositions of transfer do not necessarily occur in sequence, but there seems to be an inherent hierarchy. The first three are considered simple transfer with minimal risk taking involved, while the last three models seem more complex and require considerable mindfulness and risk taking.

However, teacher and learner knowledge about and awareness of the levels of transfer by themselves increase the likelihood of moving learning along. In other words, once you know about the levels and cues to transfer, you can't *not* know! The awareness is there. The level of transfer starts to be consciously monitored with even this relatively minor attention to it. Interestingly, this self awareness also seems to be accompanied by a sense of responsibility. Once aware of transfer, learners seem to feel accountable to attempt transfer and to use new ideas. In addition, once teachers and learners put their radar out for evidence of transfer, transfer gets more attention.

———

REFERENCES

Bellanca, J., & Fogarty, R. (1990). *Blueprints for thinking in the cooperative classroom.* Palatine, IL: Skylight Publishing, Inc.

Beyer, B. (1987). *Practical strategies for the teaching of thinking.* Boston: Allyn and Bacon.

Brandt, R. (1988). On teaching thinking: A conversation with Arthur Costa. *Educational Leadership, 45*(7), 11.

Costa, A. (1991). The search for intelligent life. In *The school as a home for the mind.* Palatine, IL: Skylight Publishing, Inc.

Cousins, N. (1981). *Human options.* New York: Norton.

Fogarty, R. (1989). *From training to transfer: The role of creativity in the adult learner.* Doctoral dissertation, Loyola University of Chicago.

Fogarty, R., & Bellanca, J. (1989). *Patterns for thinking: Patterns for transfer.* Palatine, IL: Skylight Publishing, Inc.

Fogarty, R., Perkins, D., & Barell, J. (1991). *The mindful school: How to teach for transfer.* Palatine, IL: Skylight Publishing, Inc.

Hunter, M. (1982). *Teach for transfer.* El Segundo, CA: TIP Publications.

Joyce, B. (1986). *Improving America's schools.* New York: Longman.

Perkins, D. (1988, August 6). Thinking frames. Paper delivered at ASCD Conference on Approaches to Teaching Thinking, Alexandria, VA, p. 14-15.

Perkins, D. (1986). *Knowledge as design.* Hillsdale, NJ: Erlbaum.

Perkins, D., Barell, J., & Fogarty, R. (1989). *Teaching for transfer* (Course Notebook). Palatine, IL: Skylight Publishing, Inc.

Perkins, D., & Salomon, G. (1989, January-February). Are cognitive skills context bound? *Educational Researcher*, pp. 16-25.

Posner, M., & Keele, S. (1973). Skill learning. In R. Travers, (Ed.), *Second handbook of research on teaching.* Chicago: Rand McNally, pp. 805-831.

Tyler, R. (1986/87). The first most significant curriculum events in the twentieth century. *Educational Leadership, 44*(4), 36-37.

Wittrock, M. (1967). Replacement and nonreplacement strategies in children's problem solving. *Journal of Educational Psychology, 58*(2), 69-74.

AUTHORS

Therese Bissen Bard has been on the faculty of the School of Library and Information Studies, University of Hawaii at Manoa for eighteen years. Her areas of specialization are library materials and services for children and young adults.

James Bellanca is president of The IRI Group and Skylight Publishing, Inc., staff development and publishing organizations dedicated to restructuring schools through research-based methods. Jim is the author of *The Cooperative Think Tank* and *Building a Caring, Cooperative Classroom*, as well as co-author of *Blueprints for Thinking in the Cooperative Classroom, Patterns for Thinking: Patterns for Transfer*, and other books on thinking and cooperative learning.

Tina Blythe taught English in public high schools for several years before moving into research at Harvard Project Zero. Her current research focuses on helping middle and high school students gain a deeper understanding of the subjects taught in school (especially literature and writing), and of the purposes for school itself. This work has led to a parallel interest in the nature of collaborations between researchers and teachers.

Faye Brownlie is a staff development consultant in British Columbia, specializing in teaching for thinking, active learning strategies, evaluation, cooperative learning, teacher as researcher, and Year 2000 initiatives. She has co-authored *Reaching for Higher Thought, Tomorrow's Classroom Today*, and *Reading and Responding—Evaluation Resources for Teachers*.

Jean Speer Cameron is assistant superintendent for curriculum and instruction at Elmhurst Community Unit School District 205, Elmhurst, Illinois. She has published journal articles, made presentations at state and national conferences, and taught graduate level classes on the subject of effective staff development.

Arthur L. Costa is professor emeritus of Educational Administration at California State University, Sacramento and past president of the Association for Supervision and Curriculum Development. He is the author of *Enabling Behaviors* and *The School As A Home For The Mind* as well as other

books on thinking and intelligent behavior, and is editor of both editions of ASCD's *Developing Minds*.

Martha E. Crosby is assistant professor in the department of Information and Computer Sciences at the University of Hawaii. Her research interests are in the areas of computer-supported cooperative work and the evaluation of the human use of computer interfaces and applications.

Steven Ferrara is director of student assessment for the Maryland State Department of Education. A specialist in educational measurement and performance assessment, and former high school teacher, he is the National Council on Measurement in Education's at-large representative to the Joint Committee on Testing Practices.

Robin Fogarty is director of training and development of The IRI Group, and serves as the Editor for Skylight Publishing, Inc., as well as COGITARE, the newsletter for the ASCD Network on Teaching Thinking. As author and co-author of numerous books, articles, and videotapes, including *Patterns for Thinking, Blueprints for Thinking in the Cooperative Classroom, Designs for Cooperative Interactions*, and *The Mindful School: How To Integrate The Curricula*, she is a leading national proponent of the thinking classroom.

Howard Gardner is professor of Education and co-director of Project Zero at the Harvard Graduate School of Education, research psychologist at the Boston Veterans Administration Medical Center, and adjunct professor of Neurology at the Boston University School of Medicine. He has written over 250 articles in professional journals and wide-circulation periodicals. Gardner has authored ten books, including *Frames of Mind* and *The Unschooled Mind: How Children Think, How Schools Should Teach*.

Dara Lee Howard, a retired Lieutenant Colonel in the U.S. Air Force, currently instructs at the School of Library and Information Studies at the University of Hawaii. Studying in the area of communications and information sciences at the University of Hawaii, her research interests include information seeking, information retrieval, and cognition.

Sharon Jeroski specializes in research, evaluation, and assessment at Horizon Research and Evaluation Affiliates, Vancouver, BC. Author of several teacher resource books and student textbooks, she has also edited three collections of contemporary short stories for high school students.

David W. Johnson is professor of Educational Psychology with an emphasis in Social Psychology at the University of Minnesota. He is the author of thirty books, including, *Learning Together and Alone: Cooperative, Competitive, and Individualistic Learning, Circles of Learning: Cooperation in the Classroom,* and *Cooperation and Competition: Theory and Research.* He is a recent past editor of the American Educational Research Journal.

Roger T. Johnson is professor of Curriculum and Instruction with an emphasis in Science Education at the University of Minnesota. He has served on task forces examining college policy, environmental quality, science education, math education, elementary education, and cooperative learning. Roger is a leading authority on inquiry teaching and science education and has co-authored numerous books and articles on cooperative learning.

Bena Kallick is a consultant who provides services to school districts, state departments of education, professional organizations, and public sector agencies throughout the United States. Her areas of expertise include group dynamics, creative and critical thinking, and alternative assessment strategies in the classroom. She is author of *Changing Schools Into Communities For Thinking* and co-author of *The Staff Development Manager.*

David Lazear is founder of New Dimensions of Learning in Chicago, Illinois. Facilitator for the ASCD Network on Teaching for Multiple Intelligences, David has had many years of international experience in the development of human capacities for both the public and private sectors. His books include: *Seven Ways of Knowing: Teaching For Multiple Intelligences* and *Seven Ways of Teaching: The Artistry of Teaching With Multiple Intelligences.*

Laura Lipton is an instructional strategist who specializes in instructional design to promote thinking and learning. She is currently director of Educational Consulting Services, and works in the areas of thinking, cooperative learning, cognitive coaching, whole language, and authentic assessment.

Frank T. Lyman is a teacher educator for the University of Maryland, College Park and the Howard County Public Schools. He is an educational inventor and developer known for milestones in teacher education, thinking, and cooperative learning. Lyman was the 1988 recipient of the National Association of Teacher Educators' Distinguished Clinician Award.

Margaret E. McCabe is an education and management consultant, part-time college instructor in teacher and administrator preparation programs, writer, and publisher. Her works include: *The Nurturing Classroom: Developing Self-Esteem* and *Thinking Skills and Responsibility Through Simple Cooperation.*

Jay McTighe works with the Maryland State Department of Education where he administers a statewide school improvement program. He has published articles on thinking in a number of leading journals and books, including *Educational Leadership, Developing Minds,* and *Thinking Skills: Concepts and Techniques,* and has consulted extensively throughout the country in the areas of thinking skills and authentic assessment.

Elliot Y. Merenbloom is director of Middle School Instruction for Baltimore County (Maryland) Public Schools. He has served that district as a classroom teacher, guidance counselor, assistant principal, principal, and curriculum leader for thirty-two years. Mr. Merenbloom wrote two best-selling books for the National Middle School Association, *Developing Effective Middle Schools Through Faculty Participation* and *The Team Process: A Handbook for Teachers.*

Marie Meyer is curriculum and staff development director for a seven-district cooperative. She serves on the conference steering committees for the National Association for Supervision and Curriculum Development and the Board of Directors for the Illinois Staff Development Council, the Illinois Association for Supervision and Curriculum Development, the Illinois Curriculum Council, and the Northern Illinois University Alumni Council.

Carol Booth Olson is director of the UCI Writing Project, and a faculty member in the Department of Education at the University of California, Irvine. She lectures frequently on the thinking/writing connection, the title of her chapter in *Developing Minds: A Resource Book for Teaching Thinking*, and has edited two books, *Practical Ideas for Teaching Writing as a Process* and *Thinking/Writing: Fostering Critical Thinking Through Writing*.

David Perkins is co-director and a founding member of Harvard Project Zero and an associate of the Educational Technology Center at the Harvard Graduate School of Education. He is author of *The Mind's Best Work, Knowledge As Design*, and *Smart Schools: From Educating Memories to Educating Minds*, and co-author of *The Teaching of Thinking*, and *The Mindful School: How To Teach For Transfer*.

Stanley Pogrow is an associate professor of Educational Administration and Foundations at the University of Arizona where he specializes in instructional and administrative use of technology. Dr. Pogrow is the developer of the HOTS general thinking program, and is the author of over sixty articles and three books including: *HOTS (Higher Order Thinking): Using Computers to Develop the Thinking Skills of At-Risk Students*.

Jacqueline Rhoades is a program specialist, educational consultant, and part-time college instructor in teacher preparation programs. She is co-author of eight books, including, *The Nurturing Classroom: Developing Self-Esteem* and *Thinking Skills and Responsibility Through Simple Cooperation*.

David Schumaker is principal of New Brighton Middle School in Capitola, California and a member of the Institute for Intelligent Behavior. He conducts trainings in thinking skills, cooperative learning, cognitive coaching, and integrated thematic instruction. He is a contributor to ASCD's *Developing Minds*.

Robert Swartz is co-director of The National Center for Teaching Thinking in Newtonville, Massachusetts, and professor of philosophy at the University of Massachusetts, Boston. He is author of numerous articles, and co-author with David Perkins of *Teaching Thinking: Issues and Approaches*.

Noel White is an educational researcher at Harvard Project Zero with a background in anthropology. He works with middle and high school teachers and students, focusing on how students become responsible for their own learning, particularly in mathematics and science.

INDEX

NOTES

NOTES